WESTMAR COLLEGE

 O9-ABG-823

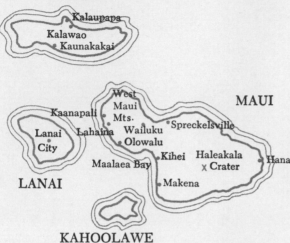

MOLOKAI

Kalaupapa
Kalawao
Kaunakakai

MAUI

West
Maui
Mts.

Kaanapali
Lanai
City
Lahaina
Wailuku
Olowalu
Spreckelsville

Kihei
Maalaea Bay
Haleakala
X Crater
Hana

Makena

LANAI

KAHOOLAWE

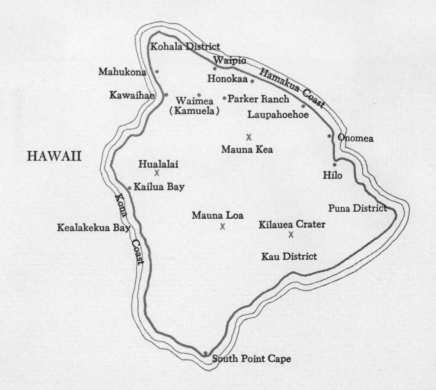

Kohala District
Waipio
Mahukona
Honokaa
Hamakua Coast
Kawaihae
Waimea
(Kamuela)
Parker Ranch
Laupahoehoe
X
Mauna Kea
Onomea

HAWAII

Hualalai
X
Kailua Bay
Hilo

Mauna Loa
Puna District
Kealakekua Bay
X
Kilauea Crater
X
Kona Coast
Kau District

South Point Cape

he name alone is the embodi-
omance and the exotic, the
of   piration of

HAWAII

A LITERARY CHRONICLE

Edited, with Commentaries by

W. STORRS LEE

Illustrations by W. Ralph Merrill

FUNK & WAGNALLS

NEW YORK

919.69
L482

DU
620.3
.L4

First Printing
Copyright © 1967 by W. Storrs Lee
All Rights Reserved.
Library of Congress Catalog Card Number: 67–28156
Published by Funk & Wagnalls, *A Division of* Reader's Digest Books, Inc.
Printed in the United States of America

Notices of Copyright Holders

Henry Adams, "So Passes the Glory of Hawaii." Reprinted by permission of Houghton, Mifflin Company from *The Letters of Henry Adams, 1858–1891,* W. C. Ford, ed., Copyright 1930.

Alexis Bachelot, "Collision of the Creeds." Reprinted by permission of the *Star-Bulletin* (Honolulu), from Father Reginald Yzendoorn, *History of the Catholic Mission in the Hawaiian Islands,* Copyright 1927 by Father Reginald Yzendoorn.

Ray Stannard Baker, "The House of Lords." Reprinted by permission of Roger D. Baker and Mrs. Rachel Baker Napier from "Wonderful Hawaii" and "Human Nature in Hawaii," *American Magazine,* November and December 1911.

Elias Bond, "Churches of Straw, Churches of Stone." Reprinted by permission of Alice Bond Alexander from Ethel M. Damon, *Father Bond of Kohala,* Copyright 1927 by Ethel M. Damon.

Rupert Brooke, "Waikiki." Reprinted by permission of Dodd, Mead and Company from *The Collected Poems of Rupert Brooke,* Copyright 1915 by Dodd, Mead and Company, Copyright renewed 1943 by Edward Marsh; also by permission of the Canadian publishers, McClelland and Stewart Ltd., Toronto.

Padraic Colum, "The Little People." Reprinted by permission of the Yale University Press from *At the Gateways of the Day,* Copyright 1924 by the Yale University Press.

Abraham Fornander, "Psalm." Reprinted by permission of the Bishop Museum Press from *The Fornander Collection of Hawaiian Antiquities and Folklore,* Thomas G. Thrum, trans., Copyright 1918–1919 by the Bishop Museum, Honolulu.

Bob Krauss, "In Defense of the Boom." Reprinted by permission of David A. Benz and the author from *Paradise of the Pacific,* December 1964.

Sister Adele Marie (Lemon), "War Correspondent on the Home Front." Reprinted by permission of the author from *To You from Hawaii,* Copyright 1950 by Sister Adele Marie.

Jack London, "The Tears of Ah Kim." Reprinted by permission of Irving Shepard, copyright owner, from Jack London, *On the Makaloa Mat.*

David Malo, "In Bondage to the Chiefs." Reprinted by permission of the Bishop Museum Press from *Hawaiian Antiquities (Moolelo Hawaii),* Dr. Nathaniel B. Emerson, trans., Copyright 1951 by the Bishop Museum, Honolulu.

William Somerset Maugham, "Meeting Place of East and West." Reprinted by permission of Doubleday and Co., The Literary Executor of W. Somerset Maugham, and William Heinemann Ltd. from W. Somerset Maugham, "Honolulu" in *The Trembling of a Leaf,* Copyright 1921 by W. Somerset Maugham.

68632

Archibald Menzies, "Frostbitten in the Tropics." Reprinted by permission of Advertiser Publishing Company Ltd., Honolulu, from Charles H. Hitchcock, *Hawaii and Its Volcanoes,* Copyright 1911 by the Hawaiian Gazette Company.

James A. Michener, "From the Sun-Swept Lagoon." Condensed from James A. Michener, *Hawaii,* © Copyright 1959 by James A. Michener. Reprinted by permission of Random House.

Eileen McCann O'Brien, "Challenge." Reprinted by permission of David A. Benz and the author from *Paradise of the Pacific,* December 1946.

Austin Strong, "His Oceanic Majesty's Goldfish." First published in the *Atlantic Monthly,* May 1944. Reprinted by permission of Brandt and Brandt, 101 Park Avenue, New York, New York, Copyright 1944 by The Atlantic Monthly Company.

Thomas G. Thrum, "Haven't Gas to Last Five Minutes." Reprinted by permission of the *Star-Bulletin* (Honolulu) from the *1926 Hawaiian Annual.*

John W. Vandercook, "Into the Melting Pot." Reprinted by permission of Harper & Row, Publishers, Inc., from John W. Vandercook, *King Cane* (pp. 53–65), Copyright 1939 by John W. Vandercook.

Armine von Tempski, "Tied to Death." Reprinted by permission of Duell, Sloan and Pearce, affiliate of Meredith Press, from Armine von Tempski, *Born in Paradise,* Copyright 1940 by Armine von Tempski.

To

MARY KAWENA PUKUI

who has rendered
greater service
than any other
living Hawaiian
in the preservation
of the native
language,
literature,
and traditions
of Hawaii

Contents

Contents

Contents

Foreword

Out of respect for those who take flight at the prospect of encountering literary samplers, symposiums, garlands, or collections of miscellany in any disguise, let me protest that this is not an anthology in the ordinary sense. The book has sequence and continuity; it tells a chronological story; it is intended to be read from the beginning, not given the dip-and-dabble treatment accorded most anthologies.

With a little joggling, it could be fitted into the category of biography, for it presents a life history of Hawaii, as reported by eye-witnesses to major events in Hawaiian annals, by participants in the events, or by qualified penmen who meticulously reconstructed them. Anyone perusing the volume from start to finish should gain at least a panoramic impression of the steps by which Hawaii emerged from primitive existence to become successively a feudal domain, a kingdom, a republic, a territory, a state.

The text is not addressed to any specialized audience. It is intended for the armchair explorer interested in the complex background of the fiftieth state; for the touring *malihini* who wants a wider-angle view of Hawaii than that presented in the one-man guide; for the *kamaaina* partial to a dosage of regional literature amply buttressed by reference to original sources; for the student not yet familiar with his legacy in local literature—the student who is constantly implored by his teachers to write about familiar subjects and places, but who needs a few examples to demonstrate that literary greats indeed found much in the home terrain to write about, entertainingly, graciously, and instructively.

Perhaps every state has a tendency to underrate the worth of its own literature simply because it is seldom packaged that way, is inaccessible, out of print, locked in library cages, buried in old magazine files. Like other states, Hawaii reaches halfway around the world for its approved secondary-school "classics" while virtually ignoring the fine writing about the home scene contributed by such notables as Henry Adams, Richard Henry Dana, Herman Melville, Padraic Colum, Robert Louis Stevenson, Mark Twain, Jack London, Isabella Lucy Bird, Ray Stannard Baker, Charles Nordhoff, and a great many others.

This volume is an attempt to help restore to circulation some of that reservoir of secluded literature on Hawaii, to help fill the gap in what should be staple fare for both educational and general consumption in the Islands. And the logical way to organize the material was to assemble it in chronological order so that it could stand as a documentary diary of Hawaii.

The most exciting approach to an investigation of regional background is through the writings of eyewitness observers. The real recording secretaries of history were the explorers, travelers, correspondents, creative writers, men of science, commerce, arts, letters, and research who passed on to us the benefit of their contemporaneous reconnaissance. The selections may serve as a invitation to explore the greater wealth of literature about Hawaii from which these are borrowed, and to investigate further the long roster of Hawaii's authors who wrote just as engagingly of other subjects and other places.

In order to keep the length of the book within bounds, many selections have been abridged. But for each author we have endeavored to present a sample of sufficient length to demonstrate his flavor, his style, and his message. Expendable passages, prolixities, and material not pertinent to the immediate subject have been excised. Excisions are indicated by ellipsis marks, which may represent deletion of a few words from a sentence (. . .), deletion of much longer passages (. . . .), or occasional juxtaposition of topical material. Since most of the selections are taken from the body of a longer piece, ellipsis marks at the beginning and end of a selection have commonly been omitted.

Represented in the text are samples of English covering a period of two centuries, and in that period grammatical usage has been modified so materially that old forms can make for halting reading or even convey unintended meaning. Accordingly, in some of the older documents spelling and punctuation have been modernized; interminable paragraphs have been broken into more digestible nuggets; obscure or outmoded abbreviations have been written out. However, this is a compromise at best; we have made no attempt to dress the selections in grammatical conformity, and where quaint spelling and other currently unacceptable usages contribute to the character of the composition, they have been retained.

For cooperation in making selections available for inclusion in the volume, the editor wishes to express his gratitude to the publishers and authors noted at the conclusion of each selection. Special recognition for assistance is extended to: Mr. Alexander Atherton, Miss Lucille Berg, Mr. Howard Cady, Mr. Ralph Merrill, Mr. James Murray, and my wife.

W. S. L.

I

James A. Michener

Though Captain James Cook is commonly credited with the discovery of the Hawaiian Islands, their real discoverers were Polynesians. To them the land was "Havaiki," named after many ancient Havaikis in the South Seas, where they and their ancestors had lived. Hundreds of years before Cook chanced upon the Islands, sailors from the South Seas had landed there on ventures far more hazardous than those of the British mariners. The Europeans came in broad-decked sailing ships with ample holds, keels, and freeboard, and possessed charts, compasses, and a knowledge of logarithms; the Polynesians came in great double canoes, piloting their craft by the stars and a sixth sense, carrying in cramped hulls the meager rations on which they must subsist, depending ultimately on the whims of their gods for guidance.

The reason for making the journey to Hawaii, the date of the original discovery, and the identity of the discoverers all remain open to conjecture, but there is no question that there *were* explorative ventures; ancient myths hint of such odysseys and modern science confirms a truth behind the myth. James A. Michener (1907–   ), author of many stories of the South Seas, the Orient, and the Middle East, in his nearly thousand-page epic novel *Hawaii* presents a fictional account of the circumstances under which the first migration might have taken place. It is dramatic, informative, exciting; and the incidents of the voyage are well within the bounds of accepted tradition.

Michener's narrative starts on one of the Society Islands, Bora Bora, where the worship of a new god Oro has been imposed by the high priests of powerful neighboring islands. The Bora Boran King Tamatoa and his brother Teroro remain loyal to the old god Tane, lead an unsuccessful revolt against the new worship, and as a result face massacre or banishment.

They choose the latter and assemble a company of fifty-eight loyal followers to sail north to legendary lands marked in the skies by the constellation "Seven Little Eyes." Their transport is *Wait-for-the-West-Wind,* an enormous seventy-nine-foot, two-masted double canoe, with a deck slung between the two hulls, capable of conveying crew and passengers, statues of the necessary gods, a sizable thatched cabin, and a bare minimum of supplies. Vague directions of a route to follow are contained in an old chant.

Included in the company are the two young chiefs: fiery, reliable, inexhaustible Mato, and wiry, shark-faced Pa, both lead paddlers; the seventy-year-old priest Tupuna, who tends the deities and reads omens; the priest's wife Teura, seer for the voyage; farmers, artisans, and veteran seamen—altogether thirty-seven men, fifteen women, and six slaves.

Compactly stowed in the canoe hulls are survival rations for the long journey: dried breadfruit, pandanus flour, dried sweet potatoes, shellfish, coconut meat, bonito, drinking coconuts, and water sealed in bamboo sections. But provisions for consumption in transit are only part of their problem in logistics; they are equally concerned with transporting the necessities for perpetuating their way of life once they reach their destination.

With the future in mind, they also carry seeds, taro corms, banana and breadfruit shoots, choice coconuts for planting, sugarcane joints; two bred sows and a boar, dogs, fowls; gourds, calabashes, fine waterproof mats, and rolls of tapa; spears, fish nets, and quantities of pearl hooks; stone adzes, chisels, *poi* pounders, a variety of farm tools—and above all, their unflagging faith in the gods: in all-powerful Tane, whose symbol is placed at the foot of one mast, and in Ta'aroa, god of oceans, whose stone is placed at the base of the other.

Perhaps their greatest encumbrance is the burden of superstition, the fear of displeasing a deity, the dread of missing or misinterpreting some sign or portent, the apprehension of not following precisely the will of Tane. Though final human authority rests with the king, the experienced navigator Teroro serves as captain, and in order to take

advantage of strong westerly winds, he orders that they embark at
night in the midst of a fierce storm which has been raging over Bora
Bora for four days. The one stop they plan to make on the long
journey is at hostile Nuku Hiva, where they hope to replenish their
supplies.

Only the bare story of the ocean crossing is presented here; omitted
from Michener's longer saga are numerous characters, incidents, and
descriptive details.

From the Sun-Swept Lagoon

And so the double canoe, *Wait-for-the-West-Wind,* loaded and
creaking with king and slave, with contradictory gods and pigs,
with hope and fear, set forth upon the unknown. . . . When
West Wind reached the reef, and stood for a moment in its last
stretch of easily navigable water, all in the canoe experienced a
moment of awful dread, for outside the coral barrier roared the
storm on splashing waves and tremendous deeps.

Just for an instant Mato, lead paddle of the left, whispered,
"Great Tane! Such waves!" But with prodigious force he led the
paddlers into a swift rhythm that bore them directly into the
heart of the storm. The canoe rose high in the sea, teetered a
moment with its shrouds whistling, then ripped down, down into
the valley of the waves. Spray dashed across all heads and the
two halves seemed as if they must tear apart. Pigs squealed in
terror and dogs barked, while in the flooded grass house women
thought: "This is death."

But instantly the powerful canoe cut into the waves, found
itself, and rode high onto the crest of the ocean, away from Bora
Bora of the muffled paddles, away from the comforting lagoon
and onto the highway that led to nothingness.

In such weather King Tamatoa led his people into exile. They
did not go in triumph or with banners flying; they fled at night,
with no drums beating. They did not leave with riches and in
panoply; they were rudely elbowed off their island with only
enough food to sustain them precariously. . . . Later ages would

depict these men as all-wise and heroic, great venturers seeking
bright new lands; but such myths would be in error, for no man
leaves where he is and seeks a distant place unless he is in some
respect a failure. . . . There was, however, one overriding
characteristic that marked these defeated people as they swept
into the storm: they did have courage. . . .

. . . They had reached, more swiftly than ever before, a point
off the north coast of Havaiki. . . . It was at this moment, when
the captains of the canoe were most agitated, that Tane and
Ta'aroa conspired to present them with an omen that erased from
all hearts memories of what had just happened. The rain came
heavily for about fifteen minutes, followed by strong winds that
blew clouds scudding ahead in darkness until the clouds parted
and the fine stars of heaven were momentarily revealed.

Then it was that the wisdom of Tapuna in setting forth at dusk
on the new day of the month became apparent, for there, rising
in the eastern sky and with no bright moon in competition,
sparkled the Seven Little Eyes. . . . With what extraordinary
joy the voyagers greeted the Little Eyes! From the grass house
women poured forth and filled their hearts with comfort. Those
crew members who had to keep the canoe headed with the wind
found new resilience in their tired muscles, and Teroro knew
that he was on course.

Then, the miracle vouchsafed, Tane drew the clouds once more
across the heavens and the storm continued, but contentment
beyond measure settled upon the canoe, for it was at last apparent that the company moved in accordance with divine laws.
How sweet the roar of the wind that bore them on, how consol-
ing the motion of the waves that carried them into the unknown;
how appropriate the world, how well ordered and secure the
heavens! On the canoe, that daring and insignificant bundle of
wood lashed together by sennit and men's wills, all hearts were
deep in peace, and the onwardness of their journey sang contentedly in all parts of the craft. . . .

The most critical part of any twenty-four-hour period came in
the half hour just before dawn, for unless the navigator could

catch a glimpse of some known star and thus check course, he would have to proceed through an entire day with only the un- reliable sun to steer by; for while it was true that master astron- omers like Teroro and Tupuna could follow each movement of the sun and take from it their heading, they could not use it to determine their latitude. For that they depended upon the stars; their sailing directions reminded them which stars culminated over which islands, and to pass the last moments of the night without seeing any constellations was not only an omen of bad luck in the future, it was also proof of present difficulty, which, if it persisted for several days, might develop into catastrophe. . . .

. . . Clouds continued to streak out of the west to meet the sun rising on the other side of the ocean. On this day dawn was neither inspiring nor refreshing, for the sun straggled reluctantly up behind many layers of cloud, half illuminated the ocean with dull gray and proved to the voyagers that they did not know where they were.

Teroro and Tupuna, having accomplished all they could, fell into immediate sleep in the stormy daylight; and it was then that the latter's wife, wizened, red-eyed old Teura, paid for her passage. She climbed out of the grass house, spattered sea water over her wrinkled face, rubbed her bleary eyes, threw her head back and started studying the omens.

In nearly two thirds of a century of living with the gods, she had unraveled many of their tricky ways. Now she watched how Ta'aroa moved the waves, how the spume rose, how the tips fell away and in what manner they tumbled back into the troughs. She marked the color of the sea and the construction of the basic swells that underlay the more conspicuous waves. . . .

But what Teura particularly appreciated were those unexpected messages from the gods which meant so much to the knowing. For example, an albatross . . . happened to fly past the canoe and she saw with gratification that he kept to the left, or Ta'aroa's side. . . . When the bird insisted upon returning to the canoe, also from the left side, and finally perched on the mast of Ta'aroa, the coincidence could no longer be termed an omen. It was a definite message that the god of the ocean had personally sent. . . .

Contentedly the old woman gathered her many omens, and they were all good. The men of her canoe might be lost, and the stars remain hidden, and the storm continue, but Ta'aroa was with them and all was well. In the late afternoon, Tupuna and Teroro, before resuming their duties, came aft to find out from Teura where they were, and she advised them that they rode much farther north than even Teroro suspected. . . .

That night it could not be proved that Teura was either right or wrong, for no stars appeared, neither in the darkness of midnight nor in the anxious dawn, and Teroro steered solely by running directly before the wind, with only a small section of sail out, trusting that the storm was steady and not blowing in circles.

On the third starless night, when the canoe could have been in real danger, Teroro reached a major decision. While consulting with Tupuna he said, "We've got to believe that the storm is blowing true."

"Arrival of the albatross is best proof of that," Tupuna pointed out.

"Then I think we'd better take full advantage of it."

"You intend hoisting the sails to the peak?"

"Yes. If it is the gods who are sending us, we ought to go forward as fast as we can."

. . . So Teroro sent Mato and Pa up the masts, and in complete darkness, while the canoe was already speeding forward into deep swells, the two young chiefs lashed fast the sturdy matting sails and with shouts of accomplishment slid down and began to play out the sails until they trapped the wind and whipped the canoe forward. Through the rest of the night and into the third disappointing dawn the canoe raced ahead on a course no man knew. . . .

More than a century ago a wise man had named the predecessor of the predecessor of this canoe *Wait-for-the-West-Wind* because he had found that when Bora Borans went forth driven by the western hurricane, they went well. And until the stars had a chance to prove the contrary, Teroro was willing to abide by this ancient wisdom. . . . "This isn't an ordinary storm," he argued.

"This is an unheard-of gale sent to the canoe of Bora Bora. . . ."

"But we are lost!" the king reasoned. . . .

"I am not lost, brother, because I am riding with the desires of Ta'aroa. I am heading with a great storm, and I am content to ride that storm."

"Do you know how to get to Nuku Hiva?"

Teroro looked at each of his companions and replied, "If we are concerned only with Nuku Hiva, I am lost. If we are going to Nuku Hiva only to get additional food and water, I am lost. But in all sense, brother, do we need to go to Nuku Hiva?"

He waited for these strong words to sink into the hearts of his seafaring companions, and he saw that he had used words they understood. Before anyone could speak he added, "What is there for us at Nuku Hiva? To get water we have to fight with those who live there, and some of us will be killed. Do we need water? To get food we must take great risks, and if we are captured, we are cooked alive and eaten. Do we need food? Hasn't Ta'aroa sent us fresh fish in abundance? Have we not disciplined ourselves as men have never done before so that each eats only a shred each day? Brother Tamatoa, if the storm is with us, what extra things do we need? . . . I cannot take you to Nuku Hiva, but I can take you to the north."

As if in support of his bold plan, a sudden force of wind ripped across the waves and spilled into the sails, whipping the canoe along in a burst of speed. Spray leaped, and dawn, still blotting out the stars and all certain knowledge, came upon the men of Bora Bora.

"We are alone on the sea," Teroro said solemnly. "We are engaged in a special voyage, and if it takes us past Nuku Hiva, then I say good, for we are doubtless being sped by the gods on some great mission. Brother, I beg you, let us keep the sails aloft."

The king . . . weighing all possibilities, sided with his brother and said, "We should get some sleep."

So for two more nights, the sixth and seventh of the voyage, the canoe sped on. . . . And then, on the late afternoon of the seventh day, red-eyed Teura spotted an omen. On the left side of the canoe came five dolphin, a propitious number in itself, followed by an albatross of some size. The creatures of Ta'aroa had come to celebrate the deliverance of this canoe from the storm, but before Teura could alert her companions to this fine intelligence, an event of transcendent importance occurred.

A shark appeared not far from the canoe and followed it lazily for a moment, trying to catch Teura's attention, and when she saw it her heart cried with joy, for this great blue beast of the sea had long been her personal god; and now while the others were blind with their work, it swam along the left side of the canoe, its blue head above the waves.

"Are you lost, Teura?" it inquired softly.

"Yes, Mano," she replied, "we are lost." . . .

"Tonight there will be stars, Teura," the shark whispered. "All the stars that you require. . . . Your men are brave, Teura, to keep the sails aloft like that."

Teura opened her eyes and smiled at the shark. "I am ashamed to tell you that I argued against it."

"We all make mistakes," the blue beast said, "but you are on the right course. You'll see when the stars come out." . . .

"Tamatoa," the old woman said quietly, "tonight there will be stars."

. . . Exactly as Teura had predicted, toward dusk the clouds disappeared and the evening sun came out. As it sank, a tremendous exhilaration filled the canoe, for trailing the sun was the bright star of evening, visible even in twilight and soon accompanied by a second wandering star of great brilliance. . . . Then, as darkness deepened over the still heaving ocean, and as the winds died momentarily from the gallant outstretched sails, the stars began to appear; first the mighty golden stars of the south . . . followed by the cold blue stars of the north, scintillating in their accustomed places and competing with the quarter moon. . . .

"The Little Eyes are still with us!" Tupuna shouted. . . . "It is true that we have been carried into far regions, but they are not off our course. We seek lands which lie beneath the Seven Little Eyes, and we are nearer to them tonight than we had a right to expect. If we do not eat too much—"

Even though Tamatoa had given permission to keep the sails aloft, and even though he had known that the canoe thus ran the risk of missing Nuku Hiva, he had nevertheless hoped that they would stumble upon that known island, and perhaps find it congenial, and possibly establish homes there. Now he was committed to a greater journey, and he was fearful. . . .

Tupuna repeated the only chant he had ever memorized for sailing to the north. In effect it said: "Keep the canoe headed with the storm until the winds cease completely. Then turn into the dead sea where bones rot with heat and no wind blows. Paddle to the new star, and when winds strike from the east, ride with them westward until land beneath the Seven Little Eyes is found."

. . . The course seemed so improbable, to head for a promised land by fleeing it, that the king cried, "Can we be sure that this is the way?"

"No," the old man confessed, "we cannot be sure. . . . I think that many canoes have left these waters, some blown by storms, others like us in exile, and no man has ever returned. Whether these canoes reached land or not, we do not know. But some man, with a vision of what might be, composed that chant."

"Then we are sailing with a dream for our guide?" Tamatoa asked.

"Yes," the priest answered. . . .

So, with the remnants of the tempest at their back . . . the voyagers sailed eastward for the ninth night, and the tenth, and the fifteenth. Their swift canoe, fleetest large craft that ever up to then had plied the oceans of the world, averaged two hundred miles a day, better than eight miles an hour, day after day. They sailed more than halfway to the lands where Aztecs were building mighty temples, and well onto the approaches of the northern land were Cheyennes and Apaches built nothing. In the direction they were then headed they could encounter no land until they struck the continent itself; but before that happened they would have perished of thirst and starvation in the doldrums. Nevertheless, they carried on, according to Teroro's plan. . . .

As the canoe reached eastward and the storm abated, the daily routine became more settled. Each dawn the six slaves stopped bailing and cleaned out the canoe, while farmers moved among the animals and fed them, giving the pigs and dogs fish caught in the early hours, plus some mashed sweet potatoes and fresh water trapped in the sails. The chickens got dried coconut and a fish to pick at, but if they lagged in eating, a slim, dark object darted out from among the freight and grabbed the food away, unseen by the slaves, for as on all such trips, some rats had stowed away, and if the voyage turned out badly, they would be the last to die. . . .

Women on such a trip did not fare well. Obviously, the food had to be reserved for men who did the hard work of paddling. The pigs and dogs also had to be kept alive to stock the new land, which left little for the women. That is why, at every opportunity, they set fishing lines and tended them carefully. The first fish they caught went to the king and Teroro, the next to Tupuna and his old wife, the next four to the paddlers, the seventh and eighth to the pigs, the ninth to the dogs, the tenth to the chickens and rats. If there were more, the women could eat.

With great niggardliness, the prepared foods were doled out, a piece at a time, but when they were distributed, how good they tasted. A man would get his stick of hard and sour breadfruit, and as he chewed on it he would recall the wasteful feasts he had once held, when abundant breadfruit, fresh and sweet, had been thrown to the animals. But the food that gave most pleasure, the master food of the islands, came when the king directed that one of the bamboo lengths of dried *poi* be opened, and then the rich purplish starch would be handed out, and as it grew sticky in the mouth, men would smile with pleasure.

But soon the *poi* was finished and the bundles of dried breadfruit diminished. Even the abundant rain ceased and King Tamatoa had to reduce his rations still further, until the crew were getting only two mouthfuls of solid food, two small portions of water. Women and slaves got half as much, so that unless the fishermen could land bonito, or trap water in the sails, all existed at the starvation level. . . .

On the eleventh night occurred an event which, in its emotional impact upon a people who lived by the stars, had no equal on this voyage. . . . As the *West Wind* crept constantly northward, it became obvious to the astronomers on board that they must lose, and forever, many old familiar stars which lay below what astronomers would later call the Southern Cross. . . . Whole constellations were washed into the sea, never to be seen again. . . . They knew that they would come upon new stars, and it was with the joy of discovery that they identified the hitherto unseen stars of the north. But in all their wisdom, they were not prepared for what they discovered on the eleventh night.

Having set their course, they were surveying the northern heavens when the old man saw, bobbing above the waves, a new star, not of maximum brightness like the vast beacons of the south—for the voyagers found the northern stars rather disappointing in brilliance in comparison with theirs—but nevertheless an interesting newcomer.

"See how it lies in a direct line from the two stars in Bird-with-a-Long-Neck," Tupuna pointed out, referring to stars which others called the Big Dipper.

At first Teroro could not catch the bright star, for it danced up and down on the horizon, now visible above the waves, now lost. Then he saw it, a bright, clean, cold star, well marked in an empty space of the sky. Speaking as a navigator, he said, "That would be a strong star to steer by . . . when it rises a little higher." . . . So on the twelfth night the two men studied the new guidepost, but as dawn appeared each was afraid to tell the other what he had seen, for each realized that he had stumbled upon an omen of such magnitude that it did not bear speaking of. . . . It was Tupuna who put it into words: "The new star does not move."

"It is fixed," Teroro agreed. . . . Suddenly and with dazzling clarity, Teroro saw an entirely new system of navigation based on Tane's gift, the fixed star, and he thought: "Life must be sweet indeed for sailors in these waters!" For he knew that northern sailors had what southerners did not: a star which could tell them, at a single glance, their latitude. "The heavens are fixed!" he cried to himself. "And I shall be free to move beneath them." . . . On what Teroro foresaw that night the navigation of the islands ahead would be built and their location in the ocean determined. . . .

Into the arid heat of the doldrums they plunged. The sun beat upon them by day and the rainless stars mocked them at night. Now not even distant squalls passed with the tantalizing hope that rain might come. They knew it would not.

Teroro planned so that Mato and Pa, the two sturdiest paddlers, would not work at the same time; also, after an hour's stint in the right hull, which tore the muscles of the left shoulder, the paddlers would shift sides and wear out the right shoulders. At each shift six men would drop out and rest. But onward the canoe went, constantly. . . .

. . . In a storm when fresh water was plentiful, the sails did most of the work, whereas now, when men sweated and strained endlessly with the paddles, there was no water. The king ordered it to be doled out in ever-decreasing portions, so that the harder the men worked, the less they had to drink.

The women, with scarcely any water, suffered miserably, while the slaves were near death. The farmers had an especially cruel task. Tenderly they would hold open the mouth of a pig and drop water inside to keep the animal alive, whereas they needed the fluid more than the animal; but the death of a farmer could be tolerated; the death of a pig would have been catastrophe.

Still the canoe bore on. At night Teroro, with his lips burning, would place on the platform near the prow a half coconut, filled with placid sea water, and in it he would catch the reflection of the fixed star, and by keeping the reflection constant in the cup, he maintained his course. . . .

Day followed day of remorseless heat, worse than anyone in the canoe had previously experienced. On the seventeenth day one of the women died, and as her body was plunged into the perpetual care of Ta'aroa, god of the mysterious deep . . . through the entire canoe there was a longing for rain and the cool valleys of Bora Bora, and it was not surprising that many began to deplore having come upon this voyage.

Hot nights were followed by blazing days, and the only thing that seemed to live in the canoe was the dancing new star as it leaped about in the coconut cup which Teroro studied; and then late one night as the navigator watched his star, he saw on the horizon, lighted by the moon, a breath of storm. It was small at first, and wavering, and Mato whispered, "Is that rain?"

At first Teroro would not reply, and then, with a mighty shout he roared into the night, "Rain!"

The grass house emptied. The sleeping paddlers wakened and watched as a cloud obscured the moon. A wind rose, and a light capping of the sea could be seen in starlight. It must be a substantial storm, and not a passing squall. It was worth pursuing, and everyone began to paddle furiously. Those with no paddles used their hands, and even the king, distraught with hope, grabbed a bailing bucket from a slave and paddled with it.

How desperately they worked, and how tantalizingly the storm eluded them. Through the remaining portion of the night, the canoe sped on, its men collapsing with thirst and exhaustion, in pursuit of the storm. They did not catch it, and as the blazing day came upon them, driving the clouds back to the horizon, and then beyond, an awful misery settled upon the canoe. The paddlers, their strength exhausted in the fruitless quest, lay listless and allowed the sun to beat upon them. Teroro was of no use. Old Tupuna was near death, and the pigs wept protestingly in the waterless heat.

Only the king was active. Sitting cross-legged on his mat he prayed ceaselessly. "Great Tane, you have always been generous to us in the past," he cajoled. "You have given us taro and breadfruit in abundance. You brought our pigs to fatness and birds to our traps. I am grateful to you, Tane. I am loyal to you. I prefer you above all other gods." . . . Then from the depth of his despair, he pleaded: "Tane, bring us rain."

From a short distance forward, red-eyed Teura heard the king praying and crept back to him. . . . In bleak despair they stared at each other and found no answer, so Teura, her eyes already inflamed from watching the merciless sun, went out to the lifeless platform and prayed for omens. . . . And as she looked, she saw a cloud, and then a disturbance ruffling the ashen sea, and then the movement of a storm, and rain. . . .

With a wild scream she cried, "Rain! Rain!" And all rushed out from the house, and dead sleepers wakened to find a storm bearing down upon them.

"Rain!" they mumbled as it marched across the ocean nearer and nearer.

"It's coming!" Tamatoa shouted. "Our prayers are answered. . . .

Almost as if by command, the near-dying voyagers began to throw off their clothes, their tapa and their shells, until each stood naked in the divine storm, drinking it into their eyes and their blistering armpits and their parched mouths. The winds rose, and the rains increased, but the naked men and women of Bora Bora continued their revel in the slashing waves. The sails came down and the mast of Ta'aroa was almost carried away, and the dogs whined, but the men in the canoe swept the water into their mouths and embraced each other. Into the night the storm continued, and it seemed as if the sections of the canoe must break apart, but no one called for the storm to abate. They fought it and drank it and washed their aching bodies with it, and sailed into the heart of it, and toward morning, exhausted in sheer joy, they watched as the clouds parted and they saw that they were almost under the path of the Seven Little Eyes, and they knew that they must ride with the easterly wind that had brought the storm. Their destination lay somewhere to the west.

It was a long leg to windward they took. For nearly two thousand miles they ran before the easterlies, covering most days more than a hundred and fifty miles. Now the fixed star remained at about the same height above the horizon, on their right, and they followed close to the path of Little Eyes. . . .

It was on this long westward leg that King Tamatoa's earlier insistence on discipline preserved the voyage, for now food had run perilously low and for some perverse reason the numerous fish in these strange waters would not bite. . . . Every woman and all men who were not paddling kept lines, long and short, in the sea, but to no avail.

There was a little coconut left and a small amount of bread-fruit, but no taro. Even the pigs, absolutely essential to the success of the journey, were famishing. But in this extremity the thirty paddlers, who worked constantly, survived amazingly. Their stomachs had long since contracted into hard little fists, shrunk to nothing under tight belly muscles. Their strong shoulders, devoid of even a trace of fat after nearly a month's steady work, seemed able to generate energy from nothing. With neither food nor adequate water, the men sweated little; through sun-reddened eyes they constantly scanned the horizon for omens.

It was old Teura, however, who saw the first substantial sign; on the twenty-seventh morning she saw a small piece of drift-wood, torn away from some distant tree, and Teroro avidly directed the canoe toward it. When it was pulled aboard it was found to contain four land worms, which were fed to the astonished chickens.

"It has been in the ocean less than ten days," Teura announced. Since the canoe could travel five or six times faster than a drifting branch, it seemed likely that land lay somewhere near; and old Teura entered into a period of intense concentration, clutching at omens and interpreting them hopefully by means of old prayers.

But *West Wind* was not to be saved by incantations. It was Mato, a trained sailor, who late one afternoon saw in a distance a flock of birds flying with determination on a set course westward. "There's land ahead. They're heading for it," he cried. . . .

In the early morning of the twenty-ninth day a group of eleven long black birds with handsome cleft tails flew by on a foraging trip from their home island, which lay somewhere beyond the horizon, and Teroro noted with keen pleasure that their heading, reversed, was his. . . . From their presence it could be deduced that land was not more than sixty miles distant, a fact which was confirmed when Teura and Tupuna, working together, detected in the waves of the sea a peculiar pattern which indicated that in the near distance the profound westerly set of the ocean was impounding upon a reef, which shot back echo waves that cut across the normal motion of the sea; but unfortunately a heavy bank of cloud obscured the western horizon, reaching even to the sea, and none could detect exactly where the island lay.

"Don't worry!" Teura reassured everyone. "When the clouds do lift, watch their undersides carefully. At sunset you'll see them turn green over the island. . . ."

As she had hoped, toward dusk the clouds began to dissipate, and it was Teura who first saw the new island looming ahead. Gasping, she cried, "Oh, great Tane! What is it?"

"Look! Look!" shouted Teroro.

And there before them, rearing from the sea like an un-dreamed-of monster, rose a tremendous mountain more massive than they had ever imagined, crowned in strange white and soaring majestically into the evening sunset.

"What a land we have found!" Teroro whispered.

"It is the land of Tane!" King Tamatoa announced in a hushed whisper. "It reaches to heaven itself."

And all in the canoe, seeing this clean and wonderful mountain, fell silent and did it reverence, until Pa cried, "Look! It is smok-ing!" And as night fell, the last sight the men of Bora Bora had was of a gigantic mountain, hung in the heavens, sending fumes from its peak. . . .

In the early light of morning it became apparent that the smok-ing mountain and its supporting island lay much farther away than had at first been supposed, and a final day of hunger and work faced the paddlers; but the visible presence of their goal spurred the famished men so that by nightfall it was certain that next morning the long voyage would end. Through the last soft tropical night, with the luminous mountain ahead, the crew of the *West Wind* followed their rhythmic, steady beat.

At they approached the end of a trek nearly five thousand miles long, it is appropriate to compare what they had accom-plished with what voyagers in other parts of the world were doing. In the Mediterranean, descendants of once-proud Phoenicians, who even in their moments of glory had rarely ventured out of sight of land, now coasted along established shores and occasion-

"This is the land. . . . This is a man's home"

ally, with what was counted bravery, actually cut across the trivial sea in voyages covering perhaps two hundred miles. In Portugal men were beginning to accumulate substantial bodies of information about the ocean, but to probe it they were not yet ready, and it would be six hundred more years before even near-at-hand islands like Madeira and the Azores would be found. Ships had coasted the shores of Africa, but it was known that crossing the equator and thus losing sight of the North Star meant boiling death, or falling off the edge of the world or both.

On the other side of the earth, Chinese junks had coasted Asia and in the southern oceans had moved from one visible island to the next, terming the act heroism. From Arabia and India, merchants had undertaken considerable voyages, but never very far from established coasts, while in the undiscovered continents to the west of Europe, no man left the land.

Only in the north of Europe did the Vikings display enterprise even remotely comparable to that of the men of Bora Bora; but even they had not yet begun their long voyages, though they had at their disposal metals, large ships, woven sails, books and maps.

It was left to the men of the Pacific, men like cautious Tamatoa and energetic Teroro, to meet an ocean on its own terms and to conquer it. Lacking both metals and maps, sailing with only the stars and a few lengths of sennit, some dried taro and positive faith in their gods, these men accomplished miracles. It would be another seven centuries before an Italian navigator, sailing under the flag of Spain and fortified by all the appurtenances of an advanced community, would dare, in three large and commodious ships well nailed together, to set forth upon a voyage not quite so far and only half as dangerous.

At dawn Teroro brought his canoe close to land at the southeastern shore of the vast volcanic island that rose from the southeast end of the rupture in the ocean floor. When the shoreline became visible, the voyagers had many thoughts. Teroro reflected in some disappointment: "It's all rocks. Where are the coconuts? Where's the water?" Mato, who paddled in the hull nearest the land, thought: "No breadfruit." But King Tamatoa mused: "It is the land Tane brought us to. It must be good."

Only Tupuna appreciated the profound problems which the next few hours would bring. In trembling apprehension he thought: "The children of my brothers are about to step upon new land. Everything depends on the next minutes, for this island is obviously filled with strange gods, and we must do nothing to offend them. But will I be able to placate them all?"

So he moved with agitation about the canoe, endeavoring to arrange things so that the unknown gods would be offended as little as possible. "Don't pick up a single stone," he warned. "Don't break a branch or eat a shellfish." Then he went to the god's house and called Pa to his side, handing him a square of flat stone. "You will follow me," he said, "because you are extremely brave." He adjusted the king's feather cape, handed Teroro a spear, and lifted into his own shaking hands the two gods, Tane and Ta'aroa.

"Now!" he cried, and the canoe touched land.

First to disembark was Tamatoa, and as soon as he had made one footprint in the sand, he stopped, kneeled down, and took that earth into his hands, bringing it to his lips, where he kissed it many times. "This is the land," he chanted gravely. "This is a man's home. This is good land to settle upon, a good land on which to have children. Here we shall bring our ancestors. Here we bring our gods."

From *Hawaii,* James A. Michener (New York: Random House, 1959).

II

David Malo

For centuries after the first Polynesian settlement was made in Hawaii, hazardous voyages between the South Seas and the new Island chain were periodically undertaken. Battered by storms, driven off course, exhausted, starved, or wrecked, many of the voyagers never reached their destination. Only the fittest and the fortunate survived. But over the years hundreds succeeded in migrating north to establish new homes and new kingdoms. Then gradually the expeditions were discontinued altogether; contact with the southern islands was broken off; and the Hawaiians were entirely on their own, isolated in mid-Pacific, independent of all outside influences.

Their cultural roots were still those of southern Polynesia, but nature, the elements, and human whimsy combined to create a society substantially different from that of their ancestors. Old gods were neglected; once-cherished customs forgotten; the language suffered slow alteration; a stronger class consciousness emerged.

Ambitious kings and chiefs built up little realms for themselves, subordinated the common people, established an oppressive feudal system, and perennially called their serfs to arms to fight bloody wars with other equally ambitious kings and chiefs. The standards of living were never high: a grass hut for shelter; *poi*, pig, and fish for a principal diet; a scrap of tapa for clothing.

All property—everything from one's own children to the home site, the canoe, and the stone ax—belonged to the king. The people owned nothing. They were kept in their place by a complicated system of taboos proclaimed by king, chief, or priests. The taboos were the law of the land. And to add to the wretchedness of everyday living, the gods all too often brought on destructive south winds and violent earthquakes, tidal waves, and devastating lava flows.

Yet despite all the adversities, the Hawaiians were a happy, playful, contented people. They loved life and could blithely shrug off their troubles in orgies of gaming, surfing, dancing, singing, frolicking, feasting. They were uncommonly content because it was the only life they knew; they had no intimation of any other form of existence with which theirs could be compared.

In their isolation they made notable progress in many arts and crafts, but they never discovered the art of writing, so the full story of their ethnology was unrecorded, except as professional raconteurs memorized important highlights. Not until the American missionaries had given them an alphabet and taught them how to read and write was an effort made to put their past on paper.

The most talented native scribe taught by the early missionaries was David Malo (c. 1793–1853). In his youth he had been exposed to court life on the Kona Coast of Hawaii, had committed to memory many of the ancient myths, chants, hula routines, and genealogies of the chiefs, had composed a few lyrics himself, and had become a popular recitalist and performer. But the direction of his life was abruptly changed in his thirties when he moved to Maui and came under the influence of the missionaries at Lahaina. Converted to Christianity, he soon developed into a star pupil and outspoken missionary advocate.

Eventually Malo was persuaded to draft a "Story of Hawaii"— *Moolelo Hawaii*—in his native language. Apparently patterned in numbered chapter-and-verse format after the Old Testament, with which he had become familiar, the book was naive, ill-organized, repetitious, contradictory, and fragmentary. Starting with the Hawaiian Genesis, it incorporated a Flood story, accounts of the origin and wanderings of various Island tribes, quaint apologies for a Leviticus and Deuteronomy, and an occasional psalm, song, and proverb. The net effect was little more than descriptive commentary on Hawaiian antiquities. Nevertheless, it stands as a Hawaiian classic.

After his conversion, Malo bitterly rejected his own pagan culture, and could not write sympathetically of his people and their past. Bitterness and bias crept into his narrative—along with the pious phrases and concepts of his teachers. Yet the thin volume is one of the few descriptions we have of Hawaiian society before it was altered by Western civilization. The passages reproduced here are selected topically from several chapters and omit the paragraph numerals.

In Bondage to the Chiefs

The physical characteristics of the chiefs and the common people of Hawaii *nei* were the same; they were all of one race, alike in features and physique. Commoners and *alii* [royalty, chiefs] were all descended from the same ancestors, Wakea and Papa. The whole people were derived from that couple. There was no difference between king and plebeian as to origin. It must have been after the time of Wakea that the separation of the chiefs from the people took place.

It is probable that because it was impossible for all the people to act in concert in the government, in settling the difficulties, lifting the burdens, and disentangling the embarrassments of the people from one end of the land to the other that one was made king, with sole authority to conduct the government and do all its business. This most likely was the reason why certain ones were selected to be chiefs. . . .

The king was appointed that he might help the oppressed who appealed to him, that he might succor those in the right and punish severely those in the wrong. The king was over all the people. . . . His executive duties in the government were to gather the people together in time of war, to decide all important questions of state and questions touching the life and death of the common people as well as of the chiefs and his comrades in arms. It was his to look after the soldiery. To him belonged the property derived from the yearly taxes, and he was the one who had the power to dispossess commoners and chiefs of their lands. . . .

He had the power to appropriate, reap or seize at pleasure the goods of any man, to cut off the ear of another man's pig [thus making it his own]. It was his duty to consecrate the temples, to oversee the performance of religious rites in the temples of human sacrifice, . . . to preside over the celebration of the *Makahiki* festival, and such other ceremonies as he might be pleased to appoint. . . .

The *Makahiki* was a time when men, women and chiefs rested and abstained from all work, either on the farm or elsewhere. It was a time of entire freedom from labor. The people did not engage in the usual religious observances during this time, nor did the chiefs; their worship consisted of making offerings of food. The king himself abstained from work on *Makahiki* days. . . . During these four months . . . the services at the royal *heiau* were suspended, and the chiefs and people who were wont to attend worship betook themselves to sports, games and the pursuit of pleasure. . . .

It was the policy of the government to place the chiefs who were destined to rule, while they were still young, with wise persons, that they might be instructed by skilled teachers in the principles of government, be taught the art of war, and be made to acquire personal skill and bravery. A young man had first to be subject to another chief that he might be disciplined and have experience of poverty, hunger, want and hardship, and by reflecting on these things learn to care for the people with gentleness and patience, with a feeling of sympathy for the common people, and at the same time to pay due respect to the ceremonies of religion and the worship of the gods, to live temperately, not violating virgins, conducting the government kindly to all. This is the way for a king to prolong his reign and cause his dynasty to be perpetuated. . . .

The great chiefs were entirely exclusive, being hedged about with many tabus, and a large number of people were slain for breaking or infringing upon these tabus. . . . If the shadow of a man fell upon the house of a tabu chief, that man must be put to death, and so with anyone whose shadow fell upon the back of the chief, or upon his robe or *malo*, or upon anything that belonged to the chief.

If anyone passed through the private doorway of a tabu chief, or climbed over the stockade about his residence, he was put to death. If a man entered the *alii's* house without changing his wet *malo*, or with his head smeared with mud, he was put to death. Even if there were no fence surrounding the *alii's* residence, only a mark or faint scratch in the ground hidden by the grass, and a man were to overstep this line unwittingly, not seeing it, he would be put to death. . . . There were many other tabus, some of them relating to the man himself and some to the king, for violating which anyone would be put to death. . . .

Likewise with the chief . . . when his food calabashes, bathing water, clothing, *malo*, or anything that belonged to him, was carried along the road, the person who at such a time remained standing was put to death in accordance with the law of the tabu relative to the chiefs. The punishment inflicted upon those who violated the tabu of the chiefs was to be burned with fire until their bodies were reduced to ashes, or to be strangled, or stoned to death. Thus it was that the tabus of the chiefs oppressed the whole people.

The edicts of the king had power over life and death. If the king had a mind to put someone to death—it might be a chief or a commoner—he uttered the word and death it was. But if the king chose to utter the word of life, the man's life was spared. The king, however, had no laws regarding property or land, regarding the payment or collection of debts, regulating affairs and transactions among the common people, not to mention a great many other things.

Everything went according to the will or whim of the king, whether it concerned land or people or anything else—not according to law. All the chiefs under the king . . . regulated land matters and everything else according to their own notions. There was no judge nor any court of justice to sit in judgment on wrongdoers of any sort. Retaliation with violence or murder was the rule in ancient times. To run away and hide one's self was the only recourse for an offender in those days. . . .

There was a great difference between chiefs. Some were given to robbery, spoliation, murder, extortion, ravishing. There were few kings who conducted themselves properly as Kamehameha I did. He looked well after the peace of the land. On account of the rascality of some of the chiefs to the common people, warlike contests frequently broke out between certain chiefs and the people, and many of the former were killed in battle by the commoners. . . .

The amount of property which the chiefs obtained from the people was very great. Some of it was given in the shape of taxes, some was the fruit of robbery and extortion. Now the people in the out-districts were, as a rule, industrious, while those about court or who lived with the chiefs were indolent, merely living on the income of the land. Some of the chiefs carried themselves haughtily and arrogantly, being supported by contributions from others without labor of their own. As was the chief, so were his retainers. On this account, the number of retainers, servants and hangers-on about the courts and residences of the kings and high chiefs was very great. The court of the king offered great attractions to the lazy and shiftless. . . .

Perhaps in the earliest time all the people were *alii* and it was only after the lapse of several generations that a division was made into commoners and chiefs. . . . The commoners were the most numerous class of people in the nation, and were known as *makaainana*. . . . The condition of the common people was that of subjection to the chiefs, compelled to do their heavy tasks, burdened and oppressed, some even to death. The life of the people was one of patient endurance, of yielding to the chiefs to purchase their favor. The plain man must not complain.

If the people were slack in doing the chief's work, they were expelled from their lands or even put to death. For such reasons as this, and because of the oppressive exactions made upon them, the people held the chiefs in great dread and looked upon them as gods. Only a small portion of the kings and chiefs ruled with kindness; the large majority simply lorded it over the people.

It was from the common people, however, that the chiefs received their food and their apparel for men and women, also their houses and many other things. When the chiefs went forth to war some of the commoners also went out to fight on the same side with them. . . . It was the *makaainana* also who did all the work on the land; yet all they produced from the soil belonged to the chiefs; and the power to expel a man from the land and rob him of his possessions lay with the chief. . . .

The people were divided into farmers, fishermen, house builders, canoe makers, etc. They were called by many different appellations according to the trades they followed. The people lived in a state of chronic fear and apprehension of the chiefs; those of them, however, who lived immediately with the chief were relieved of this apprehension. . . .

The task of providing food and eating under the *kapu* system in Hawaii *nei* was very burdensome, a grievous tax on husband and wife, an iniquitous imposition, at war with domestic peace. The husband was burdened and wearied with the preparation of two ovens of food, one for himself and a separate one for his wife. The man first started an oven of food for his wife, and when that was done, he went to the house *mua* and started an oven of food for himself.

Then he would return to the house and open his wife's oven, peel the taro, pound it into *poi,* knead it and put it into the calabash. This ended the food cooking for his wife. Then he must return to *mua,* open his own oven, peel the taro, pound and knead it into *poi,* put the mass into a [separate] calabash for himself and remove the lumps. Thus did he prepare his food; and thus was he compelled to do so long as he and his wife lived.

Another burden that fell to the lot of the man was thatching the houses for himself and his wife, because the houses for the man must be other than those for the woman. The man had first to thatch a house for himself to eat in and another house as a sanctuary in which to worship his idols. And that accomplished, he had to prepare a third house for himself and his wife to sleep in. After that he must build and thatch an eating house for his wife, and lastly he had to prepare a *hale kua,* a place for his wife to beat tapa in. . . .

The burdens that lay upon the woman were even greater than those allotted to the man. During the days of religious tabu, when the gods were specially worshipped, many women were put to death by reason of infraction of some tabu. . . . She always ate in her own house, and the man ate in the house called *mua.*

As a result of this custom, the mutual love of a man and his wife was not kept warm. . . .

Among the articles of food that were set apart for the exclusive use of man, of which it was forbidden the women to eat, were pork, bananas, coconuts, also certain fishes. . . . If a woman was clearly detected in the act of eating any of these things, as well as a number of other articles that were tabu, which I have not enumerated, she was put to death. . . .

The out-of-door work fell mostly upon the man, while the in-door work was done by the woman—that is, provided she was not a worthless and profligate woman. . . . The wives of the country people were sometimes appropriated by the men about court; even the men were sometimes separated from their country wives by the women of the court, and this violence was endured with little or no resistance, because these people feared that the king might take sides against them. In such ways as these the people of the country were heavily oppressed by the people who lived about court.

From *Hawaiian Antiquities* (*Moolelo Hawaii*), David Malo. Translated by Nathaniel B. Emerson (Honolulu: Bishop Museum Press, 1951).

III

William Ellis

By the seventeenth or eighteenth century the population of the Islands may have reached as high as half a million people. So great was the congestion in desirable waterfront villages that thousands of commoners were forced far back into the valleys and onto the mountain plateaus to carry on their agricultural pursuits. Tiny patches for taro plantings were carved in hill slopes, terraced, and filled with soil laboriously carried by the calabashful from more fertile lowlands. To meet the demand for food, hundreds of mountain acres were converted into agricultural lands and irrigated ingeniously from paved ditches that wound for miles back to a dammed water source.

Theoretically the estate of every chief was triangular-shaped, with the base on the shore and the legs of the triangle meeting on the crest of a mountain, so that all could benefit from an equitable division of the land and its produce at different altitudes, but the theory did not always work out in practice. There were highly productive parcels and less productive parcels; the inequality invariably led to jealousies, jealousies to dispute, dispute to combat, until a state of war became the natural mode of existence, chief fighting against chief, king against king, island against island.

This was the kind of society that William Ellis (1794–1872) reconstructed long after Hawaiians by the thousands had perished on their battlefields and the population had been reduced to a fraction of its former total by the wars, diseases, and the "benefits of civilization" brought by white intruders. Ellis was a veteran British missionary who had served in the Society Islands under the London Mission Society before the first New England missionaries arrived in Hawaii. In the Society Islands he had worked out a form of writing for the native language and established the first printing press in the South Seas. He was a scholar as well as a forceful evangelist, and had made himself an authority on Polynesian history, language, and culture.

In 1822, en route back to England, he called at Honolulu, where his experience proved so valuable to the American missionaries that they persuaded him to remain for two years. He at once advocated that a thorough survey be made of their field, and himself set out on a tour of the Big Island. A few weeks later he could report: "We have ascended its lofty and majestic mountains, entered its dark caverns, crossed its deep ravines and traversed its immense fields of rugged lava. . . . We traveled to the south, the east and the north; twice crossed the interior in different parts; remained a night and a day at the great volcano of Kilauea; visited all the principal settlements both on the coast and in the interior."

Ellis' knowledge of Tahitian enabled him to converse with natives everywhere he went. He made a special study of Island warfare, interrogated chiefs, old warriors, ex-priests, weapons craftsmen, professional raconteurs on the subject, and later incorporated a summary of his findings in *The Narrative of a Tour Through Hawaii*, the most accurate and detailed compendium on early Hawaii that had yet been assembled. However, he evidently declined to accept the spelling of Hawaiian words that American missionaries had agreed to adopt.

In Battle Array

The Sandwich Islands, like many other parts of the world, have frequently felt the cruel scourge of war. Their traditional history, so far as we have been able to trace it, is distinguished by nothing so much as accounts of the murderous and plundering expeditions of one island against another, or the sanguinary battles between the inhabitants of different parts of the same island.

The whole group have seldom, if ever, been united under one

authority; but, in general, separate governments and independent kings or chiefs have existed in each of the large islands; and sometimes the six great divisions of Hawaii have been under as many distinct rulers or chieftains. Their inclinations or interests often interfered, and almost every dispute terminated in an appeal to arms. Indeed, a pretext for war was seldom wanting, when one party thought themselves sufficiently powerful to invade with success the territories of their neighbors and plunder their property.

Their modes of warfare must, therefore, necessarily exhibit much of their national character. . . . Their armies were composed of individuals from every rank in society. There was no distinct class of men trained exclusively to the use of arms and warriors by profession, yet there have always been men celebrated for their courage and martial achievements, . . . men who left their peaceful home and employment as agriculturists or fishermen, to follow their fortunes in the field, and resumed their former pursuits on the cessation of hostilities.

Before the introduction of firearms and gunpowder almost all the men were taught to use the various weapons employed in battle, and frequently engaged in martial exercises or warlike games. One of the exercises consisted in slinging stones at a mark. They threw stones with great force and precision, and are supposed to have been able to strike a small stick at fifty yards' distance four times out of five.

They also practiced throwing the javelin, and catching and returning those thrown at them, or warding them off so as to avoid receiving any injury. In this latter exercise they excelled to an astonishing degree. We know some men who have stood and allowed six men to throw their javelins at them, which they would either catch and return on their assailants, or so dexterously turn aside that they fell harmless to the ground.

Wrestling was also practiced by the more athletic youth as a preparation to the single combats usual in almost every battle. Sometimes they had sham fights when large numbers engaged and each party advanced and retreated, attacked and defended, and exercised all the maneuvers employed in actual engagement.

Admirably constituted by nature, with fine-formed bodies, supple joints, strong and active limbs, accustomed also to a light and cumberless dress, they took great delight in these gymnastic and warlike exercises, and in the practice of them spent no inconsiderable portion of their time.

Whenever war was in contemplation, the *poe kiro* (diviners and priests) were directed to slay the accustomed victims and consult the gods. Animals only were used on these occasions, generally hogs and fowls. The priests offered their prayers and the diviners sacrificed the victims, observed the manner in which they expired, the appearance of their entrails and other signs.

Sometimes when the animal was slain, they embowelled it, took out the spleen and, holding it in their hands, offered their prayers. If they did not receive an answer, war was deferred. They also slept in the temple where the gods were kept and, after the war god had revealed his will by a vision or dream, or some other supernatural means, they communicated it to the king and warriors, and war was either determined or relinquished accordingly.

If the expedition in contemplation was of any magnitude or importance, or the danger which threatened imminent, human sacrifices were offered to ensure the co-operation of the war gods in the destruction of their enemies. They do not appear to have imagined these gods exerted any protecting influence over the devotees, but that their presence and their power destroyed the courage and strength of their enemies, and filled their hearts with terror and dismay.

Sometimes the priests proposed that human victims should be slain; sometimes the gods themselves were said to require them to promise a victory on condition of their being offered, and at other times they were slain after having consulted the gods as their oracle, and not having received a favorable answer, they were desirous to consult them again before they abandoned the enterprise. If any of their enemies had been taken captive, the victims were elected from among their number; if not, individuals who had broken tabu or rendered themselves obnoxious to the chiefs were fixed upon.

A message was sent to the chief under whose authority they were, and at the appointed time he sent his men, who generally dispatched them with a stone or club without any notice, and then carried them away to the temple. Sometimes they were bound and taken alive to the *heiau* and slain in the outer court immediately before being placed on the altar. It does not appear that they were slain in the idol's presence or within the temple, but either on the outside or at the place where they were first taken; in both cases they appear to have endeavored to preserve the body entire, or mangled as little as possible.

The victims were generally dispatched by a blow on the head with a club or stone; sometimes, however, they were stabbed. The number offered at a time varied according to circumstances: two, four, or seven, or ten, or even twenty, we have been informed, have been offered at once. When carried into the temple, every article of clothing they might have on was taken off and they were laid in a row with their faces downward on the altar immediately before the idol.

The priest then, in a kind of prayer, offered them to the gods; and if any offerings of hogs were presented at the same time, they were afterward piled upon them, lying at right angles across the human bodies, where the whole were left to rot and putrefy together.

War was seldom declared without the approbation of the gods, obtained through the medium of the priests, though it is probable the answer of the diviners was given with due regard to the previously known views of the king and chiefs. Sometimes the question of war or peace was deliberated in a public meeting of chiefs and warriors, and these popular assemblies furnished occasion for the most powerful displays of native eloquence which . . . from specimens we have heard repeated, was, like that of their neighbors of the southern isles, at once bold in sentiment, beautiful in imagery and powerful in effect, . . . heightened by the conciseness of their language and the euphony with which it abounds; and probably on one side of the place where they were assembled the rocks arose and the waves dashed; while on the other groves of stately breadfruit trees appeared or towering coconuts, seventy or eighty feet high, waved over their heads.

When war was declared, the king and warrior chiefs, together with the priests, fixed the time and place for commencing and the manner of carrying it on. In the meantime, the *Runapai* (messengers of war) were sent to the districts and villages under their authority to require the services of their tenants, in numbers proportionate to the magnitude of the expedition. These were ordered to come with their weapons, candle nuts for torches, light calabashes for water, dried fish or other portable provisions.

The summons was in general obeyed with alacrity, and as their spears, clubs, javelins and slings were usually suspended in some convenient part of every house, they armed with these and soon joined the forces at the appointed rendezvous. . . . These messengers of war . . . generally traveled at a running pace and in cases of emergency are reported to have gone round the island of Hawaii in eight or nine days, a distance which, including the circuitous route they would take to call at different villages, exceeds three hundred miles.

When the different parties arrived at the place of rendezvous, the chief of the division or district, with some of inferior rank, waited on the king or commanding chief, and reported the number of warriors they had brought. They then selected a spot for their encampment . . . near an open space, and they generally selected the most broken and uneven ground, frequently rugged tracts of lava as their field of battle. . . . They do not appear to have thrown up lines or other artificial barriers around their camp; they did not, however, neglect to station piquets at all the passes by which they were likely to be approached.

Each party usually had a *pari* or *pa-kaua*, natural or artificial fortress, where they left their wives and children and to which they fled if vanquished in the field. . . . When the *pari* was an eminence, after they had closed the avenues, they collected large stones and fragments of rock on the edges of the precipices overhanging the paths leading to the fortification, which they rolled down on the heads of their enemies.

Sometimes they engaged in fleets amounting to upward of one

hundred canoes on each side. At a distance they fought with slings and stones and other missiles, and at close quarters with club and spear. The fleets were not lashed together like those of the Society Islands. The Sandwich Islands, not being surrounded with coral reefs, there is but little smooth water; and the roughness of the sea most likely induced them generally to select terra firma for their theater of war. . . .

Their weapons consisted of the *pololu,* a spear made of hard wood, from sixteen to twenty feet long and pointed at one end; the *ihe,* or javelin, about six feet in length, made of a species of hard red wood resembling mahogany, pointed and barbed; the *raau parau,* a weapon eight or nine feet long, between a club and a spear, somewhat resembling a halberd, with which they were accustomed to thrust or strike; and the *pahoa,* or dagger, eighteen inches or two feet in length, made of hard wood, sometimes pointed at both ends and having a string attached to the handle, which passed around the wrist to prevent their losing it in action.

Besides these they employed the sling, and their stones were very destructive. The slings were made of human hair, plaited, or the elastic fibers of the coconut husk; the stones they employed were about the size of a hen's egg, generally ponderous pieces of compact lava from the bed of a stream or the sea beach, where they had been worn smooth by the action of the water.

They had no shields or weapons of defense, except the javelin, which they used in warding off those that might be thrown at them; they were very expert in avoiding a stone, if they saw it thrown, and the spearmen excelled in parrying the thrusts of their enemies' spears. The warriors seldom went to battle with any other dress than a maro or narrow girdle round their loins. Some, however, wore a quantity of cloth bound round their heads . . . and the chiefs were frequently dressed in warcloaks and helmets.

The cloaks, though they gave the wearers an imposing appearance, must have proved an encumbrance, without affording much protection. Some of the helmets were made of close wickerwork, exactly fitted to the head, and were ornamented along the crown. But those worn by the high chiefs only . . . were made in the form of the Grecian helmet with towering crest, and were thickly covered with the glossy red and yellow feathers of a small paraquet found in the mountains. . . . Though they did not appear adapted to defend the head any more than the cloaks were to guard the body, they increased the effect of the towering height and martial air of the chiefs, whose stature was generally above that of the common people.

The long cloaks, reaching to the knees or even to the ankles, were worn only by the king and principal chiefs. The royal color was yellow, and no one besides the king was allowed to wear a cloak made entirely of yellow feathers. Those of the other chiefs were of red and yellow rhomboidal figures intermingled or disposed in alternate lines, with sometimes a section of dark purple or glossy black. . . .

The diviners were consulted immediately before they engaged; they slew their victims, noticed also the face of the heavens and passage of clouds over the sun, the appearance of the rainbow; and if they augured well, the principal war god was brought out in front of the whole army and placed near the king.

The priest then addressed a prayer to the gods, urged them to exercise their power and prove themselves in the ensuing engagement mightier than the gods of their enemies, promising at the same time hecatombs of victims in the event of victory. The king or commander-in-chief now addressed the assembled warriors, and if they were to attack, gave the signal for the *hoouta,* or onset, and they rushed to *hui,* or mix in fight. They did not employ any banners or colors, but in their warlike expeditions were attended by their idols.

The national war god was elevated above the ranks and carried by the priest near the person of the king or commander-in-chief. Nor was this the only idol borne to the battle: other chiefs of rank had their war gods carried near them by their priest; and if the king or chief were killed or taken, the god himself was usually captured also. The presence of their deities inspired the warriors with courage, who supposed their influence essential to victory. . . .

At times the whole army, except the reserve, engaged at once, but their battles were most commonly a succession of skirmishes or partial engagements. The *hooparau,* single combat, was not unusual. A haughty and boastful warrior would advance beyond the line of his companions and *toho* or *aa,* insult, in opprobrious terms the whole army of his enemies. A warrior from that army would hasten to meet him, and the encounter was continued till one was disabled or slain. . . .

Their battles were with confused noise and boastful shouts. The first that either party slew they called *erehua;* frequently the victor jumped upon the expiring body or, spurning it contemptuously, dedicated its spirit to his gods. He then cut or tore off the hair from the top of the forehead and, elevating it in the air, shouted aloud, *"He oho,"* a frontlet. . . .

"He oho! He oho!" was reiterated through the ranks of the victor, while he despoiled the fallen warrior of his ornaments and then dragged the *heana,* slain body, to the king or the priest, who in a short address offered the victim to his god. . . .

Their conflicts were sometimes continued for several successive days before either army retreated; and on some occasions both parties discontinued the contest as if by mutual consent, from despair of victory or an evil omen revealed by the diviners. . . . This, however, was a rare occurrence; they generally fought till one of the armies was vanquished and fled.

When routed in the field some fled to the *pahu tapu,* sacred enclosure, called also *puhonua,* or place of refuge; others repaired to their *pari* or fortress; and when those were distant or the way to them intercepted, they all fled to the mountains, whither they were pursued by the victors for weeks or even months afterward. When discovered, they were cruelly massacred on the spot or brought down to the king and chiefs . . . to be slaughtered, . . . perhaps spared only to be slaves or to be sacrificed when the priests should require human victims.

The persons of the captives were the property of the victors and their lives were entirely at their disposal. A chief taken in the field or during the retreat was sometimes spared and allowed to return to his home. The victors usually buried their dead; but the bodies of the slain, belonging to the vanquished, were generally left unburied on the field, and were devoured by dogs and hogs or suffered to rot. Small heaps of stones were afterward piled over their bones or on the spot where they had fallen, probably as trophies of victory. . . .

When the vanquished were completely routed or nearly cut off, their country was *hoopahora*, portioned out, by the conqueror among the chiefs and warriors who had been his companions in the war, by whom it was settled. The wives and children of those whom they had defeated were frequently made slaves and attached to the soil for its cultivation and, together with the captives, treated with great cruelty. But when there had been a great loss on both sides or one party wished for peace, an ambassador with a young plantain tree and a green branch of the ti plant was sent with proposals for peace. If they were accepted, the preliminaries were arranged and the chiefs and priests of both parties met to adjust the particulars.

When the conditions of peace were agreed to, they all repaired to the temple. There a pig was slain, its blood caught in a vessel, and afterward poured on the ground, probably to signify that thus it should be done to those who broke the treaty. A wreath of *mairi*, a sweet-scented plant, was then woven by the leading chiefs of both parties and deposited in the temple. Peace was ratified; feasting, dances and public games followed. The warriors returned to their lands and the king's heralds were sent round his districts to announce *ua pau ka kaua*, ended is the war.

From *Journal of William Ellis, The Narrative of a Tour Through Hawaii* (London, 1827).

IV

Abraham Fornander

Pagan though they were by Christian standards, the Hawaiian Polynesians were as prayerful and godly a people as ever existed, constantly
in touch with divine beings. But instead of venerating one omniscient
god, they worshiped four principal deities and countless minor ones.
There was a different god for every phase of activity, for every form
of life, for every individual. The gods populated the earth, the sky,
the sea, the underground—fish gods, household gods, gods of war and
gods of sports, of planting and harvest, of hula dancing, and tapa
beating, of vegetation and volcanoes, major gods, less important gods,
and demigods, with galaxies of hobgoblins, guardian angels, ghouls,
and ogres to fill all gaps in the natural and supernatural world.

Hawaiian reckoning went only to 400,000; so the priests acknowledged allegiance to 400,000 gods, but that was an underestimate, for
there were many more gods than people, and no god-fearing individual
would undertake any action of consequence without first consulting
some divinity. In the 1860's before this idolatry had entirely passed
from memory, Abraham Fornander (1812–1887), a Swede who had settled in Hawaii in 1842, began to make a collection of ancient Hawaiian
tales. His marriage to an Island princess and his employment in a
number of government positions, including a circuit judgeship on
Maui, gave him trusted access to all levels of society. With the assistance of several respected Hawaiians, who did most of the actual col-
lecting and recording, over a period of twenty years he assembled

a mass of manuscript which was eventually published as *The Fornander Collection of Hawaiian Antiquities and Folklore.*

That collection still stands as the most important documentation of Hawaiian mythology ever made. Although it is a superior source of information on many facets of early Island culture, the stories themselves are not as stirring now as they were to audiences of past centuries. References to the gods, of course, are ever recurrent, and one story, "The Legend of Kamapuaa," contains what may perhaps be considered a typical pagan psalm which can be read today for its poetic quality and rhythm rather than for any profound meaning. The Hawaiian's relationship to his gods was very personal, and those Kamapuaa addressed in rapid succession could be expected to convey messages only to him.

Psalm

The small god is mine,
The large god is mine,
The long god is mine,
The short god is mine,
The god that smacks the lips is mine,
The god that whispers is mine,
Kookoona is ahead,
The *awa* drinker of Kanaloa is ahead,
Here is Opuaanuenue,
Whose sound reaches heaven,
It is carried here and there,
Along the *lehua* grove.
Dig it up, fence it up.
O that sky, O this sky,
The sky up above,
The sky in the heaven.
The folding of it is his,
The wide leaf is sacred,
Roll it up,
Dry it out.

The small night,
The large night,
The long night,
The short night,
The night with the sun that has passed.
The small cloud is here,
The large cloud is here,
The long cloud is here,
The short cloud is here.
The cloud stands close to heaven.
The assembly of gods,
Make offerings to *the* god,
Of Kahaka, of Keluea,
Of Kulia who is at war,
Lonomakaihe,
Kanaiahuea,
Kepolohaina.
The god with the piercing eyes,
Ohumuhumu,
Hawanawana,
Kanikawi,
Kanikawa,
The gods with the body,
Of the head,
Hoeu, Hoomalana,
The piece of the head, the head scalped.
Of the ear,
The ear wax, the hearing,
Lonoikiaweawealoha.
Of the grinders,
The yellow grinders,
The unclean grinders.
Of the buttocks.
Of *palala,*
Pipikauanana.
Of the knee.
Out of joint, misstep.

The back, the feet,
For fleetness.
There were the forty thousand gods,
The abode of the gods,
The creaking,
The cracking,
Kumahumahukole,
Of *kole* the laughter.

From *The Fornander Collection of Hawaiian Antiquities and Folklore,* Abraham Fornander. Translated by Thomas G. Thrum. Memoirs of the Bernice Pauahi Bishop Museum. Volume V (Honolulu: Bishop Museum Press, 1918–19).

V

Padraic Colum

The ancient Hawaiians were bold warriors, expert sailors, good crafts-men, and ingenious agriculturalists, but among them also were poets, spellbinding narrators, spinners of yarns, and superb dancers. As a race, they were natural actors. "Tie a Hawaiian's hands and he can't talk," was a cliché later applied to their descendants by white men. Not only were hands used for emphasis and nuance, but dramatic facial expression and arm, shoulder, head, and torso movements also. The common people picked up their theatrics from the performances of professional storytellers and chanters who acted as well as recited an endless repertoire of sagas and legends.

Few examples of this unwritten literature survived to be recorded, though several attempts were made by amateur anthropologists of the nineteenth century to get it on paper before it was entirely forgotten. Then belatedly in 1922 the Hawaiian legislature appointed a com-mission to take inventory of stories and *meles* still in circulation, and the Irish poet and dramatist Padraic Colum (1881–), who had earned an international reputation as a sympathetic and sensitive folk-lorist, was summoned to translate the collection into stories in English for children.

Colum spent four months in Hawaii sorting over the old material and traveling about the Islands in search of new, interviewing aged grandfathers and grandmothers, and occasionally encountering a raconteur who had not forgotten his histrionics. "What impressed me most in these recitals," he wrote, "was the gesture of the storyteller. Every feature, every finger of the man or woman becomes alive, becomes dramatic as the recital is entered into. The gesture of the Hawaiian makes the telling of the story a dramatic entertainment. . . . It was trained, as was the gesture in the hula. . . . Old men and women still have that wonderful command of their features and their hands—a command that made them the greatest ballet performers that the world, I believe, has ever had."

In almost inaccessible valleys and along remote beaches, still relatively unspoiled by the intrusion of Western civilization, Colum declared that he sometimes found "a real scholarship, a delight in poetry, and the possession of such a quantity of it as would put to shame a cultivated American, Englishman or Frenchman."

The stories that the famed Irish poet collected were originally for adult entertainment, not for children, and he admitted that details had to be "suppressed" in retelling them for a youthful audience. His account of the *Menehune* was representative. The Hawaiians were never quite convinced that they were the only tenants of the Islands. Awed perhaps by the stupendous feats of construction, the straight paved trails, the dams, irrigation projects, and monumental temples completed by their ancestors, they gradually attributed them to mysterious Menehune—the Little People, not unlike the Little People accredited to primitive civilizations in other parts of the world. Many a Hawaiian, even today, believes as firmly in the past accomplishments of the Menehune as in the recurrent wiles of Pele, mistress of the volcanoes.

The Little People

The Menehune folk worked only at night. . . . They were all very great workers . . . all little men, and none of them was higher than the legs of one of us—no, not even their Kings and Chiefs. Little men, broad-shouldered and sturdy and very active—such were the Menehune in the old days, and such are the Menehune today. . . .

A long time ago, when the Menehune were very many in our

land . . . they lived then in the Valley of Lanihula. There they planted taro in plants that still grow there—plants that they brought back with them from Kahikimoe after they had been there. It was they who planted the breadfruit tree first in that valley.

Our fathers say that when the men-folk of the Menehune stood together in those days they could form two rows reaching all the way from Makaweli to Wailua. And with their women and children there were so many of them that the only fish of which the Menehune could have one was the shrimp, the littlest and the most plentiful fish in our waters.

For the rest of their food they had *haupia,* a pudding made of arrowroot sweetened with the milk of coconut; they had squash and they had sweet potato pudding. They ate fern fronds and the cooked young leaves of the taro. They had carved wooden dishes for their food. For their games they had spinning tops which they made out of kukui nuts, and they played at casting the arrow, a game which they called *keapua.* They had boxing and wrestling, too, and they had tug of war: when one team was about to be beaten all the others jumped in and helped them.

They had sled races; they would race their sleds down the steep sides of hills; if the course were not slippery already, they would cover it with rushes so that the sleds would go more easily and more swiftly.

But their great sport was to jump off the cliffs into the sea. They would throw a stone off the cliff and dive after it and touch the bottom as it touched the bottom. Once, when some of them were bathing, a shark nearly caught one of the Menehune. Aaka was his name. Then they all swam ashore, and they made plans for punishing the shark that had treated them so. Their wise men told them what to do. They were to gather the morning-glory vine and make a great basket with it. Then they were to fill the basket with bait and lower it into the sea. Always the Menehune worked together; they worked together very heartily when they went to punish the shark.

They made the basket; they filled it with bait, and they lowered it into the sea. The shark got into the basket, and the Menehune caught him. They pulled him within the reef, and they left him there in the shallow water until the birds came and ate him up.

One of them caught a large fish there. The fish tried to escape, but the little man held bravely to him. The fish bit him and lashed him with its tail and drew blood from the Menehune. The place where his blood poured out is called Kaalele to this day—for that was the name of the Menehune who struggled with the fish.

Once they hollowed out a great stone and they gave it to their head fisherman for a house. He would sit in his hollow stone all day and fish for his people.

No cliff was too steep for them to climb; indeed, it was they who planted the wild taro on the cliffs; they planted it in the swamps too, and on cliff and in swamp it grows to this day. When they were on the march they would go in divisions. The work of the first division would be to clear the road of logs. The work of the second division would be to lower the hills. The work of the third division would be to sweep the path. Another division had to carry the sleds and the sleeping mats for the King. One division had charge of the food, and another division had charge of the planting of the crop.

One division was composed of wizards and soothsayers and astrologers, and another division was made up of story-tellers, fun-makers, and musicians who made entertainment for the King. Some played on the nose flute, and others blew trumpets that were made by ripping a ti leaf away from the middle ridge and rolling over the torn piece. Through this they blew, varying the sound by fingering. They played stringed instruments that they held in their mouths, and they twanged the strings with their fingers. Others beat on drums that were hollow logs with shark skin drawn across them.

It would have been wonderful to look on the Menehune when they were on the march. That would be on the nights of the full moon. Then they would all come together, and their King would speak to them. . . .

A long time ago a King ruled in Kauai whose name was Ola. His people were poor, for the river ran into the stony places and left their fields without water. "How can I bring water to my people?" said Ola the King to Pi, his wizard. "I will tell you how you can do it," Pi said. And then he told the King what to do so as to get the help of the Menehune.

Pi, the wise man, went into the mountains. He was known to the Menehune who had remained on the land, and he went before their Chief, and he asked him to have his people make a watercourse for Ola's people: they would have to dam the river with great stones and then make a trench that would carry the water down to the people's fields—a trench that would have stones fitted into its bed and fitted into its sides.

All the work that takes us days to do can be done by the Menehune in the space of a night. And what they do not finish in a night is left unfinished. "*Ho po hookahi, a ao ua pau,*" "In one night and it is finished," say the Menehune.

Well, in one night all the stones for the dam and the watercourse were made ready: one division went and gathered them, and another cut and shaped them. The stones were all left together, and the Menehune called them "the Pack of Pi."

Now King Ola had been told what he was to have done on the night that followed. There was to be no sound and there was to be no stir among his people. The dogs were to be muzzled so that they could not bark, and the cocks and the hens were to be put into calabashes so that there should be no crowing from them. Also a feast was to be ready for the Menehune.

Down from the mountain in the night came the troops of the Menehune, each carrying a stone in his hand. Their trampling and the hum of their voices was heard by Pi as he stayed by the river; they were heard while they were still a long way off. They came down, and they made a trench with their digging tools of wood. Then they began to lay the stones at the bottom and along the sides of the trench; each stone fitted perfectly into its place. While one division was doing this the other division was building the dam across the river. The dam was built, the water was turned into the course, and Pi, standing there in the moonlight, saw the water come over the stones that the Menehune had laid down.

Pi, and no one else, saw the Menehune that night: half the size of our men they were, but broad across the chest and very strong. Pi admired that way they all worked together; they never got into each other's way, and they never waited for someone else to do something or to help them out. They finished their work just at daybreak; and then Pi gave them their feast. He gave a shrimp to each; they were well satisfied, and while it was still dark they departed. They crossed the watercourse that was now bringing water down to the people's taro patches. And as they went the hum of their voices was so loud that it was heard in the distant land of Oahu. . . .

There was once a boy of your age, O my younger brother, and his name was Laka. As he grew up he was petted very much by his father and his mother. And while he was still a young boy his father took a canoe and went across the sea to get a toy for him. Never after did Laka see his father.

He grew up, and he would often ask about his father. His mother could tell him nothing except that his father had gone across the sea in a canoe and that it was told afterward that he had been killed in a cave by a bad man. The more he grew up the more he asked about his father. He told his mother he would go across the sea in search of him. But the boy could not go until he had a canoe. "How am I to get a canoe?" he said to his mother one day.

"You must go to your grandmother," said she, "and she will tell you what to do to get a canoe."

So to his grandmother Laka went. He lived in her house for a while, and then he asked her how he might get a canoe.

"Go to the mountains and look for a tree that has leaves shaped like the new moon," said his grandmother. "Take your axe with you. When you find such a tree, cut it down, for it is the tree to make a canoe out of."

So Laka went to the mountains. He brought his axe with him. All day he searched in the woods, and at last he found a tree that had leaves shaped like the new moon. He commenced to cut through its trunk with his little axe of stone. At nightfall the trunk was cut through, and the tree fell down on the ground.

Then, well content with his day's work, Laka went back to his grandmother's. The next day he would cut off the branches and drag the trunk down to the beach and begin to make a canoe. He went back to the mountains. He searched and searched through all the woods, but he could find no trace of the tree that he had cut down with so much labor.

He went to the mountains again the day after. He found another tree growing with leaves shaped like the new moon. With his little stone axe he cut through the trunk, and the tree fell down. Then he went back to his grandmother's, thinking that he would go the next day and cut off the branches and bring the trunk down to the beach.

But the next day when he went to the mountains there was no trace of the tree that he had cut down with so much labor. He searched for it all day, but could not find it. The next day he had to begin his labor all over again: he had to search for a tree that had leaves like the new moon, he had to cut through the trunk and let it lie on the ground. After he had cut down the third tree he spoke to his grandmother about the trees that he had cut and had lost sight of. His wise grandmother told him that, if the third tree disappeared, he was to dig a trench beside where the next tree would fall. And when that tree came down he was to hide in the trench beside it and watch what would happen.

When Laka went up the mountain the next day he found that the tree he had cut was lost to his sight like the others. He found another tree with leaves shaped like the new moon. He began to cut this one down. Near where it would fall he dug a trench.

It was very late in the evening when he cut through this tree. The trunk fell, and it covered the trench he had made. Then Laka went under and hid himself. He waited while the night came on.

Then, while he was waiting, he heard the hum of voices, and he knew that a band of people were drawing near. They were singing as they came on. Laka heard what they sang.

> O the four thousand gods,
> O the forty thousand gods,
> O the four hundred thousand gods,

O the file of gods,
O the assembly of gods!
O gods of these woods,
Of the mountain, the knoll,
Of the dam of the watercourse, O descend!

Then there was more noise, and Laka, looking up from the trench, saw the clearing around him was all filled with a crowd of little men. They came where the tree lay, and they tried to move it. Then Laka jumped out of the trench, and he laid hands upon one of the little people. He threatened to kill him for having moved away the trees he had cut.

As he jumped up, all the little people disappeared. Laka was left with the one he held.

"Do not kill me," said the little man. "I am of the Menehune, and we intend no harm to you. I will say this to you: if you kill me, there will be no one to make the canoe for you, no one to drag it down to the beach, making it ready for you to sail in. If you do not kill me, my friends will make the canoe for you. And if you build a shed for it, we will bring the canoe finished to you and place it in the shed."

Then Laka said he would gladly spare the little man if he and his friends would make the canoe for him and bring it down to the shed that he would make. He let the little man go then. The next day he built a shed for the canoe.

When he told his Grandmother about the crowd of little men he had seen and about the little man he had caught, she told him that they were the Menehune, who lived in hollow logs and in caves in the mountains. No one knew how many of them there were.

He went back, and he found that where the trunk of the tree had lain there was now a canoe perfectly finished; all was there that should be there, even to the light, well-shaped paddle, and all had been finished in the night. He went back, and that night he waited beside the shed which he had built out on the beach. At the dead of the night he heard the hum of voices. That was when the canoe was being lifted up. Then he heard a second hum

"In pursuit of profitable traffic"

of voices. That was when the canoe was being carried on the hands of the Menehune—for they did not drag the canoe, they carried it. He heard a trampling of feet. Then he heard a third hum of voices; that was when the canoe was being left down in the shed he had built.

Laka's grandmother, knowing who they were, had left a feast for the Menehune—a shrimp for each, and some cooked taro leaves. They ate, and before it was daylight they returned to the mountain where their caves were. The boy Laka saw the Menehune as they went up the side of the mountain—hundreds of little men tramping away in the waning darkness.

His canoe was ready, paddle and all. He took it down to the sea, and he went across in search of his father. When he landed on the other side he found a wise man who was able to tell him about his father, and that he was dead indeed, having been killed by a very wicked man on his landing. The boy never went back to his grandmother's. He stayed, and with the canoe that the Menehune had made for him he became a famous fisherman. From him have come my fathers and your fathers, too, O my younger brothers.

And you who are the youngest and littlest of all—gather you the kukui nuts as we go down; tonight we will make strings of them and burn them, lighting the house. And if we have many kukui nuts and a light that is long-lasting, it may be that I will tell more stories.

From *At the Gateways of the Day*, Padraic Colum (New Haven: Yale University Press, 1924).

VI

John Ledyard

The isolated existence that the Hawaiians had known for centuries—laborious, oppressive, bellicose, yet lighthearted and sometimes idyllic—could not last forever, not with white adventurers scouring the face of the globe for new realms to conquer. It all came to a sudden end early in 1778 when England's famed navigator Captain James Cook sighted on the horizon the gray outline of mountainous islands where no terra firma was shown on his charts.

Captain Cook made three voyages of exploration to the Pacific. The major objective of his final expedition was to find a Northwest Passage across the top of North America, a shortcut from the Pacific to the Atlantic. It was on a leg of this voyage, sailing north from Tahiti toward the Arctic, that he spotted, on January 18, 1778, the insular dots which he named the Sandwich Islands, in honor of his sponsor, the Earl of Sandwich, First Lord of the British Admiralty.

He landed at Waimea, Kauai, and remained in the area long enough to learn that the natives were friendly, to establish a brisk barter in nails and scrap iron for pork and yams—and to contaminate the Islanders with some of the most malignant European diseases. But it was a cursory pause; he was eager to get on with the prime purpose of his mission, and after a few days resumed the voyage north.

The attempt to find a waterway across the American continent, of course, was unsuccessful, and after spending eight months in chill North Pacific waters, Cook decided to postpone a final try at locating the Passage until the following season and return meantime to the newly discovered Sandwich Islands to repair his vessels, refresh the crews, and check his discovery more thoroughly.

The two ships, *Resolution* and *Discovery*, were back in Hawaiian waters by late November, and as islands not seen on the previous visit came into view, Cook was increasingly impressed. For several weeks he maneuvered around the southern islands of the group, mapping the shores, bucking contrary winds and currents, searching for a protected harbor, occasionally trading offshore with the natives.

To superstitious Hawaiians, who had never before seen a great sailing vessel, the *Resolution* and *Discovery* were "floating islands" manned by the gods, and the mysterious tacking of the ships a zig-zag course that only deities would take. It was the height of the *Makahiki* festival, and since the white sails roughly resembled outsized replicas of their symbol for Lono, they naturally concluded that the god was about to pay them a visit.

Swiftly the rumor spread around the island of Hawaii that Lono and his retinue were coming: "The men are white; their skin is loose and folding; fire and smoke issue from their mouths; they have openings in the sides of their bodies and draw out iron, beads and other treasures." Priests even predicted where the visitors would land —at Kealakekua Bay, the Pathway of the Gods.

The natives were not disappointed. On January 17, 1779, the two ships cautiously moved into the Bay, the best shelter the navigators had been able to find. On board, as a member of the marine guard, was the Yankee Marco Polo of the day, John Ledyard (1751–1789). Of all the notable witnesses who later reported the turn of events at Kealakekua Bay, he wrote the most vivid and entertaining version.

White Gods with Loose Skins

While we were entering the bay, which they called Kirekakooa [Kealakekua], we were surrounded by so great a number of canoes that Cook ordered two officers into each top to number them with as much exactness as they could, and as they both exceeded 3,000 in their amounts, I shall with safety say there was 2,500, and as there were upon an average six persons at least in each canoe, it will follow that there were at least 15,000 men, women and children in the canoes, besides those that were on floats, swimming without floats, and actually on board and hanging round the outside of the ships.

The crowds on shore were still more numerous. The beach, the surrounding rocks, the tops of houses, the branches of trees and the adjacent hills were all covered, and the shouts of joy and admiration proceeding from the sonorous voices of the men, confused with the shriller exclamations of the women dancing and clapping their hands, the over-setting of canoes, cries of the children, goods on float, and hogs that were brought to market squealing, formed one of the most tumultuous and the most curious prospects that can be imagined.

God of creation, these are thy doings, these are our brethren and our sisters, the works of thy hands, and thou are not without a witness even here where for ages and perhaps since the beginning it has been hid from us, and though the circumstance may be beyond our comprehension, let it not lessen the belief of the fact.

Among all this immense multitude of people there was not the least appearance of insult. They had heard of our riches by those who had come off to us and traded, and from the people at Attowai [Kauai], and, concluding from our hovering round the island that we should visit them on shore, had prepared to meet us with supplies and give us a welcome. This previous preparation was the reason of this vast assemblage of people and provisions, and every one wanting to make the first bargain occasioned their coming all together. We purchased as many hogs that and the following day or two as we did for two months after, and had besides the advantage of refusing any but such as were of the best kind.

As soon as the *Resolution* was moored, Captain Cook went on shore in his pinnace, attended only by his barge crew and two of the chiefs, and landed upon a fine beach before the western part of the town of Kirekakooa. His crew were without arms and had himself only his hanger [short sword], which he never went without; the chiefs had each two long white poles which they held upright and waved to the people in the canoes, to make room, and as they passed through the throng, the chief cried out in their language that the great Orono [Lono] was coming, at which they all bowed and covered their faces with their hands until he was passed. But the moment this was done, they resumed their clamorous shouts, closed the vacant places astern, and as many as could, crowded upon his rear to the shore.

The two chiefs first landed and joined many other of their brother officers, who had also white rods in their hands, and, observing the transactions of the two chiefs in the pinnace, had also made an avenue among the people on shore.

Cook, in the meantime, improving the awful respect he saw paid him among the natives, permitted himself to be carried upon the shoulders of his bargemen from the boat to the summit of the beach, the bargemen uncovered. As soon as he was set down, the multitude on the beach fell prostrate with their faces to the ground, and their arms extended forward.

Those upon the adjacent hills, upon the houses, on the stone walls and in the tops of the trees also hid their faces while he passed along the opening, but he was no sooner past them than they rose and followed him. But if Cook happened to turn his head or look behind him, they were down again in an instant, and up again as soon, whenever his face was reverted to some other quarter. This punctilious performance of respect in so vast a throng being regulated solely by the accidental turn of one man's head, and the transition being sudden and short, rendered it very difficult even for an individual to be in proper attitude.

If he lay prostrate but a second too long, he was pretty sure not to rise again until he had been trampled upon by all behind him, and if he dared not to prostrate himself, he would stumble over those before him who did. This produced a great many laughable circumstances, and as Cook walked very fast to get off from the sand into the shades of the town, it rendered the matter still more difficult. At length, however, they adopted a medium that much better answered a running compliment, and did not displease the chiefs; this was to go upon all fours, which was truly curious among at least ten thousand people.

This concourse, however, did not continue long, for after passing through a small part of the town only to the *morai* [*heiau* or temple] . . . this being a sanctified spot, and the people in general forbid to approach it, Cook was left, much to his satisfaction, attended only by a few chiefs and their domestics. . . .

The first business Cook wished to accomplish was to obtain a commodious spot to erect his tents upon, particularly the astronomical tents, and observing a square potato patch between the southeast side of the *morai* and the sea that particularly struck his fancy, he addressed the chief concerning it. They immediately made him the offer of it, which Cook accepted . . . [but] it was no sooner agreed that Cook should have liberty to possess the before-mentioned ground, than the chiefs required that Cook's people should never after sunset proceed without the limits prescribed, and that their own people should at all times be utterly excluded from entering them, and as a ratification of what they had promised, they directly fixed on the top of the wall that surrounded the ground, a number of the white rods before mentioned.

The chiefs on our side were made an exception to this agreement, and those among the natives were to be admitted as we pleased. These propositions surprised Cook . . . but when he contemplated the good sense by which they were dictated, and the harmony they were calculated to produce, he acquiesced. After this Cook returned on board, taking with him several of the chiefs. . . .

In the afternoon I was sent with a guard of marines, selected for the purpose from both ships, to take possession of our intended encampment, and in receiving my orders particular care was taken to mention at large the above-mentioned agreement, which I was enjoined carefully to maintain uninfringed.

The ardor of curiosity was now somewhat abated, but I had no sooner landed with the marines in complete uniform, than the town began to pour fourth its thousands again, but landing within the limits notified by the white rods, not a single individual approached beyond them, and our tents were pitched and sentries posted before sunset without annoyance.

I could not but reflect in this situation how much I was indebted either to the timidity or real innocence, hospitality and generosity of these people, whose immense numbers, had they all been women, would have trampled me to atoms. The intrinsic difference between us and them in every respect was certainly great, but the greatest difference was imaginary respecting them, and imputed to us. The moment, therefore, that this supposed superiority of ours should cease to exist or be diminished, our consequence and importance would be at an end, or at least could only be supported by the worst of all aids, an appeal to arms, which in our situation would ruin us though we conquered.

As soon as the sun set I ordered some additional sentries, and though the wondering Indians did not entirely evacuate the surrounding walls until dark, yet they retired in the greatest peace and good order.

The next morning, as soon as the sun rose, they began again to assemble upon the walls, where they continued until night in the same manner they had done the preceding day . . . [but] at length some of those difficulties Cook had foreseen and endeavored to provide against began to discover themselves. The people at the tents complained that according to orders they were secluded the society of the fair, while the people on board were not, and that it was a just matter of complaint. . . .

There was in short no alternative but for our people to go without the lines and meet their mistresses upon neutral ground. This was at first done by officers with the utmost secrecy—but what can be hid from jealous love, and the sleepless eyes of anxiety? Our soldiers and sailors saw it and practiced it. It was impossible for a number of men upon half an acre of ground to go out and return all upon the same business and not have some rencounter that would lead to a discovery, which was soon the case, both between officers and men, and then the covenant was no more.

This matter was at last well known among the inhabitants, but as it had never been productive of any misunderstandings on either side, it was taken no other notice of by people in general; but the chiefs thought differently. They knew it was a breach of covenant. . . . It was the beginning of our subsequent misfortunes, and acknowledged to be so afterward when it was too late to revert the consequences.

In a few days the white rods were taken down by some of the inhabitants, and a free egress and regress took place: the inhabitants had access to our tents, viewed our conduct in private and unguarded hours, had every opportunity to form an opinion of our manners and abilities, and contrast them with their own, nay, were even instructed in the nature and use of our firearms, and permitted to prove our own personal prowess in wrestling, boxing and other athletic exercises, and in some instances with success on their side. It also flung temptations in their way to theft, which they diligently improved and we resented.

It was not, however, until some time after our arrival that we saw these appearances, and not till near our final departure that we saw the evils which resulted from them.

The third day after our acquaintance, Captain Cook was invited on shore by a number of the chiefs, among whom was a priest, to a kind of entertainment or rather ceremony that he could not understand; as they either could or would not explain it to him, he was obliged to comply at a hazard with their requests, to come at the knowledge of a circumstance they were more anxious to communicate than he to receive.

Cook was attended by three of his lieutenants, and a draftsman, uniformly dressed. As they passed the tents after landing, I was invited by Lieutenant King to make one of the party. Our route led to a romantic, silent spot west of the *morai*, which was the residence of the priest that conducted the ceremony. It consisted of a circle of large coconut and other trees that stood upon the margin of a pond of water, in the center of which was a bathing place. . . .

On the east side under the wall of the *morai* was a thick arbor of low-spreading trees, and a number of ill-carved images interspersed throughout. To this retreat we were all conducted, and Captain Cook was placed by one of those images which was hung round with old pieces of their cloths and some viands. When the company were all seated, the natives formed a semicircle in front of Cook, who with his lieutenants on each side composed the base.

The priest, who had been very busy in forming this arrangement, now proceeded to the most important part of duty, and began to anoint the head of Cook with coconut-oil infused with a milky juice that is obtained from the breadfruit, uttering at the same time with a jargon we knew nothing of, some kind of speech, the chiefs at certain periods vociferating with a strong sonorous voice a kind of amen.

This part of the ceremony lasted about twenty minutes, and was succeeded by a long, uninterrupted, formal oration by the priest, which was run over with the greatest rapidity, and lasted about half an hour. Notwithstanding, the language here is almost verbally the same as at Otaheite [Tahiti] and the other islands, we could not understand a word this Levite had spoken.

At the end of the speech the rest of the natives gave a shout, and this was succeeded by a song of a slow, majestic composition, and was short. The song ended and was succeeded by a barbicued hog and breadfruit, but however ceremonious the natives had been in the preceding part of the exhibition, they now were of a different opinion, and made the most strenuous efforts of dispatch.

It was at this time about ten o'clock in the morning, and we did not partake with our friends, except in a drink of coconut milk; they, however, finished the hog, and then rose to wait upon Cook into town.

We had now been here several days, and had been waiting with anxiety the arrival of their . . . greatest Chief, whose name was Kireeaboo [Kalaniopuu, king of the island of Hawaii and uncle of Kamehameha I], whom we expected every day and every hour, according to the reports of the natives, from the island of Mauwee [Maui], where he had been at war with the chief of that island, . . . but it was not until the 25th that Kireeaboo came. He was attended by a number of double canoes, the largest we have ever seen, being between 60 and 70 feet in length, and a large retinue of stout, comely, bold-looking hardy chiefs, besides other attendants and about 30 men with paddles. . . .

They took little notice of the ships as they entered the bay, but

landed immediately on the beach near our encampment, which
Cook observing, and being anxious to salute Kireeaboo, rowed in
his pinnace directly to the tents, from whence he went out to meet
him. The interview was worthy Cook and Kireeaboo, and they
seemed from that moment to conceive an uncommon attachment
to each other. Kireeaboo was an old man and very feeble, about
five feet eight inches high, and of slender make; he had a countenance very expressive of conscious dignity and merit, and conducted himself at all times worthy a ruler of the people.

After the ceremonies of the first salutation were over, Cook
invited Kireeaboo and led him by the hand to his markee [mar-
quee or field tent], attended by a concourse of his chiefs, who
expressed the liveliest sense of honor done their king. Our astronomers were at this time rectifying their mathematical apparatus
in the front of their observatory. It was a bright day, and the appearance was even brilliant to us, but much more so to Kireeaboo
and his attendants, who even expressed a superstitious fear as they
approached it.

They had heard what terrible things our guns were, and therefore were particularly apprehensive of danger from our two tele-
scopes that stood elevated above the rest. The quadrants did not
appear to be dangerous instruments, but both from their construction and use were a perfect mystery, about which they made
endless inquiries, and would have idolized if one might judge from
their extravagant exclamations and gestures.

A great part of the forenoon was spent in satisfying the curiosities of these untutored sons of men, and in endeavoring to inform
them of our knowledge, and judge of the capability of theirs. But
after all, the only conclusion they made was that as we had so
much to do with the sun and the rest of the planets, whose motions we were constantly watching by day and night, and which
we had informed them we were guided by on the ocean, we must
either have come from thence, or be some other way particularly
connected with these objects, and to strengthen this inference,
they observed that the color of our skins partook of the red from
the sun and the white from the moon and stars; besides, they
said we dealt much with fire that we could kill others with, but

that it would not hurt us, though we were close by it, and that we rendered it in all things entirely subservient to us.

When the usual hour of dining arrived, Cook invited Kireeaboo and his attendants on board, and as his table was no otherwise ornamented than with the productions of Owhyhee [Hawaii], his guests were the better accommodated. . . . After dinner they were conducted upon deck, where they were again highly entertained with a new scene, and one much better adapted to their understanding than that they had lately been at on shore. Some of them were employed in measuring the ship's length, and others her breadth, which they did with a line, and then measured it into fathoms as we do, and some of them ventured as far aloft as the man and fore-tops. . . . Others again were in the ship's hold, at which they expressed the utmost admiration. Kireeaboo was on the quarter deck with Cook, and had every minute some of the chiefs running to him and relating what they had seen for his information.

After this the pinnace was manned with the crew in black caps and white shirts, and rowed uniformly to the *Discovery*, the French horn playing. The evening was spent on board with Captain Clerke.

Kireeaboo was so much pleased with the attention that had been shown him and his chiefs that he desired Cook and Clerke would spend the next day with him and his chiefs on shore . . . and the next morning both Captains and all the officers that could attend dressed in their uniforms and went to Kiverua [Kaawaloa], where Kireeaboo generally resided.

They all dined together in Kireeaboo's house. The dinner consisted of a hog and potatoes baked after their manner spread in green plantain leaves, round which they all seated themselves cross-legged. There was no ceremony, except that of washing the mouth and hands both before and after dinner with clean water, and the only utensils at the feast were pieces of bamboo, which were used as knives. . . .

After dinner they went out to take the air under an adjacent shade, where they were entertained with a dance by the women while they were voluptuously stretched along the grass or reclined against the trees. One of the gentlemen from the *Discovery* brought his violin with him, and one from the *Resolution* a German flute, and as the company seemed to want a variety, they played upon each in turn.

The violin produced the most immoderate laughter among the natives, who seemed to relish it as many do the bagpipes, or much more indifferently. But when we accompanied it by a voluntary dance or cotillion, they had a different opinion. The flute they much admired and examined very curiously. The drum and fife, though not present, is the music they most delight in.

When the sun was upon the decline, Kireeaboo and his suite crossed the bay at Kirakakooa in order to complete the entertainment of his guests by an exhibition of the gymnastic kind, at which a large concourse of people of all denominations were present. The disposition of the assembly was an extensive circle in the midst of which was performed wrestling, boxing and other athletic exercises. . . . At sundown the sports ended, and after the victors had gone off in triumph with the insignia of victory, the assembly dissolved. . . .

The next evening Cook invited Kireeaboo and his people to another entertainment, which they afterward justly called "the fiery one." This was the exhibitions of some of the fireworks we had brought from Woolwich. The fame of this intended entertainment and the manifest preparations that had been making on the beach at Kireekakooa by our gunner and yeomen extended the report far and near, by which means there was an immense number of spectators.

As soon as it was well dark, Cook landed at the spot where the preparations were, attended by Kireeaboo and a great number of men and women in their canoes. The natives had been, some of them, all day waiting, and their expectations were wound up to the last extremity. Some of them had begun to jeer us, and express a great contempt of our *heiva* [musical entertainment], as they called it. Cook expected some laughable circumstances, and was willing to improve it; he therefore took the necessary precautions, and when everything was ready, and the people as silent as the night, he ordered a skyrocket off.

I do think this part of the scene undescribable—Cook and the officers near him certainly could not do it, they were so entirely overcome with laughter. They could hardly hold the old feeble Kireeaboo and some elderly ladies of quality that sat among them, and before they had any ways recovered themselves from this paroxism, nearly the whole host that a moment before surrounded them had fled, some towards the town, some to the hills, and some into the water; many they did not know where, and many had been trampled underfoot and remained motionless. . . .

. . . The terrors of those who fled, as well as the few who remained behind, subsided, and Kireeaboo rose and called himself to the hindermost of the people to return, and sent after the rest. This had such an effect that many did return, and wait the remaining part of the evening, but there were many who were frightened past recovery, and did not appear any more that night.

However, when we came to proceed and fire another rocket, though those that had returned saw their king and the rest of the company safe, and themselves unhurt, yet they could not resist the former impulse, and again took to their heels, and though they soon returned, they continued to do so occasionally through the whole ceremony. . . . When all was over they parted with us highly pleased, shouting our greatness and goodness.

We had now been nineteen days in the bay Kireekakooa. . . . We had repaired our ships, had regaled and refreshed our people, and had lain in a supply of pork that would probably support us six months. The only article we wanted in particular was water, which was here very brackish and bad. In order therefore to procure a supply of this necessary article, we determined to visit the island of Mauwee, where, we were informed by the natives, we might get plenty of it, and that there was a good harbor.

On the 6th of February we unmoored and came to sail, standing along the south side of Owhyhee, intending to visit Mauwee and water our ships. On the 7th we had a hard gale of wind, and being close in with the southern and western shore of Owhyhee, which being high land, occasioned the wind that came partly off the land to come in irregular and most terrible gusts, such as we had never seen.

On the 8th the gale became not only more violent but more irregular and embarrassing, and before night was improved into a mere hurricane. We wrenched the head of our foremast and sprung it about 9 feet below the hounds, and also made a great deal of water. During this severe night the *Discovery* had lost us.

On the 9th the violence of the gale, or rather the tornado, ceased, but the excessive mutability of the wind and the irregular set was such as demanded our best skill and unremitted attention to keep the ship under any kind of command.

On the 10th the weather became tolerably settled, and hauling off the land, we saw the *Discovery* in the southeast quarter, and before night spoke her all well. We informed her of our situation, and that in consequence of the misfortune, it was determined to return again to our old harbor at Kireekakooa.

On the 11th of February we again entered Kireekakooa bay, and moored both ships in their old berths. On the 12th we got the foremast out and sent it on shore with the carpenters. We also sent our two observatories on shore, and a markee for the guard of marines.

Our return to this bay was as disagreeable to us as it was to the inhabitants, for we were reciprocally tired of each other. They had been oppressed and were weary of our prostituted alliance, and we were aggrieved by the consideration of wanting the provisions and refreshments of the country, which we had every reason to suppose from their behavior antecedent to our departure would now be withheld from us or brought in such small quantities as to be worse than none.

What we anticipated was true. When we entered the bay, where before we had the shouts of thousands to welcome our arrival, we had the mortification not to see a single canoe, and hardly any inhabitants in the towns. Cook was chagrined and his people were soured. Toward night, however, the canoes came in, but the provisions both in quantity and quality plainly informed us that times were altered, and what was very remarkable was the exorbitant price they asked, and the particular fancy they all at once took to iron daggers or dirks. . . .

It was also equally evident from the looks of the natives, as well as every other appearance, that our former friendship was at an end, and that we had nothing to do but to hasten our departure to some different island where our vices were not known, and where our extrinsic virtues might gain us another short space of being wondered at, and doing as we pleased, or, as our tars expressed it, of being happy by the mouth. . . .

On the 13th at night the *Discovery's* large cutter, which was at her usual moorings at the bower buoy, was taken away. On the 14th the captains met to consult on this alarming occasion, and the issue of their opinion was that one of the two captains should land with armed boats and a guard of marines at Kiverua, and attempt to persuade Kireeaboo, who was then at his house in that town, to come on board upon a visit, and that when he was on board he should be kept prisoner until his subjects should release him by a restitution of the cutter, and if it was afterward thought proper, he or some of the family who might accompany him should be kept as perpetual hostages for the good behavior of the people, during the remaining part of our continuance at Kireekakooa, and this plan was the more approved of by Cook, as he had so repeatedly on former occasions to the southward employed it with success.

Clerke was then in a deep decline in his health, and too feeble to undertake the affair; . . . he therefore begged Cook to oblige him so much as to take that part of the business of the day upon himself in his stead. This Cook agreed to. . . .

Cook landed at Kiverua about nine o'clock in the morning with the marines in the pinnace, and went by a circuitous march to the house of Kireeaboo in order to evade the suspicion of any design. This route led him through a considerable part of the town, which discovered every symptom of mischief, though Cook, blinded by some fatal cause, could not perceive it, or, too self-confident, would not regard it.

The town was evacuated by the women and children, who had retired to the circumadjacent hills, and appeared almost destitute of men, but there were at that time 200 chiefs and more than twice that number of other men detached and secreted in different parts of the houses nearest to Kireeaboo, exclusive of unknown numbers without the skirts of the town, and those that were seen were dressed many of them in black.

When the guard reached Kireeaboo's house, Cook ordered the lieutenant of marines to go in and see if he was at home, and if he was, to bring him out. The lieutenant went in and found the old man sitting with two or three old women of distinction, and when he gave Kireeaboo to understand that Cook was without and wanted to see him, he discovered the greatest marks of uneasiness, but arose and accompanied the lieutenant out, holding his hand. When he came before Cook he squatted down upon his hams as a mark of humiliation, and Cook took him by the hand from the lieutenant, and conversed with him.

The appearance of our parade both by water and on shore, though conducted with the utmost silence and with as little ostentation as possible, had alarmed the towns on both sides of the bay, but particularly Kiverua, who were in complete order for an onset. . . . Cook did not see twenty men in passing through the town, yet before he had conversed ten minutes with Kireeaboo he was surrounded by three or four hundred people, and above half of them chiefs.

Cook grew uneasy when he observed this, and was the more urgent in his persuasions with Kireeaboo to go on board, and actually persuaded the old man to go at length, and led him within a rod or two of the shore, but the just fears and conjectures of the chiefs at last interposed. They held the old man back, and one of the chiefs threatened Cook when he attempted to make him quit Kireeaboo.

Some of the crowd now cried out that Cook was going to take their king from them and kill him, and there was one in particular that advanced towards Cook in an attitude that alarmed one of the guard, who presented his bayonet and opposed him, acquainting Cook in the meantime of the danger of his situation, and that the Indians in a few minutes would attack him, that he had overheard the man whom he had just stopped from rushing in upon him say that our boats which were out in the harbor had just killed his brother, and he would be revenged.

Cook attended to what this man said, and desired him to show him the Indian that had dared to attempt a combat with him, and as soon as he was pointed out, Cook fired at him with a blank. The Indian, perceiving he received no damage from the fire, rushed from without the crowd a second time, and threatened anyone who should oppose him.

Cook . . . fired a ball, which entering the Indian's groin, he fell and was drawn off by the rest. Cook, perceiving the people determined to oppose his designs, and that he should not succeed without further bloodshed, ordered the lieutenant of marines (Mr. Phillips) to withdraw his men and get them into the boats, which were then laying ready to receive them. This was effected by the sergeant, but the instant they began to retreat, Cook was hit with a stone and, perceiving the man who hove, shot him dead.

The officer in the boats, perceiving the guard retreating and hearing this third discharge, ordered the boats to fire. This occasioned the guard to face about and fire, and then the attack became general. Cook and Mr. Phillips, . . . perceiving the general fire without orders, quitted Kireeaboo and ran to the shore to put a stop to it, but not being able to make themselves heard, and being close pressed upon by the chiefs, they joined the guard and fired as they retreated.

Cook, having at length reached the margin of the water between the fire of the boats, waved with his hat to cease firing and come in, and while he was doing this, a chief from behind stabbed him with one of our iron daggers just above the shoulder blade, and passed quite through his body. Cook fell with his face in the water and immediately expired.

From *A Journal of Captain Cook's Last Voyage to the Pacific Ocean* . . . , John Ledyard (Hartford: Nathaniel Patten, 1783).

VII

George Dixon

The pursuits of explorers and the pursuits of merchant adventurers were never very carefully differentiated; traders went out of their way to add new landmarks to their sketchy charts; professional explorers unhesitatingly indulged in commerce on the side. The mission of the *King George* and the *Queen Charlotte*, sent to the Pacific in 1785 by the King George's Sound Company of London, was no exception.

Under the command of British mariners Nathaniel Portlock and George Dixon, this was primarily a fur trade expedition, with orders to follow the itinerary that had already been established between Nootka Sound and China. But while searching out new trading posts on the West Coast, the mariners also engaged in the business of discovery and made several notable additions to their maps, such as Queen Charlotte's Islands and Norfolk Bay.

The ships also took three trips to Hawaii during 1786 and 1787. Captain Dixon (c. 1755–1800) and his supercargo William Beresford were particularly interested in determining exactly what the Sandwich Islands had to offer by way of goods and supplies for Pacific traders, and presented the first comprehensive report on the Islands as a potential marketplace.

All for the Price of a Tenpenny Nail

The circumstance which renders Owhyhee [Hawaii] peculiarly eligible to touch at is the great number of fine hogs it affords. Fowls too are in great plenty here. In regard to vegetables, bread-fruit, potatoes and plantains are the most plentiful; taro is more scarce and rather indifferent, and there are very few yams to be met with. . . .

Among the various curiosities brought by the natives to sell were a kind of basket, about eighteen inches high and five or six inches in diameter, of a circular form and exceedingly neatly made. The wicker work of which they are made was frequently variegated with twigs of red color and had a pretty effect. . . .

Besides a variety of fish lines . . . they have various other kinds of cordage, and made of different materials. The worst sorts were found useful in rounding our cables; that of the better kind was appropriated to other purposes, and the fishing lines made excellent tackle falls, top-gallant haulyards, etc. . . .

Mats are made with a degree of neatness equal to any of European manufacture, and prettily diversified with a variety of figures stained with red. Those used to sleep on are plain, and of a coarser kind, but made with an equal degree of neat-ness and regularity.

Cloth is another article which gives these Indians scope for fancy and invention. It is made from the Chinese paper mul-berry tree, and when wet (being of a soft, pliable substance) is beat out with small square pieces of wood, to from twelve to eigh-teen inches wide, and afterward stamped with various colors and a diversity of patterns, the neatness and elegance of which would not disgrace the window of a London linen draper. . . .

Atoui [Kauai] is certainly the second island for refreshments, and is in some respects superior to Owhyhee; it produces fine hogs, the greatest abundance of excellent taro, together with potatoes and plantains. Coconuts are met with here in greater abundance, than, perhaps, at all the other islands together; and there is plenty of fine salt, which is peculiarly useful in curing pork for sea store. . . . Plenty of excellent water is easily procured and at least a temporary supply of wood. The chiefs are easily attached to your interest and by that means every business is carried on with the greatest order and regularity. . . .

In Wymoa [Waimea] Bay . . . we were surrounded by a number of canoes, most of them well loaded with taro, potatoes, sugar cane and coconuts, and a good number of fine hogs. This plainly showed us that the inhabitants knew we were come for a supply of provisions and had prepared themselves accordingly. We found roots much cheaper and in greater supply than at Whahoo [Oahu] and . . . bought the largest hogs for one large or two middling-sized toes [nails]. . . . Coconuts we found in the greatest plenty; the settled price for them was five for an eightpenny nail. The sugar cane was exceeding fine and equally cheap. The taro was by far the finest of any we met with and very plentiful; we commonly got five fine roots for an eightpenny or tenpenny nail. . . .

Besides this traffic, which was carried on for necessities, the natives had a brisk trade for curiosities of various kinds, such as cloaks, caps, mats, fishing lines and hooks, necklaces, etc. . . . They likewise brought great numbers of beautiful bird skins in excellent preservation; these were generally made up in parcels of ten each by a wooden skewer run through their beaks. On our wishing to procure some of them alive, we soon found plenty of bird catchers, and the living birds were sold nearly as cheap as the preserved ones. . . .

By this time the wood . . . began to grow short, on account of the constant fires we were obliged to keep for heating water to scald hogs, and various other purposes. On this we applied to the natives for some, though without any sanguine hopes of our application being successful, as the mountains where the woods grow are farther up in the country on this island than at any of the others.

However, our application was very successful, the natives to a man engaging in the traffic, and every individual bringing us more or less the article we wanted, though it was evident from many poles and rafters brought for sale, and which had been recently pulled out of the ground, that their fences, and perhaps houses, had been demolished for our accommodation and, I may say, their profit. Yet this proceeding serves to show that anything whatever on this island, or indeed any of the group affords, may easily be obtained, so great is the value set on iron. . . .

Whahoo, though greatly inferior to either of the islands just mentioned in regard to hogs and vegetables . . . confessedly claims a first place for supplying those most necessary articles, wood and water; and I have reason to think that in a few years it will equal Atoui in point of fertility. A spirit of improvement seems to animate the people to a very great degree. . . . Whititte [Waikiki], in particular, is crowded with new plantations, laid out in the most regular order, and which seem to be in a very flourishing state of cultivation. . . .

In a bay on the south side of Whahoo . . . our captains went on shore in order to find a watering place. . . . They soon met good water, but the access to it was very difficult, occasioned by the reef of rocks which run almost the length of the bay at a considerable distance from the shore . . . but Captain Dixon, taking notice that most of the people in the canoes had several gourds or calabashes full of water, he directed us to purchase them, which we easily did for nails, buttons and such like trifles.

Indeed, so fond were they of the traffic that every other object was totally abandoned and the whole island, at least that part which lay next to us, were employed in bringing water. For a small or middling-sized calabash containing perhaps two or three gallons, we gave a small nail, and for larger ones in proportion. Thus, in this very singular and, I may venture to say, unprecedented manner, were both ships completely supplied with water, not only at a trivial expense, but also saving our boats, casks and tackling, and preserving the people from wet and the danger of catching cold. . . .

Many of the gourds or calabashes are very wide at the top and used by the natives for various purposes, and particularly to hold a kind of pudding made of taro. So eagerly did they pursue this profitable traffic that they seldom washed their vessels and we unavoidably got taro pudding mixed among the water; but we found it of little or no prejudice, though the sight would perhaps not have been altogether pleasing to an epicure. . . .

They also brought us a great quantity of fruit, somewhat resembling a nectarine. . . . They eat very agreeably, and are cool, juicy and refreshing. . . . The *ava* is a root somewhat resembling our liquorice in shape and color, but totally different in taste. None but the . . . chiefs are permitted to use it, and they never prepare it themselves, but always keep a servant whose sole business is to prepare and administer this delicious potation to his master.

He first begins by chewing a sufficient quantity till it is well masticated; this is put [spit] into a neat wooden bowl made for the purpose, and a small quantity of water being poured over, it is well squeezed and the liquor afterward strained through a piece of cloth. This delicious beverage is now complete and is drank with highest relish. The root is of an intoxicating nature, but seems to stupify rather than exhilarate the spirits. Its effects are very pernicious, if we may judge by an old priest who appeared greatly emaciated and his body was covered with a white scurf, which had the appearance of the leprosy. . . .

Oneehow [Niihau] is remarkable for the great quantity of excellent yams it produces. . . . The inhabitants brought us a plentiful supply, which we purchased for nails and such like trifles. Indeed this place produces no great plenty of anything besides, there being but few inhabitants here, compared with Attoui, Whahoo, etc. . . . We got very few hogs here and these were brought chiefly from Attoui. . . . There is also a sweet root called tee or tea [ti] found here; it is generally about the thickness of a person's wrist, but sometimes much larger, and is generally baked by the natives previous to their bringing it for barter. This root is of a wet, clammy nature, and with proper management makes excellent beer.

The other islands in general produce a few hogs, together with potatoes, breadfruit, taro, plantains and salt, which last article renders these islands superior to Otaheite [Tahiti] or any of the beautiful islands of the Southern Pacific Ocean, none of them producing any of this very useful article. Hogs and dogs are the only quadrupeds we saw here. The dogs appear to be of the cur kind, dull and heavy; they have sharp pointed ears projecting toward the nose. . . .

The people in their temper and disposition are harmless, inoffensive and friendly, not subject to passion or easily provoked; in their manners they are lively and cheerful, ever ready to render any little service in their power even to strangers, and pursue everything they undertake with unremitting diligence and application. . . . It must be confessed that they are guilty of theft, and will not scruple to plunder whenever they have an opportunity . . . yet with all this propensity to thieving, we never met with an instance of dishonesty whenever anything was committed to their charge, however valuable it might be to them. . . .

Besides nails, we found buttons very useful in our traffic with these people. To the credit of the men, be it spoken, they looked on them as things of no value, but the females saw them in a very different point of view and were exceedingly fond of wearing them round their wrists and ankles as bracelets. . . . As gallantry is perhaps equally prevalent here as in more civilized nations, the men frequently preferred buttons to nails (contrary to their better judgment) in their traffic. This is an incontestable proof that the power of beauty is not confined within the narrow limits of our polite European circles, but has equal influence all over the world. . . .

Owhyhee is by far the most plentiful island of the whole. We may indeed assign as one reason for this that it is larger than any two of the rest, but then its inhabitants are equally numerous in proportion to its extent, and I am inclined to think they are much more so, consequently the land is more universally cultivated than at any of the other islands, which accounts for the great plenty . . . we met with here.

Excerpts from *A Voyage Round the World*, George Dixon, compiled largely from letters written by William Beresford (London: Goulding, 1789).

VIII

James Jackson Jarves

By the ordinary trader and merchant adventurer, the inhabitants of any uncivilized lands were treated as unworthy barbarians, whether they were Africans or Eskimos, Fijians or American Indians. They were all savages, to be mistrusted, tricked, and exploited—but traded with if they had anything to exchange for the white man's pretty ribbons, glass beads, cheap knives, and mirrors, and arbitrarily put out of the way when they showed resistance or blocked the path of Progress.

The first traders were inclined to rank the Hawaiians with all other savages of the world. But veterans in intercontinental barter soon learned that these Islanders were a cut above the natives they dealt with elsewhere; the Hawaiians had a knack for detecting a trader's wiles, quickly learned the foreign art of shortchanging, and put it into practice, returned shoddy tapa and cordage for shoddy tinware and canvas. They had a sense of humor, mimicked the *malihini* hucksters, and made jokes about them. They were clever at distinguishing genuineness from deception, honesty from underhandedness. Yet their eagerness to barter also led them to put unwarranted trust in the traders.

Yankee skipper of the *Eleanora*, Simon Metcalfe, a pioneer in transpacific and South American coastal trade and a tough, truculent ship's master who believed implicitly in the white man's superiority, was one of the first Americans to touch at the Sandwich Islands, and he made such an indecorous impression on Hawaii that no early historian failed to chronicle the event.

James Jackson Jarves (1818–1888), who in later life became famous as author, art critic, and collector in Italy, served his apprenticeship in journalism at Honolulu. Arriving there in 1837 at the age of 19, he founded and edited the weekly newspaper *Polynesia,* assembled a vast assortment of fact and anecdote about Hawaii, and in 1843 published a lively *History of the Hawaiian or Sandwich Islands,* including, of course, his version of Metcalfe's 1790 "Olowalu Massacre." Though there was considerable variance among annalists in reporting the incidentals, Jarves at least had the advantage of being able to pick up facts from aged survivors of the atrocity.

Massacre of the Innocents

The rapid growth of trade and the general and increasing good will that prevailed is sufficient evidence that the Islanders appreciated the value of foreign commerce. . . . However, a few of the foreign commanders were men of little or no principle; the discipline preserved on board their vessels corrupted their own crews and excited the cupidity and dislike of the natives. Disturbances arose in consequence, and the captains, seeking justice, and oftener mere retaliation for real or fancied wrongs, too frequently, without due inquiry, vented their rage in deeds scarcely inferior in wanton barbarity or abuse of power and confidence to the customs of the savages themselves.

Men there were of that day, and the race is not altogether extinct, whose characters could be resolved into two principles, lust and gain. To accomplish their desires, no action was too base or cruel. Such may be properly termed pirates, for their selfishness spared neither friend nor foe, the useful servant or profitable ally: all were equally their prey. . . .

In the autumn of 1789 the American snow *Eleanor,* commanded by a man of the name of Metcalf, arrived at Hawaii and remained there trading during most of the succeeding winter. In the month of February, 1790, she anchored at Honuaula, Maui. Two of the chiefs of a neighboring place called Oloalu [Olowalu], having heard of her arrival, went to Honuaula and in the night stole her boat, which was moored under her stern.

A watchman was in it, but had fallen asleep. So adroit were they, that he did not awake until they were near the shore. He then attempted to give the alarm, but was not heard; before he could cry out again, one of the thieves killed him. The boat was taken ashore and broken up for the sake of the iron, which was manufactured into awls and fishhooks. The chiefs returned to their own village and for a while Honuaula was made to bear the brunt of a revengeful attack.

One man was killed and two made prisoners, one of whom, being from Oloalu, gave information of the real criminals. Metcalf weighed anchor and proceeded thither. At the time of his arrival a tabu existed, which prevented any indivdual from putting off in a canoe, under pain of being burnt to death.

The bones of the murdered seaman and the remains of the boat, for which a reward was offered, had been delivered up; and the natives, supposing the anger of the captain appeased by the attack he had already made, innocently asked for the promised reward. This he said they should have.

As soon as the tabu was annulled, multitudes of people from all parts of the island flocked to the ship to trade. They were all ordered to lie with their canoes on the starboard side, which they did, not perceiving the means preparing for their destruction. If any lay off the bows or stern, they were pelted with stones until they took the prescribed situation.

The ports, which had been closed, were then hauled up and the battery, charged with musket balls and nails, and depressed to bear into the thickest of the fleet, run out and fired among them. Metcalf stood on the gangway to witness the awful effect and directed the volleys of musketry and small arms which were poured in to complete the destruction.

One hundred individuals were said to have been killed outright and vast numbers wounded. The natives dragged for their bodies with fishhooks, and collected the mangled masses upon the beach, where, to use their own expression, "their brains flowed out of their broken skulls."

After this horrible massacre of innocent wretches—the more aggravated as consummated by a treachery such as only the worst of savages would have gloried in—Metcalf sailed the same day for Hawaii, where, owing to the hostility which existed between the two islands, he was well received. An awful retribution awaited him.

In connection with the *Eleanor* was a small schooner of twenty-six tons, a tender manned with only five seamen and commanded by Metcalf's son, a lad of eighteen years of age. This vessel arrived off Kawaihae Bay in March, but did not fall in with her mate, which was then a little farther to the westward.

Kameeiamoku, a high chief who for some trifling cause had received a flogging from the elder Metcalf while on board of his vessel, had resolved to revenge the insult upon the first whites that came within his reach. The smallness of the schooner and the inexperience of her commander afforded too favorable an opportunity to be overlooked. Without the powerful motive which actuated his mind, she would have proved an almost irresistible temptation to the cupidity of savages when away from her consort.

Accordingly with a number of his people he boarded her and carried many presents. While the attention of the youth and crew were occupied in receiving them and in hearing news of his father, the savages pressed on board. Suddenly the chief seized young Metcalf and threw him overboard, where he soon perished. All the others were massacred, excepting one, Isaac Davis, who after being handled with the greatest inhumanity until they were wearied with their cruelties, was spared by one of the party, who bound up his wounds. He was then taken ashore and kindly treated. The schooner was stranded and plundered.

John Young, boatswain of the *Eleanor*, on the 17th had gone ashore, but to his surprise, upon attempting to leave, he was forbidden by Kamehameha, and in the evening learnt of the capture of the schooner. The snow remained two days off Kealakekua Bay, firing guns for Young to return. This the king, after he heard of the massacre, would not permit, nor would he allow a canoe to go alongside, lest Metcalf should revenge himself as at Maui. Consequently he sailed without hearing of his loss.

It is painful to record the depravity of untutored heathen: how

much more the vile passions of a civilized being whose outward
form marks him for a man, while his actions prove him a devil!
For the credit of humanity, such cases in comparison with justice
and benevolence toward the South Sea Islanders are rare; and in
the annals of Hawaii the foul deed of Metcalf stands alone. . . .

Kamehameha was highly indignant at the outrage committed
by Kameeiamoku. Though the dominant chief, his authority was
not sufficiently established to authorize him to punish this viola-
tion of his policy. He rebuked him severely and took possession
of the schooner, which he caused to be hauled up and carefully
preserved, to be returned to her owner, should he reappear. . . .

The two prisoners, Young and Davis, though rude and ignorant
seamen in moral education and religious knowledge, were far in
advance of the most enlightened of those who held them in
bondage. . . . Kamehameha found in them tried and faithful
servants who more than repaid his protection, and the oppressed
serf ever had reason to bless the humane influence they exerted
on the mind of their arbitrary master. . . . Equal consideration
is due to them from ther own countrymen and the mariners of
other nations who traded to their shores.

They both rose to be chiefs of consequence, possessing to the
last the confidence of high and low; and their history, particularly
that of Young, will be found to be closely interwoven with that
of their royal guardian. There were other white men on the islands
at the time, runaways from ships, but mostly of bad character;
their influence, however, greatly modified by the superior address
and intelligence of these prisoners and by the comparison which
the natives necessarily drew between the two, which gave them
their first definite notions of goodness. . . .

The two seamen were immediately taken into the confidence
of their patron, and both from him and from other high chiefs
received valuable presents of estates on the seaside. They made
themselves so beloved that popular opinion would not have permitted their departure, had the king been inclined to let them go.

From *History of the Hawaiian or Sandwich Islands*, James Jackson Jarves (London: Moxon, 1843).

IX

George Vancouver

Next to Captain Cook, the most celebrated British navigator and explorer of the late 1700's was George Vancouver (1758–1798). He had accompanied Cook on two voyages, and in 1792 was back in the Pacific with two ships under his own command—the *Discovery* and the *Chatham*—and with orders from King George III to continue the exploration of the Northwest Coast, to make a more complete survey of the Sandwich Islands, and to "aid so far as possible in the improvement of the early nationalities"—the primitive natives.

Vancouver took the latter charge most seriously. On the tour he visited Hawaii three times between 1792 and 1794, formed a fast friendship with King Kamehameha, and did his conscientious best to improve political relations among warring chiefs, as well to improve the economic conditions of the common people. Recognizing the deficiency of the Hawaiian animal kingdom, he imported cattle from California, the first cows that natives had ever seen; he brought in sheep, goats, geese, a great variety of garden seeds, grapevines, and orange and almond trees.

He was a visiting humanitarian, the like of whom Hawaiians had not previously met. Instead of seeking revenge for the murder of his former commander, he sought conciliation; instead of defrauding kings, chiefs, and commoners, he tried to be their benefactor. Kamehameha was so flattered by the attentions of the great *haole* from England, and so appreciative of the benefactions that he had to be generous

too: after overwhelming Vancouver with gifts and spectacular entertainment, he impetuously ceded his entire kingdom to Vancouver's
sovereign—a bestowal that Great Britain had the good grace not to
recognize.

But Vancouver had his problems in shipping cattle to Hawaii.
Early in January 1793, the *Discovery* took on four cows and two bulls
at Monterey, California, "for the purpose of establishing a breed of
those valuable animals in the Sandwich Islands . . . which, if effected, could not fail of being highly beneficial, not only to the resident inhabitants, but also to all future visitors."

Vancouver left Monterey on January 14, but sailing for the Islands
was delayed for two weeks by severe coastal storms, by efforts to
find deserters from his crew, and by an unsuccessful attempt to locate
offshore islands that had been reported by the Spaniards. Not until
February 13 did the ships approach Hawaii. On the passage several
of the cattle had perished and the rest were on a starvation diet. Their
survival depended either on an immediate landing or obtaining fresh
fodder. But for almost another week the vessels were detained off
Kawaihae by a strict taboo and a series of gales. Chief Kahowmotoo,
whom Vancouver had met on a previous visit, finally came on board
and escorted the captain ashore, principally to meet the chief's four
wives who were "waiting on shore with much anxiety." No one except Vancouver appeared to have much interest in the starving California longhorns.

A Kingdom for a Cow

Kawaihae is situated in a grove of cocoanut trees just behind a
sandy beach. . . . The village consisted only of straggling houses
of two classes; those appropriated to the residence of the inhabitants were small, mean, miserable huts, but the others, allotted to
the purpose of shading, building and repairing their canoes, were
excellent of their kind. In these occupations several people were
busily employed, who seemed to execute their work with great
neatness and ingenuity.

In about the middle of the village is a reservoir of salt water,
nearly in the center of a large enclosure made by walls of mud

and stones. Between these walls and the reservoir, the whole space is occupied by shallow earthen pans . . . the exposure of which to the influence of the sun soon causes evaporation and crystallization. . . . This is their process of making salt, which is always white in proportion to the care bestowed in gathering it. They have large quantities, equal in color and in quality to any made in Europe, but the crystals are much larger. . . .

Paying our respects to Kahowmotoo's wives and inspecting this salt pond occupied most of our time and claimed most of our attention. Having rendered our visit pleasant to the former by distributing such articles as we knew they held in high estimation, we returned toward the boats. . . .

Calms and light baffling winds detained us in an inactive situation, which was rendered extremely unpleasant by a heavy irregular swell and by oppressively hot sultry weather. A circumstance now occurred that contributed to make me infinitely more dissatisfied with this irksome detention from the shore. The only bull that remained, and a cow that had brought forth a dead calf, were no longer able to stand on their legs, and it was evident that if a speedy opportunity did not offer itself for relieving them by sending them on shore, their lives could not possibly be preserved.

The loss, particularly of the bull, would have been a cruel disappointment to my wishes, but as favorable circumstances often take place when least expected, so it was on this occasion. In the afternoon of Tuesday, the 19th, we were visited by many canoes, though at the distance of eight or nine leagues from the land. In one of these was a chief named Crymanahoo, half brother to Kamehameha and chief of the district of Ahiedo.

To him and to his friends I made such presents as were considered by Kahowmotoo highly suitable to his rank, and which were accepted with marks of great approbation and content. This induced me to hope that by his good offices I should be enabled to get these poor animals conveyed to the shore. As his canoe was sufficiently large and roomy, I requested he would consent to their being put into it, but to my great surprise a thousand evasions and excuses were immediately started.

Anxious for the future advantages these people would derive by the propagation of these animals, I probably discovered much earnestness whilst endeavoring to prevail with Crymanahoo to lend me his assistance in securing to himself and countrymen so important a benefit. This he certainly perceived, but possessing no desire to oblige, nor any patriotic zeal, he was only studious to turn my entreaties to his own particular advantage.

After Kahowmotoo had anxiously interfered, but with the same success, I offered Crymanahoo—well knowing that avarice is a predominant passion with many of these islanders—a moderate recompense, only for allowing his canoe to perform this service. He instantly waved all his former objections and the bull and cow were soon comfortably placed in his canoe, in which there were some vegetables that the bull ate, seemingly with much appetite; this gave me great pleasure, as I was now in hopes that he would soon recover by the help of proper nourishing food, which the shore abundantly supplied. . . .

A southwest breeze springing up [on the 21st] enabled us to steer toward Kealakekua. About noon I was honored with the presence of Kamehameha, the king of Hawaii, whose approach had been announced some time before his arrival. Not only from Captain King's description, but also from my own memory, as far as it would serve me, I expected to have recognized my former acquaintance by the most savage countenance we had hitherto seen amongst these people. But I was agreeably surprised in finding that his riper years had softened that stern ferocity which his younger days had exhibited, and had changed his general deportment to an address characteristic of an open, cheerful and sensible mind, combined with great generosity and goodness of disposition. . . .

Kamehameha came on board in a very large canoe, accompanied by John Young, an English seaman who appeared to be not only a great favorite but to possess no small degree of influence with this great chief. Terrehoa, who had been sent to deliver the bull and cow to the king, was also of the party, and informed me that the cow had died in her passage to the island, but that the bull arrived safe and was lodged in a house where he ate and drank heartily.

After the usual ceremonies and assurances of friendship had passed between Kamehameha and myself . . . the remaining live stock I had on board [the *Chatham*, as well as the *Discovery*], consisting of five cows, two ewes and a ram, were sent on shore in some of his canoes. These were all in a healthy state, though in low condition, and as I flattered myself the bull would recover, I had little doubt of their succeeding to the utmost of my wishes.

I cannot avoid mentioning the pleasure I received in the particular attention paid by Kamehameha to placing of these animals in the canoes. This business was principally done by himself, after which he gave the strictest injunctions to his people who had the charge of them to pay implicit obedience to the directions of our butcher, who was sent to attend their landing.

At the departure of these canoes I was unacquainted with the extent of Kamehameha's intended compliment. In addition to his magnificent present of provisions, other canoes were now ordered alongside, from which a large quantity of cloth, mats and other articles of their own manufacture were delivering into the ship. But we were so incommoded that there was no possibility of taking care of these valuables, and on promising to receive them on a future day, the king permitted them to be returned to the shore, giving particular charge to one of his attendants, to whom they were intrusted, to be very careful of them, as they belonged to me and not to himself.

Having promised to give the king an entertainment with fireworks, that exhibition was fixed for Monday evening, and that he might contribute to the pleasures of the day, he proposed to have a sham battle on shore in the afternoon between such of his best warriors as could be assembled on so short a notice.

On Monday, the 4th [of March 1793], as soon as dinner was over, we were summoned to this review, and as Kamehameha considered all ceremonies and formalities on my part as adding to his consequence, he requested that I would be attended on shore by a guard.

We found the warriors assembled toward the north corner of the beach, without the limits of the hallowed ground. The party consisted of about a hundred and fifty men armed with spears. These were divided into three parties nearly in equal numbers; two were placed at a little distance from each other. That on the right was to represent the armies of Titeeree and Taio; that on the left the army of Kamehameha. Their spears on this occasion were blunt pointed sticks, about the length of their barbed ones, whilst on each wing we were to suppose a body of troops placed to annoy the enemy with stones from their slings.

The combatants now advanced toward each other, seemingly without any principal leader, making speeches as they approached, which appeared to end in vaunts and threats from both parties, when the battle began by throwing their sham spears at each other. These were parried in most instances with great dexterity, but such as were thrown with effect produced contusions and wounds which, though fortunately of no dangerous tendency, were yet very considerable, and it was admirable to observe the great good humor and evenness of temper that was preserved by those who were thus injured.

This battle was a mere skirmish, neither party being supported nor advancing in any order but such as the fancy of the individuals directed. Some would advance even from the rear to the front, where they would throw their spears, and instantly retreat into the midst of their associates, or would remain picking up the spears that had fallen without effect. These they would sometimes hurl again at the foe, or hastily retreat with two or three in their possession.

Those, however, who valued themselves on military achievements marched up toward the front of the adverse party and in a vaunting manner bid defiance to the whole of their adversaries. In their left hand they held their spear, with which in a contemptuous manner, they parried some of those of their opponents, whilst with their right they caught others in the act of flying immediately at them, and instantly returned them with great dexterity.

In this exercise no one seemed to excel his Hawaiian Majesty, who entered the lists for a short time and defended himself with the greatest dexterity, much to our surprise and admiration. In one instance particularly, against six spears that were hurled at him nearly at the same instant, three were caught as they were flying, with one hand; two he broke by parrying them with his spear in the other; and the sixth, by a trifling inclination of his body, passed harmless.

This part of the combat was intended to represent the king as having been suddenly discovered by the enemy in a situation where he was least expected to be found; and the shower of darts that were instantly directed to that quarter were intended to show that he was in the most imminent danger; until advancing a few paces, with the whole body of his army more closely connected, and throwing their spears with their utmost exertion, he caused the enemy to fall back in some little confusion, and he himself rejoined our party without having received the least injury.

The consequences attendant on the first man being killed or being so wounded as to fall on the disputed ground between the contending armies were next exhibited. This event causes the loss of many lives and much blood in the conflict that takes place in order to rescue the unfortunate individual who, if carried off by the adverse party, dead or alive, becomes an immediate sacrifice at the *morai*. On this occasion the wounded man was supposed to be one of Titeeree's soldiers, and until this happened, no advantage appeared on either side.

But now the dispute became very serious, was well supported on all sides and victory still seemed to hold a level scale, until at length the supposed armies of Taio and Titeeree fell back, whilst that of Kamehameha carried off in triumph several supposed dead bodies, dragging the poor fellows, who had already been much trampled upon, by the heels some distance through a light loose sand, and who, notwithstanding that their eyes, ears, mouth and nostrils were by this means filled, were no sooner permitted to use their legs than they ran into the sea, washed themselves, and appeared as happy and as cheerful as if nothing had happened. . . .

These military exploits finished toward sunset, and as soon as it was dark we entertained the king and a large concourse of his people with a display of fireworks. Kamehameha and some of the chiefs recollected to have seen a few indifferent ones that were fired by Captain Cook . . . but ours, being in higher preservation, of greater variety and in a larger quantity, were viewed by the several chiefs, who were the only persons admitted within our tabooed precincts, with the greatest mixture of fear, surprise and admiration; and by the repeated bursts of acclamation from the numerous body of the inhabitants assembled on the occasion, it was hard to determine which of these passions most generally preponderated.

The following morning . . . the chief of Kailua, who was of our party the preceding evening, informed me that on his return home, the inhabitants of that village at first considered what they beheld as a diversion only, but from the time it lasted, and the continual clamor that they had heard, they had become very much alarmed and suspected that some misunderstanding had taken place between us and Kamehameha, and that we were destroying him with all his people and houses on this side of the country. The same opinion had prevailed with most of the women who were on board the vessels, and who were not easily persuaded to believe otherwise.

These intimations afforded me an opportunity, which I did not suffer to escape, to impress on their minds the very great superiority we possessed, should we ever be obliged to act toward them as enemies. The sky and water rockets, balloons, hand grenades, etc., I represented to be like guns fired without shot when designed for entertainment, but like them capable of being rendered formidable and destructive weapons when occasion might require. Of this they seemed to entertain no doubt. . . .

In the forenoon of Tuesday, the 25th [of February 1794], the king and queen, accompanied by [a large delegation of chiefs] . . . all assembled on board the *Discovery* for the purpose of formally ceding and surrendering the island of Hawaii to me for his Britannic Majesty, his heirs and successors. . . . Kamehameha opened the business in a speech which he delivered with great moderation and equal firmness. He explained the reasons that had induced him to offer the island to the protection of Great

Britain and recounted the numerous advantages that himself, the chiefs and the people were likely to derive by the surrender they were about to make.

He enumerated the several nations that since Captain Cook's discovery of these islands had occasionally resorted hither, each of which was too powerful for them to resist; and as these visitors had come more frequently to their shores and their numbers seemed to increase, he considered that the inhabitants would be liable to more ill treatment and still greater impositions than they had yet endured, unless they could be protected against such wrongs by some one of the civilized powers with whose people they had become acquainted; that at present they were completely independent, under no sort of engagement whatever, and were free to make choice of that state which in their opinion was most likely by its attention to their security and interests to answer the purpose for which the proposed surrender was intended.

For his own part he did not hesitate to declare the preference he entertained for the king of Great Britain, to whom he was ready to acknowledge his submission; and he demanded to know who had any objection to follow his example. This produced an harangue from each of the five chiefs, all of whom had some ideas to offer on this important subject. . . .

It was clearly understood that no interference was to take place in . . . their religion, government and domestic economy . . . ; that Kamehameha, the chiefs and priests were to continue as usual to officiate with the same authority as before in their respective stations and that no alteration in those particulars was in any degree thought of or intended.

These preliminaries being fully discussed and thoroughly understood on both sides, the king repeated his former proposition, which was now unanimously approved of, and the whole party declared their consent by saying that they were no longer *Tanata no Owhyhee* (the people of Hawaii) but *Tanata no Britannee* (the people of Britain). This was instantly made known to the surrounding crowd in their numerous canoes about the vessels and the same expressions were cheerfully repeated throughout the attending multitude.

Mr. Puget, accompanied by some of the officers, immediately went on shore, there displayed the British colors, and took possession of the island in his Majesty's name, in conformity to the inclination and desire of Kamehameha and his subjects [action never officially acknowledged or accredited by a British sovereign]. On this ceremony being finished, a salute was fired from the vessels, after which the following inscription on copper was deposited in a very conspicuous place at the royal residence:

On the 25th of February, 1794, Kamehameha, king of Hawaii, in council with the principal chiefs of the island, assembled on board his Britannic Majesty's sloop *Discovery* in Kealakekua Bay, and in the presence of George Vancouver, commander of the said sloop; Lieutenant Peter Puget, commander of his said Majesty's armed tender the *Chatham;* and other officers of the *Discovery,* after due consideration, unanimously ceded the said island of Hawaii to his Britannic Majesty and acknowledged themselves to be subjects of Great Britain.

Such a distribution of useful and ornamental articles was now made to the principal chiefs, their favorite women and other attendants as Kamehameha and myself esteemed to be suitable to their respective ranks and stations on this memorable occasion.

Thus concluded the ceremonies of ceding the island of Hawaii to the British crown; but whether this addition to the empire will ever be of any importance to Great Britain, or whether the surrender of the island will ever be attended with any additional happiness to its people, time alone must determine. It was, however, a matter of great satisfaction to me that this concession had not only been voluntary but general; that it had not been suggested by a party, nor been the wish of a few, but the desire of every inhabitant with whom we had any conversation on the subject.

From *A Voyage of Discovery to the Pacific Ocean and Round the World,* Volumes III and V, George Vancouver (London: Stockdale, 1801).

X

Archibald Menzies

Accompanying the Vancouver expedition was one of the most distinguished botanists of the day, Archibald Menzies (1754–1842), to whom was left much of the responsibility for exploring the interior of the Islands. In January 1794 he led a party to the summit of the 8,251-foot dormant volcano Hualalai, which rose conspicuously above Kailua Bay, and continued still further inland in an attempt to ascend Mauna Loa. Rough lava and impenetrable jungle forced a retreat.

Upon their return to Kealakckua, Kamehameha assured Menzies that the only feasible approach to the top of Mauna Loa was from the south side. In apparent sympathy with the aims of the botanist, the king offered the use of two of his double canoes and the services of Chief Rookea as guide, recruited twenty paddlers for each canoe, organized a supply line, and even dispatched a string of bearers overland with two hundred coconuts.

The party proved to be so unwieldy that it took them almost a week to complete the fifty-mile canoe trip to South Point and make the preliminary part of the ascent into the foothills. As with all such Island journeys, the mountaineers attracted a throng of curious natives who insisted on joining the expedition, burdened with calabashes of *poi*, quantities of dried fish, coconuts, woven sleeping mats, and rolls of tapa, so that the march was inevitably retarded.

Snow was far down the mountain that winter, and its white crest looked formidable and uninviting even from the hot, dry desert lands

around South Point. Not until February 13 did the real climbing begin
—over a trail that still bears Menzies' name. Kilauea was a dreaded,
sacred area, and very active at the time; the guides skirted it accordingly, depriving the scientist of witnessing the spectacle that would
have interested him most.

Unaccountably Menzies' journal of this trip was not incorporated
in Vancouver's *Voyages* and was not published until it was dug out
of London archives by another scientist, Charles H. Hitchcock, in
1911.

Frostbitten in the Tropics

Though we had much reason to be satisfied, every step we went,
with the kind attentions and unbounded hospitality of the natives, yet we could not help being a little out of temper with
them at the great distance they were taking us, as it were, round
the foot of the mountain, till in the afternoon we reached a fine
plantation called Tepapala, belonging to the king, from which,
they told us, we were to ascend the mountain. . . .

We were now within a few miles of the Volcano [Kilauea], of
which there seemed to be this day a considerable eruption, and
as the wind blew from that direction, the smoke, dust and ashes
arising from it proved very troublesome to our eyes, in traveling
with our faces toward it.

Before we set out on the morning of the 13th, I observed . . .
our height at this place [to be] 1800 feet above the level of the
sea. The thermometer was at the same time 67°. After breakfast,
everything being got ready and the party arranged, we continued our march through the plantation for two or three miles
further and then began our ascent up the southeast side of
Mauna-roa [Mauna Loa], in an easy slanting direction, passing
through groves of trees and clear spots alternately, by a narrow,
rugged path. . . .

Toward sunset we came to two or three old huts where our
guides told us we must encamp for the night. The chief no longer

depended on his knowledge of the path, but brought men with him from the last plantation to conduct the whole party up the mountain, which now lay between us and Karakakooa [Keala-kekua]. We had the volcano to our right most part of this day and in the forenoon the smoke and ashes arising from it made the air very thick, which at times proved very tormenting to our eyes. At sunset the thermometer was 54° and . . . our height 3510.

At sunrise next morning the thermometer was so low as 41°. . . . The air was at this time so chilly, and the natives complained so much of the cold that we did not stir from the place of our encampment till after breakfast, when we again set forward up the mountain, in a reversed oblique direction to what we came the day before, but in so winding and circuitous a manner and through such pathless and rugged tracts, avoiding the clumps of forests here and there, that had we not had good guides with us, we should have met with insurmountable difficulties.

We had sight now and then of the lower edge of the snow, which did not appear to be far above us. We therefore began to entertain the most sanguine hopes of reaching it at least, should we not be able to accomplish the full extent of our object in getting to the summit. In the afternoon we turned our faces more directly up the mountain, when we found the ascent very steep and rugged and consequently more fatiguing.

Toward evening we reached the upper verge of the forest . . . where we encamped for the conveniency of having wood at hand to burn and erect our huts with. The natives, having pitched upon a clear spot overgrown only with strong, tall grass, they all set to work and in the course of about two hours erected a small village of huts sufficient to shelter themselves and us comfortably for the night. These huts, though finished with such hurry, were neatly constructed and well-thatched all over with long grass. A large one was built in the middle of the village for us to eat and set in, besides a small one for each of us to sleep in, where they spread our bedding on a thick layer of long grass, so that we enjoyed our repose comfortably as we could wish. . . .

At six in the evening . . . 6,500 feet in altitude, the thermometer . . . was at 41°, and as we had heated ourselves a good deal in this day's march up the mountain, we felt the air after sunset remarkably chilly and cold, which induced us to keep large fires burning near our huts during the whole night. Notwithstanding this precaution, many of the natives were so restless with the cold and continued coughing, that they enjoyed very little repose, and not indeed without cause, for when we got up next morning the thermometer was at 28° and the grass which grew about our huts was stiff and whitened by hoar frost, and the earth that was anywise moist and swampy was encrusted with icy concretions about our encampment. . . .

The natives, who were all barefooted, could not stir out of their huts in the morning until after breakfast, when the cheering influence of the sun dispersed the frost, but they greatly dreaded its consequences higher up the mountain, where they said the cold was so intense that it would certainly kill us and them too, and they described its effects by contracting and shivering themselves, and cautioned us very strongly against going higher up or exposing ourselves and them to such danger.

Even the old chief Rookea was so strongly prepossessed of this opinion that he now entreated us in the most earnest manner to relinquish the idea of going higher, for that he and several others were already nearly overcome with the fatigue of the journey, and that the cold on the mountain would kill them. We endeavored to soothe their minds by promising them that we should not attempt to go higher up than the edge of the snow, which we did not conceive to be far from us, and after accomplishing that, which we should undoubtedly be able to do in the heat of the day, we should return again to the encampment in the evening.

They appeared so far satisfied with this declaration that we set out after breakfast, followed by the whole party, in a direct line up the mountain. But we soon found that many of them came on so slow and reluctantly that about ten in the forenoon we proposed to the Chief that he and most of the party should return back and encamp on the edge of the forest, whilst we should go on with the guides and a few stout volunteers of the natives to carry some little refreshment and some of our bedding to wrap round us and them in case the cold should be found too powerful to withstand.

The Chief, finding his former entreaties of no avail, readily agreed to this proposal and parted with us with tears in his eyes, after he and our guides had fixed upon the place where they were to wait our return. Having made this arrangement, we continued our progress up the rugged steep, which now became naked, dreary and barren, with only here and there little tufts of grass in the crevices of the rocks. By noon, finding that vegetation had entirely ceased, not a blade of grass, moss, or even lichen was to be seen anywhere around us for some time, I observed the barometer to ascertain our height . . . 10,543 feet above the level of the sea. . . .

While we were resting and refreshing ourselves after making these observations, one of the natives who struggled higher up the mountain, came running back to us with snow in his hand, and though we were much fatigued, for the ascent was very steep, yet this gave us fresh encouragement and we continued to ascend till we passed several patches of snow, when in the evening, finding that we were not likely to gain the summit of the mountain with daylight, for every height seemed lengthening as we went on, we did not perceive it prudent to go far into the snow and therefore stopped short to consult with one another on what was to be done, whether we should go back to the encampment for the night and come up next day better provided, or whether we should venture to remain where we were all night, at the mercy of the weather on the bleak slope of this immense mountain, and on the small pittance of provisions we had with us.

Everyone was so fatigued with this day's journey . . . that the dread of descending and ascending again such a rugged steep made us at all hazards, prefer the latter. . . . We were not, as might naturally be expected, at this time without our apprehensions that our constitutions, which were for some time inured to the scorching heats of the tropic climate below, would be greatly affected by this sudden transition to the upper snowy region of the mountain, for since we began our ascent, we may be said to have gone through all the variety of climates between the equator and the pole . . . yet, after all, we were so inconsiderate of our own safety as not to make any particular provision of warm clothing to prevent the baneful effects of this sudden change. . . .

We had nothing here wherewith we could keep up a fire, and all the provisions we had remaining was a small quantity of chocolate, a few ship's biscuits and near a quart of rum, together with a few coconuts. Of these articles we carefully preserved the best half for the next day and divided the other half as equal as we could amongst the party which was now about a dozen in number.

We managed to boil the chocolate in a tin pot over a small fire made of our walking sticks, and each had his share of it warm, with a small quantity of rum in it, before he went to bed. We had no other water than what we melted from the snow, which we thought greatly improved the chocolate.

For our bed we made choice of a flat even rock on which we could all huddle close together, and after marking out the exact space we should occupy of it, we raised a small parapet round it with the lava to break off the wind, which after sunset blew very keen and penetrating. All the bed clothes we hitherto required were a few folds of the Sandwich Island cloth over us, with a mat under us . . . but this night, after spreading a mat on the bare rock, as it was agreed we should all sleep together to keep ourselves warm, we joined together everything we had for a general covering, made pillows of hard lava, and in this we passed the night tolerably comfortable, though we could not sleep much, nor was it indeed to be expected.

At this time, so many thousand feet high, reclined on the hard rock for our bed, with no other shelter than the grand canopy of heaven, our minds were variously occupied, sometimes in meditating on the dreadful consequences of a snowstorm coming on whilst we were thus situated, at other times in contemplating the awful and extended scene around us, where the most profound stillness subsisted the whole night, not even interrupted by the least chirp of a bird or an insect.

The moon rose out of the sea at an immense distance and her

orb appeared uncommonly large and brilliant, and the sky, being perfectly clear overhead, the assemblage of stars appeared very numerous and shone with unusual brightness. These led the imagination to the utmost stretch and afforded objects of both wonder and admiration.

Next morning at sunrise the thermometer was at 26° and the air was excessively keen and piercing. We made a scanty meal of the remainder of our provisions before we set out, but for want of fuel had the greatest difficulty in getting our chocolate boiled, though we burnt mats and everything we could think of. Those of the natives who appeared less able to withstand the cold or further fatigue were sent down to the encampment, and at the same time we set forward with the rest of them up the mountain, carrying with us the remainder of the liquor and a few coconuts as our only resource of refreshment in case of emergencies.

As we went, we soon found the ascent become less steep and everywhere chequered over with large patches of snow, which was so hard that we walked over it with ease, and we marched a pretty quick pace to keep ourselves warm.

We found the summit of the mountain nearly flat for several miles, strewed over with huge lumps of loose lava, and here and there deep snow. About 11 in the forenoon, we arrived at the mouth of an immense crater at least three miles in circumference, and looking round us we conceived the western edge of it to be the highest part of the mountain. . . . To get to this eminence we had to cross over a large hollow full of hideous chinks and chasms in all directions, and strewed over with large masses of broken and peaked lava in irregular piles, exhibiting the most rugged and disruptive appearance. . . .

By noon we got to the highest part of the mountain . . . 13,634 feet above the level of the sea. . . . I regretted much not having a spirit-level or some other instrument to ascertain whether this mountain or Mawna-Kaah [Mauna Kea] is the highest, though the peak of the latter, being at this time more whitened with snow, I am inclined to think it would have the pre-eminence. . . .

The sides of the crater (which was, as near as we could guess, about a mile in diameter), were quite perpendicular and, as we conjectured, about 400 yards in height all around, excepting opposite to the hollow. . . . The bottom of it was quite flat, being filled up with lava with a wavy roughness on its surface, apparently in the state in which it cooled in this immense furnace. At the edge of it we observed some smoke in two or three places, which we conceived to issue from hot springs, as on our way back we visited the entrance to a cavern out of which there issued a very hot steam.

In undergoing our struggle again across the rugged hollow, we all felt less or more exhausted with fatigue. . . . Overwhelmed, spiritless and faint, we threw ourselves down upon the bare rocks and for some moments revolved our melancholy situation in silence. The distance we were from the party, which was considerably more than half the height of the mountain; the ruggedness and steepness of the declivity; and our weakness and inability to undergo fatigue without some miraculous support, all obtruded themselves on our minds in the most ghastly shapes.

On further inquiry we found that our trusty friends had still a reserve of three coconuts. The liquor of these we gradually sipped, and it greatly revived us, and after eating some of the kernels, which were carefully divided amongst us, we set out on our return to the encampment, where we were so fortunate as to arrive safe at ten at night, after the most persevering and hazardous struggle that can possibly be conceived.

From the manuscript account of Archibald Menzies, as published in *Hawaii and Its Volcanoes,* Charles H. Hitchcock (Honolulu: Hawaiian Gazette Co., 1911).

XI

Richard J. Cleveland

The most direct influences of Western civilization were reaching Hawaii, for better or for worse, from the two shores of the Atlantic, but less direct benefits were also coming from the American West Coast—from the string of Catholic missions planted along the littoral of Upper and Lower California and Mexico. In name these missions were Spanish, but they were supervised by Franciscan friars who had been recruited from many European countries. Altogether the friars' outlook was international and humanitarian; they had been educated in the great continental universities, represented a high order of Western culture and scholarship, and had among them notable men of learning: scientists, linguists, philosophers.

Geographically these men of the cloth were the closest contact Hawaii had with Western culture, and despite the later repudiation of the Catholic fathers, the Islanders were deeply indebted to them. Anonymously they contributed a wealth of ideas and assets; through traders, explorers, and early settlers they sent to Hawaii a great variety of plants and seeds which they had gathered from the far corners of Christendom, and from them came much of the barnyard menagerie. Vancouver had brought from the missions the first cows; Richard J. Cleveland (1773–1860) shipped in the first horses.

Cleveland was a Yankee from Salem, Massachusetts, born to the sea. He took his initiatory cruise as able seaman at the age of fourteen, and five years later was bound for Calcutta as master of his own ship.

Before he was thirty he had sailed into most of the important ports of Europe, the Orient, and the Americas on small trading ships, and the spring of 1803 found him on the Lower California coast with a cargo destined for China by way of Hawaii.

On a previous visit to Kealakekua Bay Cleveland had discovered to his astonishment that the Islanders had never heard of the most indispensable animal known to civilization—the horse. He had resolved to remedy that deficiency, and before leaving Baja California for China he cleared deck space to take on board a modest stable of steeds which he intended to present to King Kamehameha.

On May 4, 1803, Cleveland sailed into a small bay far down the California peninsula and anchored at the landing used by Mission San Borgia. Father Mariano Apolonario headed the mission, and it was from him that Captain Cleveland received the first of a series of equestrian gifts that were eventually to upset Hawaiian sociology, turn a pedestrian people into a nation of hard-riding horsemen, cause Hawaiians everywhere to give up their surfboards for saddles, convert Kanakas into irresponsible galloping roughriders, and very nearly upset the Island kingdom. But the consequences of his benefaction were not on Cleveland's conscience when he appealed to the generous Father Mariano to contribute a mare and stud to take to horseless Kamehameha.

First Horse to Trod the Soil of Hawaii

The more intimately we became acquainted with Padre Mariano the more we were convinced that his was a character to love and respect. . . . His countenance beaming with the love and benevolence, which were his prevailing motives of action, inspired immediate and perfect confidence. . . . His mild and humane treatment of his domestics made their intercourse more like that of father and children than of master and servants. His regular observance, morning, noon and evening, of his devotional duties with his uncouth-looking domestics assembled around him, and on bended knee, and with the utmost decorum, participating in his prayers to the throne of grace, was affecting. . . .

Our visit here was protracted, much beyond our intentions, by the persuasions of the Padre and the promise of two horses, which we had unsuccessfully endeavored to procure at the other missions, as a present to the King of the Sandwich Islands. These arrived at the encampment on the 19th, a male and a female, and were presented to us by the Padre. In return for these and a flagon of wine and some dried fruits, we gave him such manufactures as he desired, to more than their value. The next day we took the horses on board and made preparation for our departure. . . .

On taking leave, he assured us that we would always be remembered in his prayers, and, accompanying us to the boat, repeated and vociferated his *a Dios* until we were too distant to hear him more. With our glass we perceived him to be waiting after we had arrived on board, and he did not move off with his retinue until we had weighed anchor.

At 10 o'clock A.M. we weighed anchor and made all sail to the southward. . . . Early the following morning we came to anchor in the bay of St. Joseph, at the southern extremity of the peninsula, and near the mission of that name [San Jose]. . . . The Padres had no scruple in supplying us with such provisions, vegetables and fruits as the place afforded, and were equally ready to trade with us to the extent of their means, which were rather limited.

In addition to a supply of stores, we purchased of them pearls to the amount of two thousand dollars and also a mare with foal. Having with difficulty taken the latter on board, on the 28th of May, we sailed immediately for the Sandwich Islands.

We experienced undeviating fine weather, fair winds and smooth sea on our passage to the Sandwich Islands, and on the 19th of June, 1803, got sight of Hawaii, its summit towering above the clouds. We passed Kohala Point with a strong breeze, and presuming the king to be at Kealakekua Bay, we proceeded directly thither, and arriving on the 21st in the morning, we lay by and fired a gun. Not a canoe, however, nor a person was seen moving. The silence and inactivity which prevailed formed a perfect contrast to all my former experience at these islands.

At length after lying by more than an hour, two persons were discovered swimming off to us. On arriving on board one of them spoke sufficient English to make us understand that there existed a taboo, and, moreover, that the king and principal men were on Maui. They piloted us to the best anchorage, passing over the coral bank, and we anchored on a sandy bottom in sixteen fathoms.

The next day John Young, who had seen us pass his residence at Kawaihae Bay, made us a visit, presuming we should anchor here. He told us that the taboo was a periodical one . . . now limited to three days. We intended to remain here no longer than was requisite to supply ourselves with a few refreshments, which Young undertook to procure for us. We improved the time, therefore, by a ramble on shore.

Among other places, we visited that *morai* where, in defiance of the prejudices of the natives, Captain Cook caused his observatory to be erected, a desecration which was the origin of the quarrel that terminated his existence. There are yet standing near the *morai* several cocoanut trees which are perforated with the balls fired from his cannon on that occasion.

We left Kealakekua Bay on the 23rd and the next morning anchored in Kawaihae Bay for the purpose of landing the mare with foal, for which Young was very urgent, professing to have a knowledge of the treatment of horses, and promising to take all possible care of the animal. In the expectation that the chance of their increase would be better secured by placing the horses in the care of different persons, we acceded to his request and landed the mare in safety near his place. This was the first horse that ever trod the soil of Hawaii, and caused among the natives incessant exclamations of astonishment.

Leaving this bay the same evening, we steered for Maui, off which island we lay becalmed a part of the next day. When the breeze sprang up, though at a long distance from the village of Lahaina, we were boarded by Isaac Davis, the European who with John Young was captured many years since in Captain

Metcalf's vessel. Soon after, a double canoe was seen coming towards us, and on arrival alongside, a large athletic man, nearly naked, jumped on board, who was introduced by Davis as Kamehameha, the great king.

Desirous of conciliating the good opinion of a person whose power was so great, we omitted no attention which we supposed would be agreeable to him. But whether he had left some duty unperformed on shore or whether he had met with something to disturb his serenity of mind, we know not; certain it was that he did not reciprocate our civilities. He appeared to be absent, and after walking round the deck of the vessel and taking only a very careless look at the horses, he got into his canoe and went on shore.

Davis remained on board all night to pilot us to the best anchorage, which we gained early the following morning, and soon after had our decks crowded with visitors to see the horses. The people showed none of that indifference on seeing them which had been manifested by the King, and which I believe to have been an affectation, but on the contrary, expressed such wonder and admiration as were very natural on beholding for the first time this noble animal.

The horses were landed safely and in perfect health the same day, and gave evidence by their gambols, of their satisfaction at being again on terra firma. They were then presented to the King, who was told that one had been also left at Hawaii for him. He expressed his thanks, but did not seem to comprehend their value.

While the crowd were apparently wondering what use they could be put to, a sailor from our ship jumped upon the back of one and galloped off amid the shouts of the natives, who with alacrity opened a way to let him pass. There existed strong apprehensions in the minds of all for the safety of the man, but when, by going back and forth, they perceived the docility of the animal, his subjection and his fleetness, they seemed to form some little conception of his utility.

The King was among the number who witnessed the temerity of the sailor, but with all his sagacity for which he has been

68632

justly praised remarked that he could not perceive that the ability to transport a person from one place to another in less time than he could run would be adequate compensation for the food he would consume and the care he would require.

As a dray or a dragoon's horse, there was no prospect of his being wanted, and hence our present was not very highly appreciated. In this we were much disappointed, but hoped, nevertheless, that the King would be influenced by our advice to have them well taken care of, that they would increase, and eventually that their value would be justly estimated.

Our supplies were received from the King, for all of which we paid the full price, and though he offered us a small present as an offset for the horses, we declined its acceptance. . . . On the 7th of July, 1803, having ascertained that we could obtain no [further] supplies without losing more time than they were worth, we made sail to the westward.

From *In the Forecastle or Twenty-five Years a Sailor*, Richard J. Cleveland (New York: Hurst and Co., c. 1843).

XII

Peter Corney

The opening of the Pacific Northwest and the international scramble for fur trade with coastal Indians, scattered all the way from California to Alaska, brought the Sandwich Islands their first commercial prominence. Principal contenders in the race were England, Russia, and the United States, fielding giant companies such as Hudson's Bay, The North West, the Russian-American, John Jacob Astor's American Fur and its subsidiary Pacific Fur, any one of which was powerful enough politically and economically to quash an insignificant little kingdom like Hawaii, if it chose.

All of the fur companies had a stake in Hawaiian affairs. The Islands offered an important source of food supplies, winter refuge from the stormy North Pacific, convenient warm-water bays for making emergency ship repairs, hospitality for the "refreshment" of crews, a stopover on the long voyage to and from China, and by 1810 a remunerative secondary commerce in sandalwood—that scented product of Hawaiian forests indispensable in the Orient for temple incense and woodcraft. In fact, it was such an important trade that the Sandwich Islands were known in China only as the Sandalwood Islands.

Sailing orders customarily took any of the English and American fur company ships first to the Pacific Northwest for a cargo of furs, exchanged by the Indians for cheap blankets, firearms, and baubles; on to Hawaii for a few tons of sandalwood, sold by the Chinese *picul* —133 pounds—for anything from overpriced straw hats and useless hosiery to glass beads and gunpowder; next to Canton where the sandalwood and furs were exchanged at enormous profit for spices, teas, crockery, exotic decorations, silks, and other textiles; then back to an Atlantic port for cash sale of the Oriental goods. A single voyage could yield a fortune—at the collective expense of American Indians, Chinese coolies, Hawaiian kings, and Kanakas.

Between 1814 and 1819, at the height of the era of fur traffic, the literate British seaman Peter Corney (d. 1836) was repeatedly in and out of Hawaiian ports, en route to China or the Columbia River region, in the employ of the North West Company. His journal, first published in the London *Literary Gazette* of 1821, gave intimate details of his voyages, as well as of the Island scene during the last years of the reign of Kamehameha the Great—when the king was already well-supplied with the trappings that foreign commerce had brought him, and trading followed an established routine.

Natives Come Off in Great Numbers

On the 16th January, 1815, made the island of Owhyee [Hawaii], ran close in shore; some natives visited us and informed us that Tameameah [Kamehameha] was at the village of Tyroa [Kailua]. We made all sail for that place and the next day ran between Owhyee and Mowee [Maui] and stood close in shore.

The natives came off in great numbers, bringing with them hogs, vegetables, rope and the cloth of the country; we allowed a few to enter the vessel and took a chief woman on board who acted as pilot. About midnight we reached Tyroa, where we anchored and . . . saluted the king. Mr. McDougal [supercargo] went on shore and returned with the king next morning.

Tameameah was dressed in a colored shirt, velveteen breeches, red waistcoat, large military shoes and worsted stockings, a black silk handkerchief round his neck, no coat. He is a tall, stout, athletic man, nose rather flat, thick lips, the upper one turned up; an open countenance, with three of his lower front teeth gone.

We weighed anchor and towed close in shore . . . ; the canoes collected from all parts, and in a short time there were no fewer than eighty of them, with from three to ten men in each, and some hundreds of men, women and children swimming about the ship, regardless of the sharks. The decks were soon covered with them. Captain Robson, being rather alarmed at having so many on board, told the king to send them on shore.

He took a handspike in his hand and said a few words, and in a moment the men flew out of the ship in all directions. The king ordered us to hoist a white flag, which here signifies taboo, or prohibition, and then ordered two of his *hikanees* [*aikanes*], or confidential men, to remain on board to keep the natives from stealing. The king, queens and principal chiefs remained with us all day, and had their dinner sent on board to them, not being allowed to eat ship provision. It is a strange custom that anything out of which the king eat or drink he had sent on shore.

In the afternoon Captain Robson landed in company with his Majesty, who gave Mr. McDougal permission to stop in his dominions as long as he pleased, and assured him that he should want for nothing. We accordingly forwarded their baggage, and the two gentlemen and a boy landed.

The king sent off a supply of hogs and tarrow [taro], some very good island rope, and the same night, January 18th, we weighed and made sail for Canton.

On the 10th of December [1815] we made the island of Owhyhee. The ship was surrounded with canoes filled with articles of trade. On the 12th we came to off the village of Tyroa, half a mile from the *morai* [temple] on the point. Found the American ship *Milwood* here purchasing sandalwood at the rate of seven dollars for 133 pounds. The king, Tameameah, came on board with the gentlemen we left last year, who had been well treated by the natives and wanted for nothing. On their first landing the king had houses built for them and gave them servants to attend on them.

His Majesty and the Queens were rejoiced to see their old friend Captain Jennings and after taking a good proportion of wine they went on shore together. The Prince Reoreo [Liholiho] and his stepsister Maroo [Kamamalu] also visited the vessel; the

Prince was accompanied by one of the chief priests; he was highly tattooed, and would not go under deck for fear the sailors or natives would walk above him. Being the greatest man on the island, no person was allowed to put even a hand above his head on pain of death. His sister was not so ceremonious, but came below and took her wine with me and pressed me very much to remain on Owhyhee. . . .

During our whole stay our decks were continually crowded with natives. We shipped a large quantity of island rope, which makes excellent running rigging; and the people were employed killing and salting pork, the King, Queens, Prince and Princess coming on board daily and remaining until evening.

Wanting to overhaul the rigging and caulk the ship, we determined to run down to Woahoo [Oahu], where there was a fine close harbor. We acquainted the King with our intentions, and he sent one of his *hikanees* or confidential men on board, named Kenepoo, to accompany us and see that we got what we wanted.

On the 16th of December we took leave of Tameameah, and with the ship full of men, women and children, made sail . . . and on the 18th arrived at Woahoo. We were boarded outside by John Young, a white man who had lived on these islands upward of 33 years. He piloted us into the harbor and we moored close to the shore, where thousands of natives were collected, and soon crowded us. . . . At sunrise we fired two muskets and sent the women out of the ship, and at sundown did the same as a signal for them to come on board. This practice we continued, and by that means kept the ship clear of natives.

By the 29th of December we had completed repairing the rigging, caulked and painted the ship inside and out, and salted a quantity of pork. We then left these friendly people and made sail towards Mooi [actually Kauai], another of the group. The 1st of January, 1816 we were close in with the village of Whymea [Waimea]. . . . We stood off and on the village all night and the next day ran in between the reefs. The natives came off in great numbers, bringing hogs, goats and vegetables to barter. The King, Tamoree [Kaumualii], did not make his appearance, but sent his head man to measure the schooner. On the 4th our gentlemen came on board and we sailed for China.

We left the [Columbia] River on the 10th day of January, 1817, for the Sandwich Islands . . . to refit the brig and cure pork. We were also to bring as many of the Sandwich Islanders to the Columbia River as we could conveniently accommodate. On the 27th we saw Owhyhee after a quick and pleasant passage. We stood along shore as usual; the natives came off in great numbers, bringing pigs, tarrow, yams, goats, plantains, rope and fruit of every description.

Next day we anchored off Tyroa, close to the king's *morai*. King Tameameah and his family came on board as usual and were rejoiced to see us. He assured us we should have everything we wished for that the islands afforded or he could command, and commenced sending hogs on board.

On the 1st of February we sailed from Owhyhee, his majesty sending a trusty man with us, named Kenepoo, to see that we got what we wanted. We had directions to touch at Mowee, where we should have plenty of hogs, salt and rope. When weighing our anchor we found it was fast under a rock, where it inevitably must have remained, had not the king sent his divers down to clear it. The depth of the water was eight fathoms.

We now made sail toward Mowee, our ship as usual full of natives. Next morning we passed Morokenee [Molokini], and made sail up Mackerey [Maalaea] Bay. Here we lay until the 6th, and took on board a great quantity of hogs, salt and vegetables. This bay is very deep and wide, and nearly divides the island, there being but a narrow neck of land and very low, keeping the two parts of the island together.

There is good anchorage, and the only danger arises from the trade winds which blow so strong at times as to drive ships out of the bay with two anchors down. It lies northeast and southwest and is well sheltered from every other wind. The neck of land is so low, and the land so high on each side that the northeast trade comes through like a hurricane. On this neck of land are the principal salt pans, where they make most excellent salt.

Our next station was in Lehina [Lahaina] Roads. This beautiful village has the appearance of a fine garden, laid out with the greatest taste in fish ponds, tarrow patches, cane patches, groves of breadfruit and plantain trees, so delightfully arranged that nothing can surpass it.

On the 9th the brig, full of hogs and natives, got under weigh from this romantic spot, bound for Woahoo. . . . On the 13th of February we were off the harbor of Honorora [Honolulu] and John Harbottle, the king's pilot, came on board, but it was not till the 20th that the trade wind suffered us to get in shore. . . .

The *Taamano* [*Kaahumanu*] was fitting out for Canton and taking sandalwood on board for the China market. . . . The crew consisted of about ten natives and ten white men. . . . To our great surprise, we found a very fine battery built on the point, mounting about 60 guns, and learned that during our absence the Russians had sent two ships from New Archangel or Norfolk Sound to these islands with Russians and Kodiaks to form an establishment. . . . As soon as they got footing on shore, they commenced building block houses and squaring out a place for a fort under the direction of Mr. Shefham. They even hoisted the Russian colors.

Mr. John Young . . . communicated this intelligence to the kings and chiefs, all of whom were on Owhyhee. The chiefs were immediately sent down to Woahoo with orders from Tameameah that the Russians should quit the islands instantly, and if they did not depart quietly that force would be used. The Russians, not finding themselves strong enough to resist, went peaceably off. The Islanders then built the fort under the direction of John Young.

A party was kept constantly on shore curing the pork. . . . While we lay here we gave half the people leave to go on shore each night. Our carpenter had frequent occasion to go to the woods to cut timber, which he did in safety, and we were extremely well treated by the natives.

On the 14th of April, being complete in provisions, repairs, etc., we took on board 60 natives, being all we could conveniently accommodate, for the Columbia River, and stood out of the harbor. . . .

November the 14th [1817] we left the Columbia River for the Sandwich Islands to sell the vessel. . . . Our passage . . . was quick and pleasant. On the 6th of December we made Owhyhee, stood along shore toward Toyhoy [Kawaihae] Bay and ran in. Finding no natives came off, we sent the whale boat on shore to know what was the reason.

The boat soon returned with an account that the natives were celebrating their annual festival, called *muckka-hitee* [*Makahiki*]. . . . We also heard that King Tameahmeah was then at the village of Tyroa, his favorite residence. We made all sail for that place, where we arrived on the 10th and came to with our only bower anchor off the *morai*.

No canoes being allowed to come off, Captain Jennings went on shore to see the king; in the evening the boat returned with some hogs and tarrow. The king Tameahmeah told Captain Jennings if we would go to the island of Woahoo and remain until the *muckka-hitee* was over, he should then be able to agree with him about the purchase of the ship. . . .

We made all sail for Woahoo and on the 14th arrived off the harbor. . . . We sent John Carpenter on shore and discharged him of the crew. The taboo was still on; consequently none of the natives came on board. On the 24th of December, the *muckka-hitee* being over, the king's prime minister, named Kreymokoo [Kalaimoku], commonly called Pitt, came on board with all the chiefs, accompanied by John Young, to inspect the vessel previous to their purchasing of her.

They seemed much astonished at our large battery guns; we got one on deck and, mounting it, fired several rounds of shot, at which the chiefs were much pleased, and the natives crowded from all parts of the island to see the *poo'nu'ee* [*pu nui*], as they call a great gun. They were all very particular in measuring its length, breadth and size of the bore.

After the chiefs had carefully inspected every part of the brig,

John Young was asked his opinion of her. He told Mr. Pitt she
would answer their purpose very well. Kreymokoo, upon this,
agreed to give twice the full of the vessel of sandalwood for her,
to be delivered in a space of time not exceeding six months, and
that we should hold possession of vessel till all the wood was
delivered, and that we were to be found in provision while we
remained on the island. The agreement was drawn up and signed
by Captain Jennings and Kreymokoo.

The next day being Christmas day, we invited all the chiefs
and respectable white men on the island to dine with us on
shore; we spent a most pleasant day, and the chiefs remained
with us to a late hour. We had a dinner cooked apart for the
chiefs' wives, as they were not allowed to eat with the men.

Next day we took on board the king's taxes, and January 11th,
1818, we sailed for Owhyhee, the brig loaded with provisions
and cloth of the country, this being the time at which the natives
pay their half-year's taxes. We had also a number of chiefs on
board and about 400 natives, men, women and children. There
was scarcely room to move on the decks or in the cabin; even
the chains, tops and bowsprit were crowded with them.

We touched at Mowee, where they all landed for a few days,
and nothing went forward but feasting and rejoicing. On the
16th the chiefs again came on board and we got under weigh for
Owhyhee, the ship as before full of natives. In crossing the channel between Mowee and Owhyhee, we were near upsetting the
vessel, being top heavy, from the number of them on deck and
about the rigging.

On the 18th we anchored off Tyroa, and Tameameah came on
board. On his approach all the natives jumped overboard and
left us clear decks. We commenced firing a salute, when the king
called out to us in a pleasant tone to stop, as the powder was
now his and he wanted it for other purposes—probably for the
Russians if they should come to trouble him. He was delighted
with the large guns; . . . the next day we landed them, and by
this means got rid of the curious natives.

They were placed in a square in front of the royal residence,
where thousands of the people were daily collected to look at

them. Tameameah found one fault with them, which was that they took too much powder (a charge being four pounds), but he took all our small arms, powder and everything he thought would be useful to him, and made the brig over to his son and heir Rieo Rieo [Liholiho]. . . . We received orders from Tameameah to proceed to the island of Atooai [Kauai] for a cargo of sandalwood. Teymotoo, or Cox, with several other chiefs came on board. We made sail and on the following day came to in Whymea Roads. One mile from the village the English ensign was displayed on a very fine fort, mounting about thirty guns.

The natives came off in great numbers; they informed us that the Russians had built the fort, in which there were dungeons, and had actually gone so far as to confine some white men and natives. The Russians advised Tamooree, king of Atooai, to shake off Tameameah's yoke and declare war against him, in which they would assist him. They made him a present of a schooner and he gave them in return a large tract of land. . . .

The Russians wished to send Tamooree to Petersburg, but could never get him on board. At length Tamooree discovered that they wished to possess themselves of the island; he consulted with his chiefs, returned their schooner (which they refused) and ordered them on board their ships, three of which were lying in a snug harbor at the west end of the island.

They resisted and a scuffle ensued, in which three Russians and several natives were killed, but the latter at last forced them on board, and Doctor Shefham [Scheffer] made his escape to Canton in an American vessel. The Russian ships went to Norfolk Sound. The fort does great credit to the engineer; it is situate on a high point at the entrance of the river and protects the whole town. The king, chiefs and about 150 warriors live within it and keep a regular guard. They have a number of white men for the purpose of working the guns, etc.

Our chiefs landed and were well received by Tamooree, and the next morning they commenced sending wood on board. About 500 canoes were employed in bringing it off, and by the 25th of March we had the ship quite full. The king behaved extremely well, and sent us off plenty of hogs and vegetables.

Our chiefs came on board, as did also some Atooai chiefs. We weighed and made sail for Woahoo, where we anchored the next day, landed our wood, and lay until the 19th, when we took on board a cargo of salt for the west end of Woahoo. Next day we sailed for Whymea Bay on the west end of the island, to get another cargo of wood . . . where we arrived on the 22nd, threw our ballast out and took on board a full cargo of wood in thirty-six hours—more than 200 canoes employed in bringing it off, day and night.

We weighed and made sail for Honororoa [Honolulu], where we arrived on the 28th, and sent the wood on shore. On the 1st of May, 1818, we had all our wood on shore and stored. On the 2nd of May we hauled down the English colors and hoisted the island colors, saluting them with seven guns. We then gave the ship up to Kreymokoo, or Pitt, and went on shore to the houses prepared for our reception.

It was with the greatest regret I left the ship, for it seemed as if I had lost my home; and in fact it was some time before I felt myself at all comfortable. I had sailed on board the *Columbia* from August, 1813, to May, 1818, a period of nearly five years; when she left England, the crew consisted of twenty-five persons, and when we sold the vessel at these islands, the steward and a black man . . . and myself were all that remained, and even these left before the vessel was given up.

From *Voyages in the Northern Pacific* . . . , Peter Corney (Honolulu: Thrum, 1896).

XIII

Opukahaia

Masters of trading vessels that anchored off Hawaiian villages made the early observation that there were no more eager sailors on the seven seas than Sandwich Islanders, and they took full advantage of it. The natives were lured aboard as replacements for deserters and ships' casualties; without being required to sign the usual papers, they were taken on as regular crewmen, as deckhands, whalers, boatmen, supernumeraries, cabin boys—and girls; a good many were impressed into service; others went as stowaways.

They made superb seamen, but they had three shortcomings: They could not endure exposure to cold weather; coming from the antiseptic Islands, they quickly picked up every germ in a crowded, filthy forecastle and died of the commonest Occidental ailments; and their wanderlust or irresponsibility, combined with the maltreatment they received, induced them to jump ship at the first port of call.

By the 1810's and 20's hundreds of homesick Hawaiians were wandering about waterfronts from Canton to Callao, from Santa Barbara to Boston. The case of Opukahaia was typical. In his boyhood on the Big Island he had witnessed the massacre of most of his family in the aftermath of an intertribal battle, but he had managed to escape, was adopted by his uncle, a priest, and was in training for the priesthood himself when the excitement of life aboard a Yankee ship suddenly seemed far more inviting than the dull routine of a *heiau*. Opukahaia wrote his own story, piecemeal, a few years later after he had acquired a fair command of English, and had added to his vocabulary some of the jargon of his pious teachers.

More Better Go Than Stay

While I was with my uncle, for some time I began to think about leaving that country to go to some other part of the globe. I did not care where I shall go to. I thought to myself that if I could get away and go to some other country, probably I could find some comfort, more than to live there, without father and mother. I thought it will be better for me to go than to stay.

About this time there was a ship come from New York—Captain Brintnall the master of the ship. As soon as it got into the harbor, in the very place where I lived, I thought of no more but to take the best chance I had, and if the Captain have no objection, to take me as one of his own servants, and to obey his word.

As soon as the ship anchored I went on board. The Captain soon enquired whose boy I was. Yet I knew not what he says to me, for I could not speak the English language. But there was a young man who could speak the English language, and he told the Captain that I was the Minister's nephew—the Minister [priest] of that place. The Captain wished me to stay on board the ship that night, and the next day to go home.

This very much satisfied me, and I consented to stay. At evening the Captain invited me to eat supper with him. And there sat another boy with us who was to be my fellow-traveler: by name Thomas Hopoo—Thomas, a name given him by the supercargo of the ship. After supper the Captain made some enquiry to see if I were willing to come to America; soon I made a motion with my head that I was willing to go. This man was very agreeable, and his kindness was much delighted in my heart, as if I was his own son and he was my own father. . . .

The next morning the Captain wished me to go shore to see my uncle, whether he was willing to let me go with him or not. . . . As soon as my uncle heard that I was going to leave him, he shut me up in a room, for he was not willing to let me go. . . . I saw a little hole in the side of the house. I got through it and went on board the ship.

When my uncle heard that I was on board the ship, he got into his canoe and came board the ship enquiring after me. No sooner after he made some enquirement, I was there discovered by one of my countrymen who had the care of the ship, and was brought forth, and come to my uncle's house. He would not let me go unless I pay him a hog for his god, for I was taken under his care to be made for a minister.

My uncle would now delay me no longer, and I took my leave of them and bid them farewell. My parting with them was disagreeable to them and to me, but I was willing to leave all my relations, friends and acquaintances; expected to see them no more in this world.

We set out on our journey toward the Seal Islands on the northwest part of America. On these Islands the Captain had left twenty or thirty men for sealing business on his way to Owhyhee. We found them safe. Among these I found a very desirable young man, by name Russell Hubbard, . . . a member of Yale College. He was a friend of Christ. Christ was with him when I saw him, but I knew it not. "Happy is the man that put his trust in God!" Mr. Hubbard was very kind to me on our passage and taught me the letters in English spelling book.

We continued on these Islands during six months, then took our course toward Owhyhee. Two of my countrymen were with me in the ship. One of them concluded to stay at Owhyhee, and the other to proceed on the voyage. The ship delayed no longer than a few days, and we set out for China, on our direct course for America.

On our way toward China my poor friend Thomas fell overboard. He was so careless, not knowing what he was about. He went outside of the ship and drew salt water to wash plates with, for he was a cabin's boy. When the ship rolled, he got in the water. The Captain calls all hands upon the deck, and ordered to have all the sails pull down, in order to let about. While we were working upon our sails, my friend Thomas was out of sight. While he was in the water he pulls all off his clothes in order to be lighter. We turned our ship and went back after him. We found him almost dead. He was in the water during the space of two and a half hours. O how glad was I then to see him, for he was already gone.

We took our direct course from hence as it was before. Soon we landed at an Island belonging to that part of China, and in the evening after the sun-down we anchored. On the next morning we fired one of our cannon for a pilot. When we had fired once or twice, there was another ship of war belonging to the British, which stood about four or five miles apart from us. As soon as they heard our cannon, they sent one of their brigs. We were then taken by it for a while. They took our Captain and he went on board the men of war's ship. He was there for a number of days. After this the Englishmen agreed to let us go.

We therefore leave that place called Mocao and directed our course to the city of Canton. We were there until we sold out all our seal-skins and loaded our ship with other sort of goods, such as tea, cinnamon, nankeens and silk, etc. At the end of six months we steered a direct course to America.

At the Cape of Good Hope, or before it, our sailors on board the ship began to terrify at us. They said that there was a man named Neptune who lived in that place and his abiding place was in the sea. In the evening the sailors began to act. One of them took an old great coat and put on him, and with a speaking trumpet in his hand, and his head was covered with sheep-skin; and he went forward of the ship making a great noise.

About this time friend Thomas and myself were on the quarter deck, hearing some of them telling about Neptune's coming with his iron canoe and iron paddle. Friend Thomas questioned whether the iron canoe will not sink down in the water. "No," said some of them, "he will make it light, for he is a god." While we were talking, the first we heard the sound of trumpet as follows—"Ship hail! From whence come you?"

The Captain immediately giving an answer in this manner: "From Canton."

"Have you got my boys?" said the old Neptune.

"Yes," answered the Captain.

"How many boys have you?" added the old Neptune.

"Two," said the Captain. That is myself and friend Thomas.

As soon as we both heard the Captain says "two," we both scared almost to death, and wished that we were at home. The old Neptune wished to see us, but we dare not come near at it. He continued calling to us to come to him, or else he would take both of us to be as his servants. We therefore went up immediately and shook our hands with him in friendly manner. I thought he was quite an old age, by seeing his long beards and his head covered with gray hairs, for his head was covered with a sheep-skin.

After our conversation with him he wished for drink, so that I went and filled two pails full of salt water, as the sailors had told us, and set them before him. Then he took his speaking trumpet and put it in my mouth for funnel, in order to make me drink the salt water which I brought. But while he stoops down to reach the pail of water, I took hold of the speaking trumpet and hold it on one side of my cheek, so that I may not drink a drop of salt water; did not anybody knew it, for it was dark. But friend Thomas was so full of scare, he took down a great deal of salt water. On the next morning he was taken sick and puked from the morning until the evening.

About this time our provisions was almost out. We had no bread, meat and water, save only one biscuit a day and one pint of water, only when the cook put in our tea. We were looking out for a vessel for a long time. Within a few days we come close to a schooner going to the West Indies, sailed from Boston. We fired at her in order to stop her. So did she. We got from them as much provisions as we wanted, and this lasted us until we got to New York.

We landed at New York in the year 1809, continued there a few weeks, and after the Captain sold out all the goods that are in the ship, we then parted with all our sailors, every one to go to their own home. But friend Thomas and myself continued with the Captain. One evening two gentlemen called on board the ship to see us. After our conversation was made with them, they wished us to go with them into a play-house, to show the curiosity.

We then went with them into the play-house and saw a great number of people as I ever saw before. We stayed during the fore part of the evening, then went on board the ship. The next morning the same two gentlemen called again and invited us to come to their house that afternoon. So that we both went. I thought while in the house of these two gentlemen how strange to see females eat with men.

Within a few days we left our ship and went home with Captain Brintnall to New Haven, the place where he lived. There I lived with him for some time. In this place I become acquainted with many students belonging to the college. By these pious students I was told more about God than what I had heard before, but I was so ignorant that I could not see into it whether it was so.

Many times I wished to hear more about God, but find nobody to interpret it to me. I attended many meetings on the Sabbath, but find difficulty to understand the minister. I could understand or speak but very little of the English language. Friend Thomas went to school to one of the students in the College before I thought of going to school.

I heard that a ship was ready to sail from New York within a few days for Owhyhee. The Captain was willing that I might take leave of this country and go home if I wish. But this was disagreeable to my mind. I wished to continue in this country a little longer. I stayed another week, saw Mr. Edwin Dwight, who first taught me to read and write.

The first time I saw him, he enquired whether I was one who came over with Thomas, for Thomas was known among many scholars in College. I told him I was one who come over with Thomas. He then asked me if I wished to learn to read and write. I told him that I was. He wished me to come to his room that night and begin to learn, so that I went in the evening and began to read in the spelling book.

Mr. Dwight wished me to come to his room at any time when

it is agreeable to the Captain, with whom I then lived. I went home that night and the next morning I mentioned all this matter to the Captain. He was pleased, and he wished me to go to school to Mr. Dwight. Thus I continued in school.

From *Memoirs of Henry Obookiah* (New Haven: Nathan Whiting, 1819).

XIV

Lucy G. Thurston

Once Opukahaia came under the influence of Yale divinity students, he ceased to typify misplaced Hawaiians in foreign ports. Following a brief indoctrination in New Haven, he was farmed out to a succession of church deacons and school preceptors, all of whom added to his religious and secular education. He joined the Congregational Church in 1815 and two years later enrolled as one of the charter pupils at a new "Foreign Mission School for the Sons of Unevangelized Barbarians" at Cornwall, Connecticut, along with Thomas Hopoo (Hopu) and a number of other Hawaiian drifters rounded up from various New England waterfronts.

The Cornwall curriculum offered a liberal education in subjects ranging from Biblical literature and mathematics to Latin, Hebrew, and natural philosophy; and Opukahaia—now answering to the Anglicized name of Henry Obookiah—excelled in them all, employing his spare time in composing a Hawaiian grammar and in translating the book of Genesis into phonetic Hawaiian. Meantime, he developed a consuming ambition to return to the Islands and convert his people to Connecticut Congregationalism. Henry clung tenaciously to that ambition during his years of Cornwall, but it was not destined to fulfillment. On February 19, 1818, after charging his fellow students to accept the task he knew he was not going to be able to carry out, he died agonizingly and pathetically of typhoid fever.

That death created a profound stir among New England church-goers, who probably constituted 95 percent of a largely Protestant population. Their doctrine decreed that they go into all the world and preach the Gospel to the whole creation; they had neglected that injunction, and the depravity of Hawaii was a prime example of that neglect. Something had to be done without delay to help Henry's benighted people.

His obituary, and the lessons of his life, were widely publicized in newspapers, church organs, and missionary journals. He was the subject of countless sermons and editorials. His former teacher at Yale, now the Reverend Edwin W. Dwight, hastily edited a sentimental little book, *The Memoirs of Henry Obookiah,* certain to wring tears —and alms—from the most callous laymen. Thousands upon thousands of copies were published and circulated. It was estimated that the heartrending treatise was read by half a million people.

Among the readers were Vermonter Hiram Bingham and Bay Stater Asa Thurston, who had just finished their course at Andover Theological Seminary. Both promptly volunteered as missionaries to the Sandwich Islands. A twenty-three-year-old school teacher, Lucy Goodale, from Marlboro, Massachusetts, read it too and heard the "call," as did two male teachers, a young doctor, a printer, and a farmer; and three of the Cornwall alumni, including Thomas Hopu, were ready to take Henry's place.

Volunteering as a missionary to any Pacific area in 1819 was an act of supreme self-sacrifice. The volunteer was literally giving his life. Chances of ever returning were too remote to be considered. The Pacific was a no-man's-land to civilized Easterners. There was not an island in the whole ocean that had what they considered a settled government. The nearest American outpost was on the Missouri River. To be sure, there were the California missions, but they were Catholic and therefore represented the archenemy. Traders, too, were to be counted as treacherous antagonists. Pacific-bound missionaries bade farewell to civilization forever, and took a one-way passage.

Nor did the American Board of Commissioners for Foreign Missions who were issuing the travel orders minimize the demands: "You are to aim at nothing short of covering these islands with fruitful fields and pleasant dwellings and schools and churches, and of raising up the whole people to an elevated state of Christian civilization." And the Board had made one humane ruling that was rigidly applied to all the Gospel bearers: They must be married.

So a few days before the designated sailing date of the first missionary band, school mistress Lucy Goodale and bachelor Asa Thurston qualified themselves for their calling by dutifully tying the nuptial knot. Mrs. Thurston (1795–1876) tells the story of the harried departure and their arrival in Hawaii.

Here We Are: Send Us

A new and powerful impulse was given to missionary enterprise in the New England States. There was a deep interest and feeling, an extended moving and melting of heart. Hasten, *hasten* was the watchword that went from church to church.

Mr. Whitney, pursuing a course of study in Yale College, being in his sophomore year, was impelled to go to the heathen *at once*. Captain and Mrs. Chamberlain, of independent property, surrounded by every comfort of a New England home, with five children, were impelled to go *at once*, taking their whole family with them. Ladies were ready to go. . . . Six marriages were solemnized; two missionaries were ordained; a band was gathered from four different states and a dozen different churches, to go forth as *messengers* of the churches, to the far distant land of Obookiah. . . .

Obookiah from on high saw that day. He saw the darkness fleeing away from Hawaii, and that that mission family, so hastily fitted out, was going forth to carry the Bible to a nation without a God. . . . Farewell, my dear friends. May the prospect of meeting you all in a world where trials, separations and sins shall be known no more, soothe the feelings and animate the hopes of your affectionate and far-distant daughter and sister, Lucy G. Thurston.

After sailing one hundred and fifty-seven days, we beheld, looming up before us, March 30, 1820, the long looked-for island of Hawaii. As we approached the northern shore, joy sparkled in every eye, gratitude and hope seemed to fill every heart. The native youths were all animation, scarcely seeking the refreshment of either sleep or food. Hopu, though he was up all night that he might enjoy a glimmering view of Mauna Kea, after eating half a meal at breakfast table, begged to be excused that he might go and see where his father lived.

To learn the state of the Islands and the residence of the king, the captain sent a boat on shore with an officer, attended by Hopu and Honolii. Nearly three anxious hours we waited their return. Every minute seemed to whet our eagerness for news. Then, as Mr. James Hunnewell hastily came over the side of the vessel, we gathered closely around him.

Quickly, with agitated lips he said: "Kamehameha is dead; his son Lihiliho is King; the *kapus* are abolished; the images are burned; the temples are destroyed. There has been war. Now there is peace." . . .

Soon the islanders of both sexes came paddling out in their canoes with their island fruit. The men wore girdles, and the women a slight piece of cloth wrapped round them from the hips downward. To a civilized eye their covering seemed to be revolt-ingly scanty. But we learned that it was a full dress for daily oc-cupation. All was *kapa* [tapa], beaten out of the bark of a certain tree, and could ill bear washing. . . .

As I was looking out of the cabin window to see a canoe of chattering natives with animated countenances, they approached and gave me a banana. In return I gave them a biscuit. "*Wahine maikai*," (good woman) was the reply. I then threw out several pieces, and from my scanty vocabulary said, "*Wahine*" (woman). They with great avidity snatched them up and again repeated, "*Wahine maikai*."

Thus, after sailing eighteen thousand miles, I met for the first time those children of nature alone. Although our communications by look and speech were limited and simple friendly pledges, received and given, yet that interview through the cabin window of the brig *Thaddeus* gave me a strengthening touch in crossing the threshold of the nation.

[Displaying a somewhat more marginal fund of fortitude in facing these "children of nature," pompous Hiram Bingham, self-appointed leader of the missionary group, was simultaneously ob-serving: "The appearance of destitution, degradation and barbarism among the chattering and almost naked savages, whose heads and feet and much of their sunburnt skins were bare, was appalling. Some of our number, with gushing tears, turned away from the spectacle. Others with firmer nerve continued their gaze, but were ready to exclaim, 'Can these be human beings! How dark and comfortless their state of mind and heart! How imminent the danger of the immortal soul, shrouded in this deep pagan gloom! Can such beings be civilized? Can they be Christianized? Can we throw ourselves upon these rude shores and take up our abode, for life, among such a people, for the purpose of training them for heaven?' "]

Approaching Kawaihae, Hopu went ashore to invite on board some of the highest chiefs of the nation. Kindly regarding the feelings of the ladies, he suggested that they put on garments. So they prepared for the occasion. Kalanimoku was the first person of distinction that came. In dress and manners he appeared with the dignity of a man of culture. He was first introduced to the gentlemen, with whom he shook hands in the most cordial manner.

He then turned to the ladies, to whom, while yet at a distance, he respectfully bowed, then came near and, being introduced, presented to each his hand. The effects of that first warm appreciating clasp, I feel even now. To be met by *such* a specimen of heathen humanity on the borders of their land was to "stay us with flagons, and comfort us with apples."

Kalakua, with a sister queen, next welcomed us with similar civilities. They were two out of five dowager queens of Kamehameha. They had limbs of giant mold. I was taught to estimate their weight at three hundred pounds, and even more. Kalakua was the mother of three of the wives of the young king. Two wives of Kalanimoku followed. They were all attired in a similar manner, a dress, then a *pa-u,* which consisted of ten thicknesses of the bark cloth three or four yards long and one yard wide, wrapped several times round the middle, and confined by tucking it in on one side. The two queens had loose dresses over these.

Trammeled with clothes and seated on chairs, the queens were out of their element; they divested themselves of their outer dresses; then the one stretched herself full length upon a bench and the other sat down upon the deck. Mattresses were then brought for them to recline in their own way. After reaching the cabin, the common sitting room for ladies and gentlemen, one of the queens divested herself of her only remaining dress, simply retaining her *pa-u*. While we were opening wide our eyes, she looked as self-possessed and easy as though sitting in the shades of Eden. . . .

From Kawaihae the chiefs and their large retinue all sailed with us to Kailua, where the king resided. They all slept on deck on their mats. While passing in the grey of evening between two rows of native men in Hawaiian costume, the climax of queer sensations was reached.

Kalakua brought a web of white cambric to have a dress made for herself in the fashion of those of our ladies, and was very particular in her wish to have it finished while sailing along the western side of the island before reaching the king. So Monday morning, April 3d, the first sewing circle was formed that the sun ever looked down upon in his Hawaiian realm.

Kalakua, queen dowager, was directress. She requested all the seven white ladies to take seats with them on mats on the deck of the *Thaddeus*. Mrs. Holman and Mrs. Ruggles were executive officers, to ply the scissors and prepare the work. As the sisters were very much in the habit of journalizing, every one was a self-constituted recording secretary. The four native women of distinction were furnished with calico patchwork to sew—a new employment to them.

The dress was made in the fashion of 1819. The length of the skirt accorded with Brigham Young's rule to his Mormon damsels —*have it down to the tops of the shoes*. But in the queen's case, where shoes were wanting, the bare feet cropped out very prominently.

Kalanimoku was prime minister of the king, and the most powerful executive man in the nation. He was sometimes called the "Iron cable of Hawaii." Last January, while we were in the region of Cape Horn, a rebel chief usurped kingly power to sustain the idols, and caused the blood of the last human sacrifice to

flow. . . . Now the great warrior was among us, learning the
English alphabet with the docility of a child. He often turned to
it, and as often to his favorite teacher, Daniel Chamberlain, a son
five years of age. . . .

April 4th, Tuesday, A.M., one hundred and sixty-three days from
Boston, the *Thaddeus* was anchored before Kailua. The queen
dowager, Kalakua, assumed a new appearance. In addition to her
newly-made white dress, her person was decorated with a lace
cap, having on a wreath of roses, and a lace half neckerchief in
the corner of which was a most elegant sprig of various colors.
They were presents we had brought her from some American
friends. When she went ashore, she was received by hundreds
with a shout.

Captain Blanchard, Messrs. Bingham and Thurston, together
with Hopu, went ashore and called on the king in his grass-
thatched house. They found him eating dinner with his five wives,
all of them in the free, cool undress of native dishabille. Two of
his wives were his sisters, and one the former wife of his father.

After completing their meal, four of the wives, with apparent
sisterly affection and great pleasure, turned to a game of cards.
. . . Hopu then introduced Messrs. Bingham and Thurston as
priests of the Most High God who made heaven and earth. The
letters were then read to the king from Dr. Worcester of Boston
. . . and the object for which they came to live among them was
explained. The visitors then retired, leaving the subject for royal
consideration.

April 6th, the king and family dined with us by invitation. They
came off in a double canoe with waving *kahilis* and twenty rowers,
ten on each side, and with a large retinue of attendants. The king
was introduced to the first white women, and they to the first king,
that each had ever seen. His dress on the occasion was a girdle, a
green silk scarf put on under the left arm, brought up and knotted
over the right shoulder, a chain of gold around his neck and over
his chest, and a wreath of yellow feathers upon his head.

We honored the king, but we loved the cultivated manhood of
Kalanimoku. He was the only individual Hawaiian that appeared
before us with a full civilized dress. After dining with the royal
family, all were gathered on the quarter-deck. There the Mission

Family, the captain and officers sung some hymns, aided by the bass-viol, played by Kaumualii, a young native chief returning with us. The king appeared with complacency and retired with that friendly *aloha* that left behind him the quiet hope that he would be gracious. . . .

The king had just put down one religion. In doing it his throne had tottered. It was a grave question for him to accept a new one. Hopu, who was apt to teach, had told them that our religion allowed neither polygamy nor incest. So when Kamamalu, the sister and marked favorite out of five queens, urged the king to receive the Mission, he replied: "If I do, they will allow me but one wife, and that will not be you." His royal father had twenty-one wives. . . .

After various consultations, fourteen days after reaching the Islands, March 12th, permission, simply for one year, was obtained from the king for all the missionaries to land upon his shores. Two gentlemen with their wives, and two native youths were to stop at Kailua; the rest of the Mission were to pass on forthwith to Honolulu.

Such an early separation was unexpected and painful. But broad views of usefulness were to be taken and private feelings sacrificed. At evening twilight we sundered ourselves from close family ties, from the dear old brig, and from civilization. We went ashore and entered, as our home, an abode of the most uncouth and humble character.

It was a thatched hut with one room, having two windows made simply by cutting away the thatch, leaving the bare poles. On the ground for the feet was first a layer of grass, then of mats. Here we found our effects from the *Thaddeus*; but no arrangement of them could be made until the house was thoroughly cleansed.

On the boxes and trunks, as they were scattered about the room, we formed a circle. We listened to a portion of scripture, sang a hymn and knelt in prayer. The simple natural fact speaks for itself. It was the first family altar ever reared on this group of islands to the worship of Jehovah.

From *Life and Times of Mrs. Lucy G. Thurston* . . . (Ann Arbor: S. C. Andrews, 1882).

XV

Elias Bond

As soon as the missionaries had found shelter for themselves, they faced the problem of erecting a church, and since the American Board in Boston had made no provision for this necessity, either financial or material, the respective apostles at their isolated stations were left to their own devices. Of course, they had visualized houses of worship modeled after familiar New England designs, but that dream was quickly abandoned when they discovered that there was no lumber, no sawmill, no hardware, no tools except the few brought in their own chests.

All the early missionaries were obliged to swallow their ecclesiastical pride and persuade native congregations to construct temples in the only way they knew, with materials at hand. The resulting creations were adaptations of the simple grass hut, immense longhouses that had to be built and rebuilt in ever increasing size as congregations multiplied, as high winds and fires swept away the first structures, as they sagged and collapsed under the weight of heavy rains, or as stray cattle devoured the thatch. Not until 1832 was the first stone church erected, at Lahaina; and Honolulu had to wait another full decade for its Kawaiahao.

The ordeals of the Reverend Elias Bond (1813–1896) at Kohala on the wet, remote, cliff-bound northern tip of Hawaii were typical of the difficulties endured by the amateur carpenters in directing church construction. As a native of the lumbering state of Maine and an ingenious jack-of-all-trades, however, he was far better equipped than most of his colleagues, and as a later arrival, he could also benefit from the lessons learned by others who had tried hewn logs for frames; *lau hala,* straw, ti leaves for thatch; coral and lava for siding.

When young Elias Bond took up his duties at Kohala, he was shown as a possible meetinghouse "an old tumble-down thatched building, only a roof really, for the hogs had pulled off all the thatch on the sides, and inside was only rubbish mixed with water." He ordered that torn down and a tidier longhouse constructed. For five years he conducted services in this hastily thatched shelter, exposed to high winds, heavy rains, and the intrusion of animals, while he was slowly assembling material for a more substantial and appropriate sanctuary. He reported his own experience, as pieced together from an assortment of letters, journal entries, and appeals for funds.

Churches of Straw, Churches of Stone

As often as I enter our shabby house to encounter the wet and wind and dirt, the idea of the neat and comfortable churches in which the congregations of New England worship always forces itself upon me. We do not indeed expect a house as good as the poorest of those in New England. Means for its erection could not be had. But my soul longs once more to sit in a dry and decent house in Jehovah's presence. . . .

I have seen *females,* young and old, enter the house of God on the Sabbath, having come six miles in the rain, over precipices and ravines, with a single scanty garment of brown cotton, and that as well as their hair and entire persons completely drenched with rain, and have seen them sit down on a stone and listen to the sermon attentively in that uncomfortable situation, whilst their garments dried on their bodies. . . .

Our house of worship is a serious obstacle to any prosperity in religious affairs. . . . A portion of the thatch has recently been blown off in a high wind, so that it is little better than no shelter at all. We have been for a long time trying to devise a way for procuring a new and more permanent house. What shall we do?

The people are, in the largest meaning of the word, *poor*. No *money* is in circulation and our remoteness from any market of any kind is painful assurance that we can get none. . . .

We proposed a heavy *ohia* frame, to be thatched, . . . drawing the timber from the mountains. . . . It was very laborious, for human muscles alone could be set to the task of dragging the heavy masses of timber a distance of from ten to fifteen miles. . . . Axes are rare among the people, and when possessed, no means are had wherewith to keep them sharp, save as the owner is able to round off the edge a little on any common rock he finds. I have accordingly known the people to fell large trees and get timber as hard as oak, twelve to fifteen inches square and forty to fifty feet long, all with two or three axes, whose edges were no sharper than the back of one's razor.

These poor creatures often thus exhibit an almost incredible amount of patience and perseverance. . . . When these timbers are cut, from eighty to one hundred and fifty persons of both sexes lay hold of a long rope made fast to one end of the timber, and after a hard day's work dragging the heavy load up and down the precipitous banks of our frequent ravines, through woods and brush, they deposit a single stick of timber on the ground for building. Oxen could do nothing if we had them, because of the thousands of ravines of all depths from thirty to 1200 feet, which continually intersect one another, thereby utterly forbidding a road for cattle. . . . One stick of fifty or more feet in length and fifteen or sixteen inches square occupied four days of the severest labor in drawing. . . .

Our people can get timber, prepare the ground and thatch the building. But *money* they cannot get in any possible way I have been able to devise. . . . I proposed recently to make an effort myself to raise the funds with which to pay some carpenter for framing the house. It will take about $600 to pay some foreigner for the job, and we are now endeavoring to find some suitable man. Meanwhile, with God's blessing, I hope to raise the needed funds. This is the *only alternative*, or you may be assured I never should have made these proposals, as I am fully convinced that the people should do all they are really able to do, and not be childishly dependent upon foreign aid. . . .

The timber, indeed, is already nearly all drawn down, ready hewn. . . . We have waited four months for the carpenter to come and erect the frame. . . . I still preach in the dripping rain, even in the pulpit, whilst the few listeners, 300 or 400, sit attentive, quite unconcerned as to the drips. It is a wonder they come. . . .

Although tremendously exhausting, the labor was gradually accomplished, and at last we had an exceedingly strong frame up, wattled on sides and ends very neatly with *ki* [ti] leaf and thatched with cane leaf on the roof. Oh, that was a palace in those days! It cost an immense amount of work. All that *ki* leaf was gathered dry, just as they get it for fishing. It was tied in bundles and moistened, then woven in figures. . . . When you take a big house, 86 by 45 feet, surrounded by a lanai six feet wide, there is a great deal of work in it. . . . There was not a single pin in the tie beams; they were just put on the plate and left. The carpenter, an old grey-haired man by the name of Castle, sent his man up to pin them, and supposed the work was all done.

The design was to floor and ceil the building, lining the sides also with *koa* boards. Pine at that time was brought from Boston and was very costly, 12 cents a foot. *Koa* was sawed by hand in Waimea Mountains and cost, delivered at Kawaihae, 4 and 4½ cents per foot. From Kawaihae it was brought on schooners to Mahukona and thence on men's backs, ten miles. We raised but small amounts of tapa cloth at any one time with which to purchase lumber—a few hundred feet at a time, to be worked up whilst the natives were raising more tapa cloth for a further supply.

This *koa* lumber was unseasoned, green and tough, so that the working of it was doubly hard. No carpenters were to be had. I broke in my good Deacon Paku to the use of plane and saw, and he, at that time the best of our 32 teachers, generously left his school and gave himself unstintingly to this work with me for six months . . . planing and putting up the boards on floor, sides and overhead, making the pulpit too, and a pew for the pastor's family.

It must be borne in mind that Paku did all this without the expectation of any pay. I had nothing to give him, and he knew it. There was no money ever seen here at that time. All I had went to buy the necessary lumber and glass for the building. Occasionally, however, some friend would send a gift of a piece of brown cotton, the then circulating medium, and this I was accustomed to divide with Paku. He never asked for anything in the way of pay, but did all as for the Lord. . . .

During the former part of the year, our Sabbath meetings were held under the broad canopy of heaven, and as we were always exposed to violent winds, with the addition of either hot sun or driving rains, the number of those who formed our congregation was very small, rarely exceeding two or three hundred. On the first Sabbath in April, however, just six months after the first blow of the carpenter's axe was struck, we assembled beneath the frame of our new house.

A part of the end exposed to the wind was thatched so as to afford us a partial shelter from the violence of the trades. It seemed good to be there. The very shadow of its beams was pleasant to our eyes. The congregation steadily increased until the house was so far finished as to afford us a comfortable place of worship, secure from wind and storm. Since then . . . the house has been well filled on the Sabbath without exception, with an ordinary and attentive assembly of worshippers of from 800 to 1000 souls. . . .

The sum total of expenditures for the building . . . was $1,580.33 cash. Besides the amount, our own people have contributed, out of the abundance of their poverty, $40 in cash. Very few could have given more had the desire existed. Several hundred were *subscribed* by the church but the *nominal* value of all subscriptions paid in articles of Hawaiian production is about $200. The available value, however, has been a mere trifle owing to the want of a market for the articles contributed. The *labor* given has been in hewing and drawing timber from the mountains, thatching the house and inclosing it with a substantial stone wall of 160 square feet, painted with lime. . . .

The wonderfully rapid and ameliorating influence which a clean and orderly house of God has excited upon the demeanor and external appearance of our congregation on the Sabbath, and I may add upon their social condition generally, is almost incredible. It is only with great difficulty at times that I can realize the decently-clad and well-behaved assembly before me on the Sabbath to be the same as that to whom I ministered but one year since. . . .

On the morning of December 21st the sanctuary of God . . . was swept from us by a violent gale from the Southwest. The stroke fell with a desolating power upon our hearts. We were totally unprepared for this afflictive dispensation. The frame of the house was of unusually large timbers and, as we believed, unusually strong, bidding fair to endure for a century . . . but our anticipations are disappointed, our hopes frustrated and we are bereaved and desolate. . . .

The house was the central point around which clustered the affections and hopes of all those who love God throughout the district, and I need not add it afforded the most effectual medium of communication possible with our people. In its loss a dark cloud is thrown across our future, for the right arm of your missionary is paralyzed.

Yet God reigns, and we may not distrust his loving kindness. . . . Just one week after the fall of our house, we met and cleared away from the floor the broken timbers and rubbish. Then we sat down there; . . . we prayed and wept, remembering Zion— Zion desolate and afflicted. After a sufficiency of talk we resolved:

I. We will build a stone church with the help of God, and begin now to collect the material, stones, lime, sand and wood.

II. We will not beg aid of any kind from anyone.

. . . It was soon evident that we had undertaken no child's play. Only one or two days' work each week could be devoted to this service. Each Land had its own *Luna* [boss]. The stones were gathered from neighboring ravines and brought on men's shoulders to the site. The lime was provided as follows: men in canoes with ropes, and sticks for loosening up the bunches of coral would go out in three, four or five fathoms of water, some diving with a stick to loosen the coral and attach the rope thereto, whilst those in the canoe would draw up the clumps into the canoe.

After being piled on the shore, it was carried on the shoulders of the people to the church site. And then the wood for burning it was brought in the same way from eight or ten miles *mauka* [from the mountains]. A fathom pile of coral required the same measure of wood for burning.

Then came the sand, hundreds of barrels. It was brought by women and children from all along the coast, from Kawaihae around to Pololu, in bits of kapa, in small calabashes, in rags if they had any, in small *lauhala* bags, pints, quarts, and gallons, from any and all places where it could be scraped up on the shore. If anyone was fortunate enough to have an old shirt (there might have been 20 in the whole district), they would tie up the sleeves, fill the shirt with sand and bring it in. So they would do also with a pair of old pants.

And so little by little materials were collected during several years. I would not agree to beginning to build till we had the materials on hand. By the time the church was finished, the time had passed when churches could be built in such fashion.

Again, the most formidable part of our task was hewing the large timber in the hills and drawing it thence a distance of eight to twelve miles. There was not a draught animal in this part of the island. There was no one save myself who could marshal the people and have them pull together, so that I was always at the large drawings, twice each week. . . .

We soon found a mason, a native from Lahaina. He was to receive $300 for putting up the walls, aided by daily relays of the people for carrying stone, sifting sand and mixing mortar. In due process of time the walls were up as they now stand.

Then for a carpenter. We got two, both loving liquor, and had great difficulty in getting the frame on. Like all earthly *pilikias*, this however passed away, and finally after a Herculean effort, the house stood completed. . . . The pulpit was a handsome *koa* structure; a pew each for good Deacon Paku and our family . . .

also all of *koa*. The whole house was filled with slips [pews] and provided with all the conveniences of those days for Divine Worship. . . .

The cost, estimating the labor at a fair figure, was not far from $8,000. Of this, something more than half was given in labor. As to the remainder, the people did nobly in devising methods for raising money to subserve the one common end. . . . And though we steadfastly kept to our Resolution and asked aid from no one in building the house, not a few friends volunteered some essential aid. . . .

As in the case of our former House of Worship, we likewise do find, and with the divine blessing shall continue to find in this, that it is worth more to us than it cost, and I have no fear that the great labor and the greater expense bestowed upon it, will in any measure diminish the disposition or the ability of this people to sustain the institutions of the Gospel amongst themselves, or to contribute for the spread of the truth in regions beyond. Rather, God helping, we may hope that the lessons of self-denial learned in preparing a house of worship for themselves and their children will continue to be of practical value and will be shown so to be in their attempts to send the blessings of the Gospel to others.

From quotations in *Father Bond of Kohala,* Ethel M. Damon (Honolulu: *The Friend,* 1927).

XVI

Hiram Bingham

To the Hawaiians, the greatest single innovation brought by the white man was the art of writing. Putting speech or thought on paper was a completely new concept to them, at first far beyond their comprehension. The nearest they had ever come to recording an idea was in chiseling or staining crude outlines of objects on lava—human figures, fish, animals, circles—usually to boast of some quaint achievement, to memorialize an event, preserve statistics, or merely to note, like Kilroy, that they had been there.

For hundreds of years their only means of retaining knowledge of past events had been in committing them to memory. And memorizing had developed into a fine art, particularly since it was practiced by specialists who made a profession of memorizing and reciting in chants everything from family genealogies to the details of famous battles.

Once the concept of writing took hold, however, laggard Hawaiians quickly recognized it as a laborsaving device: A person had only to learn how to read and write and he would no longer have to go through the laborious process of learning long narratives by heart and everlastingly rehearse them lest they be forgotten.

All of the early missionaries had a hand in converting oral Hawaiian into a written language, but the coordinator of this monumental effort was the Reverend Hiram Bingham (1789–1869), self-appointed leader of the first deputation of New England apostles. A practical, no-nonsense, thirty-year-old Vermonter, he assumed command of the mission while en route from Boston, and during his two decades in Hawaii never relinquished it. Between 1820 and 1840 all of the missionaries felt the authority of this stubborn disciplinarian and idealist devoted to the cause of righteousness, as he saw the right. No one foreigner of the missionary era exerted a stronger influence.

Though he had the standard ministerial background in Latin, Greek, and Aramaic, Bingham was not a distinguished linguist, and he took a great many liberties with the Hawaiian tongue in transforming it from a spoken to a written language. He even contradicted the king. When the monarch insisted that his name was Rihoriho, Bingham defiantly insisted that it was Liholiho—and Liholiho it was thereafter. But despite Bingham's autocratic and obstinate nature, he had to be given major credit for bringing literacy to the Islands. In *A Residence of Twenty-one Years in the Sandwich Islands* he presented his account of how the language was alphabetized.

The Remaking of a Language

During the first year, no suitable system of orthography was fixed upon for writing the language of the country. It was difficult even to write out in native the meaning of words and sentences of English lessons. It was no small labor not only to teach simply the enunciation of a lesson, but to teach the meaning of a column of words or a page of sentences constituting their English lesson, which without such an interpretation must have been to such pupils too forbidding. But this was so far accomplished as to make the school pleasant to most of those who attended, partly by means of the slate, and partly by writing out short lessons on paper, with an imperfect orthography. . . .

To one unacquainted with the language it would be impossible to distinguish the words in a spoken sentence, for in the mouth of a native a sentence appeared, like an ancient Hebrew or Greek manuscript, all one word. It was found that every word and every syllable in the language ends with a vowel; the final vowel of a word or syllable, however, is often made so nearly to coalesce or combine with the sound of the succeeding vowel as to form a

diphthongal sound, apparently uniting two distinct words. . . .
There were also frequent reduplications of the same vowel sound,
so rapid that by most foreigners the two were taken for one.

To avoid all arbitrary spelling, all silent letters and the representation of the same monosound by several different letters, and
many sounds by the same letter, as in the English, seemed to be
due even to the philosophy of the unlettered Hawaiians. To make
the spelling and reading of the language easy to the people and
convenient to all who use it was a matter of great importance, almost indispensable to our success in raising the nation.

It was, therefore, a part of our task to secure to the people a
perfect alphabet, literal or syllabic, of all the sounds which were
then in use, and which would need soon to come into use in the
progress of the nation. Those who had attempted to write the
names of places and persons in the islands had materially failed
even in the most plain and common. No foreigner or native at the
islands could illustrate or explain the peculiarities and intricacies
of the language. . . .

We found the dialect in use by foreigners often materially mis-
led us, so that none could be trusted as to accuracy; and it required time to detect and unlearn errors. In the oft-recurring
names of the principal island, the largest village, and of the king
of the leeward islands, "Owhyhee," "Hanaroorah," and "Tamoree,"
scarcely the sound of a single syllable was correctly expressed
either in writing or speaking by voyagers or foreign residents.

Had we, therefore, followed the orthography of voyagers, or in
adopting an alphabet made a single vowel stand for as many
sounds as in English, and several different vowels for the same
sound, and given the consonants the ambiguity of our *c, s, t, ch,
gh*, etc., it would have been extremely difficult, if not impracticable, to induce the nation to become readers in the course of a
whole generation, even if we had been furnished with ample
funds to sustain in boarding schools all who would devote their
time and labor to study. . . .

Aiming to avoid an ambiguous, erroneous and inconvenient
orthography, to assign to every character one certain sound, and
thus represent with ease and exactness the true pronunciation of

the Hawaiian language, the following five vowels and seven consonants have been adopted: *a, e, i, o, u, h, k, l, m, n, p, w*. These twelve letters, and possibly eleven, omitting either *u* or *w*, will express every sound in the pure Hawaiian dialect. . . .

In the few diphthongal combinations *ae, ai, ao*, and *au*, whether more close or more open, each letter retains its original mono-sound. . . . Consonants are not doubled, and never end a word or syllable. Double or triple vowels are never used to express a single sound, and where they occur, are sounded separately, as *a-a, e-e, i-i, o-o, u-u*. . . .

It could hardly be possible to write any language in the world with a more simple or limited alphabet and at the same time equally intelligible to the children who use it. A syllabic alphabet of ninety-five characters would have been tolerably convenient for all native sounds, but not so simple or convenient as the alphabet adopted.

There were some difficulties to be encountered in distinguishing several consonant sounds, and to determine which of two characters in the Roman or English alphabet to adopt for certain sounds that appeared somewhat variable in the mouths of the natives. The following appeared sometimes to be interchangeable: *b* and *p*, *k* and *t*, *l* and *r*, *v* and *w*, and even the sound of *d*, it was thought by some, was used in some cases where others used *k*, *l*, *r* or *t*. For purely native words, however, *k*, *l*, *p*, and *w* were preferred.

Though five vowels and seven consonants would well express the Hawaiian language unmixed with foreign terms, yet there were reasons for introducing other letters abounding in kindred Polynesian dialects and in the names of persons, places and things of other countries, with which the Hawaiians needed to become acquainted. Eleven or twelve letters must be too limited to be the representatives of general knowledge. To preserve the *identity* of foreign or scripture names was deemed of some importance. We could not in good conscience throw out every consonant in the names of Obed, Boaz, Ruth, David, Ezra, Russia and Gaza, and nearly all out of such names as Sabbath, Christ, Moses, Joseph,

Boston and Genessaret, simply because such consonants could be dispensed with in writing the words familiar to the people.

The following additional consonants, therefore, were adopted: *b, d, f, g, r, s, t, v* and *z.* These form the third class of letters in the Hawaiian alphabet, which is arranged according to ease and importance, allowing the native pupil to learn to spell and read pure native words first. . . . C, J, Q, X and Y we omit. . . . When two consonants, joined in a foreign word, need both to be preserved, we interpose the vowel *e,* and after a final consonant add usually the vowel *a*—as Bosetona for Boston.

Sibilants and compound consonants are exceedingly difficult, if not impracticable, to the unlettered Hawaiian. Had we made the Hawaiian people, as we found them, pass through the Israelitish ordeal of distinguishing and pronouncing correctly the words *Sibboleth* and *Shibboleth,* to save their lives, it is not probable that one in a thousand would have succeeded, even if each had been allowed a whole day with patient instruction, in the trial to adjust and control the vocal organs right. . . .

On the 7th of January, 1822, a year and eight months from the time of our receiving the governmental permission to enter the field and teach the people, we commenced printing the language in order to give them letters, libraries and the living oracles in their own tongue, that the nation might read and understand the wonderful works of God. . . . It was like laying a cornerstone of an important edifice for the nation. A considerable number was present, and among those particularly interested was Keeaumoku, who after a little instruction . . . applied the strength of his athletic arm to the lever of a Ramage press, pleased thus to assist in working off a few impressions of the first lessons.

These lessons were caught at with eagerness by those who had learned to read lay manuscript. Liholiho, Kalanimoku, Boki and other chiefs, and numbers of the people called to see the new engine, the printing press, to them a great curiosity. Several were easily induced to undertake to learn the art of printing, and in time succeeded. Most of the printing done at the Islands has been done by native hands. When the king first examined the press, a sheet of white paper being laid on, he pulled the lever round, and was surprised to see the paper instantly covered with words in his own language. He had some shrewdness and, for a Hawaiian, an uncommon share of confidence in his own attainments and abilities. . . .

The introduction of printing in the language of the country not only awakened curiosity among the chiefs and people, but gave a new and decided impulse to our schools and the cause of education. From sixty to seventy pupils were at once furnished with copies of the first sheet, as they could not wait until the work was finished. They found the lessons easy. They not only soon mastered them, but were able to teach them to others. In a few months there were not less than 500 learners. . . .

We rejoiced to see the king's thatched habitation under the guns of the fort at Honolulu become a primary school for the highest family in the land . . . but the female of highest rank had not yet deigned to give her attention to a book, though many others were in earnest to learn without her acquiring it; and it was still very doubtful whether she would condescend to learn the alphabet.

She was nearly fifty years of age. She was tall and portly, . . . had black hair, a swarthy complexion, a dark commanding eye, a deliberate enunciation, a dignified and measured step, an air of superiority, and a heathen queen-like hauteur; yet sometimes a full-length portrait of her dignity might have presented her stretched out prostrate on the same floor on which a large black pet hog was allowed unmolested to walk or lie and grunt for the annoyance or amusement of the inmates.

She would amuse herself for hours at cards or in trimming and stringing the bright yellow nuts of the pandanus for odoriferous necklaces or rude coronets, listen to vile songs and foolish stories, and sometimes make interesting inquiries. Her stiffness toward the missionaries, to whom her little finger, instead of a right hand, had been sometimes extended, had unbent. . . . Mrs. Bingham and myself called at her habitation in the center of Honolulu.

She and several women of rank were stretched upon the mats playing at cards, which were introduced before letters. It was not uncommon for such groups to sit like tailors or to lie full length with the face to the ground, the head a little elevated, the breast resting on a cylindrical pillow, the hands grasping and moving the cards, while their naked feet and toes extended in diverging lines toward the different sides or extremities of the room.

Being invited to enter the house, we took our seats without the accommodation of chairs, and waited till the game of cards was disposed of, when the wish was expressed to have us seated by her. We gave her ladyship one of the little books, and drew her attention to the alphabet neatly printed in large and small Roman characters.

Having her eye directed to the first class of letters—the five vowels, she was induced to imitate my voice in their enunciation: a, e, i, o, u. As the vowels could be acquired with great facility, an experiment of ten minutes, well directed, would ensure a considerable advance. She followed me in enunciating the vowels one by one, two or three times over in their order, when her skill and accuracy were commended. Her countenance brightened.

Looking off from her book upon her familiars with a tone a little boasting or exulting, and perhaps with a spice of the feeling of the Grecian philosopher, who in one of his amusements thought he had discovered the solution of a difficult problem, leaped from the bath exclaiming "*Eureka!* I have found," the queen exclaimed, "*Ua loaa iau!* I have got it.". . . She had passed the threshold, and now unexpectedly found herself entered as a pupil. Dismissing her cards, she accepted and studied the little book, and with her husband asked for forty more for her attendants. . . .

Elementary instruction in reading, writing, morals, religion, arithmetic, geography, sacred song and sacred history spread rapidly over the whole group of islands, extending more or less, in the course of a few years from this important forming period, to a third of the whole population. In the meantime, the heathen sports of the nation nearly disappeared. . . .

To us it was a consolation in the toil of bringing a nation to an acquaintance with letters, morals and the true religion, to find at length that a large portion of the people of all ages could be induced to collect in schools, and to have ourselves the exclusive privilege of furnishing them with reading matter, and putting into their hands and bringing into contact with their minds such books only as were designed to have a salutary tendency, or were on the whole favorable to the service of God.

From *A Residence of Twenty-one Years in the Sandwich Islands,* Hiram Bingham (Hartford: H. Huntington, 1848).

XVII

Alfred, Lord Tennyson

One of the most notable triumphs for the missionary cause occurred in December 1824, when the distinguished high chiefess Kapiolani, an early convert to Christianity, determined to dramatize her new-found faith by publicly defying the volcano goddess Pele, who continued to be worshiped by many Hawaiians after their other gods had been abandoned.

Accompanied by a retinue of half a hundred terrified followers, she climbed Kilauea, violating en route the ancient taboo against eating red *ohelo* berries, which were considered sacred to Pele, and then descended into Kilauea Crater, sacrosanct playground of the gods, where she allegedly cried: "Jehovah is my God. He kindled these fires. If I perish by the anger of Pele, then you may fear the power of Pele; but if I trust in Jehovah, and he shall save me from the wrath of Pele, when I break through her taboos, you must fear and serve the Lord Jehovah." To the astonishment of the Hawaiians, Pele failed to respond to the insolent challenge. The missionaries had won a singular victory and a great many converts.

The story of Kapiolani's heroism spread around the world, to be incorporated in countless sermons and recounted again and again by moralists, orators, philosophers, and poets. More than half a century after the event, England's poet laureate Alfred, Lord Tennyson (1809–1892) recalled it and wrote his tribute to Kapiolani, to the rhythm of a now-forgotton Hawaiian chant—not a great poem, but nevertheless a significant memorial to the courageous chiefess.

Kapiolani

I

When from the terrors of nature a people have
    fashioned and worship a spirit of evil,
Blest be the voice of a Teacher who calls to them,
    "Set yourselves free!"

II

Noble the Saxon who hurled at his idol a valorous
    weapon in olden England!
Great, and greater, and greatest of women, island
    heroine Kapiolani
Clomb the mountain, flung the berries and dared
    the Goddess, and freed the people
Of Hawa-i-ee!

III

A people believing that Peele the Goddess would
    wallow in fiery riot and revel
      On Kilauea,
Dance in a fountain of flame with her devils or
    shake with her thunders and shatter her island,
Rolling her anger
Thro' blasted valley and flowing forest in blood-red
    cataracts down to the sea!

IV

Long as the lava light
    Glares from the lava-lake,
    Dazing the starlight;

Long as the silvery vapor in daylight
   Over the mountain
Floats, will the glory of Kapiolani be mingled with
   either on Hawa-i-ee.

V

What said her Priesthood?
   "Woe to this island if ever a woman should
   handle or gather the berries of Peele!
Accursed were she!
And woe to this island if ever a woman should
   Climb to the dwelling of Peele the Goddess!
Accursed were she!

VI

One from the sunrise
Dawned on His people and slowly before him
   Vanished shadow-like
   Gods and Goddesses,
None but the terrible Peele remaining, as Kapiolani
   Ascended the mountain,
Baffled her priesthood,
   Broke the Taboo,
   Dipt to the crater,
Called on the Power adored by the Christian and
   crying, "I dare her, let Peele avenge herself!"
Into the flame-billows dashed the berries, and drove
   the demon from Hawa-i-ee.

From *Works of Alfred, Lord Tennyson,* Vol. VI (London and New York: Macmillan, 1903).

XVIII

Otto Von Kotzebue

Christianity and its New England spokesmen had found a home in Hawaii, and the impact of their persuasion was revolutionary, but it was not to the exclusion of other revolutionary influences. Suddenly these dots in the middle of an ocean were becoming involved in the events, business schemes, and political affairs of countries and capitals, the very existence of which the Islanders had never heard.

Three attractions—a year-round temperate climate, the strategic location, and the potential productivity—made the Sandwich Islands attractive to an increasing number of nations with interests in the Pacific. Foremost on the list were England, France, the United States, and Russia. The Muscovites had a special yearning to acquire a warm-water base, for their major Pacific commerce was in furs gathered on the frigid shores of Alaska. A little colony they had established at Sitka showed promise of becoming the richest fur center in the world, yet it could not prosper because the settlers there were starving.

It was impossible to sledge all the supplies they required across Siberia. They needed grains, fruit, vegetables, meat, and the two most convenient places to acquire them were in California or Hawaii, so they proceeded to seize territory in both. But while planting fields or trading for food, characteristically they were also building forts. A few miles north of San Francisco, Fort Ross was constructed in 1812, and five years later they were boldly erecting substantial stone fortifications at both Honolulu and Waimea, Kauai. The Spanish tried to drive the intruders out of California with appeals, bluffs, and threats, but were entirely unsuccessful. Kamehameha used sterner methods; once he realized what the Russians were up to, he not only called a halt to the construction but ousted them bodily.

Not until 1824 were relations with the Russians patched up. That year an important emissary arrived at Honolulu from St. Petersburg in the person of Otto Von Kotzebue (1787–1846), captain of the Imperial Navy, revered Russian explorer, and thrice circumnavigator of the globe. It was his second visit; he had met Kamehameha and his wives on the Big Island several years before and been sumptuously entertained. Now he returned in humility and with an apology.

Building those forts, he forswore, was all a terrible mistake and misunderstanding. The fur company people had done it without the knowledge and against the wishes of the Czar. The Russians had no desire to establish settlements in the Islands; they wanted only peace and commerce with the Hawaiians. And in the typical Hawaiian manner, the Russians were graciously forgiven and Von Kotzebue again royally received—though he must have observed with chagrin that the Honolulu fort, which his countrymen had started, had been completed by the Hawaiians and the guns mounted on its walls pointed toward his ship in the harbor.

The King (Liholiho) had gone off on his fatal trip to England and Dowager Queen Kaahumanu was visiting other parts of her realm, so Queen Namahana had to substitute as hostess, and with her the suave, sophisticated, courtly Von Kotzebue made a tremendous hit. However, he was not above having a little fun at her expense, and in his account of the visit subjected her to scurrilous burlesque. He had no use for what the missionaries were doing either, nor for the new written language they were giving the Hawaiians; preferring his own phonetic spelling, he, or his translators, represented Kamehameha as "Tameamea," Kinau as "Chinau," Kaahumanu as "Kahumanna," the Spanish interpreter-adviser Don Francisco Marin as "Marini," the Reverend Bingham as "Bengham"; Oahu became "Wahu"; Hawaii, "O Wahi"; Maui, "Muwe"; Honolulu, "Hanaruro."

Queen in Silks and Sailor's Boots

On the morning after our arrival I rowed ashore with some of my officers to pay my respects to the Queen Nomahanna, and on landing was met by the Spaniard Marini, who accompanied us to her Majesty as interpreter. On the way I was recognized by several old friends with whom I had become acquainted on my former visit. They saluted me with a friendly *"Aroha."* I cannot say there was much room for compliment on any visible improvement in their costume, for they still wore with much self-complacency some ill-assorted portions of European attire.

The residence of Nomahanna lay near the fortress on the seashore. It was a pretty little wooden house of two stories, built in the European style with handsome large windows and a balcony very neatly painted. We were received on the stairs by Chinau, the governor of Wahu, in a curious dishabille. He could hardly walk from the confinement his feet suffered in a pair of fisherman's shoes, and his red cloth waistcoat would not submit to be buttoned because it had never been intended for so colossal a frame.

He welcomed me with repeated "Arohas," and led me up to the second floor, where all the arrangements had a pleasing and even elegant appearance. The stairs were occupied from the bottom to the door of the Queen's apartments by children, adults, and even old people of both sexes, who, under her Majesty's own superintendence, were reading from spelling books and writing on slates—a spectacle very honorable to her philanthropy. The Governor himself had a spelling book in one hand and in the other a very ornamental little instrument made of bone, which he used for pointing to the letters. Some of the old people appeared to have joined the assembly rather for example's sake than from a desire to learn, as they were studying, with an affectation of extreme diligence, books held upside down.

The spectacle of these scholars and their whimsical and scanty attire nearly upset the gravity with which I had prepared for my presentation to the Queen. The doors were, however, thrown open and I entered, Chinau introducing me as the captain of the newly arrived Russian frigate. The apartment was furnished in the European fashion with chairs, tables and looking glasses. In one corner stood an immensely large bed with silk curtains; the floor was covered with fine mats, and on these, in the middle of the room, lay Nomahanna, extended on her stomach, her head turned toward the door and her arms supported on a silk pillow.

Two young girls lightly dressed sat cross-legged by the side of the Queen, flapping away the flies with bunches of feathers. Nomahanna, who appeared at the utmost not more than forty years old, was exactly six feet two inches high, and rather more than two ells [90 inches] in circumference. She wore an old-fashioned European dress of blue silk; her coal-black hair was neatly plaited at the top of a head as round as a ball; her flat nose and thick projecting lips were certainly not very handsome, yet was her countenance on the whole prepossessing and agreeable.

On seeing me she laid down the psalm book in which she had been reading and, having with the help of her attendants, changed her lying for a sitting posture, she held out her hand to me in a very friendly manner, with many *"Arohas!"* and invited me to take a seat on a chair by her side. Her memory was better than my own; she recognized me as the Russian officer who had visited the deceased monarch Tameamea on the island of O Wahi. On that occasion I had been presented to the Queens; but since that time Nomahanna had so much increased in size that I did not know her again.

She was aware how highly I esteemed her departed consort; my appearance brought him vividly to her remembrance and she could not restrain her tears in speaking of his death. "The people," said she, "have lost in him a protector and a father. What will now be the fate of these islands, the God of the Christians only knows." She now informed me with much self-gratulation that she was a Christian and attended the prayer meeting several times every day.

Desirous to know how far she had been instructed in the religion she professed, I inquired through Marini the grounds of her conversion. She replied that she could not exactly describe them, but that the missionary Bengham, who understood reading and writing perfectly well, had assured her that the Christian faith was the best; and that, seeing how far the Europeans and Americans, who were all Christians, surpassed her compatriots in knowledge, she concluded that their belief must be the most reasonable.

"If, however," she added, "it should be found unsuited to her people, we will reject it and adopt another."

Hence it appears that the Christianity of the missionaries is not regarded with the reverence which, in its purity, it is calculated to inspire in the most uncultivated minds. In conclusion, Nomahanna triumphantly informed me that the women might now eat as much pork as they pleased, instead of being, as formerly, limited to dog's flesh. At this observation an intrusive idea suddenly changed her tone and the expression of her features. With a deep sigh she exclaimed, "What would Tameamea say if he could behold the changes which have taken place here? No more Gods—no more Marais: all are destroyed! It was not so in his time; we shall never have such another king!"

Then, while the tears trickled down her cheeks, she bared her right arm and showed me, tattooed on it in the O Wahi language, "Our good King Tameamea died on the 8th of May 1819." This sign of mourning for the beloved monarch, which cannot be laid aside like our pieces of crape, but accompanies the mourner to the grave, is very frequent in the Sandwich Islands, and testifies the esteem in which his memory is held; but it is still more striking proof of the universal grief for his loss that on the anniversary of his death all his subjects struck out one of their front teeth, and the whole nation have in consequence acquired a sort of whistle in speaking.

Chinau had even had the above words tattooed on his tongue, of which he gave me ocular demonstration; nor was he singular in this mode of testifying his attachment. It is surprising that an operation so painful, and which occasions a considerable swelling, should not be attended with worse consequences.

Nomahanna spoke with enthusiasm on the subject of writing. Formerly, she said, she could only converse with persons who were present; now, let them be ever so far distant, she could whisper her thoughts softly to them alone. She promised to write me a letter, in order, she said, that I might prove to everyone in Russia that Nomahanna was able to write.

Our conversation was interrupted by the rattling of wheels and the sound of many voices. I looked from the window and

saw a little cart in which a number of active young men had
harnessed themselves with the greatest complacency. I inquired
of Marini what this meant and was informed that the Queen
was about to drive to church. An attendant soon after entered
and announced that the equipage was ready. Nomahanna graciously proposed my accompanying her; and rather than risk her
displeasure by a refusal, I accepted the invitation with many
thanks, though I foresaw that I should thus be drawn in as a
party to a very absurd spectacle.

The Queen now put on a white calico hat decorated with
Chinese flowers, took a large Chinese fan in her hand and, having
completed her toilette by drawing on a pair of clumsy sailor's
boots, we set out. In descending the stairs, she made a sign that
the school was over for the present—an announcement that
seemed very agreeable to the scholars, to the old ones especially.

At the door below a crowd had assembled, attracted by
curiosity to see me and their Queen drive out together. The
young men in harness shouted for joy and patiently waited the
signal for the race. Some delay, however, occurred in taking our
seats with suitable dignity. The carriage was very small and my
companion very large, so that I was fain to be content with a seat
upon the edge, with a very good chance of losing my balance,
had not her Majesty, to obviate the danger, encircled my waist
with her stout and powerful arm and thus secured me on my seat.
Our position, and the contrast presented by our figures, had no
doubt a sufficiently comical effect.

When we were at length comfortably settled, the Governor
Chinau came forth and, with no other addition than a round hat
to the costume already described, mounted a meager unsaddled
steed and off we went at full gallop, the Queen taking infinite
pains to avoid losing me by the way. The people came streaming
from all sides, shouting *"Aroha maita!"*—our team continually
increasing while a crowd behind contended for the honor of
helping to push us forward. In this style we drove the whole
length of Hanaruro and in about a quarter of an hour reached
the church, which lies on an ugly flat and exactly resembles that
at O Tahaiti both in external and internal appearance.

The congregation was very small. Nomahanna and an old lady were the only individuals of their sex; and Chinau, myself, and a few others, the only males present. Even the people who had drawn us did not enter the church, from which I infer that the influence of the missionaries is by no means so considerable as at O Tahaiti; and certainly the converts are not yet driven with a stick into the house of prayer. . . .

The Sandwich Islanders are engaged in constant intercourse with foreign sailors, mostly of licentious character, who indeed profess the Christian religion; but, brought hither by the desire of gain or the necessity of laying in provisions for their ships, are generally wholly occupied in driving crafty bargains and certainly are no way instrumental in inspiring the islanders with ideas of religion or morality, but on the contrary, set them examples which have a direct tendency to deprave their minds.

Such among these crews as have been guilty of offenses on board ship frequently run away and settle on the islands. This was severely prohibited in Tameamea's time, but is now permitted, from Christian charity. Such characters as these, reckless of everything sacred, do not hesitate to make a jest of the missionaries, whose extraordinary plans and regulations offer many weak points to the shafts of ridicule.

When Mr. Bengham had concluded a discourse in the O Wahi language, which might possibly have been highly edifying, but that it was addressed to little else than empty benches—for I did not understand him, and the minds of the other few persons present were evidently occupied with very different matters—we returned to the palace in the same style that we had left it. I then took my leave, having received a promise of being amply supplied with provisions. . . .

Bengham, who has usurped the absolute control of the spiritual administration, will have everything accommodated to his whims. . . . That Bengham's private views may not be too easily penetrated, religion is made the cloak of all his designs, and the greatest activity and strictness prevail in its propagation and in the maintenance of church discipline. The inhabitants of every

house or hut in Hanaruro are compelled by authority to an almost endless routine of prayers, and even the often dishonest
intentions of the foreign settlers must be concealed under the
veil of devotion.

The streets, formerly so full of life and animation, are now
deserted; games of all kinds, even the most innocent, are sternly
prohibited; singing is a punishable offense; and the consummate
profligacy of attempting to dance would certainly find no mercy.
On Sundays no cooking is permitted, nor must even a fire be
kindled. Nothing, in short, must be done; the whole day is devoted to prayer, with how much real piety may be easily
imagined. . . .

[Bengham] meddles in all the affairs of government, . . . pays
particular attention to commercial concerns, in which he appears
to take great interest, and seems to have quite forgotten his
original situation and the object of his residence in the islands,
finding the avocations of a ruler more to his taste than those of
a preacher. . . .

We had no cause to complain of our situation. Everything was
to be had for money, and Nomahanna overwhelmed us with
presents of fat hogs and the finest fish, putting all the fishermen
into requisition to provide abundantly for our table. We had all
reason to be grateful for her attention and kindness. . . . But I
can also bear testimony to another qualification of equal importance in her estimation—she has certainly the greatest appetite
that ever came under my observation. I usually visited her in the
morning and was in the habit of finding her extended at full
length upon the floor, employed in inditing her letter to me,
which appeared to occasion her many a headache.

Once, however, I called exactly at dinner time and was shown
into the eating room. She was lying on fine mats before a large
looking glass, stretched as usual on her prodigious stomach. A
number of Chinese porcelain dishes containing food of various
kinds were ranged in a semicircle before her, and the attendants
were busily employed in handing first one and then another to

her Majesty. She helped herself with her fingers from each in its turn and ate most voraciously, whilst two boys flapped away the flies with large bunches of feathers.

My appearance did not at all disturb her. She greeted me with her mouth full and graciously nodded her desire that I should take my seat in a chair by her side, when I witnessed, I think, the most extraordinary meal upon record. How much had passed the royal mouth before my entrance, I will not undertake to affirm, but it took in enough in my presence to have satisfied six men!

Great as was my admiration at the quantity of food thus consumed, the scene which followed was calculated to increase it. Her appetite appearing satisfied at length, the Queen drew her breath with difficulty two or three times, then exclaimed, "I have eaten famously!" These were the first words her important business had allowed her time to utter. By the assistance of her attendants, she then turned upon her back and made a sign with her hand to a tall, strong fellow, who seemed well practiced in his office. He immediately sprang upon her body and kneaded her as unmercifully with his knees and fists as if she had been a trough of bread.

This was done to favor digestion; and her Majesty, after groaning a little at this ungentle treatment and taking a short time to recover herself, ordered her royal person to be again turned on her stomach, and recommenced her meal. . . .

One of our officers obtained the Queen's permission to take her portrait. The limner's art is still almost a novelty here, and many persons of rank solicited permission to witness the operation. With the greatest attention they watched every stroke of the outline and loudly expressed their admiration as each feature appeared upon the paper. The nose was no sooner traced than they exclaimed, "Now Nomahanna can smell!" When the eyes were finished—"Now she can see!"

They expressed especial satisfaction at the sight of the mouth, because it would enable her to eat; and they seemed to have some apprehension that she might suffer from hunger. At this point, Nomahanna became so much interested that she requested

to see the picture also. She thought the mouth much too small
and begged that it might be enlarged.

[While the ship was anchored in the harbor, one day there]
came an ambassador from Nomahanna with instructions to demand an audience of me. I received him in the cabin. His only
clothing, except a pocket of plaited reeds that hung around his
neck, was a shirt and very broad-brimmed straw hat. The fellow
looked important and mysterious, as if he had a mighty secret to
impart; but converse with each other we could not, for he understood only his mother tongue, of which I was entirely ignorant.
He therefore informed me by signs that his pocket contained
something for me, and drew from it a packet.

One by one a multitude of envelopes of the paper manufactory
of the country were removed, till at length a letter came to light,
which he handed to me with the words, *"Aroha Nomahanna!"*—a
salutation from Nomahanna. He then explained to me, in pan-
tomime, that it was the Queen's intention to visit me today, and
that she requested I would send my boat to fetch her. After saying
a great deal about *"Pala pala,"* he left me and I summoned
Marini, who gave me the following translation of the letter:

"I salute thee, Russian! I love thee with my whole heart, and
more than myself. I feel, therefore, on seeing thee again in my
country, a joy which our poor language is unequal to express. Thou
wilt find all here much changed. While Tameamea lived, the country
flourished, but since his death all has gone to ruin. The young
king is in London. Karemaku and Kahumanna are absent; and
Chinau, who fills their place, has too little power over the people to
receive thee as becomes thy rank.

"He cannot procure for thee as many hogs and sweet potatoes
and as much tarro as thou hast need of. How sincerely do I regret
that my great possessions lie upon the Island of Muwe, so far across
the sea! Were they nearer, thou shouldst daily be surrounded by
hogs. As soon as Karemaku and Kahumanna return, all thy wants
shall be provided for. The King's brother comes with them, but he
is yet only an inexperienced boy, and does not know how to distinguish good from evil.

"I beg thee to embrace thine Emperor in my name. Tell him that I would willingly do so myself but for the wide sea that lies between us. Do not forget to carry my salutation to thy whole nation. Since I am a Christian and that thou art also such, thou wilt excuse my indifferent writing. Hunger compels me to close my letter. I wish that thou also mayst eat thy hog's head with appetite and pleasure.

I am,

With royal constancy

And endless love, thine

Nomahanna."

This curious epistle . . . had taken her many weeks to complete. . . . According to Nomahanna's request, I sent off an officer with the shallop to fetch her. . . .

For a lady of the Sandwich Islands, Nomahanna was this day very elegantly attired. A peach-colored dress of good silk, trimmed at the bottom with black lace, covered her Majesty's immense figure, which a very broad many-colored sash with a large bow in the front divided exactly in two halves. She had round her neck a collar of native manufacture made of beautiful red and yellow feathers, and on her head a very fine Leghorn hat ornamented with artificial flowers from Canton and trimmed round the edge with a pendant flounce of black lace, her chin lying modestly hidden behind a whole bed of flowers that bloomed on her mountain bosom.

In somewhat striking contrast to all this finery were the clumsily accoutred feet and stout, ill-shaped, brown, unstockinged legs, which the shortness of her Majesty's petticoats, proportioned originally to the stature of a European belle, displayed to a rather unsightly extent.

As yet the shoemaker's craft does not flourish in the Sandwich Islands, so that all the shoes and boots worn there are imported from Europe and America. But as neither of these continents can produce such a pair of feet as those of Queen Nomahanna, the attempt to force them into any ready-made shoes would be hopeless, and her Majesty is therefore obliged, if she would not go barefoot, which she does not consider altogether decorous, to content herself with a pair of men's galloshes. . . .

In these splendid habiliments, with a parasol in her hand, slowly and with difficulty she climbed the ship's stairs, on which with some of my officers I was in waiting to receive her. On the highest step she endeavored already to give us a proof of her acquaintance with our customs by making a courtesy, which was intended to accord with the most approved rules of the art of dancing, though the feet, not perfectly tutored in their parts, performed in rather a comic style. In attempting this feat, she lost her balance and would have fallen into the water if a couple of strong sailors had not caught her illustrious person in their arms.

She was much delighted with all she saw on board, especially with my cabin, where the sofa paid dearly for the honor of her approbation. She sat upon it and broke it down. The portrait of the Emperor Alexander attracted her particular attention; she sat down opposite to it upon the floor, where she could cause no further destruction and said, after gazing upon it for some minutes with much interest, *"Maitai, Yeri nui Rukkini!"* (The great Governor of the Russians is beautiful!)

She told me that she knew a great deal about Russia. A Sandwich Islander named Lauri, who in 1819 had made the voyage thither in the Russian ship *Kamtschatka* . . . had told her that it was necessary to envelope the body entirely in fur, and that even this would not obviate all danger of losing the nose and ears; that the cold changed the water into a solid substance resembling glass in appearance, but of so much strength that it was used for a high road, people passing over it in huge chests drawn by horses, without breaking it; that the houses were as high as mountains and so large that he had walked three days in one of them without coming to the end of it.

It was evident that Lauri had stretched a little, but Nomahanna had no notion of incredulity . . . and thought that if she were at Petersburg, she would not go out at all during the cold weather, but would drive her carriage about the house. . . . She now overwhelmed me with a host of questions, some of them very absurd. . . . I endeavored to cut the matter as short as possible; and, in order to divert her thoughts to other subjects, set wine before her. She liked it very much and I therefore presented her with a bottle. But her thirst for knowledge was not thus to be quenched and during a visit of two hours she asked such incessant questions that I was not a little relieved when at length she proposed to depart.

In taking leave she observed, "If I have wine, I must have glasses, or how can I drink it?" So saying, she took the bottle that had been given her, in one hand and with the other, seizing without ceremony the glasses that stood on the table, she went upon the deck. There she made a profound courtesy to all present and again took her seat in the shallop.

Thus ended this condescending visit—with the royal appropriation of my wine glasses. Nomahanna had, however, been so liberal to us that she had a right to suppose she would be welcome to them.

From *A Voyage Round the World in the Years 1823, 1824, 1825 and 1826,* Vol. II, Otto von Kotzebue (London: Colburn and Bentley, 1830).

XIX

Alexis Bachelot

The parent of the millions of *kiawe* trees that gird the lower reaches of the Islands was a single algarroba planted in 1827 from seed brought to Honolulu from the Royal Gardens of Paris by Father Alexis Bachelot (d. 1837). The *kiawe* trees perpetuate his memory, but his intentions were to plant a lasting faith, for which he might be remembered, rather than the thorny tree.

Bachelot and his companion, Father Patrick Short, arrived un-heralded in Honolulu on July 9, 1827, to be greeted by Congregational *haoles* with as much enthusiasm as a similar delegation would have been received in a puritanical New England village. In Connecticut, where a majority of the missionary families had been brought up or educated, Congregationalism was the established state religion until 1818, and long after that Catholics were regarded as undesirable citizens; as late as 1835 Connecticut Protestants could boast that there were only two Catholic churches in the entire commonwealth.

The "Romanists" were no more popular in other parts of New England, and since it was the Yankee way of life that the missionaries hoped to transplant in Hawaii, the same religious intolerance prevailed there. The Reverend Bingham and his associates brought their biases with them, and having reached the Islands first, they felt it was their prerogative to limit the infiltration of other faiths.

The priests did not remain for long. Their spirit of self-sacrifice, their devotion, and their eagerness to serve humanity were no less deep-seated than the same qualities in the Congregationalists, and their humility perhaps exceeded that of the Yankees, but these virtues failed to impress the Protestants. Image worship of any kind had been outlawed in the kingdom after the breaking of the taboo system and the destruction of the ancient gods, and it took little coaching on the part of the missionaries to convince the chiefs that the Catholic system was another form of image worship. The priests did win over a few natives, but as fast as they were converted, they were imprisoned, sentenced to hard labor, or tormented—by the Hawaiians themselves.

"Go to another Pacific Island where the Christian gospel has not yet been heard," was the constant plea directed at the priests. It was taken up by a less partial Englishman, Joshua Hill, posing as a representative of the London Missionary Society, en route to the South Pacific. Hill urged Bachelot to leave, insisting that his coming to Hawaii made as much sense as sending "a Baptist missionary to Africa to convert the Methodist Liberians." To Hill the priest addressed the letter quoted below, plaintively setting forth his case.

But despite the earnestness, Father Bachelot and his associate were deported. "This is a decree of banishment," read the order signed by six chiefs. "Begone from this land. Dwell not upon these Hawaiian Islands, for your doctrine is at variance with the religion which we profess. . . . We did not invite you. But you came of your own accord. Therefore we send you away. Begone. . . ."

Late in December 1831, after four and a half uncomfortable years in Honolulu, Father Bachelot sadly walked out of the mission premises, took a last look at the now spreading algarroba, and remarked to the onlookers: "As this tree has grown and spread, so will the Catholic religion grow and spread in these Islands." He was ushered to a ship and then sailed for California to take charge of Mission San Gabriel.

Collision of the Creeds

None is more anxious than I to promote the true blessedness of this people, who have endeared themselves to us by their happy natural qualities. None desires more than I the progress of religion. What other motive, sir, could have made me abandon my

family, friends and all that was dear to me in France, to se-
quester myself in these islands, without further guarantee as to
the necessities of life than the word of Him who feeds the birds
of the air, arrays with splendor the lilies of the field, forbids his
disciples to be solicitous for the needs of the body, and commands them what to do when they will be sent either directly by
Himself or by his representatives on earth. . . .

As a reason that we ought to withdraw, you put forward, sir,
the maintenance of the peace of the Sandwich Islands. I desire
it as much, and, if I may judge by their conduct, more than
others. A true minister of religion is essentially a minister of
peace. But certainly, sir, you are not of those who—that peace
may be preserved—wish to leave men in the creeds they adhere
to, whatever they may be. This would be closing the door to
the propagation of the Gospel, which cannot take place without
creating a schism between those that embrace the truth and
those that persevere in their errors.

Such was not the foundation of peace laid by Him who declared that He had come to set a man at variance against his
father, and the daughter against her mother, and the daughter-in-
law against her mother-in-law. He has announced this conflict
between truth and error, and to the Truth he has allotted persecu-
tions for its portion in this world as its distinctive feature.

Do not imagine, sir, that the diversity of religious denominations is incompatible with the peace you recommend. If any
trouble is to be feared, we have elsewhere to look for its cause
to study and prevent it. It may be perhaps the lesion of some
private interest, someone's feelings hurt, a sustained prejudice,
a nourished animosity, a secret jealousy, in a word, any other
cause which surely is not founded upon the Gospel, and is not in
favor of the religion which indulges in it.

Behold what must be eliminated, and where we ought to direct
our blows. Avoid the invectives, the calumnies, the slanderous
insinuations, especially when they become personal. Do not foster
them even by silence. Let us avoid approving, by as little as a
smile, those tales which are spread either by malice or by ignorance. Teach these poor people, who listen with so much docility

and whom it is so easy to persuade, that violence makes hypocrites and no Christians. Then no trouble will have to be feared; the Truth can be spread quietly and peace will reign. . . .

You say: "We ought not to kick against the goad." If by that goad, sir, you mean the prohibitions of men and their opposition, I will ask you with Peter and John, consider whether it is right to obey men rather than God, and whether the apostles and their successors, the evangelical laborers in China and elsewhere, have read in the Gospel that they ought to abandon the work of God because it was prohibited by the great ones of the earth, whom the low and poor have always preceded in their adhesion to the truth.

If by this goad you mean the Spirit of God, I answer that we shall obey it, following the examples of our Fathers and models in the Faith; that without forgetting that we have to unite the wisdom of the serpent with the simplicity of the dove, we shall never listen to motives of purely human prudence; neither shall we forget that only the hireling flies when he sees the wolf coming, whilst the good shepherd gives his life for his sheep. . . .

You say: "An immense field is open where we can exercise our zeal without conflict or opposition." We know it, sir. But that is' not the field which the Father of the family has ordered us to till. Evangelical laborers require a special *mission*. The very name of *missionary* tells it. To have a right to reform the work of God, it is not sufficient, like some make themselves believe, to take the Bible in one's hands. Neither can this essential and indispensable mission be imparted by some private individuals, nor even by certain societies, which have merely the right and power to provide for the temporary wants of the missioners. It is an ecclesiastical mission given by an authority, which itself has received it with power of delegating it which comes through an uninterrupted succession from the very Founder of the Church. The Apostle teaches the necessity of this mission which cannot be found except in the Catholic Church, because She alone can trace back her pedigree to the Founder. . . .

After this remark, you will understand, sir, that the choice of the field to be tilled is not entirely left to the whims of the evangelical laborer. The field for which he has received this essential mission, must be the only theater of his labors. He cannot change it at will, without going beyond the limits of his power and duty.

From Letter of Alexis Bachelot to Joshua Hill, as quoted in *History of the Catholic Mission in the Hawaiian Islands,* Father Reginald Yzendoorn (Honolulu: *Star-Bulletin,* 1927).

XX

Henry M. Lyman

More disruptive than the Russians, the Catholic padres, the traders, and the *haole* beachcombers now beginning to settle on Oahu were the whalers, who discovered Hawaii as a Pacific base of operations in the same year that the first missionaries appeared. There was only one ship in 1820; whalers were just beginning to move in numbers from Atlantic to Pacific waters, but they formed such a tight brotherhood that any intelligence of prolific catches was soon an open secret. Within a few years anchorages like those at Honolulu, Lahaina, Hilo, and Koloa were crowded, and for the next half century everyone in Hawaii was involved one way or another with whalers and whaling.

Kings and chiefs were kept at wit's end settling brawls started by unruly crews. Green-thumbed natives turned to agriculture, raising Irish potatoes, corn, and squash for ships' commissaries. *Paniolos*, in an effort to rid the Islands of some of the destructive herds that Vancouver's cattle had sired, went into the slaughtering business to provide crews with beef. Hordes of sportive *wahines* found seasonal employment in entertaining the whalers, and almost as many footloose males boarded the ships as deckhands and boatmen.

Though the morals of whalers and missionaries were often at odds, each played into the hands of the other. Many a whaler captain made liberal contributions to the missions while in port, and in turn at least temporary thoughts of salvation were conveyed by the missionaries to unregenerate lads from Nantucket and New Bedford. For two or three months in spring and fall they offered each other the only contact there was in the Pacific with Yankee civilization. The whaling ships brought mail from Connecticut and Massachusetts to homesick apostles; they brought flour, books, secondhand suits, and lumber— even the frame for a sizable church, and they brought whole companies of newly dedicated missionary replacements.

In fact, traveling steerage on a whaler was the only form of transportation most of the missionaries could afford. Going and coming they were exposed to the gory business of catching the great monsters of the deep. In an emergency captains were prevailed upon to ship ailing, spent divines or their wives back to the States, and a great many missionary sons and daughters went home to college on the cluttered ships.

That was the only transportation available to mission son Henry M. Lyman (1835–1904), who spent his boyhood at Hilo and Punahou, and was destined to shape for himself a distinguished career in medicine following his higher education in New England. He left Hawaii on the *Bartholomew Gosnold*, bound for New Bedford, and like other American residents in the Islands, was introduced in transit to the untidy, glamorous occupation that supported the economy of the Islands.

Thar She Blows!

About four o'clock, as under a blue sky we slowly sailed over the quiet water without a white-cap in sight, we were suddenly aroused by the stirring cry "There she blows!"

Everyone rushed on deck—the Captain with his spy-glass, followed by the dogs, dancing and barking, as full of excitement as any human being. The crew immediately cast loose the lashings that had secured the boats during the storms of the Southern Pacific, and the officers prepared their harpoons and lances for the fray.

It was a school of sperm whales, presently visible from the deck at a distance of about two miles north of our position, hundreds of them, sporting on the surface of the water, breathing forth fountains of spray at every expiration from their nostrils, sometimes leaping into the air and creating an immense surge of white foam as they fell back among the waves.

The ship was soon hove to, and the three boats were lowered and started in pursuit of the gigantic game. In the course of a few minutes they were among the whales, and we saw the mate's boat-steerer stand up with a harpoon, which he poised for a moment, and then darted downward into the back of one of the wallowing monsters. Almost at the same time the other boats made fast in like manner, and we could see them dragged furiously through the water by the terrified creatures to which they were attached.

The foremost boat soon lost its whale by the drawing or breaking of the harpoon, but it succeeded in planting a fresh iron in the side of a second whale, which rushed on, though now compelled to drag two boats in its effort to escape. Nothing could better illustrate the vigor of the powerful animal than the rapid rate with which it swam through the water, nearly swamping the boats that clung to the harpoon lines, almost smothered by the foam that was dashed upon them in their wild rush over the sea.

The first whale had received a serious wound, and soon ceased the attempt to follow its companions. The mate cautiously drew his boat by its harpoon line to the side of the monster and plunged his slender lance again and again into its flank, causing blood to fly from its blow-hole. The boat then drew off to a safe distance, while the whale slowly swam round in a narrow circle, furiously striking the waves with its broad flukes, then rolling over and over, opening and snapping its jaws as it rolled, finally making one convulsive spring and falling back lifeless on the water.

It was now sunset, and the other boats, scarcely discoverable on the northern horizon, were still dragging in the wake of their prey. Their position and course were carefully noted and all our energies were directed to getting the dead whale lashed alongside of the ship. This was accomplished by eight o'clock in the evening, and the ship's head was then turned in the direction of the boats.

We now learned that in the hurry of departure the boat-kegs had been left on board, and the absent crews were without light, compass or means of signaling in the dark. The Captain was much alarmed by this discovery and immediately ordered a bon-fire of tar-barrels on the try-works amidship. This furnished a magnificent illumination, lighting up every sail and spar and thread of rigging from stem to stern, so that the boats could not fail to find the ship if anywhere within twenty miles' distance. After sailing as far as the boats were thought to have run, the vessel was hove to and the mate's boat was sent out—this time well provided with lanterns—on a scouting expedition.

While thus prowling in the darkness, about ten o'clock, the second mate's boat suddenly came in sight, pulling slowly into the circle of light around the ship. The crew brought the news that they had killed their whale, and that the third boat was lying by the carcass about three miles away under a certain star which must be our guide to the spot.

The two boats were immediately taken up and we proceeded in the indicated direction till the Captain estimated that we had covered the prescribed distance. We again hove to and threw a fresh tar barrel on the fire, keeping a sharp lookout in every direction. The moonless night was clear but very dark, and the wind was nearly calm, so that we experienced darkness visible and silence audible on that expanse of ocean.

Presently, as I leaned over the quarter-rail, striving to discover some sign of the boat, I heard a faint and distant cry coming out of the black night across the water. I notified the Captain, and almost immediately the mate came aft with the announce-ment that he also heard a shout. One of the sailors—a gigantic mongrel, half Negro and half Cape Cod Indian, gifted with a voice like a foghorn—was ordered into the rigging to answer the call of his messmates, and the two boats were sent to aid in towing the dead whale.

The three crews soon joined forces and, guided by their lan-terns, the ship moved slowly toward the spot. By midnight both whales were securely lashed alongside, the boats were hoisted up and we all turned in for a few hours of sleep before entering upon the arduous task of "cutting in" the blubber. The Captain was so overjoyed by the recovery of his boats and by the magnitude of their prize—two seventy-barrel whales worth at least five thousand dollars apiece—that he never uttered a word of reproach for the negligence of the officers in leaving the ship without their boat-kegs.

At an early hour in the morning all hands were called on deck; a huge block-tackle was swung between the fore and main tops; a staging was rigged outside of the ship above the nearest whale; and from this a sailor with a "spade"—a chisel-shaped instrument on a long spearlike handle—dug a hole through the layer of blubber eight or ten inches thick that invested the entire body of the creature.

Another boat-steerer—Portuguese Andrew, a nimble, muscular young fellow—then leaped down upon the back of the whale with a long rope tied around his waist and held by a gang of men on board to keep him from slipping off into the water. The hook of the huge tackle that hung between the masts was lowered to him, and after a tremendous struggle with the heaving mass, as it rose and fell upon the waves, he succeeded in thrusting the curved iron into the opening through the blubber.

The sailors immediately hauled him on board, thoroughly drenched with ice-cold water, and turned him over to the steward for his reward—a glass of whiskey and a suit of dry clothes; while the other boat-steerers with their spades proceeded to cut two parallel lines through the blubber, beginning at the hook and advancing spirally around the body of the whale.

The crew on board carried to the windlass the cable that ran through the blocks of the tackle and began hauling it in. The tension thus produced caused the loosened strip to peel from the carcass, coming off in a spiral ribbon like the skin of an orange, as the whale slowly rolled around its axis in response to the efforts of the men at the rope.

When the end of the strip reached the masthead, it was cut off at the level of the deck and was lowered into the blubber-room, to be slashed into smaller pieces, while the crew on deck hooked on again to the remainder.

Having thus divested the entire body of the whale of its tallowy covering, the lower jaw was cut off and hauled on board for the sake of its ivorylike teeth; and the nose, with its contents of liquid spermaceti, forming a mass ten feet long and four or five feet thick, was in like manner secured. The sailors worked with a will and completed the arduous task at a late hour in the evening, to the great satisfaction of the Captain, who was in constant dread of interruption by a storm before he could secure the fruits of his toil.

Early next morning a fire was lighted in the try-works and the kettles were soon filled with boiling oil and seething fragments from the blubber-room, where the huge "blankets" and "horse-pieces" were carved into manageable cubes. The whole process resembled, only on a larger and coarser scale, the preparation of lard from the fat of the hog.

When sufficiently boiled, the oil was drained from the scraps and was "run off" into casks that were made ready near the works by the hard-working cooper. Thus produced, the oil was tasteless, odorless, and as edible as freshly melted lard—in fact, the sailors considered doughnuts fried in boiling sperm oil one of the greatest dainties obtainable. To satisfy our curiosity, the Captain had a piece of whale's flesh cooked; but we found it coarser than the strands of a hempen cable, and utterly destitute of agreeable flavor.

The following week favored us with fine weather, which we improved to the utmost. The whole ship, and everybody on board excepting the Captain and his passengers, were thoroughly saturated with grease. Fortunately there was no disagreeable smell, and we contemplated the black smoke from the try-works with serene satisfaction.

The Captain walked the quarter-deck, his face continually beaming with smiles that grew more radiantly expansive with each report from the boiler and the cooper. There was indeed good reason for his elation, for this catch would put into his pocket an additional thousand dollars beyond what he would otherwise receive at the end of his voyage.

From *Hawaiian Yesterdays*, Henry M. Lyman (Chicago: McClurg, 1906).

XXI

Henry T. Cheever

Honolulu developed so rapidly as one of the whaling capitals of the globe that even the oil barons of New Bedford grumbled at the substantial slice in Pacific revenues they were losing. The little Oahu port was still a sprawling village of grass shacks, reminding every captain who sailed into the harbor of an immense field of haystacks. But among the haystacks gradually rose handsome frame houses, fronted with stately columns and topped with widow's walks, indistinguishable from similar mansions in New England ports, and occupied similarly by wealthy merchants and sea captains. And nearer the waterfront were immense warehouses for storage and sea supplies, owned, for the most part, by shipping companies and chandlers on another side of the world.

The great advantage the Islands offered to the whaling industry was the possibility of doubling or tripling the length of stay for a whale ship in the Pacific; a vessel was no longer limited to a single bumper cargo. After filling the holds with oil, a captain could put in at Honolulu, transfer the cargo to a fast clipper bound for the Atlantic, replenish supplies, and head north or south for another go at the grounds. Profits could be doubled with every such venture.

None of the other Island ports could offer the variety in ship's supplies or the facilities for repair and wharfage that Honolulu boasted, and in season scores of vessels were anchored there. But Honolulu also brought upon itself a reputation for charging all the traffic could bear, levying exorbitant port and wharfage fees, curbing the activities of obstreperous crews, jailing drunkards and rakes, and impoverishing them with fines.

So more and more of the whaling vessels, after conducting necessary business in Honolulu, or avoiding that port altogether, moored in less-frequented bays of the other islands for their "refreshment." Of these, Lahaina Roads, off the west coast of Maui, offered the best protection, and the town of Lahaina became the notorious hangout for crews in search of shore leave with minimum restraint from native authorities. There the traveling parson-historian Henry T. Cheever (1814–1897) saw them in the early 1840's and made a cursory survey of Lahaina's industry.

One of the Breathing Holes of Hell

The roadstead of Lahaina, as usual in spring and fall, is anchored in all over by large whale ships that have come in from the different cruising grounds of the Pacific to recruit, where supplies of all kinds can be obtained on more advantageous terms, and with less detriment to the men than at any other place in this ocean.

It has been visited the last two seasons, fall and spring, by about 400 ships that spend on an average, at a very moderate estimate, $300 each, making the sum total of $120,000 yearly disbursements at this port. The estimated value of the whale ships and cargoes entered at Lahaina and Honolulu between 1844 and 1845 was $17,733,411; of disbursements there, $150,000.

The supplies furnished by the natives are goats, hogs, poultry, fruit and vegetables, especially Irish potatoes, for which they get money and cloth or other articles of exchange. Fresh beef also is supplied by foreigners. Other supplies, as of salt provisions, bread, cordage and ship chandlery in general, are furnished almost exclusively by one American house, that takes bills drawn upon ship owners in America and Europe at a rate of 20 percent for exchange.

The concurrence here of such large whaling fleets makes Lahaina a most desirable place of labor for a seaman's chaplain.
Estimating twenty-five seamen only to a ship, the port is visited
by 10,000 annually: not, indeed, 10,000 different seamen, but
that number in two different times. . . .

It is painful to go out among them here at sundown when
liberty expires and, drunk or sober, they must be off to the ships
or into the fort. Liquor and lust have done their best to inflame
many of them, and your ears would be shocked by ribald oaths
and the language of lewdness, caught up and repeated by native
boys; and you see some reeling to and fro at their wit's end, and
hustled along by some less drunken comrade; and others without
shame caressed and hung upon by native girls, who flock here
in the ship season from other parts to get the ready wages of sin.

The populace of both sexes were out to see what was a-going,
and to catch the contagion and cant of vice. It was a scene of
vileness, disgust and abomination which no virtuous man, if
possible, would see but once. You seemed to behold busy devils
scouting about one of the breathing holes of hell, running into the
drunken herd and chuckling with Satanic glee over the human
victims which they were making ten-fold more the children of
hell than themselves. It was a sight to make a missionary weep,
and any foreigner in whom virtue and shame have not become
extinct, to blush.

From *Life in the Sandwich Islands,* Henry T. Cheever (New York: Barnes,
1851).

XXII

Jonathan S. Green

Morals and manners, native employment and political order, health and general welfare were all included in the scope of activity with which the missionaries had been charged by the American Board. They had therefore to offer solutions to problems brought not only by whalers, but by every other kind of intruder. Any long-range accomplishment in "raising up the whole people to an elevated state of Christian civilization," they realized, would have to come through schooling, so they went into education with the same zest they applied to their spiritual labors.

Within ten years after ther arrival there were over a thousand elementary schools in the Islands, and fifty thousand pupils, taught largely by newly trained native teachers. The fact that most of the students were adult men bothered the missionaries not in the least, for men were the first to receive the benefits of learning in any emerging society; even in enlightened New England the best school facilities were still reserved for males.

The Yankee mentors in Hawaii, however, were well ahead of their time, and were soon planning programs of education for all—vocational schools, high schools, tutorial schools for the pampered sons and daughters of chiefs, a college preparatory school for white children, boarding and day schools, an English school for young *hapa haoles* (part-white children), normal schools, special schools for gifted students, and Lahainaluna, an advanced school for Hawaiian men and boys that combined a high school and college curriculum and even offered "graduate" work in theology and medicine.

Although women did attend many of these schools, the female sex in general was slighted. Hawaii's most vocal pioneer-advocate of women's education—its Emma Willard—was a man: the Reverend Jonathan S. Green (1796–1878), a Yankee visionary with a disarming sense of humor, a sense of fitness, and a green thumb that later made him just as strong an advocate of Island wheat growing.

The Troy Female Seminary, founded by Mrs. Willard in upstate New York, was less than fifteen years old when Green started campaigning for a similar institution, the Wailuku Female Seminary, on the island of Maui. At first only very young pupils were admitted, but Green gradually modified his conception to include girls of all ages, so that they would be enrolled as tots and kept under the watchful eye of the seminary preceptress until they reached a marriageable age.

The Neglected Female

At our general meeting [at Honolulu] in June 1836, the mission thoroughly canvassed the subject of boarding schools, and unanimously adopted the following resolution: "That in order to secure the greater amount of influence of the students of the High School eventually in favor of civilization, corresponding efforts should be made to raise the character of the females of the country, and to train up in a special manner suitable companions for them, who may take part with them in giving an elevated and consistent character to the nation, which it can never possess without the aid of an extensive salutary female influence, Resolved, that a Central Female Boarding Seminary be established at Wailuku."

The reasons which weighed in the minds of the mission and led to the adoption of the above resolution are many. . . . The resolution contemplates the training of females who may become suitable companions for the young men educated in the Seminary at Lahainaluna. This is a consideration of incalculable importance. Unless suitable companions can be found for them, the probability is that much of the labor and expense bestowed upon them will be lost.

Those young men will, of course, marry, and connecting themselves with illiterate females, they will soon lose the influence of their training, and sink rapidly to an equality with their companions. On the contrary, if they obtain for companions females of cultivated minds and civilized manners, and especially of industrious habits and pious dispositions, there is much reason to hope that the labor at the school for boys will not be in vain, and that the institution will prove a purified fountain, sending forth to every nook of this moral desert the waters of life.

The want of suitable training of females at these islands calls loudly for special efforts in their behalf. Children, and especially females, are at present almost wholly neglected by parents and guardians. Want of employment lies at the bottom of the evil. What employment, suited to their sex, can a Hawaiian parent give to his daughters? They have neither loom nor wheel—and if they had both, their instruction in the use of them is at present exceedingly limited. They have very little cloth to require the use of the needle, and of household employment for females there is almost none.

Look into a Hawaiian habitation. If occupied by a chief, you may see several young females sitting about as waiting maids; but the service which they here render is of little value to others, and has anything but a good influence on themselves. Now they will fill up an hour or two in "shampooing" the foot of a chief, and anon a half day is consumed in making a useless vegetable wreath for the neck. But much the greater part of the time is spent in lounging on the mats with the most worthless fellows found on the islands. . . .

Enter into the cottage of penury. Our compassion is awakened on beholding the female children, half clad, unwashed, ungoverned and unemployed. As they seldom have anything to do, they sally forth bare-headed, and half famished it may be, to seek sustenance or pleasure. They are thus exposed to temptation —become vicious and in their turn tempt others to sin.

Another thing may not be omitted. Social intercourse at these islands is corrupting to a high degree. . . . In the lower ranks of life, and among those who have not been particularly instructed, nothing is too low and obscene to be the subject of conversation between the sexes! Nor are they at all restrained by the presence of their children. Nothing like restraint is practiced by Hawaiian parents. The houses of nearly all the inhabitants of the islands have no partitions, or only slight mat ones. Hence all, men, women and children eat, converse and sleep on the same floor, and commonly in the same apartment. Hence very young children hear much that is exceedingly improper, and their minds become vitiated; so that when they grow up, they are but poorly prepared to oppose effectual resistance to sin.

The fact is as indisputable as it is distressing that there is a constant decrease in the population of these islands. . . . The cause must be sought in the vices of the people. Disease, not indigenous, but transplanted from other climes . . . has here found a congenial soil. The blood of the entire population seems poisoned, and multitudes are actually suffering from the crimes of their ancestors. More than half who enter the marriage state do not bear children. . . . Now we would stay this desolation. We would dry up this source of misery. We would see the land in the length and breadth of it teaming with a busy, intelligent, happy population—not of men from other lands, but her own sons and daughters.

Nothing at present so much prevents this as their domestic habits. And where must a reformation of these habits be expected to commence but with their women? . . . In the hope of arresting the tide of population, and turning it back, we look, under God, to the system of boarding schools of both sexes. . . .

For these and other reasons which might be mentioned, we concluded that . . . special efforts must be made to save a portion at least of the female population of these islands—to remove them from the corrupting influence of their parents, friends and associates, and place them under our direct and constant supervision, watch and instruction, and to retain them till they mature a character and enter the marriage state.

On returning from general meeting, July 1836, the principal of the school . . . commenced immediately the erection of a suitable building for the school . . . 56 feet by 24 inside, two stories high. The mason work was chiefly performed by native workmen, and the house is a plain but substantial one, covered with native material. . . . We have concluded to appropriate this building to recitation rooms; and we are now erecting at a small expense a doby [adobe] house which we think will answer a very good purpose for sleeping rooms.

On the 6th, July, 1837, the school was opened; six little girls being present. It has been increasing till the present time, and now consists of thirty, from the age of ten down to four years. Of these, one is from Oahu, one from Lanai, five from Molokai, four from Hawaii and the remainder from Maui. Others are soon expected from Hawaii, and perhaps a few more from Oahu. Many have applied whom we could not admit at present.

. . . Justice requires the teachers to say that they are greatly encouraged in witnessing . . . the desire of children, and of parents also in their behalf, to avail themselves of the benefits of the school. Children plead with their parents to seek for them admittance to the school, and parents plead with us to admit their children. The apprehensions . . . that suitable children could not be obtained for boarding schools is proved to be utterly without foundation in fact. Probably a hundred children of suitable age could be obtained on Maui alone. . . .

All appear exceedingly happy—incomparably more so than we had dared to hope. Some of the little girls having parents in the immediate neighborhood have been in school three months, yet not one of them has requested to go home even for a night. . . . One little girl we dismissed for disobedience and for exhibiting a quarrelsome temper. No other case of difficulty has yet occurred. On the whole, we can truly say that we have never had less occasion of complaint in any school which we have taught in the United States. . . . They are at present attending to reading, writing on the slate, mental arithmetic and sacred chronology. On the question of their capacity we have not the least possible concern. . . .

The second quarter of the Central Female Boarding Seminary at Wailuku closed January 30, 1838. The instructors feel that

"*A most desirable place of labor for a seaman's chaplain*"

they have great occasion for gratitude to God for his special favor during the term. Miss [Maria] Ogden has become connected with the school and she is devoting herself with much cheerfulness and ardor to the superintending of the department of labor and to the business of instruction in other departments, as she finds opportunity.

The little girls, of whom there are now 42, spend two hours daily in sewing and braiding; they are taught to arrange their sleeping apartments, prepare the table for eating, and wash their dishes. They are becoming industrious and are making considerable progress in their studies and in the knowledge of the usages of civilized life. But the apparent change in the moral character of several of the pupils demands an expression on the part of the teachers of the school of unfeigned thanksgiving to God.

[October 1838] . . . God has greatly blessed the pupils by giving them a docile temper. They have been contented, happy and easily governed. . . . Twelve of the oldest and most promising girls have been admitted to the fellowship of the church. Thus far they adorn their profession—seem humble, prayerful and obedient. . . .

The building erected in 1837 has been fitted up for the better accommodation of the school. It is a stone building . . . built at a cost of $2,000. In the upper story Miss Ogden has a pleasant and commodious room, which she occupies to the great benefit of the school. She has also very obligingly consented to take her meals at the table with the children. This secures perfect order and promises very happy results. The remainder of this story, thirty-four by twenty-four feet, is appropriated as a chapel, being sufficiently large to accommodate one hundred and fifty pupils.

The lower story is divided into three apartments, one of which is occupied at present as an eating hall, the other two as recitation rooms. A row of adobe buildings has been erected during the year at an expense of $150. It contains nineteen rooms, eight by ten feet, neatly plastered and whitewashed, and is now occupied as sleeping rooms. A dining hall, thirty-eight by fourteen feet, with a pantry, and a hospital, eighteen by fourteen feet, of adobes, are in progress. When these are completed we shall be very comfortable. . . .

At the annual examination, July 10th, there were present thirty-four children, who sustained an honorable examination in reading, arithmetic, mental and written, history, natural and Hawaiian, and vocal music. Sacred geography and chronology will be introduced early in the next term. The study of the Bible, with frequent appeals to the conscience, will be made prominent in communicating instruction. . . .

In addition to the manual labor performed by the children the past year, viz: braiding, sewing, washing, ironing and mending their own clothes, etc., we are making preparation for the spinning of cotton. . . . We are also cultivating the mulberry, and shall, as soon as possible, commence feeding the silk worm. We hope at no very distant day . . . to be able to sustain the school independent of foreign aid.

The little girls have been decently clad during the year, in blue cotton by day and white cotton by night; have been regularly and comfortably fed on native produce at less expense than was anticipated—probably something less than twenty dollars each. No effort on our part shall be wanting to enable these daughters of Hawaii, by seeking "wool and flax and working willingly with their hands," to sustain and perpetuate this rising institution.

From the *Hawaiian Spectator*, "Female Education at the Sandwich Islands," by J. S. Green (January 1838), and reports entitled "Central Female Boarding Seminary, Wailuku, Maui," published in the *Spectator*, April 1838 and October 1838.

XXIII

Richard Henry Dana

While derelict seamen and fugitives from the West were gathering on Hawaiian shores, vagrant Hawaiians were assembling in even larger numbers on foreign shores—though they were usually swallowed up in a heterogeneous port population and seldom made themselves conspicuous.

Richard Henry Dana (1815–1882) observed them particularly on the California coast in the 1830's—before he had distinguished himself as writer, maritime lawyer, and political reformer. Convinced that common American seamen as a laboring class were not getting a fair deal and sorely needed a spokesman, he withdrew from Harvard at the end of his sophomore year and shipped out as deckhand on a Pacific-bound merchant vessel to learn for himself how grim their lot was—to qualify himself to present, as he put it, "a voice from the forecastle."

That voice proved to be eloquent; it sounded a vigorous, unsentimental appeal for the improvement of the seaman's welfare, a protest against "the hardships of their daily life," and incidentally supplied one of the most lucid and exciting descriptions of the days of the sailing ship and its merchant mariners ever written. The narrative of his voyage, *Two Years Before the Mast*, published in 1840, almost immediately became an American classic and has continued to rank as one for over a century.

Dana formed his first attachment for Sandwich Islanders at San Diego, where his ship *Pilgrim*, a trader in cattle hides, anchored on May 8, 1835.

Kanakas

All the hide-houses on the beach, but ours, were shut up, and the Sandwich Islanders, a dozen or twenty in number, who had worked for the other vessels and been paid off when they sailed, were living on the beach, keeping up a grand carnival. A Russian discovery ship, which had been in this port a few years before, had built a large oven for baking bread, and went away leaving it standing.

This, the Sandwich Islanders took possession of, and had kept ever since undisturbed. It was big enough to hold six or eight men—that is, it was as large as a ship's forecastle; had a door at the side, and a vent-hole at top. They covered it with Oahu mats for a carpet; stopped up the vent-hole in bad weather, and made it their headquarters. It was now inhabited by as many as a dozen or twenty men, who lived there in complete idleness— drinking, playing cards, and carousing in every way.

They bought a bullock once a week, which kept them in meat, and one of them went up to the town every day to get fruit, liquor and provisions. Besides this, they had bought a cask of ship-bread and a barrel of flour from the *Lagoda* before she sailed. There they lived, having a grand time and caring for nobody.

Captain T____ was anxious to get three or four of them to come on board the *Pilgrim*, as we were so much diminished in numbers; and went up to the oven and spent an hour or two trying to negotiate with them. One of them, a finely built, active, strong and intelligent fellow, who was a sort of king among them, acted as spokesman. He was called Mannini—or rather, out of compliment to his known importance and influence, Mr. Mannini—and was known all over California.

Through him, the captain offered them fifteen dollars a month, and one month's pay in advance; but it was like throwing pearls before swine, or, rather, carrying coals to Newcastle. So long as they had money, they would not work for fifty dollars a month, and when their money was gone, they would work for ten.

"What do you do here, Mr. Mannini?" said the captain.

"Oh, we play cards, get drunk, smoke—do anything we're a mind to."

"Don't you want to come aboard and work?"

"*Aole! aole make make makou i ka hana.* Now, got plenty money; no good, work. *Mamule,* money *pau*—all gone. Ah! very good, work!—*maikai, hana hana nui!*"

"But you'll spend all your money in this way," said the captain.

"Aye! me know that. By-'em-by money *pau*—all gone; then Kanaka work plenty."

This was a hopeless case, and the captain left them, to wait patiently until their money was gone.

We discharged our hides and tallow, and in about a week were ready to set sail again for the windward. We unmoored and got everything ready, when the captain made another attempt upon the oven.

This time he had more regard to the *"mollia tempora fandi,"* and succeeded very well. He got Mr. Mannini in his interest, and as the shot was getting low in the locker, prevailed upon him and three others to come on board with their chests and baggage, and sent a hasty summons to me and the boy to come ashore with our things and join the gang at the hide-house.

This was unexpected to me; but anything in the way of variety I liked; so we got ready and were pulled ashore. I stood on the beach while the brig got under weigh and watched her until she rounded the point, and then went up to the hide-house to take up my quarters for a few months.

Here was a change in my life as complete as it had been sudden. In the twinkling of an eye I was transformed from a sailor into a beachcomber and a hide-curer; yet the novelty and the comparative independence of the life were not unpleasant. Our hide-house was a large building, made of rough boards, and intended to hold forty thousand hides. In one corner of it, a small room was parted off, in which four berths were made, where we were to live with mother earth for our floor. It contained a table,

a small locker for pots, spoons, plates, etc., and a small hole cut
to let in the light. . . . The boy was to act as cook; while myself, a giant of a Frenchman, and four Sandwich Islanders were
to cure the hides. Sam, the Frenchman and myself lived together
in the room, and the four Sandwich Islanders worked and ate
with us, but generally slept at the oven. . . . The Sandwich
Islanders deserve particular notice.

A considerable trade has been carried on for several years between California and the Sandwich Islands, and most of the
vessels are manned with Islanders, who, as they for the most part
sign no articles, leave whenever they choose, and let themselves
out to cure hides at San Diego, and to supply the places of the
men of the American vessels while on the coast. In this way,
quite a colony of them had become settled at San Diego, as their
headquarters. . . .

During the four months that I lived here, I got well acquainted
with all of them, and took the greatest pains to become familiar
with their language, habits and characters. Their language I
could only learn orally, for they had not any books among them,
though many of them had been taught to read and write by the
missionaries at home. They spoke a little English, and by a sort
of compromise, a mixed language was used on the beach, which
could be understood by all.

The long name of Sandwich Islanders is dropped, and they are
called by the whites all over the Pacific Ocean "Kanakas" . . . in
distinction from whites, whom they call "Haole." This name
"Kanaka" they answer to both collectively and individually. Their
proper names in their own language, being difficult to pronounce
and remember, they are called by any names which the captains
and crews may choose to give them.

Some are called after the vessel they are in; others by common
names, as Jack, Tom, Bill; and some have fancy names, as Banyan, Fore-top, Rope-yarn, Pelican, etc. Of the four who worked at
our house, one was named "Mr. Bingham," after the missionary
at Oahu; another Hope, after a vessel that he had been in; a
third, Tom Davis, the name of his first captain; and the fourth

Pelican, from his fancied resemblance to that bird. Then there was Lagoda-Jack, California-Bill, etc.

But by whatever names they might be called, they were the most interesting, intelligent and kind-hearted people that I ever fell in with. I felt a positive attachment for almost all of them; and many of them I have to this time a feeling for, which would lead me to go a great way for the mere pleasure of seeing them, and which will always make me feel a strong interest in the mere name of a Sandwich Islander.

Tom Davis knew how to read, write and cipher in common arithmetic; had been to the United States, and spoke English quite well. His education was as good as that of three quarters of the Yankees in California, and his manners and principles a good deal better, and he was so quick of apprehension that he might have been taught navigation and the elements of many of the sciences with the most perfect ease.

Old "Mr. Bingham" spoke very little English—almost none, and neither knew how to read nor write; but he was the best-hearted old fellow in the world. He must have been over fifty years of age, and had two of his front teeth knocked out, which was done by his parents as a sign of grief at the death of Tamahamaha [Kame-hameha], the great king of the Sandwich Islands.

We used to tell him that he ate Captain Cook and lost his teeth in that way. That was the only thing that ever made him angry. He would always be quite excited at that and say—"*Aole!*" (no) "Me no eat Captain Cook! Me pikinini—small—so high—no more! My father see Captain Cook! Me—no!" None of them like to have anything said about Captain Cook, for the sailors all believe that he was eaten, and that they cannot endure to be taunted with.—"New Zealand Kanaka eat white man;—Sandwich Island Kanaka—no. Sandwich Island Kanaka *ua like pu na haole—* all 'e same a' you!"

Mr. Bingham was a sort of patriarch among them and was always treated with great respect, though he had not the education and energy which gave Mr. Mannini his power over them. I have spent hours in talking with this old fellow about Tama-hamaha, the Charlemagne of the Sandwich Islands; his son and successor Riho Riho . . . whose funeral he remembered perfectly; and also about the customs of his country in his boyhood, and the changes which have been made by the missionaries.

He never would allow that human beings had been eaten there; and, indeed, it always seemed like an insult to tell so affectionate, intelligent and civilized a class of men that such barbarities had been practiced in their own country within the recollection of many of them. Certainly the history of no people on the globe can show anything like so rapid an advance. . . .

Their customs and manner of treating one another show a simple, primitive generosity which is truly delightful; and which is often a reproach to our own people. Whatever one has, they all have. Money, food, clothes they share with one another; even to the last piece of tobacco to put in their pipes.

I once heard old Mr. Bingham say with the highest indignation to a Yankee trader who was trying to persuade him to keep his money to himself—"No! We no all 'e same a' you!—Suppose one got money, all got money. You—suppose one got money—lock him up in chest—No good!—Kanaka all 'e same a' one!" This principle they carry so far that none of them will eat anything in sight of others without offering it all around. I have seen one of them break a biscuit which had been given him, into five parts, at a time when I knew he was on a very short allowance, as there was but little to eat on the beach.

My favorite among them, and one who was liked by both officers and men and by whomever he had anything to do with, was Hope. He was an intelligent, kind-hearted little fellow, and I never saw him angry, though I knew him for more than a year, and had seem him imposed upon by white people, and abused by insolent officers of vessels. He was always civil and always ready, and never forgot a benefit. I once took care of him when he was ill, getting medicines from the ship's chests, when no captain or officer would do anything for him, and he never forgot it.

Every Kanaka has one particular friend whom he considers himself bound to do everything for, and with whom he has a sort of contract—an alliance offensive and defensive—and for whom he will often make the greatest sacrifices. This friend they call *aikane*, and for such did Hope adopt me. I do not believe I could have wanted anything which he had that he would not have given me. In return for this I was always his friend among the Americans, and used to teach him letters and numbers, for he left home before he had learned how to read.

He was very curious about Boston—as they call the United States, asking many questions about the houses, the people, etc., and always wished to have the pictures in books explained to him. They were all astonishingly quick in catching at explanations, and many things which I thought it utterly impossible to make them understand, they often seized in an instant, and asked questions which showed that they knew enough to make them wish to go farther.

The pictures of steamboats and railroad cars, in the columns of some newspapers which I had, gave me great difficulty to explain. The grading of the road, the rails, the construction of the carriages they could easily understand, but the motion produced by steam was a little too refined for them. I attempted to show it to them once by an experiment upon the cook's coppers, but failed, probably as much from my own ignorance as from their want of apprehension; and, I have no doubt, left them with about as clear an idea of the principle as I had myself. . . .

A map of the world which I once showed them kept their attention for hours, those who knew how to read pointing out the places and referring to me for the distances. I remember being much amused with a question which Hope asked me. Pointing to the large irregular place which is always left blank around the poles to denote that it is undiscovered, he looked up and asked, *"Pau?"* (Done? ended?). . . .

They smoke a great deal, though not much at a time, using pipes with large bowls and very short stems, or no stems at all. These they light, and, putting them to their mouths, take a long draught, getting their mouths as full as they can hold, and their cheeks distended, and then let it slowly out through their mouths and nostrils. The pipe is then passed to others, who draw in the same manner, one pipeful serving for a half a dozen.

They never take short, continuous draughts like Europeans, but one of these "Oahu puffs," as the sailors call them, serves for an hour or two, until someone else lights his pipe, and it is passed round in the same manner. Each Kanaka on the beach had a pipe, flint, steel, tinder, a hand of tobacco and a jackknife, which he always carried about with him.

That which strikes a stranger most peculiarly is their style of singing. They run on, in a low, guttural, monotonous sort of chant, their lips and tongues seeming hardly to move, and the sounds apparently modulated solely in the throat. There is very little tune to it, and the words, so far as I could learn, are extempore. They sing about persons and things which are around them, and adopt this method when they do not wish to be understood by any but themselves; and it is very effectual, for with the most careful attention I never could detect a word that I knew.

I have often heard Mr. Mannini, who was the most noted *improvisatore* among them, sing for an hour together, when at work in the midst of Americans and Englishmen, and by the occasional shouts and laughter of the Kanakas, who were at a distance, it was evident that he was singing about the different men he was at work with. They have great powers of ridicule and are excellent mimics, many of them discovering and imitating the peculiarities of our own people before we have seen them ourselves. . . .

The Mexican hermaphrodite brig *Fazio* one day got under weigh with a light breeze and was floating out of the harbor, when two horsemen came dashing down to the beach at full speed and tried to find a boat to put off after her; but there being none on the beach, they offered a handful of silver to any Kanaka who would swim off and take a letter on board.

One of the Kanakas, a fine, active, well-made young fellow, instantly threw off everything but his duck trousers and, putting the letter into his hat, swam off after the vessel. Fortunately the wind was very light and the vessel was going slowly, so that, although she was nearly a mile off when he started, he gained on her rapidly. He went through the water leaving a wake like a small steamboat. I certainly never saw such swimming before.

They saw him coming from the deck, but did not heave to, suspecting the nature of his errand, yet, the wind continuing light, he swam alongside and got on board and delivered his letter. The captain read the letter, told the Kanaka there was no answer and, giving him a glass of brandy, left him to jump overboard and find the best of his way to the shore. The Kanaka swam in for the nearest point of land, and in about an hour made his appearance at the hide-house. He did not seem at all fatigued, had made three or four dollars, got a glass of brandy, and was in fine spirits. . . .

. . . For several days we went down to the Point and caught a quantity of cod and mackerel. On one of these expeditions we saw a battle between two Sandwich Islanders and a shark. "Johnny" had been playing about our boat for some time, driving away the fish and showing his teeth at our bait when we missed him and in a few moments heard a great shouting between two Kanakas who were fishing on the rock opposite to us: *"E hana hana make i ka ia nui! E pii mai Aikane!"* etc., and saw them pulling away on a stout line, and "Johnny Shark" floundering at the other end.

The line soon broke, but the Kanakas would not let him off so easily, and sprang directly into the water after him. Now came the tug of war. Before he could get into deep water, one of them seized him by the tail and ran up with him upon the beach, but Johnny twisted round, turning his head under his body and, showing his teeth in the vicinity of the Kanaka's hand, made him let go and spring out of the way.

The shark now turned tail and made the best of his way, by flapping and floundering, toward deep water; but here again, before he was fairly off, the other Kanaka seized him by the tail, and made a spring toward the beach, his companion at the same time paying away upon him with stones and a large stick. As soon, however, as the shark could turn, he was obliged to let go his hold; but the instant he made toward deep water, they were both behind him, watching their chance to seize him. In this way the battle went on for some time, the shark in a rage splashing

and twisting about, and the Kanakas in high excitement yelling
at the top of their voices; but the shark at last got off, carrying
away a hook and line, and not a few severe bruises.

It has been said that the greatest curse to each of the South
Sea islands was the first man who discovered it; and everyone
who knows anything of the history of our commerce in those
parts knows how much truth there is in this, and that the white
men, with their vices, have brought in diseases before unknown
to the islanders, and which are now sweeping off the native population of the Sandwich Islands at the rate of one-fortieth of the
entire population annually. They seem to be a doomed people.

The curse of a people calling themselves Christian seems to
follow them everywhere; and even here in this obscure place lay
two young islanders . . . wasting away under a disease which
they would never have known but for their intercourse with
Christianized Mexico and people from Christian America. One
of them, . . . my friend and *Aikane*—Hope, was the most dreadful object I had ever seen in my life: his eyes sunken and dead,
his cheeks fallen in against his teeth, his hands looking like
claws; a dreadful cough, which seemed to rack his whole shattered
system, a hollow, whispering voice, and an entire inability to
move himself.

There he lay upon a mat on the ground, which was the only
floor of the oven, with no medicine, no comforts, and no one to
care for or help him but a few Kanakas, who were willing
enough, but could do nothing. The sight of him made me sick and
faint. Poor fellow! During the four months that I lived upon the
beach we were continually together, both in work and in our
excursions in the woods and upon the water. I really felt a strong
affection for him, and preferred him to any of my own countrymen there; and I believe there was nothing which he would not
have done for me.

When I came into the oven he looked at me, held out his hand
and said in a low voice, but with a delightful smile, "*Aloha,
Aikane! Aloha nui!*" I comforted him as well as I could, and
promised to ask the captain to help him from the medicine

chest, and told him I had no doubt the captain would do what he could for him, as he had worked in our employ for several years, both on shore and aboard our vessels on the coast. I went aboard and turned into my hammock, but I could not sleep.

Thinking, from my education, that I must have some knowledge of medicine, the Kanakas had insisted upon my examining him carefully, and it was not a sight to be forgotten. One of our crew, an old man-of-war's-man of twenty years' standing, who had seen sin and suffering in every shape and whom I afterwards took to see Hope, said it was dreadfully worse than anything he had ever seen or even dreamed of. He was horror-struck, as his countenance showed; yet he had been among the worse cases in our naval hospitals. I could not get the thought of the poor fellow out of my head all night, his horrible suffering and his apparently inevitable, horrible end.

The next day I told the captain of Hope's state and asked him if he would be so kind as to go and see him.

"What? a Kanaka?"

"Yes, sir," said I; "but he has worked four years for our vessels, and has been in the employ of our owners, both on shore and aboard."

"Oh! he be damned!" said the captain, and walked off.

This same man died afterward of a fever on the deadly coast of Sumatra, and God grant he had better care taken of him in his sufferings than he ever gave to anyone else! Finding nothing was to be got from the captain, I consulted an old shipmate who had much experience in these matters, and got from him a recipe, which he always kept by him. With this I went to the mate and told him the case. Mr. Brown had been entrusted with the general care of the medicine chest, and although a driving fellow and a taught hand in a watch, he had good feelings and was always inclined to be kind to the sick. He said that Hope was not strictly one of the crew, but as he was in our employ when taken sick, he should have the medicines; and he got them and gave them to me, with leave to go ashore at night.

Nothing could exceed the delight of the Kanakas when I came bringing the medicines. All their terms of affection and gratitude were spent upon me, and in a sense wasted (for I could not understand half of them), yet they made all known by their manner. Poor Hope was so much revived at the bare thought of anything's being done for him that he was already stronger and better. I knew he must die as he was, and he could not die under the medicines, and any chance was worth running. An oven exposed to every wind and change of weather is no place to take calomel; but nothing else would do, and strong remedies must be used or he was gone.

The applications, internal and external, were powerful, and I gave him strict directions to keep warm and sheltered, telling him it was his only chance for life. Twice after this I visited him, having only time to run up, while waiting in the boat. He promised to take his medicines regularly until we returned, and insisted upon it that he was doing better. . . .

I would have trusted my life and my fortune in the hands of any one of these people; and certainly had I wished for a favor or act of sacrifice, I would have gone to them all in turn before I should have applied to one of my own countrymen on the coast, and should have expected to have seen it done before my own countrymen had got half through counting the cost.

From *Two Years Before the Mast,* Richard Henry Dana, Jr. (Boston and New York: Houghton Mifflin Company, 1895).

XXIV

Thomas Jefferson Farnham

The idea that Hawaii might make an attractive haven for tourists, a pleasant place in which to relax for a holiday, and a region to investigate merely for its charming scenery and native lore was yet to be broached. Someone had to promote such a novel conception, to be the precursor, the pioneering tourist whom millions would follow, and no one was better qualified to fill that role than Thomas Jefferson Farnham (1804–1848).

Toward midcentury Farnham was America's most esteemed writer on the West, popular among armchair travelers and footworn wayfarers alike. He wrote from a wealth of firsthand experience at sightseeing: *Travels in the Californias and Scenes in the Pacific Ocean, Travels in the Great Western Prairies, Life and Adventures in California.* For years after his death, the books went into edition after edition.

A son of Maine, afflicted with wanderlust at an early age, he migrated to Peoria, Illinois, temporarily hung out a lawyer's shingle there, and then was routed from his legal routine by the urge to go still further west. In 1839 he led a company to the Northwest over the Oregon Trail. Even that was not far enough. To him the Sandwich Islands were merely an offshore extension of the West, so upon reaching the mouth of the Columbia River he kept on going.

Down the years thousands of correspondents, amateur and professional, have tried to put on paper some representation of the excitement they felt on approaching the Islands. Farnham set a high standard on the subject that few have ever equaled.

Where Away the Land?

Our latitude and longitude were taken daily at twelve M., and the report of these and the distance from the islands always gave rise to some prophetic announcements of the day and hour when we should anchor in the dominions of Kamehameha. The evenings also furnished a few diversions and pleasant objects of contemplation. Bathing was one of the former. After the shadows of night had set in, we used to present ourselves at the mainstays and receive as much of the Ocean as our love of the sublime by the gallon or our notions of cleanliness demanded. And when the hooting, leaping and laughing of the ceremony were silenced, the cool comfort of the body left the mind in listless quietude, or to its wanderings among the glories of a tropical sky.

It was the 24th of December—the mid-winter hour. But the space over us was as mild and soft a blue as ever covered a September night in the States. The stars sent down a delicate sprinkling light on the waters. The air itself presented some peculiar aspects. It was more nearly transparent than any I had ever breathed; and there seemed to be woven into all its thousand eddies a tissue of golden and trembling mist, streaming down from the depths of heaven. . . .

We retired to rest this evening in unusually fine spirits, for with the aid of a good breeze piping down from the northwest we expected sight of land by the next sunset. Our sleep, however, was not remarkably deep, for I recollect that the wind freshened during the night, as it generally does on the edge of the trades, and compelled the morning watch to take in sail. The noise occasioned by this movement was construed by the wakeful ear of our desires into a shortening canvas to prevent running on land, and we turned out to see it. But it was yet beyond view.

The night, however, was worth beholding. It was one o'clock; the sky overhead was clear and starry; around the northwestern horizon hung a cluster of swollen clouds, like Moorish towers, faintly tipped with the dim light. In the southwest lay another mass, piled in silent grandeur, dark battlement-like, as if it were the citadel of the seas. The waters were in an easy mood. The ship moved through them evenly, save that she cut the long smooth swells more deeply than the space between them, and occasionally started from its slumber a porpoise or a whale.

We turned in again and slept till the breakfast dishes clattered on the table and Tom informed us that Mr. Newell supposed he had seen at sunrise the looming of the land to the southeast. That announcement brought us to our feet. . . . "On deck! on deck! where away the land?" and we tasked our eyes with the utmost effort to scan the nature of the dark embankment on which the mate had founded his auguries.

The excitement at length draw all the passengers and officers to the starboard quarter; each man looked and expressed himself in his own way. To *guess* was the Yankee's part; to *look and doubt* was John Bull's pleasure; to *wuss it might be true* was the Scotch contribution; and *to reckon awhile and commend himself to be dumbfounded if anything could be known about it* was the Carolinian carpenter's clincher. The matter left standing thus, we obeyed Tom's summons to breakfast.

While engaged in filling our countenances with the realities of life, we were startled with a bird's note from the deck. It proved to come from one of those winged songsters of the islands which often greet the toiling ship far at sea, and with their sweet voices recall to the soul, weary with the rough monotony of an un-natural life, the remembrance and anticipation of the land—the green and beautiful land, where the glorious light brightens the flowers, where the flowers shed their perfume in the air and the fruits of trees and shrubs and plants are poured into the lap of the ripened year. . . .

This one—perched in the rigging of the ship in which we had been imprisoned for weeks—a messenger from the glens and hills sweetly chanting our welcome to them, was an object of the tenderest interest. It had the cordial greeting of our hearts, and while talking about it, we could not forbear reaching our hands toward it and grieving that we had no intelligible language wherewith to convey our salutations, and ask the tidings from its beautiful home. The captain consulted his reckoning and found that we lay about one hundred miles northwest-by-north from the island of Hawaii.

The breeze, instead of decreasing with the ascent of the sun, as it had done for a number of days past, held on; and with all the weather studding-sails out, we made about ten knots during most of the morning. About ten o'clock Mr. Newell, who had been watching that embankment of cloud in the southwest, which had excited our hopes at sunrise, touched his hat to Captain Duncan and remarked, "That cloud retains its bearing and shape very much like the looming of land, sir. We must be in sight of some of the islands; we made ten knots by the log, sir, during my watch."

The Captain had expressed his belief that he could sail his ship under that cloud without lead line or copper bottom, and it was still his opinion that an English commander like himself, an old salt of thirty years' standing, would be as likely to know the complexion of the land as any gentleman with less experienced optics. However, he sent Tom for his glass and peered into it with the keenest search.

It was delightful, meantime, to us land lubbers, to watch the workings of his face. There was a gleam of triumph creeping over it as he first brought his glass to bear upon the object. But as the highest part of the pile came into the field of vision, his cheeks dropped an instant, then curled into the well-known lineaments of chagrin, and then into those of rage, as if he would rather all the land were sunk than he be found mistaken in a matter so purely professional.

"Damn the land!" he at length exclaimed. "I suppose it must be Mauna Kea," and gave the glass to a passenger.

The breeze piped up and we moved on merrily. Merrily flew the gladdening waters from the prow, steadily as the masts stood out the canvas on the clear blue sky; and brightly beamed the warm and mellow day on the sea. The Scotch mate, who swore by any dozen of things that his memory happened to seize, affirmed by his blood and the whisky that had been buried seven comfortable years at his auld aunt's homestead, that he would see the lassies of Honolulu before he was a day older; the professor of psalmody sung, "Here's a health to thee, Tom Moore"; the Hawaiian Island servants of the Hudson's Bay Company began to count their money preparatory to the purchase of *poi*.

The crew began to tell yarns about sprees they had enjoyed in Chili, New Holland, Liverpool, Vera Cruz, St. Petersburgh and Montevideo; the six-foot boatswain began to whistle; Tom began to grin; a former cabin boy began to think of his mother whom he expected to meet in the islands; the visitor bird chirped in the rigging, and all for joy! For now the lofty peaks of Hawaii loomed above the clouds, the seaweed gathered on the prow and the odor of the land puffed over us.

At five o'clock the breeze slackened again, and until nightfall the ship barely moved enough to obey her helm. Near ten in the evening it freshened, but as we were in the neighborhood of a lee shore, the captain thought it prudent to keep good sea room, and accordingly shortened sail and lay off a part of the night.

This was Christmas Eve, that nucleus of so much social and religious joy throughout the Christian world, and a merry one it was to us. Not so in the ordinary sense of the trencher and cup, the music, dance, and the embrace of kindred, nor rendered such by the pealing anthem or the solemn prayer swelling up through the lofty arches hung with boughs of evergreen and the prophetic star of Bethlehem. But nature herself seemed worshipping. The heavens were unmarred by a single breath of mist, except what rested on the heights of Hawaii; and on all its vault the stars shone, not as brightly as in the frosty skies of the temperate zones, but with a quiet subdued luster, as if they were the watch fires of angels assembled to celebrate the earth's great jubilee.

The Pacific, too, lent the scene its most charming condition. Wide and gently curved swells rolled down from the north, smooth and noiseless, except when they dashed upon our noble ship or were broken by the dolphin coursing through and dotting them with phosphorescent light. The seabirds were hailing each other a Merry Christmas, the gray and mottled albatross, flying from billow to billow, occasionally clipped the waves with its sword-shaped wings, and shouted gladly to the elements.

The gulls and other birds sat in countless flocks in every direction, sinking, rising and chattering on the panting sea. And schools of tiny fish with bright golden backs swam by the side of the ship, as children after long absence gather with cherished remembrances around the old homestead on this blessed night.

At dawn on the 25th one of the islands lay six miles distant in the southeast. The sky was clear; the sea smooth; the porpoises blowing about us; a right whale was spouting a hundred yards astern; and our Hawaiians, looking from the mainstays at the land, were uttering their beautiful language of vowels with great volubility. . . . Poor fellows! They had been five years absent from their *poi;* five years separated from the brown beauties of their native isles; five years away from their venerated sovereign. No wonder, therefore, they were charmed with the dim outline of their native land.

A mass of vapor hung along its heights and concealed them from view, save here and there a volcanic spire which stood out on the sky, overlooking cloud, mountain and sea. As the light increased to full day, this cloudy mass was fringed on the edge nearest us with delicate golden hues; but underneath it and inward toward the cliffs the undisturbed darkness reached far eastward, a line of light belting the mountains mid-heaven.

Downward from this line to the sea sloped red mountains of old lava on which no vegetable life appeared. On a few little plains near the beach the cocoa tree sent up its bare shaft; and as the clouds broke away, we discerned clumps of rich foliage on the heights. But generally the aspect was that of a dreary broken desert.

We sailed past the western cape of Molokai and laid our course for the southeastern part of Oahu. At two o'clock our good ship lay becalmed under the lofty piles of extinct craters, six miles northeast of Honolulu. At four the breeze freshened and bore us down abreast of the town. Soon after a boat came rapidly from the shore with a pilot on board by the name of Reynolds, a generous, jolly old American gentleman of long residence in the islands. He greeted his countrymen with great kindness, and having brought the ship to anchor outside the reef invited us to go ashore in his boat.

It was manned with islanders. They rowed to the entrance of the channel, rested on their oars while the angry swells lifted us at one instant on the summit of the waters and at another dropped us into the chasm between them, till the third and largest came, when by a quick and energetic movement they threw the boat upon the land side of it and shot us into the harbor with the rapidity of the wind.

We passed the American whalers which crowded the anchorage; ran under the guns of the fort, struck the landing at the pier, leaped ashore among crowds of natives, besprinkled with an occasional European face; followed an overgrown son of John Bull to another man's house, took a glass of wine, and scattered ourselves in various quarters for the night.

Thus terminated our voyage from the Columbia River to the Kingdom of Hawaii. The distance between Oregon and these islands is about three thousand miles. We had sailed it in twenty-one days.

From *Travels in the Californias and Scenes in the Pacific Ocean,* Thomas Jefferson Farnham (New York: Sheldon, 1844).

XXV

Charles Wilkes

The United States Government was tardy in joining the international exploration parade to the Pacific. Finally in 1838 a Federal expedition was organized by the Navy, and a squadron of six ships went forth to scout for undiscovered terrain and to look over what had already been mapped. Staffed by eminent American scientists, the Government Exploring Expedition aimed to make up for lost time. "Commodore" Charles Wilkes (1798–1877), a mere lieutenant, whose principal prior achievement had been to complete an exemplary survey of Narragansett Bay, was in charge.

The squadron roamed through the South Pacific and the North Pacific, carrying out important research; it touched a section of the shores of Antarctica, which was later named Wilkes Land, explored Fiji and other islands, surveyed the Northwest Coast, visited the Sandwich Islands, and wound up circumnavigating the globe.

Hawaiians of the time seemed to consider Wilkes's call as great an occasion as the coming of Captain Cook—or Hiram Bingham. Teams of scientists, always followed by a string of native admirers, fanned out over the interior of the Islands to study flora and fauna, valleys and volcanoes, local customs and living conditions. The Islanders were impressed and enormously flattered by all the attention given them. Amphibious Hawaiians assisted in underwater research on reefs and marine life, and hundreds were engaged as bearers for the greatest expedition yet made to the summit of Mauna Loa, where a tent village was erected and occupied by geologists for several weeks.

Wilkes's five-volume report of the expedition appeared in 1844, and more than half of one volume was devoted to Hawaii. He reported in detail on every phase of his observations, but the most interesting writing of this naval scientist turned out to be his asides on sociology—especially his commentary on native sports, games, and amusements. Only a generation after the first horses had been imported from California, he noted that a craze for horseback riding was sweeping through the Kingdom.

Heathenish Enjoyments

In regard to the energies of the natives, as far as my own observations extended, they are always willing to work for a reasonable compensation; and it is not remarkable that they should prefer their own ease to toiling for what they consider, in the one case, unnecessary, and, in the other, for an inadequate reward.

Having little motive for industry, they expend their physical energies in various athletic sports. A favorite amusement of the chiefs was sliding down hill on a long narrow sled: this was called *holua;* it is not unlike our boys' play when we have snow. The sled was made to slide on one runner, and the chiefs prostrated themselves on it. For this sport they had a trench dug from the top of a steep hill and down its sides to a great distance over the adjoining plain. This being made quite smooth, and having dried grass laid on it, they were precipitated with great velocity down it, and, it is said, were frequently carried a half and sometimes a whole mile. Diamond Hill [Head] and the plain of Waikiki was one of these localities for this pastime.

Playing in the surf was another of their amusements, and is still much practiced. It is a beautiful sight to see them coming in on the top of a heavy roller, borne along with increasing rapidity until they suddenly disappear. What we would look upon as the most dangerous surf, is that they most delight in. The surf-board which they use is about six feet in length and eighteen inches wide, made of some light wood.

After they have passed within the surf, they are seen buffeting the waves to regain the outside, whence they again take their course with almost the speed of an aerial flight. They play for hours in this way, never seeming to tire; and the time to see a Hawaiian happy is while he is gamboling and frolicking in the surf. I have stood for hours watching their sport with great interest and, I must say, with no little envy.

Next in interest to the foregoing amusements were their dances. Some of these consisted, as among other islanders, in gesture to a monotonous song, whose lascivious meaning is easily interpreted. Many persons were engaged in these dances, of which some are said to have been graceful; and if so, the people must have sadly changed since their first intercourse with the whites. Their music consisted of drumming on various hollow vessels, calabashes, etc., but the instrument most used by those who could afford one, was a piece of shark's skin drawn tight over a hollow log.

Since the introduction of Christianity, these amusements have been interdicted; for though the missionaries were somewhat averse to destroying those of an innocent character, yet such was the proneness of all to indulge in lascivious thoughts and actions, that it was deemed by them necessary to put a stop to the whole in order to root out the lasciviousness that pervaded the land. They therefore discourage any kind of nocturnal assemblies. . . .

The principal games now in vogue among them are cards, of which, as they minister to their love of gambling, they are passionately fond and often indulge in. They had likewise the amusement of see-saw, which has not yet quite gone out of fashion. . . . A forked stick is placed in the ground; on this a long pole is placed, which admits several on each side. After two or three ups and downs, they try which shall give the opposite party a tumble. This is, at times, adroitly done, and down they all fall, to the infinite amusement both of their adversaries and the bystanders, who indulge in loud laughter and merriment at the expense of those who are so unlucky as to get hurt. They are particularly ungallant in this respect to their female associates. . . .

The governor was kind enough, at my request, to have the game of *maika* played. This was formerly a favorite amusement of the chiefs, and consists in the art of rolling a stone of the above name.

I had heard many extraordinary accounts of the distance to which this could be thrown or rolled, which was said to be sometimes upward of a mile.

In some places they had trenches dug for this game upward of a mile in length, about three feet wide and two deep, with the bottom level, smooth and hard. The game is still practiced (although none of the trenches remain) on any level ground that may be suitable. In the present instance, the governor selected the road in front of the house I occupied. There was a large concourse of spectators, and several men were chosen by the governor to throw.

The *maika* is a piece of hard lava in the shape of a small wheel or roller, three inches in diameter and an inch and a half thick, very smooth and highly polished. The greatest distance to which they were thrown by the most expert player was four hundred and twenty yards. Many were extremely awkward, and it was necessary for the spectators to stand well on the side of the road for fear of accidents. All of them threw the *maika* with much force, which was evident from its rebounding when it met with any obstruction.

The crowd, which amounted to three thousand persons, were greatly amused. This was their great gambling game, and such was its fascination that property, wives, children, their arm and leg bones after death, and even themselves while living, would be staked on a single throw. . . .

They have another game, which I was told is now more in vogue than it has been for some years. The revival of it is attributed by some to the visit of the French frigate *Artemise*. . . . It is called *buhenehene* [*puhenehene*] and consists in hiding a stone under several bundles of tapa, generally five. He who conceals it, sits on one side of the bundles, while those playing occupy a place opposite to him. The bundles are usually of different colors and about the size of a pillow.

Each player has a stick three feet long, ornamented with a feather or cloth, with which each in turn designates the bundle under which he thinks the stone is hidden, with a blow. If the guess is correct, it counts one in his favor; if wrong, he who has concealed it gains one. He who first counts ten wins the game.

The game appears very simple, and one would be inclined to believe it luck until the game is witnessed; it is really amusing to a bystander. . . . So satisfied are they that the eye betrays the place of concealment that the hidder covers his eyes until he hears the stroke of the rod. The expert is rarely deceived, however often the hand may be passed to and fro under the bundles. This game is now played for pigs, tapa, taro, etc.

The governor gave us an exhibition of throwing the lance, which he said had formerly been a favorite amusement of all the people, but was now practiced only by the soldiers. The lance or spear is formed of a pole of the hibiscus, from seven to nine feet in length, on the larger end of which is a small roll of tapa. The exhibition was in the fort where several soldiers had prepared themselves for the exercise.

One of them placed himself at a distance of fifteen or twenty paces from three or four others, who endeavored to hit him. He evaded the spears by throwing his body on one side, stooping and dodging, in a very graceful manner. After this, they were ordered to divide, and began throwing at each other, until, when one or two had been hit rather severely, the contest waxed warm, and blows were dealt without ceremony, while the combatants came to close quarters, when the sport ended in a scuffle, which it required the authoritative voice of the governor to terminate.

This scene was highly amusing, and was the only occasion during my stay at the islands in which I saw any temper shown, or any disposition to fight. The natives, indeed, are remarkably good tempered. . . . When they see another in a passion they generally laugh, although they themselves may be the object of it. . . .

I was much struck with the absence of sports among the boys and children. On inquiry I learned that it had, after mature deliberation and experience, been considered advisable by the missionaries to deprive them of all heathenish enjoyments, rather than allow them to occupy their minds with anything that might recall old associations.

The consequence is that the Hawaiian boys are staid and demure, having the quiet looks of old men. I cannot doubt that they possess the natural tendency of youth toward frolicsome relaxations; but the fear of offending keeps a constant restraint over them. It might be well, perhaps to introduce some innocent amusements; and indeed I believe this has been attempted, for I occasionally saw them flying kites. . . .

At the schools it has been observed that the scholars are extremely fond of calculations in arithmetic, and possess extraordinary talent in that way. So great is their fondness for it that in some schools the teachers have had recourse to depriving them of the study as a punishment. . . .

There are several schools under the superintendence of the missionaries, besides the school for the chiefs . . . and a charity school for half-breeds. I attended their examinations, and the natives performed better than I anticipated. At an examination in the old church there were seven hundred children and as many more parents. The attraction that drew together such numbers was a feast, which I understand is given annually. . . .

On my arrival at the church, I found several tables set out, one for the accommodation of the chiefs, furnished as we see for a 4th of July lunch at home, with hams, turkeys, chickens, pies, etc. The common people's children took their poe [*poi*] and raw fish on the floor. . . . The governor became master of ceremonies, and with his numerous aides endeavored to direct the throng; but all were too eager to get the most convenient seats to heed his commands, and the uproar was great. Some stopped short of their allotted place, and the church soon became a human hive.

The governor did his utmost to maintain order and silence, but his voice was not heard, for in such a moment the anxiety he was under to have things conducted in good order caused him for a time to lose sight of his usual urbanity and decorum of behavior. He in fact showed that a little of the unbridled ferocity of former times was still within him, which moved him repeatedly to use his fist, and that too upon the fair sex, tumbling them over amidst calabashes of poe, raw fish, etc. . . .

Order was at last restored for a few minutes, during which grace was said by the Rev. Mr. Smith, which, being ended, the clatter of tongues, clashing of teeth and smacking of lips began. It was a joyous sight to see 1500 human beings so happy and gratified by their molasses feast: poe and raw fish were the only additions. The latter are every-day food, so that the molasses constituted a special treat. So great is the fondness of the natives for it, that I was told many are induced to send their children to school merely to entitle them to be present at this feast.

It was not a little amusing to see the wistful faces without, contrasted with the joyous and happy ones within; in one place might be a sturdy native biting a piece from a raw fish, and near him another sucking the poe off his fingers, with much grace and sleight of hand. The molasses was either drunk with water or sucked from the fingers. . . .

Of the molasses there was "short commons"; but all things considered, the feast went off well. . . . While this was going forward among the common people, those at the table of the old and young chiefs were not idle. The turkeys, pies, etc. appeared quite acceptable, though they were not so great a rarity to them as the molasses feast to the others. As far as enjoyment went, I should have preferred to have been one of the poor scholars. . . .

Saturday in Honolulu is a gala day, and all ages of both sexes devote themselves to amusement. Toward the afternoon, they may be seen wending their way toward the east end of town, in every variety of costume, and borne along in every possible manner. All who have health enough must engage in this day's sport, and every horse is in requisition.

The national taste, if I may so speak, is riding horses, and the more break-neck and furious the animal is, the better. Nicety of equipment is not thought of: anything answers for a saddle and bridle, and as for stirrups, they are considered quite unnecessary. By four o'clock the crowd is well collected, and feats of horsemanship are practiced, consisting generally of those involuntary tumblings that inexpert riders are wont to indulge in.

The great gathering is on the eastern plain, the road to which is well covered with dust. The whole looks, when the crowd has possession of it, not unlike a rag fair, the prominent color being yellow. They are generally well behaved, and the only sufferers are the poor horses, who are kept running, not races only, but for the amusement of the riders, whose great delight is to ride at full speed.

At times there are races, in which the crowd is increased by the addition of foreigners, many of whom are in a state of intoxication. The uproar is proportionately great, and the natives are less conspicuous, their places being occupied by those whose morals and enjoyments are far from being as innocent. When his majesty and suite are present, much more order and decorum are observed, and the whole affords a pleasing and amusing sight.

The returning throng is headed by the king and his party, after whom follow the crowd in a somewhat uproarious style: those on horses indiscriminately mixed, racing and hallooing; the fair riders being borne along amidst clouds of dust so thick that, were it not for the rustling of flowing silks and tapas, one would be at a loss to know their sex. By the evening, all is quiet again, and the streets are nearly deserted.

Sunday is ushered in with a decorum and quietness that would satisfy the most scrupulous Puritan. I have often had occasion to speak of the strict observance of the Sabbath among the Polynesian islands, and this strictness is no less remarkable here. Such is the force of example that even the least orderly of the foreigners are prevented from indulging in any excesses, which, considering the worthless population the town of Honolulu contains, is a proof of the excellence of the police regulations and the watchfulness of the guardians of the law.

From *Narrative of the United States Exploring Expedition, 1838–1842*, Vol. IV, Charles Wilkes (Philadelphia: Lea and Blanchard, 1845).

XXVI

Manley Hopkins

Affection for the American missionaries was far less pervasive than their own reports to patrons in the States intimated. They were berated as political meddlers by all *malihinis* who wanted to do the meddling themselves; they were an abomination to most merchants, planters, and traders, because they had taught the natives to read, reason, and suspect sly foreigners; they were hated by the whaler crews, whose fun and "refreshment" programs had been curtailed; they were resented by innumerable chiefs who saw their power and great estates shrinking under the new influences; they were despised by the French, who begrudged the intrusion of Protestants on territory that might easily have been swung to Catholicism and Gallic control, if only the curés had arrived first; and most of all the upstart Yankee do-gooders were loathed by the British, who had not yet forgotten the Revolution and the War of 1812.

The leading iconoclast for the British point of view was the English Consul General in Honolulu, Manley Hopkins (1817–1897). The diplomat had an undiplomatic gibe for any and all of the missionaries, as typified in his scorn for the Reverend William Richards, who had made himself so unpopular with the whalers at Lahaina that his mission was actually bombarded with cannon shot in 1827. Nevertheless, Hopkins had to concede that the missionary meddlers gave Hawaii its first respectable government.

Conscience to the King

In the year 1836 the American missionaries became more intimately and more openly connected with the Hawaiian government. It has been a reproach used toward them that some of the
number who went forth to those heathen islands to save souls by
their teaching and preaching, remained there to put away their
missionary character and assume the part of amateur statesmen,
much occupied thereafter in secular matters, and not altogether
foregoing such secular honors as their connection with that small
state could bestow.

The missionaries have considered it necessary to reply to this
reproach, and to justify the course they took. The substance of
their apology is that a necessity lay upon them to act as they did;
that an opportunity presented itself of gently guiding the ruling
powers of Hawaii to construct a government upon enlightened
principles, of which the Christian religion should be the directing
star, and which should be free from foreign influence; that this
was the wish of the chiefs, who in their darkness and incom-
petency to build on a model they had never seen, endeavored to
procure the needful assistance where it was to be found; that to
this end they sent one of the missionary establishment, Mr.
Richards, to the United States with an invitation to some public
man to come to the aid of the Hawaiian kingdom, one who could
assist and advise in founding a new constitution and in making
new laws. . . .

Mr. Richards failed in the endeavor, and could not persuade
any "right man" that by going to the center of the Pacific he
should be in the "right place," as far as his own prospects in life
were concerned; and in consequence of this failure there was no
other alternative than that the missionaries should detach some
from their own ranks to be associated with the chiefs in guiding,
henceforth, the vessel of State. . . .

The Rev. W. Richards, who formed one of their number, was a man originally distinguished by his insignificance. He was a well-meaning, pious, industrious person, without any great intellectual power, who during his twelve years' residence in the islands as a religious teacher had acquired the native language very correctly, and was principally employed by the mission in translating.

He was selected to go to the United States on the errand previously mentioned, which proved unsuccessful. Returning to the islands in 1838, after an absence of two years, a new line of life opened itself to the former humble missionary. He became the adviser of the sovereign—a sort of conscience to the king; resided with him, accompanied him wherever he went, and acted as his interpreter—or rather as his spokesman.

He had put off his definite character of a minister of religion to assume the task of making laws and governing a people. Alas! ambition sometimes dwells beneath unstarched white cravats and suits of black alpaca. In 1842 Mr. Richards was accredited to the United States and the Courts of London and Paris as a Minister Plenipotentiary and Ambassador Extraordinary.

He was not the only member of the mission who dropped the purely spiritual office for the secular. Whilst employees of the American Board of Commissioners for Foreign Missions, these teachers of religion were supported by the Board in a liberal manner, but they were expected to attend exclusively to the duty which had been assigned them, and they could not appropriate any property which might fall into their hands, but which was to belong to the Board itself.

Thus the American missionaries were comfortably provided for against the common needs of life, and their children were educated by the Society; but whilst in the capacity of its missionaries, they could not call house or furniture, land or cattle, their own. A means was found of liberating themselves from this too parental tutelage, and of passing from bondage into a position in which they could acquire and hold money, land and every sort of property.

This was effected by representing to the Board that they desired to be no longer a burden on the funds of the Society; that they

On the sugar plantations coolies earned $4 a month

were able to maintain themselves in the sphere of their labors. They thus partially detached themselves from the Board and its rigorous system, whilst they retained the character of missionaries. Many of their number are supported by the congregations among whom they live by subscriptions in money, provisions and labor. Some of the missionaries passed into government employ; and not a few of the number showed considerable alacrity in the search of wealth, seeking it diligently, and investing it in very remunerative securities. . . .

Up to the year 1838 the government of the Hawaiian Islands was a despotism. The King's power was absolute; and, as is usually the case with absolutisms, his chiefs in their separate spheres were smaller despots. . . . The oppressive system of tabu made itself felt as an immemorial and inevitable condition of life. Usage was almost the only system.

The American missionaries and ex-missionaries . . . had obtained a considerable influence over Kamehameha III; and they began to exert it in endeavoring to obtain the King's consent to govern the nation constitutionally. The endeavor was bold and humane. It is said that the King felt great repugnance, and made some resistance, at parting with the absolute unquestioned power which had always been the right of kings of Hawaii. The missionaries, however, gained their point, and a sketch of a constitution, occupying a sheet or two of foolscap paper, was produced. . . .

Whoever might have been the first investigator of this essential departure from an ancient despotism, Mr. Richards . . . took a leading part afterward in constructing the constitutional edifice. On the 7th of June, 1839, the King signed a Bill of Rights; and on the 8th of October, 1840, he voluntarily conferred on the people a constitution which recognized the three grand divisions of a civilized monarchy—king, legislature and judges, and defined in some respects the general duties of each. . . .

The Declaration of Rights and the Constitution were led to by a series of lectures upon Political Economy delivered to the chiefs by Mr. Richards. The organic laws, although depriving the chiefs of several of their old privileges and immunities, were passed by

them unanimously, nor were they afterward resisted; but the
severity and the system of espionage which they induced caused
much dissatisfaction to the common people. . . .

It is worthy of remark that the missionaries, who were Americans, who had lived under and perhaps loved republican institutions, never went so far as to attempt to introduce a republic in
the Hawaiian Islands. Such an idea they knew to be preposterous;
and they were wise enough to aim at what might be within
reach. . . .

Their eyes, however, traveled farther than mere earthly types,
and, consistently with their former profession as teachers of
religion, they introduced into their scheme the theocratic element.
In the preamble of "The Constitution of the Hawaiian Islands,"
borrowed partly from Scripture and partly from the American
Declaration of Independence, they start with the assertion that
"God hath made of one blood all nations of men to dwell on the
earth in unity and blessedness. God has bestowed certain rights
alike on all men, and all chiefs, and all people of all lands." We
are not to be surprised at religious language introduced into a
State paper, when the document is drawn up by a preacher.

From *Hawaii: The Past, Present and Future of Its Island Kingdom,* Manley
Hopkins (London: Longman, 1862).

XXVII

Laura Fish Judd

The first two medical missionaries sent to Hawaii by the American Board did not stay long. Dr. Holman remained for only eighteen months; his successor, Abraham Blatchely, stuck it out for three years. For half the period between 1820 and 1828 there was no trained physician anywhere in the Islands. Then on March 30, 1828, arrived Dr. Gerrit P. Judd and his wife Laura—both endowed with a whirlwind of energy, both with a lifelong commitment to Hawaii.

For fourteen years Dr. Judd doled out pills to the natives, raced from mission station to mission station trying to keep up with the steady multiplication of missionary babies, performed operations that would have taxed the skill of better surgeons in Boston or Baltimore, fought one grim epidemic after another, and covered thousands of miles with his satchel on horseback, in pushcarts, in outriggers, on interisland schooners. But in 1842 he was convinced that an ailing government needed his services more than his list of regular patients, so he gave up his practice to take over from Hiram Bingham and William Richards as the power behind the throne—the "White King."

His witty, vivacious wife, Laura Fish Judd (1804–1872), inevitably became "First White Lady" of the realm and frequently was as much involved in governmental squabbles as her husband. While he was drafting state papers of moment, she was jotting down her own views of events. Of course, her perspective was still that of a professional missionary and of a conservative American gentlewoman, but of all the accounts of three major political crises in Honolulu, hers had the most sparkle.

Ah, Those Were Dark Days!

In the years 1838 and 1839 the success of the schools and prosperity of the churches were at the culminating point; the latter were crowded with willing worshipers. Thousands of children were taught in Sunday Schools and instructed in separate congregations. The "cold water army" embraced legions of valiant champions who mustered occasionally in holiday dress and marched with flaunting standards of "Down with Rum," "Cold Water Only." Life and property were everywhere safe, and it was seldom that persons could be found who did not regard themselves as Christians. . . .

In the midst of so much prosperity there was one dark cloud casting its shadow over our sunny sky. The antagonism of certain foreign officials sat like an incubus upon the rulers, to which was added a determined perseverance on the part of France to thrust brandy and Romanism upon the nation.

On the arrival of the first French priests, who asked permission to remain, Kaahumanu said: "We do not want you. We have put away our idols and abandoned our old system of religious forms and penances. We have received the Word of God by the hand of teachers whom we love and with whom we are satisfied. Our kingdom is a little one. We do not wish the minds of our subjects distracted by any other sect. Go away and teach destitute countries which have not received the Bible."

They, not obeying her mandate, she fitted out a vessel to carry them to the coast of California, but this was a waste of money, for others followed, more or less disguised, to fill their places. The "Société de Propaganda Fide" of France resolved to place one of their priests by the side of every Protestant clergyman in the Sandwich Islands. The good queen of Louis Philippe was zealous in their cause, and French ships of war landed the graduates of the College of Picpus on many shores of the Pacific. They were sustained by French guns—meet arguments for kings, perhaps, but not so appropriate for the ambassadors of the Cross.

It was unfortunate that the first proselytes of the new faith were persons disaffected toward the chiefs. Some of them were excommunicated members of the Protestant churches, or had been denied admission. When Kaahumanu discovered that they wore crosses and images around their necks as distinguished badges of their creed, she demanded their surrender. "Do you not know that the king's first law forbade image worship? Take those from your necks."

The silence maintained by most of the priests, and the answer of one, that they would not relinquish them, even if their bodies were thrown into the fire or boiling water, alarmed and astonished the chiefs. Accustomed as they had always been to implicit obedience, they inferred very naturally that such an element in their little kingdom would prove very dangerous, if permitted to increase. They did not regard these neophytes as religious people, or punish them for any truly religious sentiment, but for obstinacy in retaining their images, which the chiefs regarded as idolatry, and could not be made to understand the difference.

They argued that their old gods, but recently destroyed by royal power, were mere representatives of the spiritual, or symbol of the thing signified, and was it not the same with the Roman Catholics? A contest for supremacy as rulers led them to adopt measures harsh and impolitic, which never were and never can be justified in suppressing a religious faith.

In July [1839] following, a French frigate of sixty guns under command of Admiral La Place entered the port and, after an interview with the French Consul, made the following demands of the Hawaiian Government:

"That the Catholic religion be declared free;
"That a site for a church be immediately granted;
"That prisoners of the Catholic faith be immediately set free;
"That twenty thousand dollars be taken on board the frigate by some person of rank, to be held as a guarantee for future good behavior."

Three days of grace were allowed, when, if the demands were not complied with, the nation would be involved in all the horrors of war. American missionaries were classed with the native rulers as instigators of the persecution against the Romanists and denied the protection of their country's flag. The American Consul had but just entered office. The Premier likewise was new in office, and both were timid.

We were absent making a tour of the island. . . . A messenger from the metropolis met us about thirty miles from home with an order from the chiefs "for all able-bodied men in the district to prepare food quickly and hasten to Honolulu, as the French had made war." The man added on his own account that the French ship carried guns which could fire around the mountains and send balls all over the island! We mounted our horses and hastened on to the next station at Kaneohe, ten miles from the city, where the gentlemen left the women and children and hastened to Honolulu.

What could the rulers do but submit? The sum required was quickly collected—a part of it borrowed from the American merchants—and taken on board the frigate. The land for the church was granted. The Catholic prisoners had been set at liberty some weeks before.

La Place evidently intended to take the islands, as he did not think it possible that so large a sum could be raised in so short a time. In a note to the foreigners he said: "I have prepared forces sufficiently strong that in giving a dreadful blow the French shall be the *masters* and the protectors of the town at the same time."

While the course pursued by the chiefs toward the proselytes cannot be justified, it did seem hard, when they had but just emerged from a sea troubles in quelling civil dissension, quenching the fires of their own distilleries and struggling for foothold, that a new creed should thus be forced upon them. They were afraid of its influence, and had reason to be.

While the king and chiefs were writhing under these humiliating exactions, an American squadron arrived from the East. . . . The corps of officers were highly intelligent and accomplished gentlemen, some of them professing Christians. On learning that American families of helpless women and children had been proscribed, and in case of hostility were to be handed over, without judge or jury, to the merciless mob, their indignation was somewhat aroused, and the regret often expressed that they had not arrived a little sooner. Pleasant and friendly intercourse during a visit of five weeks encouraged the desponding chiefs and obliterated in some degree the idea that we were defenseless exiles from our native land.

In February, 1843, an English man-of-war, the *Carysfort*, under command of Lord George Paulet, came into port. It had been ordered here by the admiral of the Pacific Squadron from the misrepresentations of the English Consul, to redress alleged injuries done to Englishmen. . . . All intercourse with the resident authorities was refused, and a demand to see the king immediately presented. He was accordingly sent for from Lahaina.

On his arrival, before he had time to change his sea apparel, an imperative demand was sent him to acknowledge the deputyconsul forthwith or prepare for the alternative—a broadside upon the town from the *Carysfort*. Eight hours of grace were granted for deliberation. The demand was acceded to, and Mr. Alexander Simpson was acknowledged as Her Britannic Majesty's representative in the Hawaiian kingdom. Then came the tug of war. The august gentleman said, as did one of olden time, Whereas my predecessor "chastised you with whips, I will chastise you with scorpions."

Daily interviews with the king were demanded, and granted, only to pour upon him insult upon insult. Decisions in the courts were required to be reversed; claims to large tracts of valuable land to be confirmed; and a great amount of hypothetical damages demanded. The king was neither judge nor constable, and was utterly ignorant of the facts in many of the cases brought before him; his knowledge of English was imperfect, and the properly-appointed translator and interpreter was treated as obnoxious. The demands which the defenseless king was obliged to acknowledge ran up in a few days to about $80,000, quite enough to cripple the nation. The ship-of-war was brought around, so that the mouths of her guns yawned continually upon the town.

Ah, those were dark days! The intention was sufficiently clear
to rob the treasury by extorting large sums of money and compel
the king to yield his sovereignty, to prevent it—they said among
themselves—from falling into the hands of the French. The sympathies of the whole foreign community were with the king; but
unfortunately each had a separate plan to propose. Some said:
"Don't yield a single iota; let them fire." Others asked, "In that
case, who will pay for the American property thus destroyed?"
One proposed a cession of the Islands to the United States and
France *pro tem.* Another inquired, "Will the United States Government accept and protect, and the French ever relinquish their
hold, if once in possession?"

The interest of some of us was identified with that of the nation;
with it we must live or die. The king and chiefs broke down; and
after a night of prayer and deliberation the king said: "I will not
die piece-meal; they may cut off my head at once. I will yield the
breath of my kingdom and trust to my commissioners in London
and to the magnanimity of the British Government to redress the
wrong and restore my rights."

Preliminaries were arranged with the belligerent party for a
cession of the Islands, under protest; and on Saturday afternoon
at three o'clock on February 25, 1843, the Hawaiian flag we loved
so well was lowered in the Fort and an English one run up in its
place and saluted by the batteries of the Fort and the guns of the
Carysfort. English soldiers marched into the Fort and the band
played "God Save the Queen," and "Isle of Beauty, Fare Thee
Well." The latter was played by the request of some lady friends
of Lord George, and regarded by us as a refined cruelty which
could only emanate from a woman.

For five long months we ground in the prison house, like poor
blind Samson. After the cession my husband came home and
threw himself down utterly exhausted in body and mind after the
sleepless week of fasting and torture. I sat by him two hours ran-
sacking heart and brain for arguments of consolation. There was
no stain on his character; he had committed no crime. No blood
had been shed. He had done his best, and what more could be
required? . . .

A commission was formed for the government of the Islands, consisting of Lord George Paulet, one of his officers . . . and G. P. Judd, the king's deputy. One of the Government schooners was immediately dispatched to bear the news to the admiral at Valparaiso. Dr. Judd was retained in the financial department and left in possession of the Government papers. The king and premier returned to Maui. Every avenue of communication with the king or foreign countries was most jealously watched and guarded by his lordship in order to prevent any statement of affairs derogatory to his own from being sent abroad.

Dispatches, prepared in the silence of midnight in the royal tomb, with Kaahumanu's coffin for a table, were sent off in canoes from distant points of the island; and once when the king's signature was required, he came down in a schooner and landed incognito at Waikiki, a neighboring village, at twilight, read and signed the prepared documents, and was on his way back across the channel, while his lordship was dining and having a pleasant time with his friends.

This lasted some three months, when Dr. Judd, finding the conditions of the cessions were disregarded by the other members of the commission, protested and withdrew the king from further participation in their councils. . . . The archives were carefully removed from the office and deposited in the royal tomb. . . .

We had just arisen from family devotions one morning, where we had been pleading for the prostrate nation in the hands of those who were crushing out its vitality and trampling in the dust its best interests, when we were startled by the native cry, "Sail ho!" An immense man-of-war hove in sight, floating the flag of an English rear admiral of the white. What was his errand? Had he brought relief, or had he come to declare our bondage perpetual? We held our very breath to await the answer.

Admiral Thomas landed and requested an immediate interview with the native authorities. The first glimpse of his mild, benevolent face inspired confidence. Negotiations were not difficult. The admiral, who had ordered the *Carysfort* here, was evidently pained at the course pursued and anxious to restore the king. Lord George had destroyed every Hawaiian flag he could find, flattering

himself they would never again be called for. The admiral had a
new one made on board the *Dublin* expressly for the restoration
ceremony.

It was on Saturday, July 31, a little more than five months after
the cession or seizure, that the marines from the *Dublin, Carysfort*
and other English ships . . . were ordered to be on the parade
ground on the plain in full uniform at eight o'clock A.M. . . . A
pavilion was erected for the ladies. Foreign residents of all classes,
missionaries, and thousands of natives assembled at an early hour.
Admiral Thomas preceded the king in the carriage of the latter.
When the king, on horseback, arrived upon the ground, the
admiral gave him a salute of twenty-one guns. . . . Lord George
was not present.

At a signal given, the English flag officer advanced toward the
king, surrounded by his guards, bowed his colors most gracefully,
while the splendid Hawaiian standard was unfurled, and, as the
breeze caught its ample folds, displaying the dove and olive
branch in the center, the guns from the *Carysfort* fired first, then
the *Dublin* and other English ships, followed by two American
ships of war. Each poured forth a salute of twenty-one guns,
which was responded to by the fort and battery of old Punchbowl.

The roar and reverberations were loud and long, and one would
think the royal slumbers in the adjacent tomb might be startled in
their long sleep. As the cannons ceased, thousands of human
voices mingled in one patriotic cheer. Men and boys, black, white
and red, shouted themselves hoarse as the king returned from the
plain. The king and chiefs proceeded to the stone church, where
in the midst of a great congregation they gave thanks to their God
for deliverance from a foreign yoke.

August 12, 1849, the French frigate *La Poursuivante,* Admiral
de Tromelin, arrived from Hilo where she had been for ten days.
The admiral called on me with Madame Dillon. . . . Sunday the
French steamer *Gassendi* arrived from Tahiti. The political atmosphere portends a storm. . . . [On the] 22d, a dispatch was received from the admiral couched in very imperative terms, de-

manding an immediate interview with the king . . . and before
it could be replied to was followed by another. . . .

The demands were as follows:

The reduction of duty on French brandy.
A rigorous equality for the two forms of Christian worship.
The adoption of the French language in official intercourse between
French and Hawaiians.
Concession and redress with reference to customs duties, and the
return of a small fine imposed on a French vessel for the infringe-
ment of custom-house regulations.
An official apology for the impious conduct of certain native pupils
of the High School at Lahainaluna (who had put their hands in
the holy water).
Indemnity to the keeper of the French hotel for property damaged
by some drunken *English* sailors.
The removal from office of the governor of Hawaii, who enforced
the payment of taxes by a person in the employ of a French priest
on Hawaii, and who evaded the policemen by sheltering himself
in the house of said priest.

Prompt compliance was required or the admiral "would resort to
the means at his disposal for coercion!"

Replies—calm, reasonable and dignified—from the king's cabinet
requesting the admiral to show cause for this extraordinary proceeding were of no avail. While the negotiations were pending,
and before the king's ultimatum was received, a French force of
sappers and miners was landed, who took possession of the fort
and magazine, and French guards were placed at the Custom
House and at the Government offices. The king's yacht and several
vessels belonging to foreigners were seized.

All the guns were thrown from the walls of the fort or spiked.
The magazine was opened and the powder poured into the sea.
All the old muskets, swords and bayonets that could be found
were broken to pieces, and every article on the premises destroyed,
not sparing the old clock on the walls of the governor's house. Two
large camphor-wood trunks containing *kahili* feathers and various
articles belonging to Kinau were carried on board the French

ships, and even the calabashes were smashed and thrown into the
well.

This glorious warfare was carried on by the soldiers of that
most chivalrous nation without the slightest resistance on the part
of natives or foreigners. The damage amounted to $100,000 at a
fair estimate. While the French were doing this mischief, not to
redress a national wrong, but in obedience to the orders of M.
Dillon, for personal revenge upon the minister, the French flag
was pulled down at the consulate, and the Hawaiian Government
held responsible for damage to French property, and Madame's
furniture removed from her residence in the valley a mile above
our dwelling to the steamer *Gassendi.*

She called on her way down, as we had always been on the most
friendly terms, and assured me of the most kindly feelings on the
part of herself, her husband and the admiral toward the king and
all his cabinet, with the exception of the Minister of Foreign Relations. . . . The consul had *power* now, and would have satisfaction for all he had suffered of insult and indignity at the hands
of the minister. She offered protection for me and the children on
board the steamer and assured me that if still harsher measures
were resorted to, great care would be taken to save our premises.
. . .

I thanked her for her kind offer, but replied that our interests
were identified with the Hawaiians, and their fate must be ours. I
could see no just cause for this destruction of property, as all the
disputed points . . . had been referred to France for adjudica-
tion, and the other complaints had been settled in our courts of
justice—the only proper place. . . . And thus we parted. Madame
Dillon took refuge on board the war steamer, and I remained at
my own quiet home.

On the evening of the same day Judge Lee and Dr. Judd went
on board the *Gassendi* with the king's dispatches to the admiral,
where they remained several hours endeavoring to negotiate a
settlement. The French guards were still at their station before
the Custom House and Government offices.

Some of my kind neighbors came in to express their sympathies,
fearing the commissioners would be detained on board as prisoners

of war or harmed in some way, and were quite surprised to find me *asleep!* . . . It is difficult to restrain the tide of indignation called forth among all classes, native and foreign. They would most willingly rush to arms, but their resistance would only afford pretext for further aggression.

September 4th—The king's yacht was manned by Frenchmen and sent to sea. We watched the little beauty as she glided out of the harbor, with no benediction on the heads of the actors in these proceedings.

The wrath of M. Dillon is appeased by the wreck of property he has caused, and after exchanging another billet-doux with the minister, he has embarked bag and baggage for San Francisco on the *Gassendi*. In order to appreciate the necessity of this manifestation of French prowess, one must know the magnitude of French interests in these islands. Aside from the priests and their missions, there are twelve French subjects, one of whom is a merchant who transacts about one-thousandth part of the commercial business of the place.

September 6th—Dr. Judd returned from Privy Council and handed me the following: "It has pleased the king to nominate G. P. Judd, his Minister of Finance, as his Majesty's Special Commissioner and Plenipotentiary Extraordinary to the Governments of France, England and the United States."

September 11th—Dr. Judd is gone. He sailed on the schooner *Honolulu* . . . bound for San Francisco, accompanied by the two princes, Alexander Liholiho and Lot Kamehameha. The king, queen, chiefs, and a large concourse of natives and foreigners accompanied them to the ship. The welkin rang with cheers for their success and a speedy return, and all the ships manned their yards to do them honor. But what consolation does it all afford to wife and children quite away from this demonstration in their own distant dwelling, weeping and watching the little craft that bears from them the joy of their hearts, the light of their home, their stay and staff.

One cargo of French merchandise has been imported and one French ship of war has visited the islands during the last five years. French schooners have occasionally brought freight for

English and American merchants, and there are a few whalers in the Pacific who touch now and then at this port.

There is no prejudice against Frenchmen as such, and the few residents among us express their unmitigated disapproval of the late proceedings. Admiral de Tromelin is only to be blamed for allowing himself to be the tool in the hands of the consul, as did Lord George Paulet. Both acted contrary to their own convictions of right, but were constrained to do the bidding of their respective consuls.

September 15th—The French ships are all gone. The war is all over, and we have visited the battleground, and what a scene is presented! Those famous old guns, used only for the exchange of friendly and national greetings . . . all thrown from their carriages, spiked and mutilated! The ground is covered with broken muskets, cartridge boxes, bayonets and swords. Every window and door of the governor's house is broken and battered, and the walls are covered with charcoal sketches. Every box, barrel and calabash is crushed to atoms. A glorious victory!

From *Honolulu: Sketches of the Life Social, Political and Religious in the Hawaiian Islands from 1828 to 1861,* Laura Fish Judd (New York: Randolph and Co., 1880).

XXVIII

Herman Melville

A New Yorker who was eventually to be ranked as one of the giants in American literature was an eyewitness to those "Dark Days" under Lord George Paulet in Honolulu—no other than Herman Melville (1819–1891), author-to-be of the masterpieces *Typee, Omoo* and *Moby Dick.* He was only twenty-three at the time, but had already seen enough of Polynesia and the whaling industry to gather authentic background for the best of his writing.

In 1841 and 1842 he spent eighteen months on the whaler *Acushnet* exposed to such unendurable hardships that he deserted in the Marquesas, where he was captured by cannibals, and fortuitously spared until rescued by an Australian whaler. The Australians put him ashore on safer Tahiti, and from there he made his way home via Honolulu.

It was on this leg of his retreat that he was first introduced to Oahu. Morale in the Islands was at a low ebb, and after having lived among natives less contaminated by Western commerce, he was not very favorably impressed with Hawaiians. Moreover, in his penniless state, he accepted temporary employment as a clerk in a British trading firm in Honolulu and quite naturally swung over to their political outlook.

He gave vent to his sentiments regarding Hawaiians and their missionary indoctrinators in a denunciation later inserted by his publishers as an irrelevant appendix to the novel *Typee.* It was a forceful, incisive, impassioned diatribe, a dialectic gem—but unfortunately it reflected the bias of the British and indicated that Melville was either misinformed or careless with facts, for Dr. Judd, whom he excoriated as a quack, had excellent credentials as a physician, and the error in labeling the missionaries "Methodist," when everyone else knew they were conspicuously Congregational, dulled the sting of his argument.

Connecticut Blue Laws Abrogated

No transaction has ever been more grossly misrepresented than the events which occurred upon the arrival of Lord George Paulet at Oahu. During a residence of four months at Honolulu, the metropolis of the group, the author was in the confidence of an Englishman who was much employed by his lordship; and great was the author's astonishment on his arrival at Boston, in the autumn of 1844, to read the distorted accounts and fabrications which had produced in the United States so violent an outbreak of indignation against the English. . . .

It is needless to rehearse all the abuse that for some time previous to the spring of 1843 had been heaped upon the British residents, especially upon Captain Charlton, Her Britannic-Majesty's consul-general, by the native authorities of the Sandwich Islands. High in the favor of the imbecile king at this time was one Dr. Judd, a sanctimonious apothecary-adventurer, who, with other kindred and influential spirits, were animated by an inveterate dislike to England.

The ascendancy of a junta of ignorant and designing Methodist elders in the councils of a half-civilized king, ruling with absolute sway over a nation just poised between barbarism and civilization, and exposed by the peculiarities of its relations with foreign states to unusual difficulties, was not precisely calculated to impart a healthy tone to the policy of the government.

At last matters were brought to such an extremity, through the iniquitous maladministration of affairs that the endurance of further insults and injuries on the part of the British consul was no longer to be borne. Captain Charlton, insultingly forbidden to leave the islands, clandestinely withdrew, and arriving at Valparaiso, conferred with Rear-Admiral Thomas, the English commander-in-chief on the Pacific station.

In consequence of this communication, Lord George Paulet was dispatched by the admiral in the *Carysfort* frigate, to inquire into and correct the alleged abuses. On arriving at his destination, he sent his first lieutenant ashore with a letter to the king, couched in terms of the utmost courtesy, and soliciting the honor of an audience.

The messenger was denied access to His Majesty, and Paulet was coolly referred to Dr. Judd, and informed that the apothecary was invested with plenary powers to treat with him. Rejecting this insolent proposition, his lordship again addressed the king by letter, and renewed his previous request; but he encountered another repulse. Justly indignant at this treatment, he penned a third epistle, enumerating the grievances to be redressed and demanding a compliance with his requisitions, under penalty of immediate hostilities.

The government was now obliged to act, and an artful stroke of policy was decided upon by the despicable councillors of the king to entrap the sympathies and rouse the indignation of Christendom. His Majesty was made to intimate to the British captain that he could not, as the conscientious ruler of his beloved people, comply with the arbitrary demands of his lordship, and in deprecation of the horrors of war, tendered to his acceptance the *provisional cession* of the islands, subject to the result of the negotiations then pending in London.

Paulet, a bluff and straightforward sailor, took the king at his word, and after some preliminary arrangements, entered upon the administration of Hawaiian affairs, in the same firm and benignant spirit which marked the discipline of his frigate, and which rendered him the idol of his ship's company. He soon endeared himself to nearly all orders of the islanders; but the king and the chiefs, whose feudal sway over the common people was laboriously sought to be perpetuated by their missionary advisers, regarded all his proceedings with the most vigilant animosity.

Jealous of his growing popularity, and unable to counteract it, they endeavored to assail his reputation abroad by ostensibly protesting against his acts, and appealing in Oriental phrase to the *wide universe* to witness and compassionate their *unparalleled wrongs*.

Heedless of their idle clamors, Lord George Paulet addressed himself to the task of reconciling the differences among the foreign residents, remedying their grievances, promoting their mercantile interests, and ameliorating, as far as lay in his power, the condition of the degraded natives. The iniquities he brought to light and instantly suppressed are too numerous to be here recorded; but one instance may be mentioned that will give some idea of the lamentable misrule to which these poor islanders are subjected.

It is well known that the laws at the Sandwich Islands are subject to the most capricious alterations, which, by confounding all ideas of right and wrong in the minds of the natives, produce the most pernicious effects. In no case is this mischief more plainly discernible than in the continually shifting regulations concerning licentiousness. At one time the most innocent freedoms between the sexes are punished with fine and imprisonment; at another the revocation of the statute is followed by the most open and undisguised profligacy.

It so happened that at the period of Paulet's arrival, the Connecticut blue laws had been for at least three weeks steadily enforced. In consequence of this, the fort at Honolulu was filled with a great number of young girls, who were confined there doing penance for their slips from virtue. Paulet, although at first unwilling to interfere with regulations having reference solely to natives themselves, was eventually, by the prevalence of certain reports, induced to institute a strict inquiry into the internal administration of General Kekuanoa, governor of the island of Oahu, one of the pillars of the Hawaiian Church, and captain of the fort.

He soon ascertained that numbers of the young females employed during the day at work intended for the benefit of the king, were at night smuggled over the ramparts of the fort—

which on one side directly overhangs the sea—and were conveyed by stealth on board such vessels as had contracted with the General to be supplied with them. Before daybreak they returned to their quarters, and their silence with regard to these secret excursions was purchased by a small portion of those wages of iniquity which were placed in the hands of Kekuanoa.

The vigor with which the laws concerning licentiousness were at that period enforced, enabled the General to monopolize in a great measure the detestable trade in which he was engaged, and there consequently flowed into his coffers—and some say into those of the government also—considerable sums of money. It is indeed a lamentable fact that the principal revenue of the Hawaiian government is derived from the fines levied upon, or rather the licences taken out by Vice, the prosperity of which is linked with that of the government. Were the people to become virtuous, the authorities would become poor; but from present indications there is little apprehension to be entertained on that score.

Some five months after the date of the cession, the *Dublin* frigate, carrying the flag of Rear-Admiral Thomas, entered the harbor of Honolulu. The excitement that her sudden appearance produced on shore was prodigious. Three days after her arrival an English sailor hauled down the red cross which had been flying from the heights of the fort, and the Hawaiian colors were again displayed upon the same staff.

At the same moment the long 42-pounders upon Punchbowl Hill opened their iron throats in triumphant reply to the thunders of the five men-of-war in the harbor; and King Kamehameha III, surrounded by a splendid group of British and American officers, unfurled the royal standard to assembled thousands of his subjects, who, attracted by the imposing military display of the foreigners, had flocked to witness the formal restoration of the islands to their ancient rulers.

The admiral, after sanctioning the proceedings of his subaltern, had brought the authorities to terms; and so removed the necessity of acting any longer under the provisional cession.

The event was made an occasion of riotous rejoicing by the king and the principal chiefs, who easily secured a display of enthusiasm from the inferior orders, by remitting for a time the accustomed severity of the laws. Royal proclamations in English and Hawaiian were placarded in the streets of Honolulu, and posted up in the more populous villages of the group, in which His Majesty announced to his loving subjects the re-establishment of his throne, and called upon them to celebrate it by breaking through all moral, legal and religious restraint for ten consecutive days, during which time all the laws of the land were solemnly declared to be suspended.

Who that happened to be at Honolulu during those ten memorable days will ever forget them! The spectacle of universal broadday debauchery, which was then exhibited, beggars description. The natives of the surrounding islands flocked to Honolulu by hundreds, and the crews of two frigates, opportunely let loose like so many demons to swell the heathenish uproar, gave the crowning flourish to the scene. It was a sort of Polynesian saturnalia.

Deeds too atrocious to be mentioned were done at noonday in the open street, and some of the islanders, caught in the very act of stealing from the foreigners, were, on being taken to the fort by the aggrieved party, suffered immediately to go at large and to retain the stolen property—Kekuanoa informing the white men, with a sardonic grin, that the laws were *hannapa* (tied up).

The history of those ten days reveals in their true colors the character of the Sandwich islanders, and furnishes an eloquent commentary on the results which have flowed from the labors of the missionaries. Freed from the restraint of severe penal laws, the natives almost to a man had plunged voluntarily into every species of wickedness and excess, and by their utter disregard of all decency plainly showed that, although they had been schooled into a seeming submission to the new order of things, they were in reality as depraved and vicious as ever.

Such were the events which produced in America so general an outbreak of indignation against the spirited and high-minded Paulet. He is not the first man who, in the fearless discharge of his duty, has awakened the senseless clamors of those whose narrow-minded suspicions blind them to a proper appreciation of measures which unusual exigencies may have rendered necessary.

It is almost needless to add that the British cabinet never had any idea of appropriating the islands; and it furnishes a sufficient vindication of the acts of Lord George Paulet, that he not only received the unqualified approbation of his own government, but that to this hour the great body of the Hawaiian people invoke blessings on his head, and look back with gratitude to the time when his liberal and paternal sway diffused peace and happiness among them.

From *Typee, a Peep at Polynesian Life*, Herman Melville (London: J. M. Dent and Sons Ltd., New York: E. P. Dutton and Company, 1907).

XXIX

R. T. Macoun

Despite the periodic chaos in political affairs, the Sandwich Islands never looked better to any outlanders than they did at midcentury to fugitives from the gold rush country of California. On the Coast the golden rule had been altered to read "Every man for himself." Its devotees were all in a hurry to get to their pickings at the mines ahead of someone else; in the absence of other law and order, a six-shooter or a noose served as the accepted means of winning justice. Food of any kind was scarce, unpalatable, and exorbitantly priced. Public lodgings were virtually nonexistent in a society where every-one was on the move. Peace and quiet were luxuries no man could purchase. With their picks and spades a throng of avaricious Argo-nauts could turn an idyllic natural setting into a scene of confused squalor in half a day.

The few who managed to wangle passage from San Francisco to Hawaii made the inevitable comparison between Pandemonium and Paradise. Lieutenant R. T. Macoun of the United States Navy, spare-time poet and correspondent for the *Knickerbocker Magazine,* was one of them. His opinion of rowdy California was the less flattering because he was unable to get shore leave to go gold-digging; he was attached to the *North Carolina,* doing patrol duty for a full year during the height of the furor.

Then unexpectedly his ship was ordered to Hawaii, and he could bid farewell to infernal San Francisco. "It was a happy day," he sighed, "when the anchor went up to our bows and we spread sails for the islands." Two weeks later the *North Carolina* hove to in "Byron's Bay"—Hilo Harbor. By contrast, here lay before him a land of aloha exchanged for a land of greed, a land of plenty for one of privation, a land of leisure for one of mad scramble—a land not entirely dominated by males.

In Communion with Bountiful Nature

Before the sails were furled, the ship was surrounded by more than fifty canoes, filled with natives and freighted with poultry and vegetables. Such a chattering and such shouts of laughter my ears were never before saluted with; they all appeared to have gone crazy with joy, and to have lost all control of themselves. . . .

The view of the shore from the anchorage was charming. Toward the south, as far as eye could reach, a verdant plain was spread out before me, whose shores were washed by the ocean; and to the northwest the land rose gradually toward the interior, until far inland the snow-capped summits of Mauna Loa and Mauna Kea reached an elevation of nearly 16,000 feet above the level of the sea.

Along the shore, the coconut tree waved its feathery branches to the refreshing tradewinds; and the thatched roofs of the village of Hilo peeped here and there from among the deep foliage in which they were imbedded; while just beyond, the landscape was occasionally studded with fields of the coffee plant and waving sugar cane. . . .

Strolling through the village and surrounding country, I passed many very pleasant days in visiting the habitations of the natives and witnessing their primitive mode of life. . . . Wherever I went I was greeted with smiling faces and received the national salutation of "Aloha" or welcome; and I scarcely ever remember to have passed a house without having been invited to enter.

I almost invariably found the family to be very numerous in proportion to the size of the domicile. They were generally quite unoccupied, some lolling about the mat floor, others fast asleep under a piece of tapa cloth. As soon as I was seated, the female part of the household, with the natural curiosity of the sex, usually approached to scrutinize the dress and appearance of the . . . stranger. They would examine me from head to foot with the utmost particularity, every now and then exclaiming, "*Mai-kai*," pretty, when they noticed anything which met with their approbation. . . .

It was quite diverting to behold a half-dozen or a dozen natives gathered round a large calabash of *poi*, and to witness with what surprising rapidity each one in his turn would dip two fingers of the right hand into the vessel and convey a large portion to his mouth, which was held wide for its reception. To give zest to this repast, a little salt fish, or salt water, is usually at hand, of which each occasionally partakes. . . . The ancient custom of eating raw fish is still continued in this island; nor is it confined only to the lower class of people. . . . Dogs are also eaten and considered a great delicacy. . . .

The young girls, though a little dark, are often quite handsome, and usually very interesting. Their glossy raven hair, fully unconfined upon the shoulders and frequently curly in natural ringlets; their dark, lustrous eyes, as soft as a gazelle's, and full of expression; their teeth of matchless whiteness and regularity, embellished faces that appeared to know only how to smile. And the villainous dress which civilization has placed upon their backs, consisting of a single loose gown, unconfined at the waist, could not altogether hide their fine figures and well-turned limbs, which they appeared very fond of displaying to the best advantage. . . .

At the edge of the village is the beautiful little river Wai-Rouka [Wailuku], which, descending rapidly over its rocky bed, through wild and picturesque mountain passes, forms two beautiful cascades just before it empties itself into the ocean. The stream above and below these cascades is the common bathing place for the whole village. From early dawn until evening, it is thronged with swimmers of both sexes, and of all ages and sizes, some of whom are seen sporting like so many porpoises in their natural element, some diving from cliffs twenty or thirty feet high, while others are reclining upon the rocks and basking themselves in the broiling hot sun.

But the greatest diversion here, especially among the young girls, was to plunge into the stream above and allow themselves to be swept down by the rapids over the cascade. Whether this preference was caused by a species of savage coquetry, arising from a desire to display their sylph-like forms to the best advantage, I will not pretend to say; but certainly these island beauties, as free from the incumbrance of dress as was their mother Eve before the fall, appeared to be highly pleased when they attracted particular attention.

I often passed an hour sitting upon the banks of the Wai-Rouka witnessing the graceful movements of these Naïads, as they fearlessly sprang into the stream, were swept down over the rocks by the boiling rapids with the speed of a race-horse, until arriving at the edge of the cascade they were launched off into the white foam, then plunged into the calm, deep basin below, and still visible, sank down, down through the crystal waters, until suddenly rising again to the surface, they shook the diamond shower from their flowing tresses, swam toward the precipitous rocky walls that shut in the stream on each side, nimbly clambered up the sides and joyously returned to perform the same feat over again. . . .

The imagination of the poet, which has pictured to us sunny climes where the blasts of winter are unknown, where the earth is clothed in perennial verdure, and man lives in communion with bountiful nature that ministers to all wants, without toil, was perhaps never more nearly realized than in the Sandwich Islands before adventure drew to their shore civilized man.

From "A Glimpse at the Sandwich Islands," R. T. Macoun, *Knickerbocker Magazine,* November 1851.

XXX

Richard Henry Dana

Richard Henry Dana never relinquished the attachment he formed for Kanakas at San Diego in 1835. Shortly after leaving them he had commented that he would go a long way to renew some of those acquaintances; and exactly a quarter of a century later he proved that he meant it by going a very long way—crossing the continent and sailing to Hawaii for a two months' visit.

But on reaching his destination, the thing that impressed him even more than the character of the natives and the attractiveness of their homeland was the character of the missionaries and what they had accomplished. Now widely recognized as a sophisticated American savant, prominent in national politics, distinguished in maritime and international law, a brilliant writer, wise to the ways of the world— and a good Episcopalian—he was hardly one that the missionaries would have deigned to choose as their defender. Even they must have been amazed at the glowing tribute—an open bread-and-butter letter —he voluntarily sent to the New York *Tribune.*

The Saviors of Hawaii

It is no small thing to say of the Missionaries of the American Board that in less than forty years they have taught this whole people to read and to write, to cipher and to sew. They have given them an alphabet, grammar and dictionary; preserved their language from extinction; given it a literature, and translated into it the Bible and works of devotion, science and entertainment, etc., etc.

They have established schools, reared up native teachers, and so pressed their work that now the proportion of inhabitants who can read and write is greater than in New England; and whereas they found these islanders a nation of half-naked savages, living in the surf and on the sand, eating raw fish, fighting among themselves, tyrannized over by feudal chiefs and abandoned to sensuality, they now see them decently clothed, recognizing the law of marriage, knowing something of accounts, going to school and public worship with more regularity than people do at home; and the more elevated of them taking part in conducting the affairs of the constitutional monarchy under which they live, holding seats on the judicial bench and in the legislative chambers, and filling posts in the local magistracies.

It is often objected against missionaries that a people must be civilized before it can be Christianized; or at least that the two processes must go on together, and that the mere preacher, with his book under his arm, among a barbarous people, is an unprofitable laborer. But the missionaries to the Sandwich Islands went out in families and planted themselves in households, carrying with them and exhibiting to the natives the customs, manners, comforts, discipline and order of civilized society.

Each house was a center and source of civilizing influences; and the natives generally yielded to the superiority of our civilization and copied its ways; for, unlike the Asiatics, they had no civilization of their own and, unlike the North American Indians, they were capable of civilization. Each missionary was obliged to qualify himself to some extent as a physician and surgeon before leaving home; and each mission house had its medicine chest, and was the place of resort by the natives for medicines and medical advice and care.

Each missionary was a school teacher to the natives in their own language; and the women of the missions, who were no less missionaries than their husbands, taught schools for women and children, instructing them not only in books, but in sewing, knitting and ironing, in singing by note and in the discipline of children. These mission families, too, were planted as garrisons would have been planted by a military conqueror in places where there were no inducements of trade to carry families, so that no large region, however difficult of access or undesirable as a residence, is without its headquarters of religion and civilization.

The women of the mission, too, can approach the native women and children in many ways not open to men—as in their sickness, and by the peculiar sympathies of sex—and thus exert the tenderest, which are often the most decisive, influences.

In the course of the two months I have spent upon these Islands, it has been my good fortune to be the guest of many of the mission families, and to become more or less acquainted with nearly all of them. And, besides fidelity in the discharge of their duties to the natives, I can truly say that in point of kindness and hospitality to strangers, of intelligence and general information, of solicitude and painstaking for the liberal education of their children, and of zeal for the acquirement of information of every sort, it would be difficult to find their superiors among the most favored families at home.

I have seen in their houses collections of minerals, shells, plants and flowers which must be valuable to science; and the missionaries have often preserved the best, sometimes the only, records of the volcanic eruptions, earthquakes and other phenomena and meteorological observations. Besides having given, as I have said, to the native language an alphabet, grammar, dictionary and literature, they have done nearly all that has been done to preserve the national traditions, legends and poetry.

But for the missionaries, it is my firm belief that the Hawaiian would never have been a written language; there would have been few or no trustworthy early records, historical or scientific; the traditions would have perished; the native government would have been overborne by foreign influences, and the interesting, intelligent, gentle native race would have sunk into insignificance, and perhaps into servitude to the dominant whites.

The educational system of the Islands is the work of the missionaries and their supporters among the foreign residents, and one formerly of the mission is now Minister of Education. In every district are free schools for natives. In these they are taught reading, writing, singing by note, arithmetic, grammar and geography by native teachers. At Lahainaluna is the Normal School for natives, where the best scholars from the district schools are received and carried to an advanced stage of education, and those who desire it are fitted for the duties of teachers.

This was originally a mission school, but is now partly a government institution. Several of the missionaries in small and remote stations have schools for advanced studies, among which I visited several times that of Mr. Lyman at Hilo, where there are nearly one hundred native lads; and all the under teachers are natives. These lads had an orchestra of ten or twelve flutes, which made very creditable music.

At Honolulu there is a royal school for natives and another middle school for whites and half-castes; for it has been found expedient generally to separate the races in education. Both these schools are in excellent condition. But the special pride of the missionary efforts for education is the High School or College of Punahou. This was established for the education of the children of the mission families and has been enlarged to receive the children of other foreign residents, and is now an incorporated college with some seventy scholars.

The course of studies goes as far as the end of the sophomore year in our New England colleges and is expected soon to go farther. The teachers are young men of the mission families, taught first at this school, with educations finished in the colleges of New England, where they have taken high rank. At Williams College there were at one time five pupils from this school, one of whom was the first scholar, and four of whom were among the first seven scholars of the year; and another of the professors at Punahou was the first scholar of his year at New Haven.

I attended several recitations at Punahou in Greek, Latin and mathematics, and after having said that the teachers were leading scholars in our colleges, and the pupils mostly children of the

mission families, I need hardly add that I advised the young men
to remain there to the end of the course, as they could not pass
the freshman and sophomore years more profitably elsewhere,
in my judgment. . . . This institution must determine in a great
measure the character not only of the rising generation of whites,
but, as education proceeds downward and not upward, also that
of the natives. It is the chief hope of the people, who have spent
their utmost upon it. . . .

Among the traders, shipmasters and travelers who have visited
these Islands, some have made disparaging statements respecting
the missionaries; and a good deal of imperfect information is carried home by persons who have visited only the half-European-
ized ports, where the worst view of the condition of the natives
is presented. I visited among all classes—the foreign merchants,
traders and shipmasters, foreign and native officials, and with the
natives, from the king and several of the chiefs to the humblest
poor, whom I saw without constraint in a tour I made alone over
Hawaii, throwing myself upon their hospitality in their huts.

I sought information from all, foreign and native, friendly and
unfriendly; and the conclusion to which I came is that the best
men, and those who are best acquainted with the history of
things here, hold in high esteem the labors and conduct of the
missionaries. The mere seekers of pleasure, power or gain do not
like their influence; and those persons who sympathized with that
officer of the American navy who compelled the authorities to
allow women to go off to his ship by opening his ports and threat-
ening to bombard the town naturally are hostile to the missions. . . .

Doubtless the missionaries have largely influenced the legislation of the kingdom and its police system; it is fortunate that they
have done so. Influence of some kind was the law of the native
development. Had not the missionaries and their friends among
the foreign merchants and professional men been in the ascendant,
these Islands would have presented only the usual history of a
handful of foreigners exacting everything from a people who
denied their right to anything. As it is, in no place in the world

that I have visited are the rules which control vice and regulate amusements so strict, yet so reasonable, and so fairly enforced.

The government and the best citizens stand as a good genius between the natives and the besieging army. As to the interior, it is well known that a man may travel alone, with money, through the wildest spots, unarmed. Having just come from the mountains of California, I was prepared with the usual and necessary belt and its appendages of that region, but was told that these defences were unheard of in Hawaii.

I found no hut without its Bible and hymn book in the native tongue, and the practice of family prayer and grace before meat, though it be over no more than a calabash of *poi* and a few dried fish, and whether at home or on journeys, is as common as in New England a century ago.

It may be asked whether there is no offset, no deduction to be made from this high estimate of the American missionaries. As to their fidelity and industry in the worst of times and their success up to the point they have now reached, I can think of none.

Quoted from *The Hawaiian Islands, Their Progress and Condition under Missionary Labors,* Rufus Anderson (Boston: Gould and Lincoln, 1865).

XXXI

Henry M. Lyman

A conspicuous by-product of the growing importance of Hawaii as a whaling and commercial center was the influx of ship deserters, outlaws, and beachcombers—the dregs of marine society, brawling, lawless gangs, at odds with the authorities, the missionaries, and frequently themselves, and abetted by groups of irresponsible native admirers. To Honolulu and Lahaina they brought insurrection and riot; to lesser ports like Hilo, occasional terror and tumult.

The sheltered son of a missionary, Henry M. Lyman (1835–1904) saw these colorful characters, along with other foreign influences, in his early youth at Hilo. They made such a vivid impression—the beachcombers, the first store, the first sugar mill, the first saloon, the first Catholic church—that half a century later, when he had gained more worldly perspective as a distinguished physician, educator, and author, he could still recall them in vivid detail, with a sparkle of humor and a touch of nostalgia.

The Beachcombers of Hilo

My father, when walking abroad for exercise or on business, frequently encouraged me to trot along by his side. One day he turned out from the road to the sea and tried a new path that led toward the Wailuku River. Presently we came to a neat thatched house, surrounded and half hidden by a dense shrubbery of coffee plants in full bloom. The cottage—for such it was—unlike the ordinary native houses, was provided with a floor and with glass windows.

An agreeably furnished reception room opened on one side into an airy bedroom, and on another into a large apartment, crossed by a wooden counter and surrounded by shelves on which were piles of cotton cloth and all manner of curious articles, for the most part quite beyond my knowledge. Here we were welcomed by a stout, gray-headed old gentleman, whose kindly features were handsomely set off by an elegant pair of white mutton-chop whiskers. . . .

On the occasion of my first introduction to a "store," I was treated with much consideration, being permitted to explore the depths of a barrel of dried apples, and to experiment upon the contents of an ancient box of raisins. When at last my father drew me away from the contemplation of a conical loaf of white sugar, the shopkeeper cordially invoked my speedy return, and presented me with a small circular mirror, about three inches in diameter—a gift as gratifying to me as it could have been to any one of the little savages for whom it was originally designed.

From that date our occasional visits to the store were reckoned among the rare privileges of existence. To our unsophisticated vision, that emporium was a museum of wonders like those of which we had read, but nowhere else in our tiny world could find.

On another day, walking a little farther, we found the new road extended beyond a dense grove of breadfruit trees to a considerable enclosure where a number of thatched houses had been recently erected. Two or three almond-eyed gentlemen, with long braids of hair coiled about their heads, were persuading a yoke of half-tamed oxen to walk in a circle, dragging after them a beam that rotated three vertical wooden rollers, between which a native boy was insinuating slender stalks of sugar cane drawn from a pile by his side.

A rivulet of juice was pouring into a wooden gutter that pene-

trated the side of an adjacent building, from which a cloud of
steam continually escaped. One of the Chinamen laid down his
goad, unrolled his queue, and led us into the boiling-house, where
three large try-pots, evidently after long service in the extraction
of oil from the blubber of the sperm whale, were set in solid
masonry over a fire that was fed with the dried stalks of cane
from which the sap had been previously pressed.

Into these cauldrons the juice flowed from the mill, and in them
it was bubbling and steaming at a furious rate. The pig-tailed
gentleman courteously explained to us, in choice Cantonese English, how to know when the process had been carried far enough;
and then he showed us the syrup, ladled hot from the kettles,
and set aside to crystallize in queer conical jars of porous Chinese
earthenware, which finally were placed in rows to drain away the
molasses that trickled into sundry rude wooden canoes, wherein
floated dead flies, cockroaches and adventurous mice without
number.

This was the first sugar mill established on the island of Hawaii.
When we visited the place next year, the old bullock-mill had
given way to a larger system of horizontal rollers, connected with
a fine overshot wheel turned by a dashing stream of water diverted
from its original course to the sea, and now compelled for the
first time in its existence to work for a living.

Besides these industrious Orientals, our village was the abode of
a small contingent of Occidentals who, in point of morality, did
not compare very favorably with the despised Asiatics. They were
for the most part ancient mariners who in some way had parted
company with the ships that bore them to our shore. One of them
was a dark-skinned fellow from the Iberian peninsula, who was
unknown by any other appellation than that of "John the Portu-
gee."

Always an object of suspicion, he finally, when the New Bedford whalers began to gather at our island, threw off all reserve
and placed over his door a board on which were rudely painted
the suggestive symbols, a bottle and a glass. This overt act aroused
the guardians of public morality, and after a long struggle the
obnoxious sign was relegated to the interior of its owner's abode;

but the actual bottle and its accompanying glass, I fear, were irrepressible.

Quite conspicuous in the little gang of beachcombers was a jovial young Englishman with blue eyes and chestnut curls, whose battered nose proclaimed him a hero in many a fistic encounter. He was really a good sailor, and was stirred with ambition to become the pilot of the harbor. Unfortunately, when ships came in sight, it was too often the case that poor Christopher had to lie under the pump before he could be made presentable as the Palinurus of our port; so he gradually sank into oblivion.

Another Englishman also dwelt near us—one of the lowest and stupidest of his kind. He lived like a pig in a miserable hovel with a slatternly native woman for a wife; and professing to have been a carpenter's mate on the ship from which his residence had been —accidentally of course—transferred to the shore, he occasionally earned a few honest dollars with the help of sundry borrowed tools that were not always returned until replevined by the lender.

After such wearisome labor he would remain in the seclusion of his stye until all supplies were exhausted, when with the regularity of the sun, he would sally forth and levy the contribution of a meal whenever he found a family that could tolerate his demands. While yet a very small boy, I once fearfully enraged him by calling him a beggar as he sat at our door munching the breakfast which my mother was daily providing at the expense of her entire stock of patience. He came no more; but it was merely a shift of the pain, for he immediately installed himself as a beneficiary of the Coans. It was a real relief when he went the way of all the earth.

Far off by himself, alone on the north point near the entrance of the bay, dwelt a red-faced, gray-haired Welshman, commonly called "John the Pilot," to distinguish him from that other John, the Lusitanian vendor of contraband spirits. On the appearance of ships heading toward the harbor, the veteran was wont to sally forth in a canoe, paddled by his half-caste children and retainers, offering service as a qualified guide to the port.

In after years, when the shipping became more abundant, and

another pilot was seeking to obtain a share in the emoluments of the business, the old man purchased a whaleboat, in which, while his rival was puffing a fragrant Manila cigar and basking in the midst of his family at home, he would lie, far out at sea, waiting for the prey. Great was the expenditure of profanity over the frequent success of the nautical maneuver!

There was also a debauched little fellow, known by the name of a very aristocratic English family, who wore a black skull-cap to conceal the disgraceful scars on his bald head. He claimed to be the possessor of a medical education, though he never prescribed, unless for the members of his own congenial set. He affected literary tastes, and was an avowed admirer of Voltaire and Thomas Paine; consequently, in the estimation of our parents, he was scarcely a shade better than the Evil One himself.

Of contemporaneous American seamen in retirement, I remember only two or three specimens. They dwelt apart from the British—for the animosities of the War of 1812 had not yet died out; and when liquor was scarce, they made some pretense of a decent life, assuming an aspect of mournful resignation, like decayed gentlemen under the stress of inevitable misfortune.

The preponderance of the Anglican party and its peculiar degradation, were due to the fact that for many years Hawaii was a haven of refuge for convicts, who, from the reservoir in Botany Bay, were continually escaping and filtering through the sands all over the broad Pacific Ocean.

Such were some of the ornaments of the beach, who in that remote period, outside the storekeepers and the missionary circles, were the sole exemplars of the white man's glorious civilization. But with the gradual increase of foreign trade, other more respectable settlers came among us, and were not without influence in favor of righteousness.

There was a period, however, about the time the New Bedford and Nantucket harpooners, fresh from pursuit of the Alaskan whale, were beginning to winter in the Hawaiian harbors, when our houses were for several months at the mercy of a band of desperadoes who deserted their ships, concealing themselves in the fern woods until the departure of the fleet. When they then came forth from their hiding, they were at once captured by the native police, and in obedience to the law were incontinently clapped into jail.

But this little ceremony did not in the least interfere with their pleasures. The jail was simply a large native house where male-factors were invited to reside at the expense of the government while under sentence of imprisonment. Our jolly jack-tars accepted the hospitality of the jailor at mealtime, or when it rained; but the balance of their time was joyously occupied with the society of their numerous friends whenever and wherever they willed. They sometimes, as a concession to uncharitable public opinion, allowed a native policeman to guide them in their walks abroad; but if not sufficiently complaisant, he was soon clubbed into sub-mission.

Finally the troop—some thirty-five or forty strong—became so audacious as to raise the piratical flag, and, armed with bludgeons, they marched around the town, roaring ribald songs and shouting defiance as they went. So dilatory were the official communica-tions with the capital that the lapse of three or four months and the opportune arrival of a ship of war were necessary before our community could be relieved of this incubus, and we could safely resume our exercise abroad.

Besides these enemies of good order, there was another foe whom our parents dreaded more than all the rest. Walking with my father one evening, we saw through the dusky twilight a strange figure drawing near under the protection of a shovel-hat and a black frock that reached to his feet. Staring blankly through a pair of spectacles into space, it made the sign of the cross and uttered a deprecatory ejaculation as it hurried past.

I instinctively shrank behind my father and, anxiously inquiring the significance of an apparition so uncanny, was informed that it was the Roman Catholic priest who had recently descended upon our fold. Ah! I knew what that meant, because as far back as I could remember, "Fox's Book of Martyrs" was one of our chief sources of Sunday recreation and joy.

A few weeks later . . . I discovered a lonely native building, newly erected in an unfrequented part of town and open to the winds of heaven. A rude cross surmounted the ridgepole, and a few tawdry colored prints looked down upon a floor of dried grass. A sort of wooden cupboard standing at the end opposite the door, and a gourd-shell of holy water fixed on the doorpost, made up the entire furniture.

Informed that this was the Roman Catholic chapel, we were stricken with terror, and fled for our lives, lest we too might somehow get burned at the stake like poor John Huss or John Rodgers and his wife with her "nine children in arms and one at the breast," whose martyrdom, depicted in certain popular volumes, made our tender flesh creep with horror as we read.

I do not know the name of the priest who ministered to the few waifs and strays who then formed the shabby island following of the Holy See, but when, at the age of sixteen or seventeen years, I made the acquaintance of Father Charles Pougot, the refined and delicate-looking Frenchman who cared for the parish of Hilo, I found him a very saintly-seeming personage.

His flock, however, consisted for the most part of the devotees of tobacco and other loose livers whom Mr. Coan would not tolerate within his church on any consideration whatever. No matter how upright and virtuous their lives, men and women who would not forsake the pipe were bundled out of the congregation of true-believers and handed over to the tender mercies of Satan and his host. All such hardened sinners were joyfully welcomed, as brands rescued from the burning, by the proselyters of the True Church, so that in a short time the papal emissaries laid claim to the souls of all who were not actually enrolled on the books of the American mission. . . .

So these good men anathematized each other, and stood asunder as long as they lived. But with their antagonisms I meddled not; and when I left home for the last time, the kindly Father gave me a little French dictionary that still stands in my library. Thirty years later, when his eyesight grew dim, I sent him a massbook, printed in the largest and clearest type that could be procured; and he responded with a cordial letter of thanks, written only a short time before his death.

From *Hawaiian Yesterdays,* Henry M. Lyman (Chicago: A. C. McClurg, 1906).

XXXII

Mark Twain

For almost half a century, nations of prestige and importance had been practicing the diplomatic art of showing contempt for a nation of little prestige and importance by accrediting third-rate representatives to Hawaii. Honolulu had put up with more than its due share of these undiplomatic agents.

And then came an unofficial ambassador from the United States who brought the Island kingdom a form of recognition that no suave, top-hatted political representative could ever have elicited. He came as an obscure, vagrant journalist, yet within a few months after his visit, audiences and the reading public across America and in England were laughing at and loving the Sandwich Islanders. Any nation that could be the subject of such amiable humor throughout the English-speaking world was above the need of acquiring ephemeral prestige and importance.

In 1866 Samuel Clemens (1835–1910) was just beginning to receive notice as a wry humorist. His story about a jumping frog, which started him on the road to fame, had been published only the year before, and the pen name "Mark Twain" meant little more to the public than "Sam Clemens." In his native town, Hannibal, Missouri, he was still remembered as a cub reporter on his brother's newspaper; in a few eastern cities he was known as a printer; along the Mississippi as a fair river pilot; in the Nevada gold country as a get-rich-quick schemer who never got rich, a greenhorn free-lance, and a not-too-

responsible reporter for the Virginia City *Enterprise;* in San Francisco
as a short-term literary hack.

It was an unexpected assignment from the Sacramento *Union* to
compose a series of letters on the Sandwich Islands that took him to
Honolulu. A half year in Hawaii marked a turning point in his life.
The letters were a conspicuous success, widely read and widely
quoted, and upon returning to the Coast, he embarked upon his
career as a popular lecturer, using his experiences in the Sandwich
Islands as a favorite topic. Fame as a wit and satirist followed quickly
after that, with such volumes as *The Innocents Abroad* (1869), *The
Gilded Age* (1873), *The Adventures of Tom Sawyer* (1876), *Life on the
Mississippi* (1883), *The Adventures of Huckleberry Finn* (1884), and
many others.

The letters from the Sandwich Islands were substantially incorporated in *Roughing It,* published in 1872, and the quotations below,
excerpted topically, are from that source. Nothing, no one, in Hawaii
was sacrosanct to Twain. His darts flew in all directions—at natives,
haoles, missionaries, whalers, traders, the government, customs, folklore, even the scenery. But the wit masked a great affection for the
Islands. To him they were "Sunday Land," "a dreamy, beautiful,
charming land," "paradise for an indolent man." He never outgrew
his desire to return—and stay; years after the 1866 visit he confessed
that the one thing he had always longed for was "the privilege of
living forever away up on one of those mountains in the Sandwich
Islands overlooking the sea."

Lampoonist at Large

On a certain bright morning the Islands hove in sight, lying low
on the lonely sea, and everybody climbed to the upper deck to
look. After two thousand miles of watery solitude the vision was
a welcome one. As we approached, the imposing promontory of
Diamond Head rose up out of the ocean, its rugged front softened
by the hazy distance, and presently the details of the land began
to make themselves manifest: first the line of beach; then the
plumed cocoanut trees of the tropics; then cabins of the natives;
then the white town of Honolulu. . . .

The further I traveled through the town the better I liked it. Every step revealed a new contrast—disclosed something I was unaccustomed to. In place of the grand mud-colored brown fronts of San Francisco, I saw dwellings built of straw, adobes, and cream-colored pebble-and-shell-conglomerated coral, cut into oblong blocks and laid in cement; also a great number of neat white cottages, with green window-shutters.

In place of front yards like billiard-tables with iron fences around them, I saw these homes surrounded by ample yards, thickly clad with green grass, and shaded by tall trees, through whose dense foliage the sun could scarcely penetrate; in place of the customary geranium, calla lily, etc., languishing in dust and general debility, I saw luxurious banks and thickets of flowers, fresh as a meadow after a rain, and glowing with the richest dyes; in place of the dingy horrors of San Francisco's pleasure grove, the "Willows," I saw huge-bodied, wide-spreading forest trees, with strange names and stranger appearance—trees that cast a shadow like a thundercloud, and were able to stand alone without being tied to green poles.

In place of gold fish wiggling around in glass globes, assuming countless shades and degrees of distortion through the magnifying and diminishing qualities of their transparent prison houses, I saw cats—Tom-cats, Mary Ann cats, long-tailed cats, bob-tailed cats, blind cats, one-eyed cats, wall-eyed cats, cross-eyed cats, gray cats, black cats, white cats, yellow cats, striped cats, spotted cats, tame cats, wild cats, singed cats, individual cats, groups of cats, platoons of cats, companies of cats, regiments of cats, armies of cats, multitudes of cats, millions of cats, and all of them sleek, fat, lazy and sound asleep.

I looked on a multitude of people, some white, in white coats, vests, pantaloons, even white cloth shoes, made snowy with chalk laid on every morning; the majority of the people were almost as dark as Negroes—women with comely features, fine black eyes, rounded forms, inclining on the voluptuous, clad in a single bright red and white garment that fell free and unconfined from shoulder to heel, long black hair falling loose, gypsy hats, encircled with wreaths of natural flowers of a brilliant carmine tint; plenty of dark men in various costumes, and some with nothing on but a battered stove-pipe hat tilted on the nose, and a very scant breech-clout;—certain smoke-dried children were clothed in nothing but sunshine—a very neat fitting and picturesque apparel indeed. . . .

Instead of cramped and crowded street-cars, I met dusky native women sweeping by, free as the wind, on fleet horses and astride, with gaudy riding-sashes, streaming like banners behind them; instead of the combined stenches of Chinadom and Brannan Street slaughter-houses, I breathed the balmy fragrance of jessamine, oleander, and the Pride of India; in place of the hurry and bustle and noisy confusion of San Francisco, I moved in the midst of a summer calm as tranquil as dawn in the Garden of Eden.

In place of the Golden City's skirting sand hills and the placid bay, I saw on the one side a frame-work of tall, precipitous mountains close at hand, clad in refreshing green, and cleft by deep, cool, chasm-like valleys—and in front the grand sweep of the ocean: a brilliant, transparent green near the shore, bound and bordered by a long white line of foamy spray dashing against the reef, and further out the dead blue water of the deep sea, flecked with "white caps," and in the far horizon a single, lonely sail—a mere accent-mark to emphasize a slumberous calm and a solitude that were without sound or limit. When the sun sank down—the one intruder from other realms and persistent in suggestions of them—it was tranced luxury to sit in the perfumed air and forget that there was any world but these enchanted islands.

On Wild Life

It was such ecstasy to dream, and dream—till you got a bite. A scorpion bite. Then the first duty was to get up out of the grass and kill the scorpion; and the next to bathe the bitten place with alcohol or brandy; and the next to resolve to keep out of the grass in future. Then came an adjournment to the bed-chamber and the pastime of writing up the day's journal with one hand and the destruction of mosquitoes with the other—a whole community of them at a slap. Then, observing an enemy approaching,—a hairy tarantula on stilts—why not set the spittoon on him?

It is done, and the projecting ends of his paws give a luminous idea of the magnitude of his reach. Then to bed and become a promenade for a centipede with forty-two legs on a side and every foot hot enough to burn a hole through a raw-hide. More soaking with alcohol, and a resolution to examine the bed before entering it, in future. Then wait, and suffer, till all the mosquitoes in the neighborhood have crawled in under the bar, then slip out quickly, shut them in and sleep peacefully on the floor till morning.

On Vegetation

We had an abundance of fruit in Honolulu, of course. Oranges, pineapples, bananas, strawberries, lemons, limes, mangoes, guavas, melons, and a rare and curious luxury called the chirimoya, which is deliciousness itself. Then there is the tamarind. I thought tamarinds were made to eat, but that was probably not the idea. I ate several, and it seemed to me that they were rather sour that year. They pursed up my lips, till they resembled the stem-end of a tomato, and I had to take my sustenance through a quill for twenty-four hours. They sharpened my teeth till I could have shaved with them, and gave them a "wire edge" that I was afraid would stay; but a citizen said "no, it will come off when the enamel does"—which was comforting at any rate. I found, afterward, that only strangers eat tamarinds—but they only eat them once. . . .

A mile and a half from town, I came to a grove of tall cocoanut trees, with clean, branchless stems reaching straight up sixty or seventy feet and topped with a spray of green foliage sheltering clusters of cocoanuts—not more picturesque than a forest of colossal ragged parasols, with bunches of magnified grapes under them, would be. I once heard a grouty northern invalid say that a cocoanut tree might be poetical, possibly it was; but it looked like a feather-duster struck by lightning. I think that describes it better than a picture—and yet, without any question, there is something fascinating about a cocoanut tree—and graceful, too.

We rode through one orange grove [on Hawaii] that had ten thousand trees in it! They were all laden with fruit. At one farmhouse we got some large peaches of excellent flavor. This fruit, as a general thing, does not do well in the Sandwich Islands. It takes a sort of almond shape, and is small and bitter. It needs frost, they say, and perhaps it does: if this be so, it will have a good opportunity to go on needing it, as it will not be likely to get it. The trees, from which the fine fruit I have spoken of came, had been planted and replanted *sixteen times*, and to this treatment the proprietor of the orchard attributed his success.

On Fashions

Passing through the market place we saw that feature of Honolulu under its most favorable auspices—that is, in the full glory of Saturday afternoon, which is a festive day with the natives. The native girls by twos and threes and parties of a dozen, and sometimes in whole platoons and companies, went cantering up and down the neighboring streets astride of fleet but homely horses, and with their gaudy riding habits streaming like banners behind them.

Such a troop of free and easy riders, in their natural home, the saddle, makes a gay and graceful spectacle. The riding habit I speak of is simply a long, broad scarf, like a tavern table cloth brilliantly colored, wrapped around the loins once, then apparently passed between the limbs and each end thrown backward over the same, and floating and flapping behind on both sides beyond the horse's tail like a couple of fancy flags; then slipping the stirrup-irons between her toes, the girl throws her chest forward, sits up like a Major General and goes sweeping by like the wind.

The girls put on all the finery they can on Saturday afternoon— fine black silk robes; flowing red ones that nearly put your eyes out; others as white as snow; still others that discount the rainbow; and they wear their hair in nets, and trim their jaunty hats with fresh flowers, and encircle their dusky throats with homemade necklaces of the brilliant vermilion-tinted blossoms of the *ohia;* and they fill the markets and the adjacent streets with their bright presences, and smell like a rag factory on fire with their offensive cocoanut oil.

At noon I observed a bevy of nude native young ladies bathing in the sea, and went and sat down on their clothes to keep them from being stolen. I begged them to come out, for the sea was rising and I was satisfied that they were running some risk. But they were not afraid, and presently went on with their sport. They were finished swimmers and divers, and enjoyed themselves to the last degree. They swam races, splashed and ducked and tumbled each other about, and filled the air with their laughter. It is said that the first thing an Islander learns is how to swim; learning to walk, being a matter of smaller consequence, comes afterward.

In the rural districts of any of the Islands, the traveler hourly comes upon parties of dusky maidens bathing in the streams or in the sea without any clothing on and exhibiting no very intemperate zeal in the matter of hiding their nakedness. When the missionaries first took up their residence in Honolulu, the native women would pay their families frequent friendly visits, day by day, not even clothed with a blush. It was found a hard matter to convince them that this was rather indelicate. Finally the missionaries provided them with long, loose calico robes, and that ended the difficulty—for the women would troop through the town, stark naked, with their robes folded under their arms, march to the missionary houses and then proceed to dress!

The natives soon manifested a strong proclivity for clothing, but it was shortly apparent that they wanted it only for grandeur. The missionaries imported a quantity of hats, bonnets, and other male and female wearing apparel, instituted a general distribution, and begged the people not to come to church naked, next Sunday, as usual. And they did not; but the national spirit of unselfishness led them to divide up with neighbors who were not at the distribution, and next Sabbath the poor preachers could hardly keep countenance before their vast congregations.

In the midst of the reading of a hymn a brown, stately dame would sweep up the aisle with a world of airs, with nothing in the world on but a "stovepipe" hat and a pair of cheap gloves; another dame would follow, tricked out in a man's shirt, and nothing else; another one would enter with a flourish, with simply the sleeves of a bright calico dress tied around her waist and the rest of the garment dragging behind like a peacock's tail off duty; a stately "buck" Kanaka would stalk in with a woman's bonnet on, wrong side before—only this, and nothing more; after him would stride his fellow, with the legs of a pair of pantaloons tied around his neck, the rest of his person untrammeled; in his rear would come another gentleman simply gotten up in a fiery necktie and a striped vest.

The poor creatures were beaming with complacency and wholly unconscious of any absurdity in their appearance. They gazed at each other with happy admiration, and it was plain to see that the young girls were taking note of what each other had on, as naturally as if they had always lived in a land of Bibles and knew what churches were made for; here was the evidence of a dawning civilization.

The spectacle which the congregation presented was so extraordinary and withal so moving, that the missionaries found it difficult to keep to the text and go on with the services; and by and by when the simple children of the sun began a general swapping of garments in open meeting and produced some irresistibly grotesque effects in the course of re-dressing, there was nothing for it but to cut the thing short with the benediction and dismiss the fantastic assemblage.

On Hawaiian Horses

You can buy a pretty good horse for forty or fifty dollars, and a good enough horse for all practical purposes for two dollars and a half. I estimate "Oahu" to be worth somewhere in the neighborhood of thirty-five cents. A good deal better animal than he is, was sold here day before yesterday for a dollar and seventy-five cents, and sold again today for two dollars and twenty-five cents; Williams bought a handsome and lively little pony yesterday for ten dollars; and about the best common horse on the island (and he is a really good one) sold yesterday, with Mexican saddle and bridle, for seventy dollars—a horse which is well and widely known, and greatly respected for his speed, good disposition and everlasting bottom.

You give your horse a little grain once a day; it comes from San Francisco, and is worth about two cents a pound; and you give him as much hay as he wants; it is cut and brought to the market by natives, and is not very good; it is baled into long, round bundles, about the size of a large man; one of them is stuck by the middle on each end of a six-foot pole, and the Kanaka shoulders the pole and walks about the streets between the upright bales in search of customers. These hay bales, thus carried, have a general resemblance to a colossal capital H.

The hay-bundles cost twenty-five cents apiece, and one will last a horse about a day. You can get a horse for a song, a week's hay for another song, and you can turn your animal loose among the luxuriant grass in your neighbor's broad front yard without a song at all—you do it at midnight, and stable the beast again before morning. You have been at no expense thus far, but when you come to buy a saddle and bridle they will cost you from twenty to thirty-five dollars. You can hire a horse, saddle and bridle at from seven to ten dollars a week, and the owner will take care of them at his own expense. . . .

There is no regular livery stable in Honolulu, or, indeed, in any part of the kingdom of Hawaii; therefore unless you are acquainted with wealthy residents (who all have good horses) you must hire animals of the wretchedest description from the Kanakas. . . . Any horse you hire, even though it be from a white man, is not often of much account, because it will be brought in for you from some ranch, and has necessarily been leading a hard life. If the Kanakas who have been caring for him (inveterate riders they are) have not ridden him half to death every day themselves, you can depend upon it they have been doing the same by proxy, by clandestinely hiring him out. . . . The result is that no horse has a chance to eat, drink, rest, recuperate, or look well or feel well. . . .

In hiring a horse from a Kanaka, you must have all your eyes about you, because you can rest satisfied that you are dealing with a shrewd, unprincipled rascal. You may leave your door open and your trunk unlocked as long as you please, and he will not meddle with your property; he has no important vices and no inclination to commit robbery on a large scale; but if he can get ahead of you in the horse business, he will take a genuine delight in doing it. This trait is characteristic of horse jockeys the world over, is it not? He will overcharge you if he can; he will hire you a fine-looking horse at night (anybody's—may be the king's, if the royal steed be in convenient view), and bring you the mate to my Oahu in the morning, and contend it is the same animal. . . .

I made one horseback trip on a mule. I paid ten dollars for him . . . added four to get him shod, rode him two hundred miles, and then sold him for fifteen dollars. I mark the circumstance . . . for up to that day and date it was the first strictly commercial transaction I had ever entered into and come out the winner.

On Hula

In old times here Saturday was a grand gala day indeed. All the native population of the town forsook their labors, and those of the surrounding country journeyed to the city. Then the white folks had to stay indoors, for every street was so packed with charging cavaliers and cavalieresses that it was next to impossible to thread one's way through the cavalcades without getting crippled.

At night they feasted and the girls danced the lascivious *hula-hula*—a dance that is said to exhibit the very perfection of educated motion of limb and arm, hand, head and body, and the exactest uniformity of movement and accuracy of "time." It was performed by a circle of girls with no raiment on them to speak of, who went through an infinite variety of motions and figures without prompting, and yet so true was their "time," and in such perfect concert did they move that when they were placed in a straight line, hands, arms, bodies, limbs and heads waved, swayed, gesticulated, bowed, stooped, whirled, squirmed, twisted and undulated as if they were part and parcel of a single individual; and it was difficult to believe they were not moved in a body by some exquisite piece of mechanism.

Of late years, however, Saturday has lost most of its quondam gala features. This weekly stampede of the natives interfered too much with labor and the interests of the white folks, and by sticking in a law here, and preaching a sermon there, and by various other means, they gradually broke it up. The demoralizing *hula-hula* was forbidden to be performed, save at night, with closed doors, in presence of few spectators, and only by permission duly procured from the authorities and the payment of ten dollars for the same. There are few girls now-a-days able to dance this ancient national dance in the highest perfection of the art.

On Missionaries

While the first missionaries were on their way around the Horn, the idolatrous customs which had obtained in the island, as far back as tradition reached, were suddenly broken up. . . . The nation was without a religion. The missionary ship arrived in safety shortly afterward, timed by providential exactness to meet the emergency, and the Gospel was planted as in a virgin soil. . . .

The missionaries braved a thousand privations to come and make them [the Hawaiians] permanently miserable by telling them how beautiful and how blissful a place heaven is, and how nearly impossible it is to get there; and showed the poor native how dreary a place perdition is, and what unnecessarily liberal facilities there are for going to it. . . . How sad it is to think of the multitudes who have gone to their graves in this beautiful island and never knew there was a hell! . . .

All the natives are Christians now, but many of them desert to the Great Shark God for temporary succor in time of trouble. . . . The Christianizing of the natives has hardly even weakened some of their barbarian superstitions, much less destroyed them. . . . To this day the natives are able to *lie down and die whenever they want to,* whether there is anything the matter with them or not. If a Kanaka takes a notion to die, that is the end of him; nobody can persuade him to hold on; all the doctors in the world could not

save him. . . . It is still a popular belief that if your enemy can
get hold of any article belonging to you he can get down on his
knees over it and *pray you to death.*

Therefore many a native gives up and dies merely because he
imagines that some enemy is putting him through a course of
damaging prayer. This praying an individual to death seems
absurd at the first glance, but then when you call to mind some
of the pulpit efforts of certain of our own ministers, the thing
looks plausible.

In former times, among the Islanders, not only a plurality of
wives was customary, but a *plurality of husbands* likewise. Some
native women of noble rank had as many as six husbands. . . . In
those days woman was rigidly taught to "know her place." Her
place was to do all the work, take all the cuffs, provide all the
food, and content herself with what was left after her lord had
finished his dinner. . . . But the missionaries broke up this satisfactory arrangement of things. They liberated woman and made
her the equal of man. The natives had a romantic fashion of bury-
ing some of their children alive when the family became larger
than necessary. The missionaries interfered in this matter, too, and
stopped it. . . .

The missionaries have Christianized and educated all the
natives. They all belong to the church, and there is not one of
them, above the age of eight years, but can read and write with
facility in the native tongue. It is the most universally educated
race of people outside of China. They have any quantity of books
printed in the Kanaka language, and all the natives are fond of
reading. They are inveterate church-goers—nothing can keep them
away. All this ameliorating cultivation has at last built up in the
native woman a proud respect for chastity—in other people. . . .

The missionaries have clothed them, educated them, broken up
the tyrannous authority of the chiefs, and given them freedom and
the right to enjoy whatever their hands and brains produce, with
equal laws for all, and punishment for all alike who transgress
them. The contrast is so strong—the benefit conferred upon this
people by the missionaries is so prominent, so palpable and so un-
questionable, that the frankest compliment I can pay them, and

the best, is simply to point to the condition of the Sandwich Islanders of Captain Cook's time, and their condition today. Their work speaks for itself.

On Government

In our country, children play "keep house"; and in the same high-sounding but miniature way the grown folk here, with the poor little material of slender territory and meager population, play "empire." There is his royal Majesty the King, with a New York detective's income of thirty or thirty-five thousand dollars a year from the "royal civil list" and the "royal domain." He lives in a two-story frame "palace."

And there is the "royal family"—the customary hive of royal brothers, sisters, cousins and other noble drones and vagrants usual to monarchy—all with a spoon in the national pap-dish, and all bearing such titles as his or her Royal Highness the Prince or Princess So-and-so. Few of them can carry their royal splendors far enough to ride in carriages, however; they sport the economical Kanaka horse or "hoof it" with the plebeians.

Then there is his Excellency the "royal Chamberlain"—a sine-cure, for his Majesty dresses himself with his own hands, except when he is ruralizing at Waikiki and then he requires no dressing.

Next we have his Excellency the Commander-in-Chief of the Household Troops, whose forces consist of about the number of soldiers usually placed under a corporal in other lands.

Next comes the royal Steward and the Grand Equerry in Wait-ing—high dignitaries with modest salaries and little to do.

Then we have his Excellency the First Gentleman of the Bed-Chamber—an office as easy as it is magnificent.

Next we come to his Excellency the Prime Minister, a renegade American from New Hampshire, all jaw, vanity, bombast and ignorance, a lawyer of "shyster" caliber, a fraud by nature, a humble worshiper of the scepter above him, a reptile never tired of sneering at the land of his birth or glorifying the ten-acre kingdom that has adopted him—salary, $4,000 a year, vast consequence and no perquisites.

Then we have his Excellency the Imperial Minister of Finance, who handles a million dollars of public money a year, sends in his annual "budget" with great ceremony, talks prodigiously of "finance," suggests imposing schemes for paying off the "national debt" (of $150,000) and does it all for $4,000 a year and unimaginable glory.

Next we have his Excellency the Minister of War, who holds sway over the royal armies—they consist of two hundred and thirty uniformed Kanakas, mostly Brigadier Generals, and if the country ever gets into trouble with a foreign power we shall probably hear from them. I knew an American whose copper-plate visiting card bore this impressive legend: "Lieutenant-Colonel in the Royal Infantry." To say that he was proud of this distinction is stating it but tamely. The Minister of War has also in his charge some venerable swivels on Punch-Bowl Hill wherewith royal salutes are fired when foreign vessels of war enter the port.

Next comes his Excellency the Minister of the Navy—a nabob who rules the "royal fleet" (a steam-tug and a sixty-ton schooner).

And next comes his Grace the Lord Bishop of Honolulu, the chief dignitary of the "Established Church"—for when the American Presbyterian missionaries had completed the reduction of the nation to a compact condition of Christianity, native royalty stepped in and erected the grand dignity of an "Established (Episcopal) Church" over it, and imported a cheap ready-made Bishop from England to take charge. The chagrin of the missionaries has never been comprehensively expressed, to this day, profanity not being admissible.

Next comes his Excellency the Minister of Public Instruction.

Next, their Excellencies the Governors of Oahu, Hawaii, etc., and after them a string of High Sheriffs and other small fry too numerous for computation.

Then there are their Excellencies the Envoy Extraordinary and Minister Plenipotentiary of his Imperial Majesty the Emperor of the French; her British Majesty's Minister; the Minister Resident of the United States; and some six or eight representatives of other foreign nations, all with sounding titles, imposing dignity and prodigious but economical state.

Imagine all this grandeur in a play-house "kingdom" whose population falls absolutely short of sixty thousand souls!

The people are so accustomed to nine-jointed titles and colossal magnates that a foreign prince makes very little more stir in Honolulu than a Western Congressman does in New York.

And let it be borne in mind that there is a strictly defined "court costume" of so "stunning" a nature that it would make a clown in a circus look tame and commonplace by comparison; and each Hawaiian official dignitary has a gorgeous vari-colored, gold-laced uniform peculiar to his office—no two of them are alike, and it is hard to tell which one is the "loudest." The King has a "drawing-room" at stated intervals, like other monarchs, and when these varied uniforms congregate there, weak-eyed people have to contemplate the spectacle through smoked glasses.

On Interisland Travel

The *Boomerang* is about as long as two street cars, and about as wide. She was so small (though she was larger than the majority of the interisland coasters) that when I stood on her deck I felt but little smaller than the Colossus of Rhodes must have felt when he had a man-of-war under him. I could reach the water when she lay over under a strong breeze.

When the Captain and my comrade (a Mr. Billings), myself and four other persons were all assembled on the little after portion of the deck which was sacred to the cabin passengers, it was full—there was not room for any more quality folks. Another section of the deck, twice as large as ours, was full of natives of both sexes, with their customary dogs, mats, blankets, pipes, calabashes of *poi,* fleas and other luxuries and baggage of minor importance. As soon as we set sail, the natives all lay down on the deck as thick as Negroes in a slave-pen, and smoked, conversed, and spit on each other, and were truly sociable.

The little low-ceiled cabin below was rather larger than a hearse, and as dark as a vault. It had two coffins on each side—I mean two bunks. A small table, capable of accommodating three persons at dinner, stood against the forward bulkhead, and over it hung the dingiest whale oil lantern that ever peopled the obscurity of a dungeon with ghostly shapes.

The floor room unoccupied was not extensive. One might swing a cat in it, perhaps, but not a long cat. The hold forward of the bulkhead had but little freight in it, and from morning till night a portly old rooster, with a voice like Baalam's ass, and the same disposition to use it, strutted up and down in that part of the vessel and crowed. He usually took dinner at six o'clock and then, after an hour devoted to meditation, he mounted a barrel and crowed a good part of the night. He got hoarser and hoarser all the time, but he scorned to allow any personal consideration to interfere with his duty, and kept up his labors in defiance of threatened diphtheria.

Sleeping was out of the question when he was on watch. He was a source of genuine aggravation and annoyance. It was worse than useless to shout at him or apply offensive epithets to him—he only took these things for applause and strained himself to make more noise. Occasionally during the day I threw potatoes at him through an aperture in the bulkhead, but he only dodged and went on crowing.

The first night as I lay in my coffin, idly watching the dim lamp swinging to the rolling of the ship and snuffing the nauseous odors of bilge water, I felt something gallop over me. I turned out promptly. However, I turned in again when I found it was only a rat. Presently something galloped over me once more. I knew it was not a rat this time, and I thought it might be a centipede because the Captain had killed one on deck in the afternoon. I turned out. The first glance at the pillow showed me a repulsive sentinel perched upon each end of it—cockroaches as large as peach leaves—fellows with long, quivering antennae and fiery, malignant eyes. They were grating their teeth like tobacco worms, and appeared to be dissatisfied about something. I had often heard that these reptiles were in the habit of eating off sleeping sailors' toe nails down to the quick, and I would not get in the bunk any more.

I lay down on the floor. But a rat came and bothered me, and shortly afterward a procession of cockroaches arrived and camped in my hair. In a few minutes the rooster was crowing with uncommon spirit and a party of fleas were throwing double somersaults about my person in the wildest disorder, and taking a bite every time they struck. I was beginning to feel really annoyed. I got up and put my clothes on and went on deck.

The above is not overdrawn; it is a truthful sketch of interisland schooner life. There is no such thing as keeping a vessel in elegant condition when it carries molasses and Kanakas.

On Haleakala

The chief pride of Maui is her dead volcano of Haleakala—which means, translated, "The House of the Sun." We climbed a thousand feet up the side of this isolated colossus one afternoon; then camped and next day climbed the remaining nine thousand feet, and anchored on the summit, where we built a fire and froze and roasted by turns all night. With the first pallor of dawn we got up and saw things that were new to us. Mounted on a commanding pinnacle, we watched Nature work her silent wonders. The sea was spread abroad on every hand, its tumbled surface seeming only wrinkled and dimpled in the distance. A broad valley below appeared like an ample checker-board, its velvety green sugar plantations alternating with dun squares of barrenness and groves of trees diminished to mossy tufts. . . .

I have spoken of the outside view—but we had an inside one, too. That was the yawning dead crater, into which we now and then tumbled rocks, half as large as a barrel, from our perch, and saw them go careering down the almost perpendicular sides, bounding three hundred feet at a jump; kicking up dust-clouds wherever they struck; diminishing to our view as they sped farther into distance; growing invisible, finally, and only betraying their course by faint little puffs of dust; and coming to a halt at last in the bottom of the abyss, two thousand five hundred feet down from where they started! It was magnificent sport. We wore ourselves out at it.

The crater of Vesuvius . . . is a modest pit about a thousand feet deep and three thousand in circumference; that of Kilauea is somewhat deeper, and *ten miles* in circumference. But what are either of them compared to the vacant stomach of Haleakala? I will not offer any figures of my own, but give official ones—those of Commander Wilkes, U.S.N., who surveyed it and testifies that it is *twenty-seven miles in circumference!* If it had a level bottom it would make a fine site for a city like London. It must have afforded a spectacle worth contemplating in the old days when its furnaces gave full rein to their anger.

Presently vagrant white clouds came drifting along, high over the sea and valley; then they came in couples and groups; then in imposing squadrons; gradually joining their forces, they banked themselves solidly together, a thousand feet under us, and *totally shut out land and ocean*—not a vestige of *anything* was left in view but just a little of the rim of the crater, circling away from the pinnacle whereon we sat (for a ghostly procession of wanderers from the filmy hosts without had drifted through a chasm in the crater wall and filed round and round, and gathered and sunk and blended together till the abyss was stored to the brim with a fleecy fog). Thus banked, motion ceased, and silence reigned.

Clear to the horizon, league on league, the snowy floor stretched without a break—not level, but in rounded folds, with shallow creases between, and with here and there stately piles of vapory architecture lifting themselves aloft out of the common plain— some near at hand, some in the middle distances, and others relieving the monotony of the remote solitudes.

There was little conversation, for the impressive scene overawed speech. I felt like the Last Man, neglected of the judgment, and left pinnacled in mid-heaven, a forgotten relic of a vanishing world.

While the hush yet brooded, the messengers of the coming resurrection appeared in the East. A growing warmth suffused the horizon, and soon the sun emerged and looked out over the cloud-waste, flinging bars of ruddy light across it, staining its folds and billow-caps with blushes, purpling the shaded troughs between, and glorifying the massy vapor-palaces and cathedrals with a wasteful splendor of all blendings and combinations of rich coloring.

It was the sublimest spectacle I ever witnessed, and I think the memory of it will remain with me always.

From *Roughing It*, Mark Twain (Samuel L. Clemens) (Hartford: American Publishing Co., 1872).

XXXIII

John W. Vandercook

To foreign intruders with a business bent—even to Hawaiian chiefs concerned about the material welfare of their kingdom—it was apparent from the earliest years of contact with the outside world that the economic survival of the Islands depended on finding new sources of income. Hawaii had to produce; Islanders had to have something to trade.

Sandalwood served as a stopgap for a few years, until the forests were stripped of that lucrative growth. Supplying fur traders and whalers with potatoes and salt and fruit and beef and firewood paid off, but that source of income was erratic and short-lived. One after another new agricultural specialties were tried on a large scale: coffee, silk, wheat, cotton, wool, rice, rum, oranges, various nuts, bananas, tobacco, cattle, sheep and horsehides, sisal, cassava, coconuts, field corn, peanuts, grapes, pineapples, sugarcane. No one could accuse the experimenters of either lack of persistence or lack of ingenuity. Fortunes were spent—and usually lost—on the trials and errors, as assorted pests, drought, gales, deluges, and labor troubles brought disaster.

Products like pineapples, rice, coffee, and macadamia nuts were to find receptive markets later, but at midcentury it was becoming increasingly evident that the real economic future for Hawaii lay in sugarcane—not in small private acreages, but in vast corporate ventures. The plantations grew larger and larger; huge mills gradually replaced the tiny factories run by mule and waterpower; irrigation canals were dug halfway around an island to bring water to parched but fertile soil; new kinds of cane that grew three times the height of "indigenous" varieties were introduced.

And as the industry expanded, the problem of finding men to work the fields and mills mounted. Hawaiians simply could not be induced to slave on the plantations for a few pennies a day when they could, with far less demanding effort, make a marginal livelihood with a fishnet, canoe, an ax, and *poi* pounder. Moreover, they were dying off at a frightful rate. If sugar were to be a success, the planters had to import foreign help.

It was this demand for men and women to produce sugar that brought a social revolution to Hawaii and converted the Islands into a racial melting pot. In *King Cane* John W. Vandercook (1902–1964) outlined factually the succession of migrations that ended the domination of Hawaii by Hawaiians. The period of major labor importation extended over half a century, and is seen in clearest perspective when considered as a whole, even at the expense of breaking continuity of the text.

King Cane was written in 1938 when there was still an element of romance in the cane and pineapple camps—before World War II had brought on a new conception of blue-collar wages, before plantation workers had been lured into the big labor unions, before living perquisites and the philosophy of paternalism went out of fashion, before the era of modern field mechanization had dawned in the Islands, before a man with a hoe had ever dreamed he could earn $25 a day.

Into the Melting Pot

In the middle of the century the Hawaiian sugar men were faced with a starkly simple situation. Through irrigation and improved technique they were bringing more and more land under cultivation. Their descendants would plow probably ten times as many acres as had ever been set out by the Hawaiians themselves in the most crowded period of native culture. But for every gain in land that farmers were making there was worse-than-proportionate loss of men. If the plantations were to survive, manpower had to be sought abroad.

The traditional place to turn to was that most crowded of countries, China. The initial move was made by the Royal Agricultural Society. In January, 1852, about 200 Chinese arrived from Hong Kong. In August 100 more arrived. They were the first of tens of thousands from many scattered lands.

The practice followed in the procurement of labor was the one customary at the time. Recruiters visited the Chinese ports, set up a kind of temporary shop and bruited the news that the far-off Hawaiian Islands wanted men. The hardiest were selected from the swarms of applicants and a contract was signed with them. The farmers promised to feed the immigrants, house them and repatriate them when their contract time was over—unless they should choose to renew their contracts or remain in the islands as free workers.

The pay—of from $3 to $6 a month—was fixed, and though the sum was small, it was more than Chinese of the "coolie" class had much chance of earning in their own country. Nor was the style of living for the workers on the farms comparable to that which distinguishes the Hawaiian properties today. But, for the period, the imported labor was well treated.

Two factors have always been at work in the relationship of the island employers to the people employed by them. The majority of managers, there seems no doubt, have been to some extent ruled by a moral attitude. Even to pretend such a thing in a business relationship seems ingenuous. Laws of profit and of power, and the law of supply and demand have more commonly been in force in fields and factories than moral laws. But in Hawaii, a by-the-book ethical attitude does appear to have been a reality. There were exceptions surely. The blacksnake-wielding, heavy-fisted, damn-your-eyes type of planter in the early days was certainly not unknown.

But there were missionaries in Hawaii, rigid, intolerant men whose pious views came close to ruling the islands. Many of the planters were their sons and grandsons. Others were their friends and neighbors. There were few who did not live in awe of them.

The missionaries' views were clear. They believed in work and there is no evidence that they did not believe in profits. But they did not believe in physical cruelty. A farmer who was brutal to his coolies was apt to find himself an outcast in the community—no trivial thing when a community is small.

Another reason for the preservation in the Hawaiian sugar industry of one of the most frictionless management-worker relationships in America was that labor on the islands was and has always remained scarce. Even $4-a-month coolies had cost a fair sum to gather and import. Due to the rapid growth of the sugar farms there were never enough of them.

The importation of Chinese continued until the end of the century. The Chinese had been familiar with the Hawaiian Islands through the sandalwood trade and there had been a few Chinese among the earliest groups of foreign settlers. Hawaii was not wholly strange. The climate was agreeable. The coolies' strength was equal to plantation tasks.

The Hawaiian Government, fully conscious of the necessity for repopulation, for a time hoped that people of their own ethnic stock might be imported. In 1855 King Kamehameha IV declared in a speech that "it becomes a question of some moment whether a class of persons more like the Hawaiian race could not be induced to settle on our shores. . . . In a few days they would speak our language with ease; they would be acclimated almost before they left the ships that conveyed them hither; and they might bring with them their wives. . . . Such immigrants, besides supplying the present labor demand, would pave the way for a future population of native-born Hawaiians, between whom and those of aboriginal parents no distinguishable difference would exist."

It seemed a reasonable hope. But it was doomed to failure. The same destructive forces had been at work in the rest of Polynesia. There were few islands in the whole of the eastern Pacific where the Polynesian stock was not dangerously dwindling. The foreign governments who held title to them were unfriendly to any scheme to diminish the population still further.

Another Hawaiian king once romantically proposed that the

half-caste descendants of the famous *Bounty* mutineers be brought *in toto* from far-off Pitcairn Island. But when a British Consul General insisted that the Pitcairn Islanders be admitted as perpetual subjects of the British crown, the scheme was dropped. In 1859 ten Polynesians were brought in by the government and put to work at Koloa. In 1878, after other attempts had led to nothing, eighty-six natives of Micronesia were induced to settle. That was all that ever came of the King's plan. Chinese, at least, were available.

A Bureau of Immigration was established in 1864 and an official was appointed to go to Asia to make the necessary contacts and to exercise judgment in the selection of immigrant material. In the next year 500 more Chinese entered the islands.

Between 1864 and 1900, it is estimated that 46,000 Chinese migrated to Hawaii. More than half had come unassisted, paying their own way, and rather more than half of the total, having served their time, went home. Oddly, about 8,000 had migrated not from China, but from the United States. "Coolie labor" had been an early fashion in California. The changing situation there made Hawaii seem more attractive and more profitable. Besides, Hawaii was a way-point toward home.

The peak of Chinese immigration came with the boom in Hawaiian sugar following the passage of the Reciprocity Treaty in 1875. Those who had come out under contract with the planters had cost in passage money and administrative expenses, apart from keep and wages, approximately $50 a head and the longest plantation work contract ran for five years. When profits were large these costs were bearable. When the price of sugar was low the Chinese seemed an expensive luxury. Their numbers on the farms would be kept constant only by renewed importations.

The Chinese were competent agricultural laborers but they preferred independence. Since most of them had been recruited from cities, the life of towns was in their blood. In 1886 it was estimated that out of a total of 20,000 Chinese then in the islands, 14,000 were in Honolulu. Chinese were in complete control of the small retail shops and of the food trades. Others had small truck farms just beyond the city limits where they grew vegetables for the town market. Too few of them had brought their wives. The Chinese population was predominantly male and despite some successful intermarriage with Hawaiian women, it was therefore a population that would automatically grow less.

The sugar men began to cast about for manpower from some other source. Oddly they hit on Portuguese from the Atlantic islands.

The choice appears to have been sheer chance. At the time of the establishment of the government Bureau of Immigration in 1865, the commissioner who was selected to go from Hawaii to Asia was a distinguished German botanist named Dr. William Hillebrand. Hillebrand had made an authoritative index of the flora of Hawaii and part of the purpose in his Asiatic trip was to collect useful plants which could be acclimated in the islands.

Though Hillebrand returned to Europe in 1871, his contacts with Hawaii remained fresh. Six years later his interest in subtropical botany had taken him to the Portuguese island province of Madeira, off the west coast of Africa. He found himself in a country climatically not unlike Hawaii, populated—indeed tragically overpopulated—by a hardy agricultural peasant people of south European stock. Through Hillebrand's offices it was arranged that a group of 180 Madeirans should emigrate to the Hawaiian Islands. . . .

Unlike the Chinese, the Portuguese Madeirans brought their wives and families with them. They made the journey half way around the world with the intention of becoming permanent settlers. They went to the sugar farms and stayed on them. The Portuguese movement continued until 1913. During that time about 20,000 men, women and children of Portuguese nationality migrated, the majority of them from the island provinces of Madeira and the Azores. . . .

The first group of Japanese laborers—148 in number—came to Hawaii in 1868. The migration had been arranged by a Hawaiian consul then residing in Japan. But no others followed for nearly twenty years.

Then, in 1885, formal arrangements were made between the two governments and a great migration began. Two thousand

Japanese entered Hawaii in 1885 and the annual total increased each year after that. When the movement ended in 1908, 180,000 Japanese had come to the islands and approximately 126,000 had left them, some to go to the mainland, the majority to return to Japan.

Most of the Japanese "shipped men," as they were called in the Nineties, came out under the then customary contracts. Negotiations were conducted by the government Bureau of Immigration, acting in cooperation with the Planters' Labor and Supply Company and the laborers were proportioned among the sugar farms. Officials in Japan examined and selected the applicants for emigration and the Consul of the Japanese Empire watched out for their well-being after their arrival in the islands. The plantations paid the expenses of transport, provided free food and housing and paid fixed wages of about $12.50 a month for men and $8 a month for women for ten hours a day in the fields, or twelve hours in the factory. By the end of the century, Japanese workers were in the majority upon all of the sugar farms.

The conditions under which the immigrants then lived and worked . . . were unquestionably crude. The farm work was hard, the houses provided were rarely more than simple barracks, and food was of the plainest sort. But there appears to have been no great discontent. The various immigrant groups were still close enough to their own backgrounds to be appreciative of what, at worst, still represented an improvement.

The extraordinary betterment in labor relations and in working conditions that the second and third decades of the Twentieth Century were to bring about had not begun. Conditions were acceptable then to both owners and workers. . . .

The Japanese in many instances had brought their wives with them, and many others, encouraged by the plantations, sent home for their wives or wives-to-be, as soon as they had surveyed the situation in Hawaii and found it to their liking. Those who did, have in most cases remained in Hawaii. Their children, and in many instances, their children's children, have been born as American citizens, with American allegiance, with their homes fixed in Hawaii, in fact and in spirit. Those Japanese who returned home or drifted elsewhere were usually the single men. They took their honestly earned and conscientiously saved money away with them, left more than its fair equivalent behind in the effects of the labor they had done. . . .

With annexation Hawaii became subject to the same immigration regulations and to the Oriental Exclusion laws that were in effect in the mainland.

After the turn of the century when improved technique and fresh discoveries brought more and more hitherto useless land under cultivation and the sugar industry grew to ever larger proportions, the question of manpower arose again. The number of Chinese field laborers had dwindled to a tiny figure. The total of native Hawaiians employed on all the farms could not have run the smallest of them. The Japanese, though they were indispensable, were declining rather than increasing in numbers, and a portion were withdrawing from plantation work and going into other occupations.

A last great movement was instituted. . . . When the Philippine Islands were ceded to the United States after the Spanish-American War, their people acquired the status of American nationals. Beginning in 1906 the sugar farmers commenced the importation of Filipino labor.

This time the migration was differently planned. The Hawaiian Sugar Planters' Association, having entered into an agreement with the Philippine government, established an office in Manila. The work that was offered, the pay, and the conditions that prospective immigrants would find awaiting them were publicized and applicants were individually examined. Filipinos who wished to make the venture had to pay their own expenses to the islands, but food and lodging were given them while they waited for transport and a certain amount of suitable clothing was issued. The only inducement—other than somewhat easier work and better wages than could be found in the Philippines—was the promise that after the completion of 720 days of work within a three-year period, the applicant could have his expenses home paid by the planters' organization.

Filipino immigration was conceived as a means of securing

temporary labor, not a scheme of settlement. In 1910 there were 2,361 Filipinos in Hawaii. By 1931 the total had risen to 66,049 and Filipino men comprised the majority of plantation labor. . . . Few women ever made the journey. Hawaii has simply been a place where a young and energetic Filipino might come, work for a few years, save, and then go home. . . .

It has been a curious procession. Those who have come to the islands to work on the sugar lands have by no means been wholly of Asiatic and Portuguese origin. Repeated efforts were made to encourage European settlement. In 1881, 615 Norwegians were recruited and 124 Germans. In 1898, 365 Galicians entered the islands as worker-colonists, and in the same year 14 American farm families took up residence on Ewa Plantation on the island of Oahu.

After the turn of the century two more considerable efforts were made to stimulate Caucasian settlement: 2,246 Spaniards from the sugar region near Malaga came to Hawaii in 1907, and between 1909 and 1912 the Bureau of Immigration, at a cost of $178,000, induced 2,056 Russians to emigrate from Russian Manchuria. A considerable group have come . . . from that other sugar island, Puerto Rico. At the beginning of the century some 5,000 workers migrated from Korea. All have funneled through the colorful port of Honolulu; all but a few, for a time at least, have been scattered to the sugar farms on the different islands.

The farms where they have lived in close communities of many thousands have turned into towns as racially cosmopolitan as any in the world. It is by no means the least of the sugar industry's accomplishments that in such towns the various groups live amiably together.

From *King Cane*, John W. Vandercook (New York: Harper and Brothers, 1939).

XXXIV

William Root Bliss

Waikiki in the 1860's was still a fishing village, backed by unsightly marshlands, Hawaiian taro patches, coolie duck farms, banana plantings, piggeries, and more piggeries. The beach itself was strewn with broken coral, dried coconuts, brown heaps of seaweed, flotsam and jetsam, and a tangle of creeping vines that seemed to thrive on the coarse sand. It was not a distinguished residential area; the odor of hogs and fish offal and the clouds of mosquitoes propagated in the nearby swamps were not conducive to unalloyed pleasure.

When the wind was right, Waikiki was a favorite destination for Honolulu horseback riders and picnickers, and it was a superb place for surfing and paddling, if one were mindful of the dangerously jagged clumps of coral offshore. Despite the unattractiveness, everyone in Honolulu visited Waikiki occasionally. The king had a rustic cottage there, for use when he wanted to loaf, drink, or play cards in private; and a few *haoles* had also thrown up shacks along the beach as shelter from the heat during fishing expeditions or picnics. But only lower-class Hawaiians and Chinese actually deigned to live there.

Never having heard of Waikiki until he reached Honolulu in 1872, author-traveler William Root Bliss (1825–1906) let his curiosity get the best of him, and he rode out one afternoon. In general, Bliss was charmed by Hawaii, but he found nothing to commend at Waikiki until he was soaking in the Pacific.

The Road to Waikiki

The favorite ride is to Waikiki. This is the name of a hamlet of plain cottages, stretching along the seashore in the edge of a grove of coconut palms, whither the white people of Honolulu go to revel in bathing clothes, mosquitoes and solitude at odd times of the year. It is not a gay watering place. Its local excitements are caused by the activity of the insect tribes and the occasional fall of a coconut.

But to the wearied dweller in Honolulu, to whose year there comes no variety of seasons, fashions or faces, Waikiki is "somewhere to go." Here he celebrates his birthday by a picnic with his friends. Here when school does not keep, he brings his children for a romp and a bath and a hunt for shells along the shore; and here he comes alone to enjoy nature and the natives.

It is a ride of three or four miles to Waikiki. Leaving the city on the eastern side, by King Street, we pass the great coral meeting house built by native labor so long ago that it is now much too large for its uses. Near by is a neighborhood whose broad street, white houses, stone walls, swinging gates and old shade trees remind me of a New England village. These large, arching algarobas are sufficiently suggestive of elms to complete the delusion. Here was the first missionary settlement in Honolulu: hence its pleasant New England complexion.

Now we enter upon a hard, level road where we can try the speed of our horse. On the right we pass the handsomest tree on the island, a huge *kamani* . . . extending its shade over half an acre. At this season its large, isolated leaves are both scarlet and green. Beyond, over a grassy flat, we see the ocean and an American whale ship, her maintopsail aback, waiting for the pilot. On the left are pleasant cottages and the plains of Kulaokahua, from which rise the volcanic hills and mountains, in whose variety of form and color we always find something to admire.

After a brisk trot of ten minutes we turn to the right, direct for the shore. . . . Hereabout is a neighborhood of white cottages within white fences, inhabited by white people, pleasantly shaded by trees. The crimson flowers of the China hibiscus, the reddening leaves of the mango, and the brown loments of the tamarind make attractive contrasts to the green foliage.

The road, now crossing a stretch of level fields, is occupied by pigs of every color except white, apparently going like ourselves to Waikiki. They swing their straight tasseled tails with so much energy as to worry our horse, who never saw such pigs at his own home in California. Fit companions to them are their owners—natives on whose civilization the era of trousers has not yet dawned. After the pigs we come to the king's *poi* factory, where *poi* is ground out by the quantity, for the subjects of his majesty to lick from their fingers as they squat around musty calabashes at their social dinner parties.

Near by, under the coconut trees, is the king's brown cottage. The royal standard is flying from a flag staff on the lawn, reflecting its red, white and blue stripes in the large silvered globe, emblematic of dominion, perched on a tripod below it. On the veranda sits his majesty, alone, while a little way off before him a dozen native women, chattering, in calico gowns, lie on their bellies in waiting.

What strange things these coconut trees are! Casting their shadows far away, never showing any signs of growth, always standing in silence—the same long, crooked, wrinkled, cylindrical stems crowned with plumy tufts. They lean and curve and point upward from every direction. . . . Under these trees are a few grass huts and wooden shanties occupied by natives; and under them also straggles the line of unpainted cottages, which is Waikiki.

The architecture of these cottages is of the sudden, spasmodic style, indicating daily diversities of mind in the same individual. They stand so near to the shore that the front door is necessarily on the back side, which our carriage must approach by a wandering by-road. From the southern verandas extends a long, broad porch made of reeds woven upon a frame, which shuts out the glare thrown up by the sun from the sea; but it cannot shut out the mosquitoes that come with the gloaming, whose visits are the sharpest ills of life.

Here is indolence all around us. It is exemplified by those native men and women lounging in scanty raiments on the grass, playing cards and talking idle tattle all day long. What specimens of human grossness and laziness! Even a silver coin is slow to induce a native boy to climb a coconut tree and throw down some nuts for us.

The sand on this shore is lava, coral and shells pulverized by the sea and bleached by the sun. Wild vines, bearing flowers, are running over it as if it were a garden soil. A mile away on our left, where the shore curves toward the south, rise the sterile sides of Diamond Head—the stump of an ancient volcano, whose southern slope is seven hundred feet high, where it juts into the sea.

Yonder in front of us is a coral reef, against which the ocean is always breaking with a moan, as if it were weary of its long endeavor to destroy the barrier. Naked natives are searching in the water for shell fish to eat; and others are paddling swift canoes, balanced by outriggers, through the surf. A company of men and women are wading toward the land, dragging a sweep of palm leaves, in which they expect to strand a skip-jack or a mullet.

The swell which rolls over the reef comes up gently to the edge of the shore. . . . A bath in this summer sea is delightful. The water is very buoyant, clear and pleasantly warm, its temperature being about seventy degrees. Once in, I am reluctant to leave it. But can we not come again tomorrow?

From *Paradise in the Pacific*, William Root Bliss (New York: Sheldon, 1873).

XXXV

Isabella Lucy Bird

The gift horses from California that King Kamehameha had grudgingly accepted in 1803, with the remark that they would never pay for their keep, multiplied within three-quarters of a century until there were more horses than Hawaiians—the reason being that the native population was rapidly declining and that new studs were shipped in occasionally to spell the originals.

The king's subjects never shared Kamehameha's prejudice; horses fascinated them. Hawaiians took to riding as avidly as American Indians, though generally the Island-bred horses were inferior stock, inhumanely treated, rarely stabled or shod, irregularly fed, often ridden to death. By the 1860's and 70's they were overrunning the Islands; virtually every native, young or old, male or female, possessed a saddle horse. The market was so glutted that a ridable dobbin could be purchased for less than a dollar.

On the shores of this horsiest of kingdoms, in 1873, arrived the vivacious British equestrienne and author Isabella Lucy Bird (1831–1904) for a six months' visit. According to her medical record, she had been a chronic invalid since childhood, afflicted with a crippling spinal disorder that frequently necessitated her wearing a steel net to support her head; and it was a secret to no one that she was a prim middle-aged spinster.

But almost on sight of Hawaii, with its display of galloping steeds, Mexican saddles, lassos, immense wood stirrups, and gaudy riding

blankets, she discarded her primness, her invalidism, and her steel
head support, and was a well woman. Her riding in England had
always been on a respectable sidesaddle, but since all the Hawaiian
damsels went astride, she donned ridiculous bloomers and mounted as
they did. Within hours after checking in at the Hawaiian Hotel, she
was off on a bridle path and spent most of the next six months on
horseback. She missed none of the common tourist sights and expanded
her itinerary with trips that few foreigners, male or female, had ever
taken.

Typical of her ventures was an expedition down the Big Island's
Hamakua Coast, at the time considered accessible only to the hardiest
of horsemen or hikers. By Miss Bird's count, on a stretch of thirty
miles between Onomea and Waipio, the rider had to scale the sides
of sixty-nine gulches ranging in depth from one hundred to two
thousand feet. Attempting the journey in dry weather was treacherous;
in wet weather it was foolhardy, for the gulches were the watershed
of Mauna Loa, and an unseen cloudburst high on the mountain could
at any time, without warning, turn a trickle into a raging Niagara.

Miss Bird set out from Onomea, a few miles north of Hilo, accompanied by a seventeen-year-old *wahine*, Deborah, and the girl's cousin
Kaluna, "a very handsome youth of sixteen," "pliable as an inver-
tebrate animal," "almost a complete savage," "the most careless and
irresponsible boy I ever saw, reckless about horses, reckless about
himself, without any manners or any obvious sense of right and
propriety." Kaluna was her guide.

The trip up the coast was made in fair weather without serious
incident, but on the return, after stopovers at Waipio Valley and the
exposed little shore village of Laupahoehoe, the rains came and the
excitement started.

Lady on Horseback

When I awoke the next morning [at Laupahoehoe] a strong
breeze was blowing, the surf was roaring so loud as almost to
drown human voices, and rolling up in gigantic surges, and to
judge from appearances, the rain which was falling in torrents

had been falling for some hours. There was much buzzing among the natives regarding our prospects for the day. I shall always think from their tone and manner, and the frequent repetition of the names of the three worst gulches, that the older men tried to dissuade us from going; but Deborah, who was very anxious to be at home by Sunday, said that the verdict was that if we started at once for our ride of twenty-three miles we might reach Onomea before the freshet came on.

This might have been the case had it not been for Kaluna. Not only was his horse worn out, but nothing could induce him to lead the mule, and she went off on foraging expeditions continually, which further detained us. Kaluna had grown quite polite in his savage way. He always insisted on putting on and taking off my boots, carried me once through the Waipio River, helped me to pack the saddle-bags, and even offered to brush my hair!

He frequently brought me guavas on the road, saying, "eat," and often rode up, saying interrogatively, "tired?" "cold?" Deborah told me that he was very tired, and I was very sorry for him, for he was so thinly and poorly dressed, and the natives are not strong enough to bear exposure to cold as we can, and a temperature of 68° is cold to them. But he was quite incorrigible, and thrashed his horse to the last.

We breakfasted on fowl, *poi,* and cocoanut milk, in presence of even a larger number of spectators than the night before, one of them a very old man looking savagely picturesque, with a red blanket tied round his waist, leaving his lean chest and arms, which were elaborately tattooed, completely exposed.

The mule had been slightly chafed by the gear, and in my anxiety about a borrowed animal . . . I put my saddle bags on my own mare, in an evil hour, and not only these, but some fine cocoanuts, tied up in a waterproof which had long ago proved its worthlessness.

It was a grotesquely miserable picture. The house was not far from the beach, and the surf, beyond which a heavy mist hung, was coming in with such a tremendous sound that we had to shout at the top of our voices in order to be heard. The sides of the great gulch rose like prison walls; cascades which had no existence the previous night hurled themselves from the summit of the cliffs directly into the sea; the rain, which fell in sheets, not drops, covered the ground to the depth of two or three inches, and dripped from the wretched, shivering horses, which stood huddled together with their tails between their legs.

My thin flannel suit was wet through even before we mounted. I dispensed with stockings, as I was told that wearing them in rain chills and stiffens the limbs. Deborah . . . does not care about rain any more than I do.

We soon reached the top of the worst and dizziest of all the *palis,* and then splashed on mile after mile, down sliding banks, and along rocky tracks, from which the soil had been completely carried, the rain falling all the time. In some places several feet of soil had been carried away, and we passed through water-rents, the sides of which were as high as our horses' heads, where the ground had been level a few days before.

By noon the aspect of things became so bad that I wished we had a white man with us, as I was uneasy about some of the deepest gulches. When four hours' journey from Onomea, Kaluna's horse broke down, and he left us to get another, and we rode a mile out of our way to visit Deborah's grandparents.

Her uncle carried us across some water to their cookhouse, where, happily, a *kalo* [taro] baking had just been accomplished in a hole in the ground, lined with stones, among which the embers were still warm. In this very small hut, in which a man could hardly stand upright, there were five men only dressed in *malos,* four women, two of them very old, much tattooed, and huddled up in blankets, two children, five pertinaciously sociable dogs, two cats, and heaps of things of different kinds.

They are most gregarious people, always visiting each other, and living in each other's houses, and so hospitable that no Hawaiian, however poor, will refuse to share his last mouthful of *poi* with a stranger of his own race. These people looked very poor, but probably were not really so, as they had a nice grass-house, with very fine mats, within a few yards.

A man went out, cut off the head of a fowl, singed it in the flame, cut it into pieces, put it into a pot to boil, and before our feet were warm the bird was cooked, and we ate it out of the pot with some baked *kalo*. . . .

We rode on again, somewhat unwillingly on my part, for though I thought my apprehensions might be cowardly and ignorant, yet Deborah was but a child, and had the attractive willfulness of childhood, and she was, I saw, determined to get back to her husband, and the devotion and affection of the young wife were so pleasant to see, that I had not the heart to offer serious opposition to her wishes, especially as I knew that I might be exaggerating the possible peril.

I gathered, however, from what she said, that her people wanted us to remain until Monday, especially as none of them could go with us, their horses being at some distance. I thought it a sign of difficulties ahead, that on one of the most frequented tracks in Hawaii, we had not met a single traveler, though it was Saturday, a special traveling day.

We crossed one gulch in which the water was strong, and up to our horses' bodies, and came upon the incorrigible Kaluna, who, instead of catching his horse, was recounting his adventures to a circle of natives, but promised to follow us soon. Deborah then said that the next gulch was rather a bad one, and that we must not wait for Kaluna, but ride fast, and try to get through it.

When we reached the *pali* above it, we heard the roaring of a torrent, and when we descended to its brink it looked truly bad, but Deborah rode in, and I waited on the margin. She got safely across, but when she was near the opposite side her large horse plunged, slipped, and scrambled in a most unpleasant way, and she screamed something to me which I could not hear.

Then I went in, and

> "At the first plunge the horse sank low,
> And the water broke o'er the saddle bow:"

but the brave animal struggled through, with the water up to the top of her back, till she reached the place where Deborah's horse had looked so insecure. In another moment she and I rolled backward into deep water, as if she had slipped from a submerged rock. I saw her fore feet pawing the air, and then only her head was above water. I struck her hard with my spurs; she snorted, clawed, made a desperate struggle, regained her footing, got into shallow water, and landed safely. It was a small but not an agreeable adventure.

We went on again, the track now really dangerous from denudation and slipperiness. The rain came down, if possible, yet more heavily, and coursed fiercely down each *pali* track. Hundreds of cascades leapt from the cliffs, bringing down stones with a sharp rattling sound. We crossed a bridge over one gulch, where the water was thundering down in such volume that it seemed as if it must rend the hard basalt of the *palis*. Then we reached the lofty top of the great Hakalau gulch, the largest of all, with the double river, and the ocean close to the ford. Mingling with the deep reverberations of the surf, I heard the sharp crisp rush of a river, and of "a river that has no bridge."

The dense foliage, and the exigencies of the steep track, which had become very difficult, owing to the washing away of the soil, prevented me from seeing anything till I got down. I found Deborah speaking to a native, who was gesticulating very emphatically, and pointing up the river.

The roar was deafening, and the sight terrific. Where there were two shallow streams a week ago, with a house and a good-sized piece of ground above their confluence, there was now one spinning, rushing, chafing, foaming river, twice as wide as the Clyde at Glasgow; the land was submerged, and, if I remember correctly, the house only stood above the flood. And, most fearful to look upon, the ocean, in three huge breakers, had come quite in, and its mountains of white surge looked fearfully near the only possible crossing.

I entreated Deborah not to go on. She said we could not go back, that the last gulch was already impassable, that between the two there was no house in which we could sleep, that the river had a good bottom, that the man thought if our horses were strong we could cross now, but not later, &c. In short, she overbore all opposition, and plunged in, calling to me, "spur, spur, all the time."

Just as I went in, I took my knife and cut open the cloak which contained the cocoanuts, one only remaining. Deborah's horse I knew was strong, and shod, but my unshod and untried mare, what of her? My soul and senses literally reeled among the dizzy horrors of the wide, wild tide, but with an effort I regained sense and self-possession, for we were in, and there was no turning.

Deborah, ahead, screeched to me what I could not hear; she said afterward it was "spur, spur, and keep up the river;" the native was shrieking in Hawaiian from the hinder shore, and waving to the right, but the torrents of rain, the crash of the breakers, and the rush and hurry of the river confused both sight and hearing. I saw Deborah's great horse carried off his legs; my mare, too, was swimming, and shortly afterward, between swimming, struggling and floundering, we reached what had been the junction of the two rivers, where there was foothold, and the water was only up to the seat of the saddles.

Remember, we were both sitting nearly up to our waists in water, and it was only by screaming that our voices were heard above the din, and to return or go on seemed equally perilous. Under these critical circumstances the following colloquy took place, on my side, with teeth chattering, and on hers, with a sudden forgetfulness of English produced by her first sense of the imminent danger we were in.

SELF.—"My mare is so tired, and so heavily weighted, we shall be drowned, or I shall."

DEBORAH (with some reason on her side).—"But can't go back, we no stay here, water higher all minutes, spur horse, think we come through."

SELF.—"But if we go on there is broader, deeper water between us and the shore; your husband would not like you to run such a risk."

DEBORAH.—"Think we get through, if horses give out, we let go; I swim and save you."

Even under these circumstances a gleam of the ludicrous shot through me at the idea of this small fragile being bearing up my weight among the breakers. I attempted to shift my saddle-bags upon her powerful horse, but being full of water and under water, the attempt failed, and as we spoke both our horses were carried off their vantage ground into deep water.

With wilder fury the river rushed by; its waters whirled dizzily, and, in spite of spurring and lifting with the rein, the horses were swept seaward. It was a very fearful sight. I saw Deborah's horse spin round, and thought woefully of the possible fate of the bright young wife, almost a bride; only the horses' heads and our own heads and shoulders were above water; the surf was thundering on our left, and we were drifting toward it "broadside on."

When I saw the young girl's face of horror I felt increased presence of mind, and raising my voice to a shriek, and telling her to do as I did, I lifted and turned my mare with the rein, so that her chest and not her side should receive the force of the river, and the brave animal, as if seeing what she should do, struck out desperately.

It was a horrible suspense. Were we stemming the torrent, or was it sweeping us back that very short distance which lay between us and the mountainous breakers? I constantly spurred my mare, guiding her slightly to the left; the side grew nearer, and after exhausting struggles, Deborah's horse touched ground, and her voice came faintly towards me like a voice in a dream, still calling "Spur, spur." My mare touched ground twice, and was carried off again before she fairly got to land some yards nearer the sea than the bridle track.

When our tired horses were taking breath I felt as if my heart stopped, and I trembled all over, for we had narrowly escaped death. I then put my saddle-bags on Deborah's horse. It was one of the worst and steepest of the *palis* that we had to ascend; but I can't remember anything about the road except that we had to leap some place which we could not cross otherwise.

Deborah, then thoroughly alive to a sense of risk, said there was only one more bad gulch to cross before we reached Onomea, but it was the most dangerous of all, and we could not get across, she feared, but we might go and look at it.

I only remember the extreme solitude of the region, and scrambling and sliding down a most precipitous *pali*, hearing a roar like cataract upon cataract, and coming suddenly down upon a sublime and picturesque scene, with only standing room, and that knee-deep in water, between a savage torrent and a cliff. This gulch, called the Scotchman's gulch, I am told, because a Scotchman was drowned there, must be at its crossing three-quarters of a mile inland, and three hundred feet above the sea. In going to Waipio, on noticing the deep holes and enormous boulders, some of them higher than a man on horseback, I had thought what a fearful place it would be if it were ever full; but my imagination had not reached the reality.

One huge compressed impetuous torrent, leaping in creamy foam, boiling in creamy eddies, rioting in deep black chasms, roared and thundered over the whole, in rapids of the most tempestuous kind, leaping down to the ocean in three grand broad cataracts, the nearest of them not more than forty feet from the crossing. . . .

Portions of two or three rocks only could be seen, and on one of these, about twelve feet from the shore, a nude native, beautifully tattooed, with a lasso in his hands, was standing nearly up to his knees in foam; and about a third of the way from the other side, another native in deeper water, steadying himself by a pole. A young woman on horseback, whose near relative was dangerously ill in Hilo, was jammed under the cliff, and the men were going to get her across.

Deborah, to my dismay, said that if she got safely over we would go too, as these natives were very skillful. I asked if she thought her husband would let her cross, and she said "No." I asked her if she were frightened, and she said "Yes;" but she wished so to get home, and her face was as pale as a brown face can be. I only hope the man will prove worthy of her affectionate devotion.

Here, though people say it is a most perilous gulch, I was not afraid for her life or mine, with the amphibious natives to help us; but I was sorely afraid of being bruised, and scarred, and of breaking the horses' legs, and I said I would not cross, but would sleep among the trees; but the tumult drowned our voices, though the Hawaiians by screeching could make themselves understood.

The nearest man then approached the shore, put the lasso round the nose of the woman's horse, and dragged it into the torrent; and it was exciting to see a horse creeping from rock to rock in a cataract with alarming possibilities in every direction. But beasts may well be bold, as they have not "the foreknowledge of death."

When the nearest native had got the horse as far as he could, he threw the lasso to the man who was steadying himself with the pole, and urged the horse on. There was a deep chasm between the two, into which the animal fell, as he tried to leap from one rock to another. I saw for a moment only a woman's head and shoulders, a horse's head, a commotion of foam, a native tugging at the lasso, and then a violent scramble on to a rock, and a plunging and floundering through deep water to shore.

Then Deborah said she would go, that her horse was a better and stronger one; and the same process was repeated with the same slip into the chasm, only with the variation that for a second she went out of sight altogether. It was a terribly interesting and exciting spectacle with sublime accompaniments.

Though I had no fear of absolute danger, yet my mare was tired, and I had made up my mind to remain on that side till the flood abated; but I could not make the natives understand that I wished to turn, and while I was screaming "No, no," and trying to withdraw my stiffened limbs from the stirrups, the noose was put round the mare's nose, and she went in.

It was horrible to know that into the chasm as the others went I too must go, and the mare went with a blind plunge. With violent plunging and struggling she got her forefeet on the rock, but just as she was jumping up to it altogether she slipped back snorting into the hole, and the water went over my eyes.

I struck her with my spurs; the men screeched and shouted; the hinder man jumped in; they both tugged at the lasso, and slipping and struggling, the animal gained the rock, and plunged through deep water to shore, the water covering that rock with a rush of foam, being fully two feet deep.

Kaluna came up just after we had crossed, undressed, made his clothes into a bundle, and got over amphibiously, leaping, swimming and diving, looking like a water-god, with the horse and mule after him. His dexterity was a beautiful sight; but on looking back I wondered how human beings ever devised to cross such a flood.

We got over just in time. Some travelers who reached Laupa-hoehoe shortly after we left, more experienced than we were, suffered a two days' detention rather than incur a similar risk. . . . We had several more gulches to cross, but none of them was dangerous; and we rode the last seven miles at a great pace, though the mire and water were often up to the horses' knees, and came up to Onomea at full gallop, with spirit and strength enough for riding another twenty miles.

From *The Hawaiian Archipelago: Six Months Among the Palm Groves, Coral Reefs and Volcanoes of the Sandwich Islands,* Isabella Lucy Bird (New York: Putnam, 1881).

XXXVI

Charles Nordhoff

Honolulu was losing its grass shack character by the 1870's and was beginning to take on the cosmopolitan appearance of a sizable American waterfront community. At least that was the way Charles Nordhoff (1830–1901) saw it in 1873, and though Nordhoff had a tendency to puff any place that caught his fancy, his observations were not to be ignored, for he was one of the most respected journalists, political commentators, and descriptive writers of his day.

Born with a penchant for globe-trotting, at the age of five he migrated with his family from Germany to Cincinnati, Ohio; at the age of fourteen, in an effort to get a broader look at the world, he talked his way into juvenile service with the United States Navy; and after a three-year hitch as a blue jacket, he continued his peregrinations with whaling and fishing fleets.

Nine Years a Sailor and *Stories of the Island World* were early products of his voyaging. He settled down long enough to become a correspondent and editor of the New York *Evening Post;* then he was off to the West to write *California: For Health, Pleasure and Residence,* and still farther afield to write *Northern California, Oregon and the Sandwich Islands.* Few contemporary journalists had a wider or more enthusiastic audience—and not the least of his distinctions was having later as grandson another Charles Nordhoff, coauthor of *Mutiny on the Bounty.*

The elder Nordhoff found far less to censure in Hawaii than professional colleagues like Herman Melville, Robert Louis Stevenson, or even Mark Twain. To him Honolulu had real charm—imported straight from New England.

Honolulu—Petty New England Village

We rounded Diamond Head, and sailing past Waikiki, which is the Long Branch of Honolulu charmingly placed amidst groves of coconut trees, turned sharp about, and steamed through a narrow channel into the landlocked little harbor of Honolulu, smooth as a mill-pond.

It is not until you are almost within the harbor that you get a fair view of the city, which lies embowered in palms and fine tamarind trees, with the tall fronds of the banana peering above the low-roofed houses; and thus the tropics come after all somewhat suddenly upon you; for the land which you have skirted all the morning is by no means tropical in appearance, and the coconut groves of Waikiki will disappoint you on their first and too distant view, which gives them the insignificant appearance of tall reeds.

But your first view of Honolulu, that from the ship's deck, is one of the pleasantest you can get; it is a view of gray house-tops, hidden in luxuriant green, with a background of volcanic mountains three or four thousand feet high, and an immediate foreground of smooth harbor, gay with man-of-war boats, native canoes and flags, and the wharf, with ladies in carriages, and native fruit-venders in what will seem to you brightly colored night-gowns, eager to sell you a feast of bananas and oranges. . . .

From the steamer you proceed to a surprisingly excellent hotel, which was built at a cost of about $120,000, and is owned by the government. You will find it a large building, affording all the conveniences of a first-class hotel in any part of the world. It is built of a concrete stone made on the spot, of which also the new Parliament House is composed; and as it has roomy, well-shaded courtyards and deep, cool piazzas, and breezy halls and good rooms, and baths and gas, and a billiard room, you might imagine yourself in San Francisco, were it not that you drive in under the shade of coconut, tamarind, guava and algaroba trees, and find all the doors and windows open in mid-winter; and ladies and children in white sitting on the piazzas. . . .

. . . Before this hotel was completed—that is to say, until 1871 —a stranger landing in Honolulu had either to throw himself on the hospitality of the citizens, take his lodgings in the Sailors' Home or go back to the ship. . . .

Honolulu, being the capital of the kingdom, contains the government offices; and you will perhaps be surprised, as I was, to find an excellent public hospital, a reform school, and other proper and well-managed charities. When you have visited these and some of the numerous schools and native churches, and have driven or ridden to Waikiki for a sea bath, and have seen the Nuuanu Valley and the precipice called the Pali, if you are American and familiar with New England, it will be revealed to you that the reason why all the country looks so familiar to you is that it is really a very accurate reproduction of New England country scenery.

The white frame houses with green blinds, the picket fences, whitewashed until they shine, the stone walls, the small barns, the scanty pastures, the little white frame churches scattered about, the narrow "front yards," the frequent school houses, usually with but little shade: all are New England, genuine and unadulterated; and you have only to eliminate the palms, the bananas and other tropical vegetation, to have before you a fine bit of Vermont or the stonier parts of Massachusetts.

The whole scene has no more breadth nor freedom about it than a petty New England village, but it is just as neat, trim, orderly, and silent also. There is even the same propensity to put all the household affairs under one roof, which was born of a severe climate in Massachusetts, but has been brought over to these milder suns by the incorrigible Puritans who founded this bit of civilization.

In fact, the missionaries have left an indelible mark upon these islands. You do not need to look deep to know that they were men of force, men of the same kind as they who have left an equally deep impress upon so large a part of our Western States; men and women who had formed their own lives according to certain fixed and immutable rules, who knew no better country than New England, nor any better ways than New England ways, and to whom it never occurred to think that what was good and sufficient in Massachusetts was not equally good and fit in any part of the world. Patiently, and somewhat rigorously, no doubt, they sought from the beginning to make New England men and women of these Hawaiians; and what is wonderful is that, to a large extent, they have succeeded.

As you ride about the suburbs of Honolulu, and later as you travel about the islands, more and more you will be impressed with a feeling of respect and admiration for the missionaries. Whatever of material prosperity has grown up here is built on their work, and could not have existed but for their preceding labors; and you see in the spirit of the people, in their often quaint habits, in their universal education, in all that makes these islands peculiar and what they are, the marks of the Puritans who came here but fifty years ago to civilize a savage nation, and have done their work so thoroughly that, even though the Hawaiian people became extinct, it would require a century to obliterate the way-marks of that handful of determined New England men and women. Their patient and effective labors seem to me, now that I have seen the results, to have been singularly undervalued at home.

. . . In 1853 the American Board of Missions determined that "the Sandwich Islands, having been Christianized, shall no longer receive aid from the Board"; and in this year, 1873, the natives of these islands are, there is reason to believe, the most generally educated people in the world. . . . Nine hundred and three thousand dollars were given by Christian people in the United States during thirty-five years to accomplish this result; and today the islands themselves support a missionary society, which sends the Gospel in the hands of native missionaries into other islands at its own cost. . . .

On your first Sunday in Honolulu you will probably attend

one or other of the native churches. They are commodious buildings, well furnished; and a good organ, well played, will surprise
you. . . . If you go to hear preaching in your own language, it
will probably be to the Seamen's Chapel where the Rev. Mr.
Damon preaches—one of the oldest and one of the best-known
residents in Honolulu. This little chapel was brought around
Cape Horn in pieces, in a whale ship many years ago, and was,
I believe, the first American church set up in these islands. . . .

The charitable and penal institutions of Honolulu are quickly
seen, and deserve a visit. They show the care with which the
Government has looked after the welfare of the people. The
Queen's Hospital is an admirably kept house. At the Reform
School you will see a number of boys trained and educated in
right ways. The prison not only deserves a visit for itself, but
from its roof . . . is one of the best views of Honolulu and the
adjacent country and ocean.

Then there are native schools, elementary and academic, where
you will see the young Hawaiian at his studies, and learn to
appreciate the industry and thoroughness with which education
is carried on all over these islands. You will see also curious evidence of the mixture of races here; for on the benches sit, and
in the classes recite, Hawaiian, Chinese, Portuguese, half-white
and half-Chinese children; and the little pig-tailed Celestial reads
out of his primer quite as well as any. . . .

Society in Honolulu possesses some peculiar features, owing in
part to the singularly isolated situation . . . and partly to the
composition of the social body. Honolulu is a capital city uncon-
nected with any other place in the world by telegraph, having a
mail once a month from San Francisco and New Zealand, and
dependent during the remainder of the month upon its own resources.

To a New Yorker, who gets his news hot and hot all day and
night, and can't go to sleep without first looking in at the Fifth
Avenue Hotel to hear the latest item, this will seem deplorable
enough; but you have no idea how charming, how pleasant, how
satisfactory it is for a busy or overworked man to be thus for a

while absolutely isolated from affairs; to feel that for a month at least the world must get on without your interfering hand. . . .

The people are surprisingly hospitable and kind and know how to make strangers at home; they have leisure and know how to use it pleasantly; the climate controls their customs in many respects, and nothing is pursued at fever heat as with us. What strikes you, when you have found your way into Honolulu society and looked around, is a sensible moderation and simplicity; . . . there is a certain amount of formality, which is necessary to keep society from deteriorating, but there is no striving for effect; there are, so far as a stranger discovers, no petty cliques or cabals or coteries, and there is a very high average of intelligence: they care about the best things. . . .

Finally, society in Honolulu is respectable. It is fashionable to be virtuous, and if you were "fast," I think you would conceal it. The Government has always encouraged respectability and discountenanced vice. The men who have ruled the Islands—not the missionaries alone, but the political rulers since—have been plain, honest, and, in the main, wise men; and they have kept politics respectable in the little monarchy. . . . I do not know, in short, where else in the world you would find so kindly, so gracefully hospitable and at the same time so simple and enjoyable a society. . . . Nothing is done in haste in Honolulu, where they have long ago convinced themselves that "tomorrow is another day." . . . Indeed, when you have passed a month in the Islands, you will have a better opinion of idleness than you had before.

From *Northern California, Oregon and the Sandwich Islands,* Charles Nordhoff (New York: Harper and Brothers, 1874).

XXXVII

C. F. Gordon-Cumming

Commentators on Hawaii could find areas of disagreement on virtually everything from the motives of the missionaries to the magnificence of the scenery, but on one subject there was complete unanimity—interisland transportation. All united in casting aspersion on the fleet that ferried freight and human beings between the Islands. The censure started in the days of Kamehameha the Great with the first vessel to hold an interisland franchise, and it lasted through the reign of Kalakaua and Liliuokalani—almost a century, during which dozens of unseaworthy arks carried countless passengers to watery graves.

The complaints of voyagers were directed not only at the unseaworthy vessels and at totally unseaworthy skippers, but also at the gross overcrowding, the inevitable nausea, the filthy decks and cabins, the swarms of cockroaches, the heat, the violence of the sea, the constant and sickening display of food—which passengers, of course, had to supply for themselves—the endless chatter, celebrating, and singing of natives, their eating, drinking, and sanitation habits.

In 1820 missionary wife Lucy Thurston boarded a brig bound for Maui from Kailua-Kona and waited three weeks for it to sail; when it finally did get under way she counted four hundred and seventy-five fellow passengers crowding a deck that would have been overladen with fifty; moreover, every family was trying to cluster about its private collection of calabashes of *poi,* fish, and beverages, restrain its retinue of dogs, while "here and there a nest of puppies served to fill up the crevices."

On a similar voyage in 1828, Laura Fish Judd, wife of the mission doctor, sailed on a schooner "stowed to its utmost capacity with men, women and children, *poi*, poultry, horses, horned cattle, pet pigs and dogs, and all manner of creeping things." "We were utterly prostrated and helpless," she added, "with that merciless malady which falls on all alike, master and servant, the *mal de mer*. . . . If I had ever dreamed of yachting by moonlight among the Isles of the Pacific, one trip dispelled the illusion forever."

In 1840 Francis Olmsted, a young Yale graduate and author of *Incidents of a Whaling Voyage,* made the run from Kawaihae to Honolulu on the *Clementine,* "one of those vessels rigged in defiance of all symmetry." But despite the lack of symmetry, the ship did have staterooms, clean and freshly whitewashed—but no beds; and after rolling around on the whitewash all night, he went on deck next morning looking as though he had been "sleeping in a flour barrel." Camping on deck was out of the question because that area had been converted into a stable occupied by forty head of bullocks; in fact, dozing off anywhere was impossible, considering "the violent motion of the vessel, the creaking of the timbers and the noise made by the stamping of the cattle upon deck."

Theo. H. Davies, founder of one of Hawaii's big companies, sailed from Honolulu to Kawaihae in 1859 on the schooner *Mary,* which he described as "not all that stomach could wish. . . . The natives were scattered about the deck in small parties," he wrote, "and in all stages of seasickness. All the ladies were carefully supplied with very small specimens of those useful items of domestic economy, mystically promulgated by modest and retiring salesmen as 'chambers.' These are held in readiness for the first attack of sickness, as I have abundant reason to testify, for one interesting young woman, being 'took bad,' was waited on by a venerable old witch who dutifully discharged the consequences over the vessel's side about six feet to windward of me, sitting qualmish at the stern. . . . After this I bore with tolerable composure such trifles as spitting and blowing of native noses, which kept dropping as the gentle rain from heaven upon my cheek."

Mark Twain in 1866 complained jocularly, but sensitively, of rats and centipedes as well as cockroaches on the *Boomerang,* and felt compelled to acknowledge that fellow passengers failed to meet his standards of hygiene.

And Isabella Lucy Bird took her trip to Hilo in 1873 on the queen of island transports, the *Kilauea*, whose keel, she reported, "had rasped off the branch coral around all the islands," and whose deck was entirely too crowded to move about on because of the confusion of "men, women, children, dogs, cats, mats, calabashes of *poi*, coconuts, bananas, dried fish, and every dusky individual in the throng garlanded with odorous and brilliant flowers." She did manage to claim a berth below in what she assumed was the "ladies' cabin," but was awakened in the morning with the inquiry from a gentleman curious to know whether she realized she had been using the head of the governor of Maui as a footrest during the night.

The interisland ships were getting a little larger, and time had brought mechanical improvements but little change in clientele or freight, as attested in 1879 by another British gentlewoman and traveling authoress, Constance Frederica Gordon-Cumming (1837–1924).

Gentle Bosom of the Pacific

The interinsular trade is carried on by upward of sixty vessels, ranging from 41 to 219 registered tonnage. These are barks, brigantines, schooners, sloops and steamers. The latter number half-a-dozen, and ply regularly between Honolulu and the other isles. They are commanded by white men and manned by Hawaiians. They vary from 190 to 218 tons, so you can understand that by the time they have shipped an indiscriminate mass of human beings—white men, Chinamen, and Hawaiians—horses, cattle, baggage, timber, sugar, coffee and sundries—there is not much elbow-room to spare, and certainly no possibility of luxury.

All these little steamers are said to be alike dingy and dirty, so the voyages from isle to isle must be anything but pleasure trips.

I have traveled in many curious varieties of ships, but nowhere have I found so strange a medley as has been crowded together on the deck of the *Like Like* for the last three days. The only berths she owns are ranged in a double row round her saloon, where the regular meals are served for such as choose to attend them. But the Hawaiian passengers prefer to carry their own provisions, and stranger than any picnic are the meals consumed by each family party, as they squat in merry groups on their mats, which they have spread on the deck.

A large bowl of *poi* is the inevitable center-piece, into which all present dip promiscuously, drawing out a finger thickly coated with the very adhesive sour paste, which by a series of most scientific twirls is safely landed in the mouth.

From baskets of plaited palm leaves and wrappings of silken banana leaves, are produced raw fish, dried octopus, pieces of roast pig—possibly dog—cooked taro, and long sticks of sugar cane, occasionally a breadfruit (but these are not abundant in Hawaii), bunches of oranges and bananas, and sometimes wonderful-looking oily puddings and sweetmeats.

All these are eaten with hearty appetite; and (I grieve to mention it) the travelers being bad sailors, and the sea rough, consequences were unpleasant. Nevertheless, with undaunted courage, the sufferers very quickly resumed their repast, which seemed to go on at intervals all day and even through the night.

If there was no food on hand, chewing sugar cane was an endless resource; but as the refuse fiber did not always reach the sea, it was not an agreeable addition to the cleanliness of the deck.

Besides the baskets of food, each party was surrounded by a litter of personal luggage—bedding, pillows, shawls. Several of the girls carried pet dogs, and both men and women had wreaths of large bright flowers round hat and neck . . . and the heavy scent of gardenia, tuberose, jessamine and orange blossoms would have been almost overpowering but for the fresh sea breeze with its own invigorating iodine.

As it would have been quite impossible to occupy the berth I had secured down-stairs, I followed the example of all my neighbors and accepted the offer of the kindly steward to spread my mattress on the middle deck, where I shortly found myself one of a closely packed mass of miserable humanity, all mingled promiscuously—men, women and children, brown, white and whitey-brown—all laid out in rows, and almost all violently sick. It was a horrible scene.

The upper or hurricane deck of the *Like Like* is large and commodious; and as an old traveler and good sailor, and moreover somewhat ungregarious, I should have preferred on this occasion to find a nook for myself on its breezy and solitary heights, but for the first time in all my traveling experience, I found the captain of the vessel so churlish and coarse-mouthed that I deemed the horrors of "the middle passage" the least evil of the two. . . .

In that mixed throng lay American ladies, half-breed cattle-drivers, sugar planters and Chinamen. I was struck by the great kindliness of everyone, even under such adverse circumstances, all ready to make the best of their miseries and of their neighbors. And a party of men with lovely voices beguiled the tedium of day and night alike by frequently singing very pleasant native choruses.

We called at many ports along the howlishly dreary volcanic shores of Isle Maui, and then of Hawaii. It may be that the stormy weather made them appear more dismal to my eyes, but to me the settlements seemed to be for the most part merely groups of native huts or poor wooden houses, clustered on cinder heaps. I never saw a more distressingly ugly coast. . . . I am told that there are some pretty and pleasant spots to be seen even on these shores, and delightful depths of cool tropical green in the deep chasms of the hills; but either they are not visible from the sea or we passed them in the night.

From *Fire Fountains,* C. F. Gordon-Cumming (Edinburgh and London: Blackwood, 1883).

XXXVIII

Titus Coan

For half a century the foremost authority on Hawaiian volcanoes was missionary Titus Coan (1801–1882), who lived in Hilo under the shadow of mighty Mauna Loa, and who, at the first shudder of an earthquake or the first explosive glare in the sky, took off for the mountains with the ardor of a firechaser, to reconnoiter the site of the latest cataclysm.

He kept fairly reliable records of volcanic activity on the Big Island, made original observations on gradient flow of lava, conducted hair-raising experiments with a pyrometer at outlets of active cones, contributed reports to learned scientific magazines, and regaled visiting journalists with tales of his adventures until they were convinced they could write authoritatively about volcanoes. Finally, a few months before his death, he incorporated in a modest autobiography a few of his exploits in the land of Pele.

Coan was an exciting preacher and evangelist, and his reports showed that he could have been an equally exciting author or scientist. He was stationed at Hilo during a long period when Kilauea and Mauna Loa were putting on their noisiest and most flamboyant exhibitions. People journeyed halfway around the world to witness the intermittent spectacle, but Coan was there and could narrate what he saw as though it were merely another incident in a life overflowing with thrills.

Fire Mountains in Action

It is widely known that the Hawaiian Islands are all of volcanic origin. They are the summits of mountains whose bases are far down in the sea. Their structure is plutonic, and the marks of fire are everywhere visible. They are scarred with hundreds and hundreds of pit and cone craters, most of which are extinct.

Mauna Loa is a vast volcanic dome, subject to igneous eruptions at any time, either from its extended summit or sides. Professor Dana estimates that "there is enough rock material in Mauna Loa to make one hundred and twenty-five Vesuviuses." About midway from its summit to the sea on the eastern flank of the mountain and on a nearly level plain is Kilauea, the largest known active crater in the world. The brink of this crater is 4,440 feet above the sea level; its depth varies from 700 to 1,200 feet, and its longer diameter is about three miles. Grand eruptions have issued from it in past ages, covering hundreds of square miles in different parts of Puna and Kau.

The first eruption from Kilauea which occurred after my arrival in Hilo, began on the 30th of May, 1840. . . . There had been no grand eruption for the previous seventeen years, so that the lavas in the crater had risen several hundred feet, and the action had at times been terrific.

The volcano is thirty miles by road from Hilo, and under favorable conditions of the atmosphere we could see the splendid light by night, and the white cloudy pillar of steam by day. It was reported that for several days before the outburst, the whole vast floor of the crater was in a state of intense ebullition; the seething waves rolling, surging, and dashing against the adamantine walls and shaking down large rocks into the fiery abyss below. . . . The heat was so intense and the surges so infernal that travelers near the upper rim of the crater left the path on account of the heat and for fear of the falling of the precipice over which the trail lay, and passed at a considerable distance from the crater.

Kilauea is about half in Kau and half in Puna, and all travelers going from Kau to Hilo by the inland road pass the very brink of the crater.

The eruption was first noticed by the people of Puna, who were living only twenty miles from it. The light appeared at first like a highland jungle on fire; and so it was, for the fiery river found vent some 1,200 to 1,500 feet below the rim of Kilauea, and flowing subterraneously in a N.E. direction for about four miles, marking its course by rending the superincumbent strata and throwing up light puffs of sulphurous steam, it broke ground in the bottom of a wooded crater about 500 feet deep, consuming the shrubs, vines and grasses, and leaving a smouldering mass instead.

The great stream forced its way underground in a wild and wooded region for two miles more, when it again threw up a jet of fire and sulphur, covering about an acre. . . . Only a little further on, an old wooded cone was rent with fissures several feet wide and about half an acre of burning lava spouted up, consuming the trees and jungle. This crevasse emitted scalding vapor for twenty-five years.

Onward went the burning river, deep underground, some six more miles, when the earth was rent again with an enormous fissure, and floods of devouring fire were poured out, consuming the forest and spreading over perhaps fifty acres. And still the passage seaward was underground for about another six miles, when it broke out in a terrific flood and rolled and surged along henceforth upon the surface, contracting to half a mile, or extending to two miles in width, and moving from half a mile to five miles an hour according to the angle of descent and the inequalities and obstructions of the surface, until it poured over the perpendicular seawall, about thirty feet high, in a sheet of burning fusion only a little less than a mile wide.

This was on June 3, 1840. It reached the sea on the fifth day after the light was first seen on the highlands, and at a distance of only seventeen and a half miles from Hilo. As this grand cataract of fire poured over the basaltic seawall, the sights and sounds were . . . indescribable. Two mighty antagonistic forces were in conflict. The sea boiled and raged as with infernal fury, while the burning flood continued to pour into the troubled waves by night and by day for three weeks.

Dense clouds of steam rolled up heavenward, veiling sun and stars, and so covering the lava flow that objects could not be seen from one margin to the other. All communication between the northern and southern portions of Puna was cut off for more than a month. The waters of the sea were heated for twenty miles along the coast, and multitudes of fishes were killed by the heat and sulphurous gases, and were seen floating upon the waves.

During this flow the sea line along the whole breadth of the fire stream was pushed out many yards by the solidified lavas, and three tufaceous cones were raised in the water where ships could once sail. . . . Imagine the Mississippi converted into liquid fire of the consistence of fused iron, and moving onward sometimes rapidly, sometimes sluggishly, now widening into a lake, and anon rushing through a narrow gorge, breaking its way through mighty forests and ancient solitudes, and you will get some idea of the spectacle here exhibited.

When the eruption was at its height, night was turned into day in all this region. The light rose and spread like morning upon the mountains and its glare was seen on the opposite side of the island. It was also visible for more than a hundred miles at sea; and at a distance of forty miles fine print could be read at midnight. The brilliancy of the light . . . was like a blazing firmament, and the scene one of unrivaled sublimity.

No lives were lost during this eruption. The stream passed over and under an almost uninhabited desert. A few small hamlets were consumed and a few patches of taro, potatoes and bananas were destroyed, but the people walked off with their calabashes, *kapas* and other chattels to seek shelter and food elsewhere. During the eruption some of the people of Puna spent much of their time in prayer and religious meetings, some fled in consternation, and others wandered along the margin of the lava stream at a safe distance, marking with idle curiosity its progress, while others still pursued their daily avocations within a mile of the fiery river as quietly as if nothing strange had occurred.

Pele on a rampage

They ate, drank, bought, sold, planted, builded, slept and waked apparently indifferent to the roar of the consuming forests, the sight of devouring fire, the startling detonations, the hissing of escaping steam, the rending of gigantic rocks, the raging and crashing of lava waves, and the bellowings, the murmurings, the unearthly mutterings coming up from the burning abyss. They went quietly on in sight of the rain of ashes, sand and fiery scintillations, gazing vacantly on the fearful and ever-varying appearance of the atmosphere illuminated by the eruption, the sudden rising of lofty pillars of flame, the upward curling of ten thousand columns of smoke, and their majestic gyrations of dingy, lurid or parti-colored clouds. . . .

Sometimes the intense heat of the stream would cause large boulders and rocks to explode with great detonations, and sometimes lateral branches of the stream would push out into some fissure and work into a subterranean gallery until they met with some obstacle, when the accumulating fusion with its heat, its gases and its pressure would lift up the super-incumbent mass of rock into a dome, or, sundering it from its surroundings, bear it off on its burning bosom like a raft upon the water.

A foreigner told me that while he was standing on a rocky hillock, some distance from the stream, gazing with rapt interest upon its movements, he felt himself rising with the ground on which he stood. Startled by the motion, he leaped from the rock, when in a few minutes fire burst out from the place where he had been. . . .

I spent nearly two days on the stream. It was solidified and mostly cooled, yet hot and steaming in many places. I went up the flow to where it burst out in volume and breadth from its subterranean chambers and continued on the surface to the sea, a distance of about twelve miles, making the entire length of the stream about thirty miles. . . . I found the place of final outburst a scene where terrific energy had been exerted. Yawning crevasses were opened, the rocks were rent and the forests consumed; the molten flood had raged and swirled and been thrown high into the air, and there had been a display of titanic fury that must have been appalling at the time of the outbreak. . . .

Numerous holes left in the hot lava bed by the gradual reduction of tree trunks to ashes afforded the means of measuring the
depth of the flow. With a long pole I was enabled to measure
from a depth of five to twenty-five feet. Some of these trunk
moulds were as smooth as the calibre of a cannon. Some of the
holes were still so hot at the bottom as to set my pole on fire in one
minute. I had seen fearful ragings and heard what seemed the
wails of infernal beings in the great crater of Kilauea, but I had
never before seen the amazing effects of a great external eruption
of lava . . . and I returned from this weary exploration . . .
with a deepened sense of the terrible dynamics of the fiery abyss
over which we tread.

The volcano of Kilauea is always in action. Its lake of lava
and brimstone rolls and surges from age to age. Sometimes these
fires are sluggish, and one might feel safe in pitching a tent on
the floor of the crater. Again the ponderous masses of hardened
lava, in appearance like vast coal beds, are broken up by the
surging floods below and tossed hither and thither, while the
great bellows of Jehovah blows upon these hills and cones and
ridges of solidified rocks, and melts them down into seas and
lakes and streams of liquid fire.

As the great volcano is within the limits of my parish, and as
my missionary trail flanks it on three sides, I may have observed
it a hundred times, but never twice in the same state. Its outer
wall remains nearly the same from age to age, but all within the
vast caldron undergoes changes. I have visited it when there was
but one small pool of fusion visible, and at another time I have
counted eighty fires in the bottom of the crater.

Sometimes I have seen what is called Halemaumau, or South
Lake, enlarged to a circuit of three miles, and raging as if filled
with infernal demons, and again domed over with a solid roof,
excepting a single aperture of about twenty feet in diameter at
the apex, which served as a vent to the steam and gases. On my
next visit I would find this dome broken in and the great sea of
fiery billows of near a mile in diameter rolling below.

On one occasion, when there with a party of friends, we found the door of entrance to the floor of the crater closed against us. A flood of burning fusion covering some fifty acres had burst out at the lower end of the path, shutting out all visitors, so that we spent the day and night upon the upper rim of the abyss.

On another occasion I found the great South Lake filled to the brim and pouring out in two deep and broad canals at nearly opposite points of the lake. . . . I have heard great avalanches of rocks fall from the outer walls of the crater some eight hundred feet into the dread abyss below with thundering uproar. At a distance of two miles I have heard the soughing and sighing of the lava waves, and upon the surface of that awful lake I have seen, as it were, gory forms leaping up with shrieks, as if struggling to escape their doom, and again plunging and disappearing beneath the burning billows.

To stand upon the margin of this lake of fire and brimstone, to listen to its infernal sounds, the rolling, surging, tossing, dashing, and spouting of its furious waves; to witness its restless throbbings, its gyrations, its fierce ebullitions, its writhing, and its fearful throes, as if in anguish, and to feel the hot flushes of its sulphurous breath, is to give one sensations which no human language can express.

It was a little before daybreak on the 17th of February, 1852, that we saw through our window a beacon light resting on the apex of Mauna Loa. At first we supposed it to be a planet just setting. In a few minutes we were undeceived by the increasing brilliancy of the light, and by a grand outburst of a fiery column which shot high into the air, sending down a wonderful sheen of light, which illuminated our fields and flashed through our windows. Immediately a burning river came rushing down the side of the mountain at the apparent rate of fifteen to twenty miles an hour.

This summit eruption was vivid and vigorous for forty hours, and I was preparing to visit the scene when all at once the valves closed and all signs of the eruption disappeared; accordingly I ceased my preparations to ascend the mountain.

On the 20th the eruption broke out laterally, about 4,000 feet below the summit, and at a point facing Hilo; from this aperture a brilliant column of fire shot up to a height of 700 feet, by angular measurement, with a diameter of from 100 to 300 feet. This lava fountain was sustained without intermission for twenty days and nights, during which time it built up a crater one mile in circumference, lacking one chain, and 400 feet high. It also sent down a river of liquid fire more than forty miles long, which came within ten miles of Hilo.

The roar of this great furnace was heard along the shores of Hilo and the earth quivered with its rage, while all the district was so lighted up that we could see to read at any hour of the night when the sky was not clouded. The smoke and steam rose in a vast column like a pillar of cloud by day, and at night it was illuminated with glowing brilliants, raising the pillar of fire thousands of feet in appearance.

When it reached a stratum of atmosphere of its own specific gravity, it moved off like the tail of a comet, or spread out laterally, a vast canopy of illuminated gases. The winds from the mountain brought down smoke, cinders, "Pele's hair," and gases, scattering the light products over houses and gardens, streets and fields, or, bearing them far out to sea, dropped them upon the decks of vessels approaching our coast.

On Monday, the 23rd of February, Dr. Whetmore and myself, taking with us four natives as assistants, set out for the mountain. . . . We passed our first night in the skirt of the forest, having taken with us long knives, an old sword, clubs and hatchets, proposing to cut and beat our way through the jungle in as straight a line as possible toward the fiery pillar. On Tuesday we rose fresh and earnest, and pressed through the ferns and vines, and through the tangled thicket. . . . At night we bivouacked in the ancient forest, hearing the distant roar of the volcano and seeing the glare of the igneous river, which had already passed us, cutting its way through the wood a few miles distant on our left.

On Wednesday Dr. Whetmore decided to return to Hilo, apprehensive that the stream might reach the sea before we could return from the crater, and that our families might need his presence. Taking one of the men, he hastened back to the village, while I pressed on. . . .

We left our mountain eyrie on the 27th, determined if possible to reach the seat of action that day. The scoriaceous hills and ridges, the plains and gorges bristled with the sharp and jagged *aa*, and our ascent was rough and difficult. We mounted ridges where the pillar of fire shone strongly upon us, and we plunged down deep dells and steep ravines where our horizon was only a few feet distant. . . . I soon found that my guide needed a leader; he lagged behind . . . but fearing we should not reach the point before night, I pressed forward alone, with an interest that mocked all obstacles.

At half-past three P.M. I reached the awful crater, and stood alone in the light of its fires. It was a moment of unutterable interest. I was 10,000 feet above the sea in a vast solitude untrodden by the foot of man or beast, amidst a silence unbroken by any living voice. . . . I was blinded by the insufferable brightness, almost petrified by the sublimity of the scene.

The heat was so intense I could not approach the pillar within forty or fifty yards, even on the windward side, and in the snowy breezes coming down from the mountain near four thousand feet above. On the leeward side, the steam, the hot cinders, ashes and burning pumice forbade approach within a mile or more.

I stood amazed before this roaring furnace. I felt the flashing heat and the jar of earth; I heard the subterranean thunders. . . . Here indeed the hills smoked and the earth melted, and I saw its gushings from the awful throat of the crater burning with intense white heat. I saw the vast column of melted rocks mounting higher and still higher, while dazzling volleys and coruscations shot out like flaming meteors in every direction, exploding all the way up the ascending column of 1,000 feet with the sharp rattle of infantry fire in battle. There were unutterable sounds as the fierce fountain sent up the seething fusion to its utmost height; it came down in parabolic curves, crashing like a storm of fiery hail in conflict with the continuous ascending volume, a thousand tons of the descending mass falling back into the burning throat of the crater, where another thousand were struggling for vent. . . .

We chose our station for the night within about two hundred feet of the crater and watched its pyrotechnics, and heard its mutterings, its detonations and its crashing thunder until morning. Occasionally our eyelids became heavy, but before we were fairly asleep some new and rousing demonstration would bring us to our feet and excite the most intense interest. In addition to the marvelous sounds, the kaleidoscopic views of the playing column were so rapid and so brilliant that we could hardly turn our eyes for a moment from it.

The fusion when issuing from the mouth of the crater was white hot, but as it rose through the air its tints underwent continuous changes: it became a light red, then a deeper shade, then a glossy gray, and in patches a shining black, but these tints and shades with many others were intermingled, and as every particle was in motion the picture was splendid beyond the power of description. Thousands and millions of tons of sparkling lava were pouring from the rim of the crater, while the cone was rising rapidly and spreading out at the base.

From the lower side of this cone a large fissure opened, through which the molten flood was issuing and rushing down the mountain, burning its way through the forest. No tongue, no pen, no pencil can portray the beauty, the grandeur, the terrible sublimity of the scenes of that memorable night.

The great eruption of 1855–56 continued fifteen months and the disgorgement of lava exceeded by millions of tons that of any other eruption we have seen. It was first observed on the evening of the 11th of August, 1855, shining like Sirius at a small point near the summit of Mauna Loa. This radiant point expanded rapidly and in a short time the glow was like that of the rising sun. Soon a deluge of liquid fire rushed down the mountainside in the direction of our town.

Day after day and night after night, we could trace this stream until it entered the deep forest. . . . On the 2nd of October, in company with a friend and several natives, I set off to visit this approaching torrent of lava. As the jungle through which it was burning its pathway was too dense to be penetrated, we chose for our track the bed of the Wailuku River. . . . We slept three nights in the great forest on the banks of the river and the fourth night in a cave on the outskirts of the forest. Early in the morning of October 6th we emerged and came to the margin of the lava stream in the open plain. We had flanked it at the distance of some two miles on our left, and its terminus was about ten miles below us on its way to Hilo.

Where we first struck it, we estimated the breadth to be about three miles, but twice that width in places. . . . Onward we went; the ascent grew steeper. We were startled; a yawning fissure was before us—hot, sulphurous gases were rushing up—the sullen swash of liquid lava was heard. We took the windward side of the opening, approached carefully, and with awe we saw the swift river of fire some fifty feet below us, rushing at white heat, and with such fearful speed that we stood amazed. The great tunnel in which this fiery flow swept down was a vitrified duct apparently as smooth as glass, and the speed, though it could not be measured, I estimated to be forty miles an hour.

Leaving this opening, we pressed forward, and once in about one or two miles we found other rents from thirty to two hundred feet in length, down which we looked, and saw the lava torrent hurrying toward the sea. These openings in the mountain are vents or breathing holes for the discharge of the burning gases, and thus perhaps prevented earthquakes and terrific explosions. They are longitudinal, revealing the fiery channel at the depth of fifty to a hundred feet below, and exposing a sight to appall the stoutest heart. To fall into one of these orifices would be instant death. . . .

In one place we saw the burning river uncovered for nearly 500 feet, and dashing down a declivity of about twenty degrees, leaping precipices in a mad rage that was indescribable. Standing at the lower end of this opening we could look up, not only along the line of fire, but also thirty-five feet or more into the mouth of the tunnel out of which it issued, and see the fiery cataract leaping over a cliff some fifteen feet high, with a sullen roar which was terrific, while the arched roof of this tunnel, some forty feet above the stream, and the walls on each side of the open space were hung with glowing stalactites. . . .

On our return we found Hilo in a state of anxious suspense, and eager to hear what we had seen and what were the probabilities that the eruption would reach the town. The light of the blazing forest was evidently drawing nearer and nearer daily. . . . The eruption made steady progress toward the town, felling the forest, filling up ravines and depressions, and licking up the streams and basins of water in its way. . . .

As the weeks went by, I made several other visits to the lava stream—eight, I think, in all—marking its rate of progress and its varied phenomena, and concluding with many others that its entrance into our town and harbor was only a question of time, unless the blast of the awful furnace on the mountain should cease. . . . The devouring enemy was within seven miles of us, its fiery lines extending two miles in width. Already it had descended on its devastated track fifty or sixty miles, persistently overcoming every obstacle; the little distance remaining was all open, and no human power could set up any barriers or arrest the oncoming destroyer. . . .

On the 12th of February . . . a party of fifty or sixty foreigners was made up to visit the eruption, then about six miles from the town. . . . We met in an opening in the forest, some distance from the main stream, but opposite an active flow of lava that had shot down the channel of a rivulet. . . . Most of them were so terrified that they could not be persuaded to approach nearer to the burning river, but those who were reassured and ventured to join the party of observation were well repaid.

Through the energy of a ship master, a fine topsail canvas tent had been set up on a high bank of the water channel overlooking a deep basin, into which a cascade was falling from a height of thirty-nine feet, and our position commanded the channel for half a mile. The fiery stream, perhaps seventy-five feet wide, filled the whole channel and drove the boiling water before it, burning the bushes and vines and ferns along the banks as it approached the fall.

Down plunged the molten lava, moving like a serpent into the depths of the basin, covering the whole surface with enormous bubbles. A dense steam which rolled upward in convolving clouds of fleecy whiteness floated away upon the wind. Sometimes the glare of the fire would so fall upon the cloud of vapor as to produce the appearance of flame mingled with blood, and again the quivering and dancing of countless prismatic colors.

By daybreak there was not a drop of water left in the basin; the space was filled with smouldering lavas, and the precipice . . . was converted into a gently sloping plane. A large slab of lava crust was tilted and stood as a monument of the accomplished work; the flow ceased; a little red-hot lava was seen amidst the smouldering heaps of rocky coal, and from that day the fearful flood did not come another foot toward Hilo.

From time immemorial earthquakes have been common in Hawaii. We have felt the jar of thousands. Most of these shocks have been harmless. A few have broken a little crockery, cracked plastering, and thrown down stone walls. But on the 27th of March, 1868, a series of remarkable earthquakes commenced. Kilauea was unusually full and in vehement action. Day after day from March 27th and onward, shocks were frequent, and growing more and more earnest.

At 4 P.M., April 2nd, a terrific shock rent the ground, sending consternation through all Hilo, Puna and Kau. In some places fissures of great length, breadth and depth opened. Rocks of twenty to fifty tons were sent thundering down from the walls of Kilauea, and massive boulders were torn from hillsides and sent crashing down upon the plains and valleys below. Stone houses were rent and ruined, and stone walls sent flying in every direction. Horses and men were thrown to the ground; houses tilted from their foundations; furniture, hardware, crockery, books and bottles, and all things movable in houses were dashed hither and thither, as of no account. It seemed as if the ribs and pillars of the earth were being shattered.

I was sitting . . . at my study table when a fearful jerk startled me, and before I could arise a jar still more terrible caused me to rush for the stairs, and while going down, such a crash shook the house that I supposed the roof had fallen. Going out of doors, I found my wife standing at a distance from the house watching with an intense gaze its swaying and trembling, while the ground rose and sank like waves, and there was no place stable where hand or foot could rest.

When the shocks intermitted a little, I went upstairs to witness a scene of wild confusion. A large bookcase, seven feet high by four wide with glass doors and filled with books, lay prostrate on the floor near where I had been sitting, with the glass broken into a thousand pieces. My study table, eight feet long and loaded with large volumes, was thrown out from the wall into the center of the room, with one leg broken square off. . . . Another bookcase, fastened to the wall, was rent from its fastenings and thrown out near the table, and three of the sleepers which supported the floor were broken by the fall of the case.

The shaking continued all night, and most or all of the Hilo people spent the night out of doors, fearing to remain in their houses. Some said they counted a thousand shocks before morning, and so rapid were these shocks that the earth seemed to be in a continuous quiver, like a ship in a battle.

But the heaviest blows fell on Kau, the district lying south of us on the other side of Kilauea. There the earth was rent in a thousand places, and along the foothills of Mauna Loa a number of land-slips were shaken off from the steep places, and thrown down with soil, boulders and trees. In one place a slide of half a mile in width was started on a steep inclined plane, till, coming to a precipice of some 700 feet, on an angle of about 70 degrees, the vast avalanche, mixing with waters of a running stream and several springs, was pitched down this precipice, receiving such fearful momentum as to carry it three miles in as many minutes. Ten houses, with thirty-one souls and five hundred head of cattle, were buried instantly, and not one of them has been recovered.

I measured this avalanche and found it just three miles long, one half a mile wide at the head, and of a supposed average depth of twenty-five feet.

At the same time the sea rose twenty feet along the southern shore of the island, and in Kau 108 houses were destroyed and forty-six people drowned, making a loss of 118 houses and seventy-seven lives in that district during this one hour. Many houses were also destroyed in Puna, but no lives lost.

During this awful hour the coast of Puna and Kau, for a distance of seventy-five miles, subsided seven feet on the average, submerging a line of small villages all along the shore. One of my rough stone meeting houses in Puna, where we once had a congregation of 500 to 1,000, was swept away with the influx of the sea, and its walls are now under water. Fortunately there was but one stone building in Hilo, our prison; that fell immediately. Had our coast been studded with cities built of stone and brick, the destruction of life and property would have been terrific.

This terrible earthquake was evidently caused by the subterraneous flow of lavas from Kilauea, for the bottom of the crater sank rapidly hundreds of feet, as ice goes down when the water beneath it is drawn off. The course and the terminus of this flow were indicated by fissures, steam and spouting of lava jets along the whole line from Kilauea to Kahuku in western Kau, a distance of forty miles, and I have found foldings and faults in several places.

During these days of subterranean passage, the earth was in a remarkable state of unrest; shocks were frequent, and it was asserted by trustworthy witnesses that in several places the ragings of the subterranean river were heard by listeners who put their ears to the ground. On the 7th of April the lava burst out from the ground in Kahuku, nine miles from the sea, and flowed rapidly down to the shore. . . . A fissure of a mile long was opened for the disgorgement of this igneous river, and from the whole length of this orifice the lava rushed up with intense vehemence, spouting jets one hundred to two hundred feet high, burning the forest and spreading out a mile wide. The rending, the raging, the swirling of this stream were terrific, awakening awe in all the beholders.

Flowing seaward, it came to a high precipice which ran some seven miles toward the shore, varying in height from two hundred to seven hundred feet, and separating a high fertile plain of a deep and rich soil. . . . Before the flow reached this precipice it sent out three lateral streams upon the grassy plain above, which ran a few miles, and ceased without reaching the sea. But the larger portion of the igneous river or its main trunk moved in a nearly straight line toward the shore, pouring over the upper end of the precipice upon the plain below, and dividing into two streams which ran parallel to each other some hundred feet apart until they plunged into the sea.

These streams flowed four days, causing the waves to boil with great violence and raising two large tufa cones in the water at their termini. They formed a long, narrow island, on which they enclosed thirty head of cattle . . . and it was ten days before the lava was hard enough to allow them to be taken out of their prison. During this time they had no water and were almost maddened by the smoke and heat. . . .

The owner of a ranch, with his wife and a large family of children, was living in a pleasant house surrounded by a wall, with a fine garden of trees and plants, near the center of this beautiful grassy plain, and while sleeping at night, unconscious of danger, one of these lateral streams came creeping softly and silently like a serpent toward them, until within twenty yards of the house, when a sudden spout of lava aroused them and all fled with frightened precipitation, taking neither "purse or scrip," but leaving all to the devouring fire. . . .

The family, crossing a small ravine, rested a few moments on a hill nearby. In ten minutes after crossing the ravine it was filled with liquid fire. Their escape was marvelous. In a few minutes the house was wrapped in flames, the garden consumed and all the premises were covered with a burning sea.

A little farther down this green lawn was the hut of a native Hawaiian. As the fiery flood came within fifty feet of it, it suddenly parted, one arm sweeping around one side of the house and the other around the opposite side, and, uniting again, left the building on a small plat of ground of some three-quarters of an acre, surrounded by a wall of fusion. In this house five souls were imprisoned ten days with no power to escape. All their food and water were exhausted. Small fingers of lava often came under the house; it was a little grass hut, and they were obliged to beat out the fire with clubs and stamp it with their feet.

Piles of burning scoria were heaped around this house as high as the eaves, and in some places within ten feet of it. I afterward visited this house and found its inmates alive and rejoicing in their deliverance.

On the 5th of November, 1880, our latest eruption from Mauna Loa broke out at a point some 12,000 feet above sea level. . . . The glare was intense and was seen at great distances. Brilliant jets of lava were thrown high in the air, and a pillar of blazing gases mounted thousands of feet skyward, spreading out into a canopy of sanguinary light, which resembled, though upon a larger scale, the so-called "pine-tree appendage" formed over Vesuvius during its eruptions. . . .

Down came a river of lava in several channels flowing in the direction of Hilo. . . . There was the sound of a continuous cannonading as the lava moved on, rocks exploding under the heat, and gases shattering their way from confinement. We could hear the explosions in Hilo; it was like the noise of battle. Day and night the ancient forest was ablaze, and the scene was vivid beyond description. By the 25th of March [1881] the lava was within seven miles of Hilo and steadily advancing. . . . By the 1st of June it was within five miles of us, and its advance, though slow, was persistent. It had now descended nearly fifty miles from its source and the action of Mauna Loa was unabated. The outlook was fearful. . . .

The flood came on until all agreed that in two or three days more it would be pouring into our beautiful bay. On the 10th of August it was but one mile from the sea and half a mile from Hilo town. On that day, nine months and five days from the outbursting of the great eruption when hope had perished in nearly every heart, the action began to abate. The raging flood, the steam, the smoke, the noise of the flow was checked; and in a day or two the great red dragon lay stiffened and harmless upon the borders of our village. The relief was unspeakable.

I estimate that the lava stream covered a hundred square miles of mountain, forest, and farm land to an average depth of twenty-five feet—enough to cover the State of Connecticut to a depth of six inches.

From *Life in Hawaii*, Titus Coan (New York: Randolph, 1882).

XXXIX

Charles Warren Stoddard

Charles Warren Stoddard (1843–1909), essayist, poet, South Seas publicist, university English professor, and secretary to Mark Twain, was touted as a major American author in the 1870's, 80's, and 90's. The editor of the *Atlantic Monthly*, William Dean Howells, one of the most highly respected critics and authors of the period, proclaimed extravagantly that there existed "few such delicious bits of literature in the language" as Stoddard's compositions. He went on further to identify Stoddard's essays on Pacific islands as "the lightest, sweetest, wildest, freshest things that ever were written about the life of that summer ocean."

But Stoddard's literary reputation was shortlived. Though he pioneered as the light lyricist in revealing the wonders of the tropics, authors of greater stature soon eclipsed him in his own specialty—including Robert Louis Stevenson, whom he persuaded to make that first Pacific pilgrimage. Stoddard belonged to the brief era of American romanticism when readers could be carried away with sentimental descriptions of bright sunsets, rollicking rivulets, mountain peaks at dawn, and moonlit surf; little of his writing outlived that era.

South-Sea Idyls, which went into several editions in the United States and England, was his most popular book—and his essay on a horseback jaunt, with his stooge Felix, into lonely, charming Waipio Valley on the Big Island, was representative of his art. "Tired out twenty times over" from the long ride to the brink of the valley, at

sunset they descend the precipitous trail into the otherworldliness of
Waipio, where their fatigue is relieved by the ancient Hawaiian art
of *lomilomi*—a form of chiropractic or massage—before they proceed to
an illegal hula performance.

Lomilomi and Hulahula

Down we dropped into fifty fathoms of the sweetest twilight
imaginable—so sweet it seemed to have been born of a wilderness
of the night-blooming cereus and fed forever on jasmine buds.
There were shelter and refreshment for two hundred souls, and
we slid out of our saddles as though we had been boned expressly
for a cannibal feast.

By this time the rosy flush on Mauna Kea had faded, and its
superb brow was pale with an unearthly pallor. "Come in," said
the host; and he led us under the thatched gable that was fragrant
as new-mown hay. There we sat, "in," as he called it, though there
was never a side to the concern thicker than a shadow.

A stream flowed noiselessly at our feet. Canoes drifted by us,
with dusky and nude forms bowed over the paddles. Each oc-
cupant greeted us. . . . They seldom paused, but called back to
us from the gathering darkness with inexpressibly tender contralto
voices. Thereupon we were summoned to dinner in another apartment, screened with vines. The faint flicker of tapers suggested
that what breath of air might be stirring came from the mountain,
and it brought with it a message from the orangery up the valley. . . .

"You are just in time," said our host.

"Why, what's up?" asked I.

"The moon will be up presently, and after moonrise you shall
see the *hula-hula*."

Felix desired to be enlightened as to the nature of the what-you-
call-it, and was assured that it was worth seeing, and would require no explanatory chorus when its hour came.

It was at least a mile to the scene of action; a tortuous stream wound thither, navigable in spots, but from time to time the canoe would have to take to the banks for a short cut into deeper water.

"I can never get there," growled Felix; "I'm full of needles and pins"; to which the host responded by excusing himself for a few moments, leaving Felix and me alone. It was deathly still in the valley, though a thousand crickets sang, and the fish smacked their round mouths at the top of the water. Evening comes slowly in those beloved tropics, but it comes so satisfactorily that there is nothing left out.

A moonlight night is a continuous festival. The natives sing and dance till daybreak, making it all up by sleeping till the next twilight. Nothing is lost by this ingenious and admirable arrangement. Why should they sleep, when a night there has the very essence of five nights anywhere else, extracted and enriched with spices till it is so inspiring that the soul cries out in triumph, and the eyes couldn't sleep if they would?

At this period, enter to us the host, with several young native girls, who seat themselves at our feet, clasping each a boot-leg encasing the extremities of Felix and myself. Felix kicked violently and left the room with some embarrassment, and I appealed to the hospitable gentleman of the house, who was smiling somewhat audibly at our perplexity.

He assured me that if I would throw myself upon the mats in the corner, two of these maids would speedily relieve me of any bodily pain I might at that moment be suffering with.

I did so: the two proceeded . . . and whatever bodily pain I may have possessed at the beginning of the process speedily dwindled into insignificance by comparison with the tortures of my novel cure. Every limb had to be unjointed and set over again. Places were made for new joints, and I think the new joints were temporarily set in, for my arms and legs went into angles I had never before seen them in, nor have I since been able to assume those startling attitudes.

The stomach was then kneaded like dough. The ribs were crushed down against the spine, and then forced out by well-directed blows in the back. The spinal column was undoubtedly abstracted and some mechanical substitute now does its best to

help me through the world. The arms were tied in bow-knots behind, and the skull cracked like the shell of a hard-boiled egg,
worked into shape again, and left to heal.

By this time I was unconscious, and for an hour my sleep
promised to be eternal. I must have lain flat on the matting, without a curve in me, when Nature, taking pity, gradually let me rise
and assume my own proportions, as though a little leaven had
been mixed in my taking over.

The awakening was like coming from a bath of the elements. I
breathed to the tips of my toes. Perfumes penetrated me till I was
saturated with them. I felt a thousand years younger; and as I
looked back upon the old life I seemed to have risen from, I
thought of it much as a butterfly must think of his grub-hood, and
was in the act of expanding my wings, when I saw Felix just recovering, a few feet from me, apparently as ecstatic as myself. . . .

Felix sprang to his feet like Prometheus unbound, and embraced
me with fervor. . . . "Did you ever see anything like it, Old
Boy?" . . .

"There wasn't much to see, but my feelings were past expression."

"What's its name?" asked Felix.

"I think they call it *lomi-lomi*," said I.

"Pass *lomi-lomi!*" shouted Felix; and then we both roared again,
which summoned the host, who congratulated us and invited us to
his canoe. . . .

Bands of fishermen and fisherwomen passed us, wading breast-
high in the water, beating it into a foam before them, and singing
at the top of their voices as they drove the fish down the stream
into a broad net a few rods below. Grass houses, half buried in
foliage, lined the mossy banks; while the dusky groups of women
and children, clustering about the smouldering flames that be-
tokened the preparation of the evening meal, added not a little to
the poetry of twilight in the tropics. . . .

The boughs of densely leaved trees reached out to one another
across the water. We proceeded with more caution as the channel
grew narrow; and, pressing through a submerged thicket of reeds,
we routed a flock of water-fowls that wheeled overhead on heavy

wings, filling the valley with their clamor. Two or three dogs barked sleepily off somewhere in the darkness, and the voice of someone calling floated to us as clear as a bird's note, though we knew it must be far away.

We strode through a cane field, its smoky plumes just tipped with moonlight, and saw the pinnacle of Mauna Kea, as spacious and splendid as a fairy pavilion . . . illuminated as for a festival. To the left, a stream fell from the cliff, a ribbon of gauze fluttering noiselessly in the wind.

"O, look!" said Felix, who had yielded again to the influences of Nature. Looking, I saw the moon resting upon the water for a moment, while the dew seemed actually to drip from her burnished disk . . . I ran to him and was silent with him, while we two stood worshiping one stately palm that rested its glorious head upon the glowing bosom of the moon, like the Virgin in the radiant aureola.

"Well," said our host, "supposing we get along!"

We got along, by land and water, into a village in an orange grove. There was a subdued murmur of many voices. I think the whole community would have burst out into a song of some sort at the slightest provocation. On we paced, in Indian file, through narrow lanes, under the shining leaves. Pale blossoms rained down upon us, and the air was oppressively sweet. Groups of natives sat in the lanes, smoking and laughing. Lovers made love in the face of heaven, utterly unconscious of any human presence. . . .

Through a wicket we passed, where a sentinel kept ward. Within the bamboo paling a swarm of natives gathered about us, first questioning the nature of our visit, which having proved entirely satisfactory, we were welcomed in real earnest and offered a mat in an inner room of a large house rather superior to the average, and a disagreeable liquor—brewed of oranges, very intoxicating when not diluted, and therefore popular.

We were evidently the lions of the hour, for we sat in the center of the first row of spectators who were gathered to witness the *hula-hula*. We reclined as gracefully as possible upon our mats, supported by plump pillows stuffed with dried ferns. Slender rushes—strung with *kukui* nuts, about the size of chestnuts, and very oily—were planted before us like footlights, which, being lighted at the top, burned slowly downward till the whole was consumed, giving a good flame for several hours.

The great mat upon the floor before us was the stage. On one side of it a half-dozen muscular fellows were squatted, with large calabashes headed with tightly drawn goat skins. These were the drummers and singers. . . . A dozen performers entered, sitting in two lines face to face—six women and six men. Each bore a long joint of bamboo, slit at one end like a broom. . . .

Taking a bamboo in one hand, they struck it in the palm of the other, on the shoulder, on the floor in front, to left and right; thrust it out before them, and were parried by the partners opposite; crossed it over and back, and turned in a thousand ways to a thousand meters, varied with chants and pauses. . . . For half an hour or more the thrashing of the bamboos was prolonged, while we were hopelessly confused in our endeavors to follow the barbarous harmony. . . .

"Now for the *hula-hula*," said the host. . . . It is the national dance, taught to all children by their parents, but so difficult to excel in that the few who perfect themselves can afford to travel on this one specialty.

There was a murmur of impatience, speedily checked, and followed by a burst of applause as a band of beautiful girls, covered with wreaths of flowers and vines, entered and seated themselves before us. While the musicians beat an introductory overture upon the tom-toms, the dancers proceeded to bind shawls and scarfs about their waists, turban-fashion. They sat in a line, facing us, a foot or two apart. The loose sleeves of their dresses were caught up at the shoulder, exposing arms of almost perfect symmetry, while their bare throats were scarcely hidden by the necklaces of jasmines that coiled about them.

Then the leader of the band who sat, grayheaded and wrinkled at one end of the room, throwing back his head, uttered a long, wild and shrill guttural—a sort of invocation to the goddess of the *hula-hula*. . . . The dance began, all joining in with wonderfully accurate rhythm, the body swaying slowly backward and forward, to left and right; the arms tossing, or rather waving, in the air above the head, now beckoning some spirit of light, so tender and seductive were the emotions of the dancers, so graceful and free the movements of the wrists; now, in violence and fear, they seemed to repulse a host of devils that hovered invisibly about them.

The spectators watched and listened breathlessly, fascinated by the terrible wildness of the song and the monotonous thrumming of the accompaniment. Presently the excitement increased. Swifter and more wildly the bare arms beat the air, embracing, as it were, the airy forms that haunted the dancers, who rose to their knees and, with astonishing agility, caused the clumsy turbans about their loins to quiver with an undulatory motion, increasing or decreasing with the sentiment of the song and the enthusiasm of the spectators. . . .

From the floor to the knees, from the knees to their feet, now facing us, now turning from us, they spun and ambled, till the ear was deafened with cheers and boisterous, half-drunken, wholly passionate laughter. The room whirled with the reeling dancers, who seemed encircled with living serpents in the act of swallowing big lumps of something from their throats clear to the tips of their tails, and the convulsions continued till the hysterical dancers staggered and fell to the floor, overcome by unutterable fatigue. . . .

This was the seductive dance still practiced in secret, though the law forbids it; and to the Hawaiian it is more beautiful, because more sensuous, than anything else in the world. . . .

A slight variation in the order of the dances followed. A young lover, seated in the center of the room, beat a tattoo upon his calabash and sang a song of love. In a moment he was answered. Out of the darkness rose the sweet, shrill voice of the loved one. Nearer and nearer it approached; the voice range clear and high, melodiously swelling upon the air. It must have been heard far off in the valley, it was so plaintive and penetrating. . . . Dramatic effect was produced by her entrance at the right moment.

She enacted her part with graceful energy. To the regular and melancholy thrumming of the calabash, she sang her song of love. Yielding to her emotion, she did not hesitate to betray all; neither was he of the calabash slow to respond; and, scorning the charms of goat skin and gourd, he sprang toward her in the madness of his soul, when she, having reached the climax of desperation, was hurried from the scene of her conquest amid whirlwinds of applause. . . . The audience began slowly to disperse. . . .

Our time was up at daybreak and, with an endless deal of persuasion, Felix followed me out of the valley to the little chapel on the cliff. Our horses took a breath there, and so did we, bird's-eyeing the scene of the last night's orgy.

Who says it isn't a delicious spot—that deep, narrow and secluded vale, walled by almost perpendicular cliffs, hung with green tapestries of ferns and vines; that slender stream, like a thread of silver, embroidering a carpet of Nature's richest pattern; that torrent, leaping from the cliff into a garden of citrons; the sea sobbing at its mouth, while wary mariners, coasting in summer afternoons, catch glimpses of the tranquil and forbidden paradise, yet are heedless of all its beauty, and reck not the rustling of the cane fields nor the voices of the charmers, because— because these things are so common in that latitude that one grows naturally indifferent!

From *South-Sea Idyls*, Charles Warren Stoddard (New York: Scribners, 1873).

XL

Bill Nye

The warm hospitality extended by Hawaiians to visitors from the Mainland, even in remote villages like Waipio, was seldom reciprocated in kind when Hawaiians visited the Mainland. The genuineness of the Island reception was ordinarily repaid in furtive mockery and condescension; common Kanakas were treated like Negroes; chiefs and royalty like circus celebrities or third-class cousins from the country. Though kings, queens, and princes—always occupying expensive suites in the best hotels—were accorded fawning deference to their faces, behind their backs they were showered with chuckles and quips.

For half a century entourages of *alii* had been sailing from Honolulu on world tours, until Hawaiian monarchs, their wives and sons, had gained a reputation for being the most traveled royalty on earth. In 1881 King Kalakaua topped the itinerancy of his predecessors by making a trip around the globe—the first king ever to undertake such an exploit. He was lavishly entertained by the emperor of Japan and the viceroy of India, had an audience with the Pope in Rome, visited Queen Victoria and Kaiser Wilhelm, toured Belgium, Austria, France, Spain, and Portugal, and on his way home was wined and dined in the United States.

That spectacular venture was soon followed by another for Queens Kapiolani and Liliuokalani, en route to Queen Victoria's Jubilee in England. On their stopover in Manhattan, Bill Nye (Edgar Wilson Nye, 1850–1896), correspondent for the *New York World* and one of

America's foremost humorists, then extremely popular for his billings as co-lecturer with James Whitcomb Riley, made the most of an opportunity to express how Americans in general regarded the dark-complexioned royalty from the little Pacific kingdom—when such guests strayed too far from their throne.

Audience with the Queen

The sun was just slipping out the back door of the West and hunting for the timber of New Jersey as Queen Kapiolani, at her rooms in the Victoria Hotel, received a plain, rectangular card, printed in two kinds of ink at the owner's steam job office, containing the following brief but logical statement:

Wilhelm Von Nyj
Littérateur and Danseuse.

On the back of the card the Von Nyj arms had been emblazoned with a rubber stamp. Downstairs, near the dais of the night clerk, stood a gayly caparisoned yet cultivated cuss pouring over a late volume of the city directory. He was the author of these lines.

Scarcely an hour had elapsed when a tinted octavo page who waits on the Queen slid down the stair rail and told me that her Royal Highness would receive me in state as soon as she could change her dress.

Later on I was ushered into the presence of Queen Kapiolani, who was at the time accompanied by her suite and another gentleman whose name I did not learn.

She is a distinguished-looking woman of middle age, but in apparent good health and with a constitution which I think would easily endure the fatigue of reigning over a much larger country than her own.

As I entered the room and made a low, groveling obeisance, an act that is wholly foreign to my nature, the Queen made a rapid movement towards the bell, but I held her back and assured her that I did not drink.

We then chatted gayly for some time in relation to the Sandwich business and court matters. . . . For a long time the Queen seemed constrained and evidently could not think of anything to say; but she soon saw that I was not haughty or reserved, and when at last she reluctantly showed me out and locked the door, I felt amply repaid for the annoyance that one naturally feels on visiting a perfect stranger.

From what she said regarding her dynasty I gather that it consists of a covey of half-grown islands in the Pacific, inhabited by people who were once benighted and carnivorous, but happy. Now they are well-informed and bilious, while they revel in suspenders and rum, with all the blessings of late hours, civilization and suicide.

The better classes of the Sandwich Islands have the same customs which prevail here, and the swallow-tail coat is quite prevalent there. The low-neck and short-sleeve costume is even carried to a greater excess, perhaps, and all opera tickets read: "Admit the Bearer and Barer."

In answer to a question of my own, the Queen said that crops in the Sandwich Islands were looking well, and that garden truck was far in advance of what she saw here. She said that they had pie plant in her garden big enough to eat before she came away, and new potatoes were as big as walnuts. Still, she is enjoying herself here first rate and says she sees many pleasing features about New York which will ever decorate the tablets of her memory.

I thanked her for this neat little compliment, and told her I should always regard her in the same manner. I then wrote a little impromptu stanza in her autograph album, wrung Her Majesty's hand, and retired with another suppliant and crouching bow, which indicated a contrite spirit, but was calculated to deceive.

I took the liberty of extending to Her Majesty the freedom of the city, and asked her to visit our press rooms and see us squat our burning thoughts into a quarter of a million copies of the paper, and all for two cents. I also asked her to come up any time and read our Hawaii exchanges, for I know how lonely anybody can be in a great city sometimes, and how one yearns for a glimpse of his country paper.

The Queen is well paid while she reigns; and even while away as she is now, with her scepter standing idly in the umbrella rack at home and a large pink mosquito net thrown over the throne, her pay is still going on night and day.

The above is substantially all that I said during the interview, though the Queen said something as I came out of the room, escorted by the janitor, which I did not quite catch. I did say, however, just before leaving the room, that I regretted sincerely the unfortunate time of the year at which Her Majesty had decided to visit us, it being rather between hay and grass, as it were, for as there was no *R* in the month, it was a little too late for missionaries and a little too early for watermelons. It was only an instant later that I joined the janitor at the foot of the stairs.

From *Bill Nye's Chestnuts Old and New* (Chicago, New York, and San Francisco: Belford, Clarke & Company, 1889).

XLI

Robert Louis Stevenson

Though Robert Louis Stevenson (1850–1894) has been limned by promotion agents as one of the grand old patrons of the Islands, the status is hardly in accord with any sentiment he ever expressed. Stevenson did not fall very hard for Hawaii. He was looking for a more primitive Polynesian paradise. "In vile Honolulu," he once sniffed, "there are too many cesspools and beastly *haoles.*" He loved the Hawaiians and became a bosom companion of King Kalakaua, but he detested the planters, the aggressive men of commerce, and the social climbers.

The ailing British novelist and poet called at the Islands twice— en route to places that interested him more; he stayed for five months in 1889 and for a shorter period four years later. At one time he did toy with the idea of purchasing a ranch on the Big Island and settling down, but it was only a passing fancy. Some of the Island setting he absorbed was worked into "The Bottle Imp" and "The Isle of Voices," but during the stopovers in Hawaii he was preoccupied most of the time with writing that had nothing to do with the Islands. Graciously he scrawled in the guest book of his Waikiki rooming house a warm endorsement of the establishment and its locale; ingraciously the manager promptly sent it to the local newspaper as a paid advertisement. That was the nearest he ever came to lauding Hawaii.

While touring the Islands, he visited the leper colony at Molokai for eight days, sympathized with the devoted Catholic priests and sisters who were trying to relieve some of the suffering, played croquet with the leprous children, constantly fought back his "horror of the horrible," developed a profound respect for the late Reverend Father J. Damien De Veuster, the Belgian peasant-priest who for sixteen years had labored among the "loathsome lepers," contracted the disease, and recently succumbed to it.

The presence of leprosy, at the time, was beginning to give the Islands a bad name. Mainlanders who knew nothing else about Hawaii seemed to be very familiar with the prevalence of that frightful pestilence. It was fixed in many minds as a symbol for the Islands, and inadvertently Stevenson enlarged that symbol.

In Australia, a few months after leaving Honolulu, the novelist picked up an American magazine containing a deprecatory letter about Father Damien written by a prominent Honolulu pastor, Dr. Charles M. Hyde, to a fellow Protestant minister, the Reverend H. B. Gage in Riverside, California. The brief letter, a scurrilous attack on revered Father Damien, was apparently being given worldwide publicity. It infuriated Stevenson. In white heat he drafted an even more scurrilous open letter to Dr. Hyde—a counterattack on the pastor and a brilliant defense of the Molokai martyr. In fact, Stevenson was so fully aware that his answer might bring on a ruinous libel suit that he declined to send it to the press until his immediate family had voted unanimously for its publication.

Sensibly Dr. Hyde did not choose to take the matter to court, and later Stevenson expressed regret at having been so "barbarously harsh." But the reply, published in newspapers around the world, reprinted in pamphlet form, and included in anthologies, became recognized as one of the famous letters in English literature.

The Martyr of Molokai

Sydney, February 25, 1890

Sir,—It may probably occur to you that we have met, and visited, and conversed; on my side, with interest. You may remember that you have done me several courtesies, for which I was prepared to be grateful. But there are duties which come before gratitude, and offenses which justly divide friends, far more acquaintances.

Your letter to the Reverend H. B. Gage is a document which, in my sight, if you had filled me with bread when I was starving, if you had sat up to nurse my father when he lay a-dying, would yet absolve me from the bonds of gratitude.

You know enough, doubtless, of the process of canonization to be aware that, a hundred years after the death of Damien, there will appear a man charged with the painful office of the *devil's advocate*. After that noble brother of mine, and of all frail clay, shall have lain a century at rest, one shall accuse, one defend him. The circumstance is unusual that the devil's advocate should be a volunteer, should be a member of a sect immediately rival, and should make haste to take upon himself his ugly office ere the bones are cold; unusual, and of a taste which I shall leave my readers free to qualify; unusual, and to me inspiring.

If I have at all learned the trade of using words to convey truth and to arouse emotion, you have at least furnished me with a subject.

For it is in the interest of all mankind and the cause of public decency in every quarter of the world, not only that Damien should be righted, but that you and your letter should be displayed at length, in their true colors, to the public eye.

To do this properly, I must begin by quoting you at large: I shall then proceed to criticize your utterance from several points of view, divine and human, in the course of which I shall attempt to draw again and with more specification the character of the dead saint whom it has pleased you to vilify: so much being done, I shall say farewell to you forever.

Honolulu, Aug. 2, 1889

Rev. H. B. Gage:

Dear Brother,—In answer to your inquiries about Father Damien, I can only reply that we who know the man are surprised at the extravagant newspaper laudations, as if he was a most saintly philanthropist. The simple truth is, he was a coarse, dirty man, headstrong and bigoted. He was not sent to Molokai, but went there without orders; did not stay at the leper settlement (before he became one himself), but circulated freely over the whole island (less than half the island is devoted to the lepers), and he came often to Honolulu. He had no hand in the reforms and improvements inaugurated, which were the work of our Board of Health, as occasion required and means were provided. He was not a pure man in his relations with women, and the leprosy of which he died should be attributed to his vices and carelessness. Others have done much for the lepers, our own ministers, the government physicians, and so forth, but never with the Catholic idea of meriting eternal life.—

Yours, etc.

C. M. Hyde

To deal fitly with a letter so extraordinary, I must draw at the outset on my private knowledge of the signatory and his sect. It may offend others; scarcely you, who have been so busy to collect, so bold to publish, gossip on your rivals. And this is perhaps the moment when I may best explain to you the character of what you are to read: I conceive you as a man quite beyond and below the reticences of civility: with what measure you mete, with that shall it be measured you again; with you, at last, I rejoice to feel the button off the foil and to plunge home. And if in aught that I shall say I should offend others, your colleagues, whom I respect and remember with affection, I can but offer them my regret; I am not free, I am inspired by the consideration of interests far more large; and such pain as can be inflicted by anything from me must be indeed trifling when compared with the pain with which they read your letter. It is not the hangman, but the criminal, that brings dishonor on the house.

You belong, sir, to a sect—I believe my sect, and that in which my ancestors labored—which has enjoyed, and partly failed to utilize, an exceptional advantage in the islands of Hawaii. The first missionaries came; they found the land already self-purged of its old and bloody faith; they were embraced, almost on their arrival, with enthusiasm; what troubles they supported came far more from whites than from Hawaiians; and to these last they stood (in a rough figure) in the shoes of God.

This is not the place to enter into the degree or causes of their failure, such as it is. One element alone is pertinent, and must here be plainly dealt with. In the course of their evangelical calling, they—or too many of them—grew rich. It may be news to you that the houses of missionaries are a cause of mocking on the streets of Honolulu. It will at least be news to you, that when I returned your civil visit, the driver of my cab commented on the size, the taste, and the comfort of your home. It would have been news certainly to myself, had anyone told me that afternoon that I should live to drag such matter into print.

But you see, sir, how you degrade better men to your own level; and it is needful for those who are to judge betwixt you and me, betwixt Damien and the devil's advocate, should understand your letter to have been penned in a house which could raise, and that very justly, the envy and the comments of the passers-by. I think (to employ a phrase of yours which I admire) it "should be attributed" to you that you have never visited the scene of Damien's life and death. If you had, and had recalled it, and looked about your pleasant rooms, even your pen perhaps would have been stayed.

Your sect (and remember, as far as any sect avows me, it is mine) has not done ill in a worldly sense in the Hawaiian Kingdom. When calamity befell their innocent parishioners, when leprosy descended and took root in the Eight Islands, a *quid pro quo* was to be looked for. To that prosperous mission, and to you, as one of its adornments, God had sent at last an opportunity.

I know I am touching here upon a nerve acutely sensitive. I know that others of your colleagues look back on the inertia of your Church, and the intrusive and decisive heroism of Damien, with something almost to be called remorse. I am sure it is so with yourself; I am persuaded your letter was inspired by a certain envy, not essentially ignoble, and the one human trait to be espied in that performance.

You were thinking of the lost chance, the past day; of that which should have been conceived and was not; of the service due and not rendered. *Time was,* said the voice in your ear, in your pleasant room, as you sat raging and writing; and if the words written were base beyond parallel, the rage, I am happy to repeat—it is the only compliment I shall pay you—the rage was almost virtuous.

But, sir, when you have failed, and another has succeeded; when we have stood by, and another has stepped in; when we sit and grow bulky in our charming mansions, and a plain, uncouth peasant steps into the battle, under the eyes of God, and succors the afflicted, and consoles the dying, and is himself afflicted in his turn, and dies upon the field of honor—the battle cannot be retrieved as your unhappy irritation has suggested. It is a lost battle, and lost forever. One thing remained to you in your defeat—some rags of common honor; and these you have made haste to cast away. . . .

Your church and Father Damien's were in Hawaii upon a rivalry to do well: to help, to edify, to set divine examples. You having (in one huge instance) failed, and Damien succeeded, I marvel it should not have occurred to you that you were doomed to silence; that when you had been outstripped in that high rivalry, and sat inglorious in the midst of your well-being, in your pleasant room—and Damien, crowned with glories and honors, toiled and rotted in that pigsty of his under the cliffs of Kalawao —you, the elect, who would not, were the last man on earth to collect and propagate gossip on the volunteer who would and did. . . .

The world, in your despite, may perhaps owe you something . . . for if that world at all remember you on the day when Damien of Molokai shall be named Saint, it will be in virtue of one work: your letter to the Reverend H. B. Gage. . . .

I imagine you to be one of those persons who talk with cheerfulness of that place which oxen and wainropes could not drag you to behold. You, who do not even know its situation on the map, probably denounce sensational descriptions, stretching your limbs the while in your pleasant parlor on Beretania Street.

When I was pulled ashore there one early morning, there sat with me in the boat two sisters, bidding farewell (in humble imitation of Damien) to the lights and joys of human life. One of these wept silently; I could not withhold myself from joining her.

Had you been there, it is my belief that nature would have triumphed even in you; and as the boat drew but a little nearer,

Pearl Harbor, 1918—foothold between coasts

and you beheld the stairs crowded with abominable deformations of our common manhood, and saw yourself landing in the midst of such a population as only now and then surrounds us in the horror of a nightmare—what a haggard eye you would have rolled over your reluctant shoulder toward the house on Beretania Street!

Had you gone on; had you found every fourth face a blot upon the landscape; had you visited the hospital and seen the butt-ends of human beings lying there almost unrecognizable, but still breathing, still thinking, still remembering; you would have understood that life in the lazaretto is an ordeal from which the nerves of a man's spirit shrink, even as his eye quails under the brightness of the sun; you would have felt it was (even today) a pitiful place to visit and a hell to dwell in.

It is not the fear of possible infection. That seems a little thing when compared with the pain, the pity, and the disgust of the visitor's surroundings, and the atmosphere of affection, disease, and physical disgrace in which he breathes.

I do not think I am a man more than usually timid; but I never recall the days and nights I spent upon that island promontory (eight days and seven nights), without heartfelt thankfulness that I am somewhere else. I find in my diary that I speak of my stay as a "grinding experience": I have once jotted in the margin, "*Harrowing* is the word"; and when the *Mololii* bore me at last toward the outer world, I kept repeating to myself, with a new conception of their pregnancy, those simple words of the song—
'Tis the most distressful country that ever yet was seen.

And observe: that which I saw and suffered from was a settlement purged, bettered, beautified; the new village built, the hospital and the Bishop Home excellently arranged; the sisters, the doctor, and the missionaries, all indefatigable in their noble tasks.

It was a different place when Damien came there, and made his great renunciation, and slept that first night under a tree amidst his rotting brethren: alone with pestilence; and looking forward (with what courage, with what pitiful sinkings of dread, God only knows) to a lifetime of distressing sores and stumps.

You will say, perhaps, I am too sensitive, that sights as painful abound in cancer hospitals and are confronted daily by doctors and nurses. I have long learned to admire and envy the doctors and the nurses. But there is no cancer hospital so large and populous as Kalawao and Kalaupapa; . . . no doctor or nurse is called upon to enter once for all the doors of the gehenna; they do not say farewell, they need not abandon hope, on its sad threshold; they but go for a time to their high calling, and can look forward as they go to relief, to recreation, and to rest. But Damien shut to with his own hand the doors of his own sepulcher. . . .

We will (if you please) go hand-in-hand through the different phrases of your letter, and candidly examine each from the point of view of its truth, its appositeness, and its charity.

Damien was *coarse*.

It is very possible. You make us sorry for the lepers who had only a coarse old peasant for their friend and father. But you, who were so refined, why were you not there, to cheer them with the lights of culture? Or may I remind you that we have some reason to doubt if John the Baptist were genteel; and in the case of Peter, on whose career you doubtless dwell approvingly in the pulpit, no doubt at all he was a "coarse, headstrong" fisherman! Yet even in our Protestant Bibles Peter is called a Saint.

Damien was *dirty*.

He was. Think of the poor lepers annoyed with this dirty comrade! But the clean Dr. Hyde was at his food in a fine house.

Damien was *headstrong*.

I believe you are right again; and I thank God for his strong head and heart.

Damien was *bigoted*.

I am not fond of bigots myself, because they are not fond of me. But what is meant by bigotry, that we should regard it as a blemish in a priest? Damien believed his own religion with the simplicity of a peasant or a child; as I would I could suppose that you do. For this I wonder at him some way off; and had that been his only character, should have avoided him in life. But the point of interest in Damien, which has caused him to be so much talked about and made him at last the subject of your pen and mine, was that, in him, his bigotry, his intense and narrow faith, wrought potently for good, and strengthened him to be one of the world's heroes and exemplars.

Damien *was not sent to Molokai, but went there without orders.*

Is this a misreading? or do you really mean the words for blame? I have heard Christ, in the pulpits of your church, held up for imitation on the ground that His sacrifice was voluntary. Does Dr. Hyde think otherwise?

Damien *did not stay at the settlement, etc.*

It is true he was allowed many indulgences. Am I to understand that you blame the father for profiting by these, or the officers for granting them? In either case, it is a mighty Spartan standard to issue from the house on Beretania Street; and I am convinced you will find yourself with few supporters.

Damien *had no hand in the reforms, etc.*

I think even you will admit that I have already been frank in my description of the man I am defending. . . . I have now come far enough to meet you on a common ground of fact; and I tell you that, to a mind not prejudiced by jealousy, all the reforms of the lazaretto, and even those which he most vigorously opposed, are properly the work of Damien. They are the evidence of his success; they are what his heroism provoked from the reluctant and the careless. . . . It was his part, by one striking act of martyrdom, to direct all men's eyes on that distressful country. At a blow, and with the price of his life, he made the place illustrious and public. . . . If ever any man brought reforms, and died to bring them, it was he. There is not a clean cup or towel in the Bishop Home, but dirty Damien washed it.

Damien *was not a pure man in his relations with women, etc.*

How do you know that? Is this the nature of the conversation in that house on Beretania Street which the cabman envied, driving past?—racy details of the misconduct of the poor peasant priest, toiling under the cliffs of Molokai?

Many have visited the station before me; they seem not to have heard the rumor. When I was there I heard many shocking tales, for my informants were men speaking with the plainness of the laity; and I heard plenty of complaints of Damien. Why was this

never mentioned? and how came it to you in the retirement of
your clerical parlor?

But I must not even seem to deceive you. This scandal, when
I read it in your letter, was not new to me. I had heard it once
before; and I must tell you how. There came to Samoa a man
from Honolulu; he, in a public house on the beach, volunteered
the statement that Damien had "contracted the disease from
having connection with the female lepers"; and I find a joy in
telling you how the report was welcomed in a public house.

A man sprang to his feet; I am not at liberty to give his name,
but from what I heard I doubt if you would care to have him to
dinner in Beretania Street. "You miserable little ____" (here is a
word I dare not print, it would so shock your ears). "You miserable little ____," he cried, "if the story were a thousand times
true, can't you see you are a million times a lower ____ for
daring to repeat it?"

I wish it could be told of you that when the report reached
you in your house, perhaps after family worship, you had found
in your soul enough holy anger to receive it with the same expressions: ay, even with that one which I dare not print. . . .
But you have deliberately chosen the part of the man from Honolulu, and you have played it with improvements of your own.
The man from Honolulu—miserable, leering creature—communicated the tale to a rude knot of beach-combing drinkers in a
public house, where (I will so far agree with your temperance
opinions) man is not always at his noblest; and the man from
Honolulu had himself been drinking—drinking, we may charitably
fancy, to excess.

It was to your "Dear Brother, the Reverend H. B. Gage," that
you chose to communicate the sickening story; and the blue ribbon which adorns your portly bosom forbids me to allow you the
extenuating plea that you were drunk when it was done. Your
"dear brother"—a brother indeed—made haste to deliver up your
letter (as a means of grace, perhaps) to the religious papers;
where, after many months, I found and read and wondered at it;
and whence I have now reproduced it for the wonder of others.

And you and your dear brother have, by this cycle of operations, built up a contrast very edifying to examine in detail. The man whom you would not care to have to dinner, on the one side; on the other, the Reverend Dr. Hyde and the Reverend H. B. Gage: the Apia barroom, the Honolulu manse.

But I fear you scarce appreciate how you appear to your fellow-men; and to bring it home to you, I will suppose your story to be true. I will suppose—and God forgive me for supposing it—that Damien faltered and stumbled in his narrow path of duty; I will suppose that, in the horror of his isolation, perhaps in the fever of incipent disease, he, who was doing so much more than he had sworn, failed in the letter of his priestly oath—he, who was so much a better man than either you or me, who did what we have never dreamed of daring—he too tasted of our common frailty. "O, Iago, the pity of it!" The least tender should be moved to tears; the most incredulous to prayer. And all that you could do was to pen your letter to the Reverend H. B. Gage.

Is it growing at all clear to you what a picture you have drawn of your own heart? I will try yet once again to make it clearer. You had a father: suppose this tale were about him, and some informant brought it to you, proof in hand: I am not making too high an estimate of your emotional nature when I suppose you would regret the circumstance? that you would feel the tale of frailty the more keenly since it shamed the author of your days? and that the last thing you would do would be to publish it in the religious press? Well, the man who tried to do what Damien did, is my father, and the father of the man in the Apia bar, and the father of all who love goodness; and he is your father too, if God had given you grace to see it.

Robert Louis Stevenson

From *The Works of Robert Louis Stevenson*, Vol. 7, *In the South Seas* (New York: National Library Co., 1906).

XLII

Henry Adams

Except in remote spots like Hawaii's Waipio Valley, Maui's Hana, Oahu's Laie, or Kauai's Hanalei, the old Hawaiians and their ancient customs were fast disappearing. *Haole* enterprise and *haole* civilization were taking over; white plantation families, white ranchers, and white merchants and shippers were the real dictators of Island affairs. Honolulu and other port towns were becoming very civilized and respectable. Comfortable accommodations in Honolulu, paved roads in and out of the city, fine carriages, and a dignified society were making Hawaii attractive and not unfashionable as a destination for travelers, particularly for escapists, for those who wanted to forget their troubles, to relax, and to rediscover themselves in a fresh environment. It was an ideal retreat for America's foremost historian, Henry Adams (1838–1918).

The death of his wife in 1885 had sent him off on a series of wanderings. A member of the illustrious Boston family of statesmen and presidents, he had lived in England, served as a professor of history at Harvard for seven years, edited the *North American Review*, written novels, biographies, and a brilliant nine-volume history of the United States; but the loss of his wife enveloped him in a cloud of despair, pessimism, and uncertainty.

His journeyings at length landed him in Honolulu on the last day of August 1890, and the great historian, who later was to acquire even greater renown as author of *Mont-Saint-Michel and Chartres* and *The*

Education of Henry Adams, began looking over Hawaii with the eyes of a reluctant tourist.

He was a distinguished gentleman, accustomed to deferential courtesies, which Islanders—possibly through ignorance of his stature—failed to accord him. Doors were politely opened to him, but most of his calls were made on his own initiative, not in response to the invitations he expected. Socially Hawaii was an enigma to him. With his traveling companion, artist John La Farge, he rented a cottage in Nuuanu Valley, spent many days on horseback, sailed to the Big Island, returned to Oahu, and from his quiet Nuuanu retreat posted letters on his reactions to the Islands to his close friend Elizabeth Cameron.

So Passes the Glory of Hawaii

The drive of about two miles [up Nuuanu Avenue] was as amusing as a comedy, and full of "Look at that!" and "What is that?" and "What good eyes she has!" and so on, but I can't stop to speak of Kanakas or palms or banyans or reds or purples or flowers or night-gown costumes or old-gold women with splashes of color, but must hurry to our house, which was reached at last over a turf avenue between rows of palms.

The place is at the mouth of a broad mountain-valley opening out behind Honolulu, and overlooking the town and harbor, to the long line of white surf some three miles away, and then over the purple ocean indefinitely southward. The sense of space, light and color in front is superb, and the greater from the contrast behind, where the eye rests on a Scotch mountain-valley, ending in clouds and mist, and green mountain sides absolutely velvety with the liquid softness of its lights and shadows.

Showers and mist perpetually swept down the valley and moistened the grass, but about us, and to the southward, the sky was always blue and the sun shining. The day was hot in the town and the air like a green-house, but up here the northeast trade wind blew deliciously. As for the grounds, they are a mass of palms, ferns, roses, many-colored flowers, creepers interspersed with the yellow fruit of the limes, and unknown trees and shrubs of vaguely tropical suggestions, all a little neglected, and as though waiting for us.

The house, when we got into it, was large . . . and there was an ample supply of all ordinary things. Both La Farge and I were eager to move in at once. Mr. Smith drove us back to town at five o'clock, and helped us to order our house-keeping necessities; and I never but once saw La Farge so much amused and delighted with everything he saw as in this afternoon's excitement, where all was new and full of life and color. We dined at the hotel, and at eight o'clock reached our house again and installed ourselves.

While our rooms were made ready, we sat on the verandah and smoked. The full moon rose behind us and threw a wonderful light as far as the ocean-horizon. On the terrace were twin palm trees, about fifty feet high, glistening in the moonlight, and their long leaves wavering, and, as Stoddard says, "beckoning" and rustling in the strong gusts, with the human suggestion of distress which the palm alone among trees conveys to me.

I have driven La Farge up the Nuuanu Valley, where we live, to the great divide or pass, Pali, five or six miles up, where the lava cliff suddenly drops down to the sea-level, and one looks northward over green valleys and brown headlands to where the ocean, two or three miles distant, is breaking in curves and curls along the coast. The view is one of the finest I ever saw, and quite smashed La Farge. Yet I am amused to think what my original idea was of what the island would be like.

I conceived it as a forest-clad cluster of volcanoes, with fringing beaches where natives were always swimming, and I imagined that when I should leave the beach I should be led by steep paths through dense forests to green glades where native girls said *Aloha* and threw garlands round your neck, and where you would find straw huts of unparalleled cleanliness always on terraces looking over a distant ocean a thousand feet below. The reality, though beautiful, is quite different.

The mountains are like Scotch moors, without woods, presenting an appearance of total bareness. One drives everywhere over hard roads, and can go to most places about Honolulu by horse-car or railroad. On the other islands, travel is more on horseback, but the stories of cockroaches and centipedes, not to mention scorpions, make one's teeth chatter; and the mosquitoes at night are as bad as at Beverly [Massachusetts].

The absence of tropical sensation is curious. One would come here to escape summer. The weather is divine, but the heat never rises above 84°, and at night the thermometer always stands at 75° with a strong breeze—too strong to sit in. After our July in Washington, I feel as though I had run away to a cool climate. . . .

The huge flat bulk of Mauna Loa stretches down an interminable slope ahead of us, with the strange voluptuous charm peculiar to volcanic slopes, which always seem to invite you to lie down and caress them; the shores are rocky and lined with palms; the mountainsides are green and packed with dark tufts of forest; the place is an island paradise, made of lava; and the native boats—queer long coffins with an outrigger on one side resting in the water—are now coming out at some new landing place, bringing mangoes, pineapples, melons and alligator pears, all of which I am somewhat too nauseated to eat.

Our steamer is filled with plaintive-looking native women—the old-gold variety—who vary in expression between the ferocious look of the warriors who worshiped Captain Cook and then killed him, and the melancholy of a generation obliged to be educated by missionaries. They have a charm in this extraordinary scope of expressions, which run from tenderness to ferocity in a single play of feature, but I prefer the children, who are plaintive and sea-sick in stacks about the decks, and lie perfectly still, with their pathetic dark eyes expressing all sorts of vague sensations evidently more or less out of gear with the cosmos.

The least sympathetic character is the occasional white man. Third-rate places seldom attract even third-rate men, but rather

ninth-rate samples, and these are commonly the white men of
tropical islands. I prefer the savages who were—at least the high
chiefs—great swells and very much gentlemen. . . .

Kilauea Volcano House. . . . Our pilgrimage is effected at last.
I am looking from the porch of the inn down on the black floor
of the crater and its steaming and smoking lake, now chilled over,
some two or three miles away, at the crater's further end. More
impressive to my fancy is the broad sloping mass of Mauna Loa,
which rises beyond, ten thousand feet above us, a mass of rugged
red lava, scored by deeper red or black streaks down its side, but
looking softer than baby's flesh in this lovely morning sunlight,
and tinged above its red with the faintest violet vapor. I adore
mountains—from below. . . .

The natives still come up here and sit on the crater's edge to
look down at the residence of their great Goddess, but they never
go down into it. They say they're not rich enough. The presents
cost too much. Mrs. Dominus, the king's sister and queen expectant, came up here in the year 1885 and brought a black pig,
two roosters, champagne, red handkerchiefs and a whole basket
of presents, which were all thrown on the lava lake.

The pig, having its legs tied, squealed half an hour before it
was thoroughly roasted, and one of the roosters escaped to an
adjoining rock, but was recaught and immersed. Only princesses
are rich enough to do the thing suitably, and as Mrs. Dominus is
a Sunday-school Christian, she knows how to treat true deities.
As for me, I prefer the bigger and handsomer Mauna Loa. . . .

Hilo. . . . If you do not know where Hilo is, don't look for it
on the map. One's imagination is the best map for travelers. You
may remember Hilo best because it is the place where Clarence
King's waterfall of old-gold girls was situated. The waterfall is
still here, just behind the Severance house where we are staying.
Mrs. Severance took us down there half an hour ago. She said
nothing about the girls, but she did say that the boys used habitu-
ally to go over the fall as their after-school amusement; but of

late they have given it up, and must be paid for doing it. The last man who jumped off the neighboring high rock required fifteen dollars. Mrs. Severance told this sadly, mourning over the decline of the arts and of surf bathing. . . . So passes the glory of Hawaii, and of the old-gold girl—woe is me! . . .

Tomorrow we start, through mud and gulches of torrents on a five days' ride to Kawaihae, eighty miles to the westward, where we take the steamer again. If you will believe it, I do this to avoid a day's seasickness.

Steamer *Kinau*. . . . I take it all back. Hawaii is fascinating, and I could dream away months here. Yet dreaming has not been my standard amusement of late. Never have I done such hard and continuous traveling as during the last ten days since leaving Honolulu. . . . Friday morning early we left Hilo, according to plan, with a circus of horses to ride eighty miles, divided into four days . . . and in an hour arrived at a lovely cove or ravine called Onomea, . . . one of the sweetest spots on earth, where the land and ocean meet like lovers, and the natives look almost natural. . . .

The road was awful, in deep holes of mud, with rocky canyons to climb down and up at every half mile; but I never enjoyed anything in travel more thoroughly than I did this. Every ravine was more beautiful than the last . . . wildly lovely in ways that made one forget life. The intensely blue ocean foamed into the mouths of small inlets, saturated with the tropical green of ferns and dense woods, and a waterfall always made a background, with its sound of running water above the surf. The afternoon repaid all my five thousand miles of weariness. . . .

At Laupahoehoe plantation . . . I dismounted before a country house, and before I realized it, tumbled up the steps into an open hall where three ladies in white dresses were seated. I had to explain that we had invited ourselves to pass the night, and they had to acquiesce. The family was named Horner, and were Americans running several plantations and ranches on the island. We passed the night of Sunday at the plantation of another son or

brother of the same family at Kukuihaele, and strolled down to
see the Waipio Valley, which is one of the Hawaiian sights.

Yesterday we rode twelve miles up the hills, stopping to lunch
at the house of one Jarrett, who manages a great cattle ranch
[Parker Ranch]. Jarrett was not there, but two young women
were, and though they were in language and manners as much
like other young women as might be, they had enough of the
old-gold quality and blood to make them very amusing to me.
They made me eat raw fish and squid, as well as, of course, the
eternal *poi*, to which I am now accustomed; then after lunch,
while La Farge and I smoked or dozed and looked across the grass
plains to the wonderful slopes of Mauna Loa and Mauna Kea,
the two girls sat on mats under the trees and made garlands of
roses and geranium, which they fastened around our necks—or
rather around my neck and La Farge's hat.

I was tremendously pleased at this, my first *lei* . . . and wore
it down the long, dusty ride to Kawaihae, where we were to meet
the steamer, and where we arrived just at dark in an afterglow
like Egypt. The girls also drove down. . . . Kawaihae seemed a
terrible spot, baked by the southern sun against a mountain of
brown lava, without a drop of fresh water for miles. When I dismounted and entered the dirty little restaurant, I found our two
young ladies eating supper at a dusky table. They had ordered for
me a perfectly raw fresh fish, and the old-goldest of the two
showed me how to eat it, looking delightfully savage as she held
the dripping fish in her hands and tore its flesh with her teeth.

Jarrett was there, and took us under his care, so that an evening
which threatened to be so awful in heat and dirt, turned out delightful. They took us to a native house nearby, where a large
platform thatched with palm leaves looked under scrubby trees
across the moonlit ocean, which just lapped and purred on the
beach a few yards away. Then they made the mistress of the
house—an old schoolmate, but a native and speaking little English—bring her guitar and sing the Hawaiian songs.

They were curiously plaintive, perhaps owing to the way of
singing, but only one—Kamehameha's war dance—was really inter-

esting and sounded as though it were real. A large mat was brought out, and those of us who liked lay down and listened or slept. The moon was half full and shone exquisitely, and Venus sank with a trail like the sun's.

From this queer little episode, the only touch of half-native life we have felt, we were roused by the appearance of the steamer at ten o'clock, and in due time were taken into the boat and set on board. I dropped my faded and tattered *lei* into the water as we were rowed out, and now while the *Kinau* lies at Mahukona doing nothing, I write to tell you that our journey has been fascinating, in spite of prosaic sugar plantations, and that I am yearning to get back to Waimea, where I might stay a month at Samuel Parker's great ranch, and ride his horses about the slopes of Mauna Kea, while indefinite girls of the old-gold variety should hang indefinite garlands round my bronze neck.

Honolulu again. . . . Now that I look back on our Hawaiian journey of the last ten days, it seems really considerable experience, and one new to common travelers in gaiters. . . . To us the volcano was positively flat, and I sympathized actively with an Englishman who, we arc told, after a single glance at it, turned away and gazed only at the planets and the Southern Cross. To irritate me still more, we are now assured that the lake of fire, by which we sat unmoved, became very active within four-and-twenty hours afterward. These are our lucks. I never see the world as the world ought to be.

In revenge I have enjoyed much that is not to be set down in literary composition, unless by a writer like Fromentin or a spectacled and animated prism like La Farge. He has taught me to feel the subtleness and endless variety of charm in the color and light of every hour in the tropical island's day and night. I get gently intoxicated on the soft violets and strong blues, the masses of purple and the broad bands of orange and green in the sunsets, as I used to *griser* myself on absinthe on the summer evenings in the Palais Royal before dining at Velfour's thirty years ago.

The outlines of the great mountains, their reddish purple glow, the infinite variety of greens and the perfectly intemperate shift-

ing blues of the ocean are a new world to me. To be sure, man
is pretty vile, but perhaps woman might partly compensate for
him, if one only knew where to find her. As she canters about
the roads, a-straddle on horseback, with wreaths of faded yellow
flowers, and clothed in a blue or red or yellow night-gown, she
is rather a riddle than a satisfaction. . . .

La Farge and I had our audience of the King yesterday. We
went to the little palace at half-past nine in the morning, and
Kalakaua received us informally in his ugly drawing-room. His
Majesty is half Hawaiian, half Negro; talks quite admirable English in a charming voice; has admirable manners; and—forgive me
just this once more—seems to me a somewhat superior Chester A.
Arthur; a type surprisingly common among the natives.

To be sure, his Majesty is not wise, and he has—or is said to
have—vices, such as whiskey and—others; but he is the only interesting figure in the government, and is really . . . amusing. I
have listened by the hour to the accounts of his varied weaknesses
and especially to his sympathies with ancient Hawaii and archaic
faiths, such as black pigs and necromancy; but yesterday he sat
up straight and talked of Hawaiian archeology, and arts as well,
as though he had been a professor.

He was quite agreeable, though not, like our own chief magis-
trate, an example of the Christian virtues. I would not be thought
to prefer Kalakaua to Benjamin Harrison, but I own to finding
him a more amusing subject.

Socially this seems a queer place. I cheerfully forgive society
for ignoring us, for I have caught glimpses enough of it to
imagine worse than Washington horrors; but I find it strange that
no one even suggests our doing anything social, or tells us of
anything to be done, or desirable to do. I make my own infer-
ences, but without much real knowledge.

After a month, I know little or nothing of Honolulu. We know
everybody of much account, but we have not even been put up
at the club. Almost no one has called on us. As for dinners or
parties, we have as yet cost Honolulu not a bottle of wine. Appar-

ently in order to see the interior of a white man's house here, one must invite oneself into it. . . . I should suppose we had given offense, except that no one seems to do more than we do, or to have more social vogue.

From *The Letters of Henry Adams, 1858–1891*, edited by W. C. Ford (Boston and New York: Houghton Mifflin Company, 1930).

XLIII

John La Farge

Artist John La Farge (1835–1910), who accompanied Henry Adams on his tour of Hawaii, was so excited by the variety of intense color in which he saw the Island landscape and seascape illuminated that he felt called upon to tell about it in words as well as record it on his sketch pad; and though his facility with a pen scarcely matched his great talent with a brush, he could at least open the eyes of nonartists to what they were missing.

Hawaii could not have induced a more accomplished American artist to serve as interpreter and teacher in 1890, but like his traveling companion, he was not fully appreciated. He was too urbane, too erudite, too elegant, to fit into a social scheme dominated by planters and the sons and daughters of Protestant missionaries—and he was an ardent Catholic. In the States he was regarded as a sort of dean of American artists. Having established a sound reputation in both landscape and portraiture, he then branched out into Church murals and stained glass and achieved such distinction that the French Government had awarded him the insignia of the Legion of Honor.

No man of his time had done more to create a worthy tradition of the fine arts in America, yet in Hawaii he was virtually ignored, so he quietly went about his business, sketching, painting, writing—finding color at every turn. His journal was flavored with the parlance of an Island tour conductor obsessed with color intensity, depths, light, shade, form, and proportion.

[352]

The Moon and the Pacific

The sun set in those silver tones that I associate with the Pacific and with Japan. The horizon was enclosed everywhere, but through it every here and there the pink and the rose of sunset came out and in the east lit up the highest of the clouds in every variety of pink and lilac and purple and rose, shut in with gray.

But the moon, "O Tsuki San," had her turn. . . . There is no way of telling you all that the moon did, for she seemed to arrange the clouds, to place them about her or drive them away, to veil herself with one hand of cloud. It was like a great heavenly play— . . . like an opera of color and shadow. . . . No Rembrandt could have more indication of gradings and of darks than these clouds had in reality. No possible palette could approximate the degrees of dark and light, for the moon, when she uncovered entirely, was the same transparent silver vase out of which poured light. . . .

It was like a sun one could look at without wincing, and canopied itself with colors that did not imitate but were merely the iridescent spectrum which belongs to the great sun. These colors, by their arrangement in the prismatic sequence, seemed to make more light, to arrange it and dispose it, as if it were recalling nature. All this must seem unintelligible. . . . But this is, at least, what we came for—the moon and the Pacific.

We sat on the veranda [in Nuuanu Valley], looking out toward the sea, I should say about two miles from us, with the same brilliant moonlight we had had the night before. The two palm trees in front of the house were gradually lit, as if the whole air had been a stage scene, seen through the smoothly shining trunks glistening like dark silver. . . . Behind them spread sky and ocean—for we are just on the summit of the hill—the sea line cutting distinctly and the air being clear enough (even when a slight drift of rain came down across the picture) to see the surf far out, and the lines of a great bar, which made a long, hooked bend into the sea.

Lights shone red on board of two English and American war vessels. Far off, a few azure clouds on the horizon; and occasionally a white patch of cloud floated, like gauze, over the palms, then sank away into the space shining far off—a little darker now than the sky, and warm and rather red in color.

Meanwhile the palm branches tossed up and down in the intermittent gale which blew from behind us in the great hills. The landscape was all below us, lying at the very foot of the palms which edge the hill upon which we are. Across the grass the moonlight came sometimes, as if a lamp had suddenly been brought in—and the color of the half-yellow grass, which was not lost in the moonlight, urged on this illusion. Even the violet of the two pillars of palm and its silveriness were strong enough to make greener the color of the sky.

When I walked out behind the house the hills were covered with cloud—I say covered, but rather the cloud rested upon them, and poured up into the sky in large masses of white; the moon shining through most of the time, out of an opening more blue than the blue sky, itself an opaline circle of greenish-blue light, with variant iridescent redness in the cloud edges. Against it the heavy trees looked as dark as green can be, and now and again the branches of other palms were like waves of grass against this dark, or against the sky, all shining and brilliant.

Occasionally it rained; the edges of the great cloud blew upon us like a little sprinkle of wet dust, and later, as it came thicker, the rustle of the palms was increased by the rustle of the rain. The grass of the hills shone as with moisture, but the grass outside, near us, was so dry that the hand put down to it felt no wet. And I went to bed . . . to think that it rained because I heard the palms.

Honolulu streets are amusing. The blocks of houses are tropical, with most reasonable lowness, and are of cement in facings; and the great number of Chinese shops and of Chinese, with some pretty Chinese girl faces and children's faces, enliven the streets.

And there are so many horses, small, with much mustang blood and good action and good heads, and ridden freely—too freely, for we saw a laborer ridden down by some cowboyish fellow.

Hawaiian women rode about in their divided skirts; they had, as well as many of the men, flowers around their hats and their necks, and among other delights, peacock-feather bands around their hats. Many of them were pretty, I thought, with animated faces, talking to mild and fierce men of similar adornments. And, as I said, there was much Chinese, and dresses of much color—for men and women—and trees with flowers, like the Bougain-villea, purplish-rose colored; gray palm trunks, and many plants of big leaves like the bananas; yellow limes, and fiercely green acacias. . . .

I walked about this morning toward the hills, of which the near ones are covered with grass of a velvet gray in the light, and dun color in the shade; but behind, the higher hills are purple and lost in the base of the cloud that has never ceased to turret them. . . . If this be tropical, it is easy to bear, and the vast feeling of air and space gives a charm even to the heat.

Off Island of Hawaii—We are lying off a little place, Keauhou, while people are landing in boats from the small steamer that carries us. The shore is broken with black lava rock in beds that do not seem high, so flat are they on top. It is about eight o'clock, and the impression is of full sunlight on the green of everything. Behind the fringe of shore rises the big slope of the mountain seen in profile, so gigantic that one only sees a slice of it at a time. . . .

The sea, of course, at the shore is glittering blue, but every-thing else that can cast a shadow throws its edges upon the next. . . . There are a few houses strung along, half in light, half in shadow; three of them are tall grass huts, hay-colored in the half-shade of the coconuts beside them. Above them are focuses, patches of sun on the green slope where the upper bank behind first flattens into the strong light.

In the shadow, faint whites and pinks and blacks are the dresses of people waiting for their friends or watching the steamer.

The horses and mules and donkeys stand in rows along the houses
—or walls—occasionally they pass into the sunshine. One girl in
red runs (why, heaven only knows—time seems of no possible
use) and as she rises over a rock in the sand, the sun catches her
feet and legs and the lower folds of her floating gown. . . .
There is loud objurgation and chattering, and keeping the children together, and holding up odds and ends of things not sent
ashore by the other boats that carry goods and household furniture. . . .

And later we have come to a great bank of black rock running
out to sea, and precipices of black spotted with a green all of one
color, which is where Cook was killed, and where they have put
up a little monument to him. This is Kaawaloa. We try the land,
for the roll of the ship is disagreeable as it waits, and we run in
over the transparent water. It is too deep just by the landing for
anchorage. The sea jumps from light aquamarine to the color of
a peacock's breast in the shadow.

We go up the black lava that looks as if it had been run out on
the road. . . . And it is hot—the heights have shut off the wind,
and all is baking. Horses and donkeys, saddled, stand about near
the shadow of fences, left to themselves while the cargo is landed.
. . . As I look around on this green and black, and the few coconuts, and the dark blue-green olive water, I think that it is not
an unlikely place for a man to have been killed in. The place has,
for Hawaiians, another interest: it was once a great place, and
the high cliffs have many holes where chiefs were buried, inaccessible and hidden. . . .

At the Volcano, Kilauea—In the morning Adams woke me out
of sound sleep; the air was cold and damp, the room decidedly
so during the night. As I came out the sun was rising. Before us
was the volcano, still in shadow, but the walls of the crater lit up
pink in the sun, and farther out the long line of Mauna Loa appeared to come right down to these cliffs, all clear and lit up
except for the shadow of one enormous cloud that stretched half
across the sky.

The floor of the crater, of black lava, was almost all in shadow, so that, as it stretched to its sunlit walls, it seemed as if all below was shadow. In the center of the space smoked the cones that rise from the bed of the crater. Through this vapor we saw the farther walls, and on the other side of the flow, as it sloped away from us, more steam. . . .

We sketched that day and lounged in the afternoon, the rain coming down and shutting out things; but in the noon I was able to make a sketch in the faint sunlight; and that was of no value, but as I looked and tried to match tints, I realized more and more the unearthly look that the black masses take under the light. A slight radiance from these surfaces of molten black glass gives a curious sheen, that far off, in tones of mirage, does anything that light reflected can do, and fills the eye with imaginary suggestions.

Hence the delightful silver, hence the rosy coldness that had made fairylands for us of the desert aridity. But nearer, the glitter is like that of the moon on a hard, cold night, and the volcano crater I shall always think of as a piece of dead world; and far away, in the prismatic tones of the mountain sides, I shall see a revelation of the landscapes of the moon.

From "Passages from a Diary in the Pacific—Hawaii," John La Farge, *Scribner's Magazine*, May 1901.

XLIV

Austin Strong

With a letter of introduction to King Kalakaua, a case of pigment tubes, and a young son still in rompers, another artist, Joseph Strong, and his wife set out from San Francisco in the late 1880's to take up brief residence in Honolulu while painting an assortment of Island scenes. Half a century later, the son—Austin Strong (1881–1957)—risen to prominence as a New York playwright, could still recall his juvenile experiences as schooner passenger, Waikiki beachcomber, and associate of Hawaiian royalty vividly enough to pen for the *Atlantic Monthly* one of the most cheerful little stories ever written about Hawaii.

His Oceanic Majesty's Goldfish

The large mustache was my father, the beautiful dark eyes my mother. I was aware of tears, champagne glasses, laughing speeches, and farewell shouts as we stood at the ship's rail looking back at Meiggs Wharf and the receding city of San Francisco.

Our heavy sails turned to iron as the northeast wind struck them with a howl, sending the tiny schooner scudding through the Golden Gate to breast the angry Pacific waiting outside to pounce on us. Suddenly everything went mad; screaming sea gulls were blown high; the vessel leaped into the air and fell on her side, half capsized by a knockdown flaw, her lee rail disappearing under a wash of green water and foaming suds.

The young couple fell to the deck clutching their small son. They laughingly held me between them as we all three slid down the careening deck to be rescued in the nick of time by grinning brown sailors smelling of tar, coconut oil, and chewing tobacco. One of them, at the request of my mother, tied a double bowline around my waist, making the end fast to a ring bolt on the white deck.

Here I was tethered, a none too safe passenger, every day for fourteen terrifying days. Tied to that slanting, heaving floor, which was half under water the whole length of the ship, I was buffeted, jerked off my feet, stung by flying spray, deafened by the never-ending roar of the wind and sea.

Green waters full of iridescent bubbles snatched at my feet when they swept by, leaving long damp stains on the deck. The winds blew up my sleeves, whipping my hair in all directions. Everywhere there was wild excitement—banging of blocks, angry shouts, sudden rushings of the crew to take in or let out the main and jib sheets. No one had to tell me that our lives were in the four hands of the two struggling men at the wheel and that the angel with the dark wings was hovering over our masts.

The large mustache would prick my cheek as my father brought his reassuring face close to mine, while my mother held me safe, and together they would sing to keep fear away from me. I would look into the eyes of my mother, searching for any sign of anxiety in the clear, quiet depths, and finding none I would breathe again, feeling the iron band about my heart relax. I caught the infection of their happiness and we would all laugh together for no reason at all.

They were filled with high hope, for riches and honors lay ahead of us. No wonder they were gay, for had not our good rich friend commissioned my father to go to Honolulu to paint a picture of the volcano Mauna Loa in full eruption? And hadn't they an important letter of introduction to a real king who sat on a real throne, wore a real crown, and lived in a real palace, His Oceanic Majesty, King Kalakaua of the Hawaiian Archipelago?

Since we were too poor to afford tickets on a Pacific liner, our benefactor had given us free passage on one of his trading schooners, the *Consuelo*, and these two babes in the wood, with their solemn offspring, were blown at last around Diamond Head under the lee of Punchbowl into the breathless heat of Honolulu Harbor, dangerous seas now far behind, fame and fortune beckoning us from the shores.

A long, graceful boat manned by singing natives in uniform shot out from the king's boathouse. She was dazzling white, with a canvas awning the length of her and a gilded crown on either side of her bow. This was the royal barge coming alongside with tossed oars to row us ashore in state.

We went to live in a wooden cottage that might have been taken from a child's picture book. It was set back from Fort Street, almost lost in a fragrant garden of big leaves and strange-looking flowers. Young attachés and their wives from all the legations annexed my parents with joy, and our wide veranda fairly glistened with naval gold lace from the British, French, Russian and Chilean men-of-war. My gay parents must have been a godsend to those exiles of every nationality.

I lived to the tune of their laughter and endless parties, but in spite of belonging to the king's set, in spite of my father's success as an artist, I was not happy. The children who lived on our street looked down their noses at me.

It was the fashion in those days to have at the entrances of one's driveway half a tub constantly filled by a pipe with fresh water for the horses. The rich people had handsome tubs painted with bright colors at their gates and, to add to their prestige, their tubs were alive with goldfish. Ours was old and unpainted, a shabby affair with rusty hoops, and, alas, contained no fish. The neighboring children made faces at me and with an ancient malice insisted that we were too poor to have goldfish in our disreputable tub. It troubled me that my hilarious parents had no idea that we were losing face with our neighbors' children, but boylike I kept my suffering to myself.

One day the Japanese attachés from the legation across the way came over for lunch. They were dressed like dark butterflies in their national costume. I stood on the outer edge of the veranda and overheard them telling about the beautiful double-tailed gold-fish the Emperor of Japan had just sent to King Kalakaua and how they had emptied them officially that morning into the lily pond of the royal Kapiolani Park. They told my mother these sacred fish were very rare and belonged to the royal family of Japan.

My heart skipped a beat; I was stabbed by a sudden over-whelming desire. In one moment I had become a thief. From then on I saw nothing but an imperial fish swimming in our battered tub, giving face to my carefree parents and despair to my enemies.

Kapiolani Park was out of town near Waikiki, and it cost five cents to go there in the mule-car. Finding I had ten cents in my tincan bank, I dashed up to the friendly old Chinese groceryman at the head of our street and for five cents bought a ball of red, white, and blue string. I then took two bright new pins from my Portuguese nurse's sewing basket and plunged into action.

This was my first adventure alone into the great out-of-doors away from the safe and protected area under my nurse's eye. With a pounding heart I hailed the mule-car, a wide open-air affair with a cool covering of white canvas and bobbing tassels. It was driven by a barefoot Kanaka with a sleepy face. I held up a timid finger and to my astonishment I was obeyed—the car stopped at my command. I felt important and apologetic at the same time when I found I was the only passenger, for it was the hot, buzzy time of the afternoon when everyone retires for a siesta.

With one wheel flat and squeaking, we swayed and bumped along through the deserted city, down freshly watered avenues kept in perpetual twilight by the shade of flowering trees over-head. The air was filled with the stinging scent of roasting coffee and burnt sugar, while over all hung the redoubtable smell of distant Chinatown, that potent mixture of teeming humanity, rotting fish, sandalwood and incense.

I heard a warning voice within as I paid my carfare with my last remaining nickel. It whispered, "How are you going to come back with no money?" But I shut my ears tight, and going forward with a pounding heart, I sat close to the driver as we came out of the city into the blinding white road which ran along the shore.

"Want to drive?" he asked, smiling through an enormous yawn as he held out the reins. I clutched the stiff hot leathers while the driver disappeared inside, curled up on a bench, and promptly fell asleep. This was my first meeting with responsibility. Though my bare feet were being burned alive by the heat of the sun on the platform, I stood motionless.

The mule, with his large ears encased in netted fly-bags, feeling the hand of inexperience, promptly relaxed and reduced his speed to a crawl. He dragged us at a snail's pace along the edge of the beach and I could see the lines on lines of charging surf running white over the hidden reefs. To the left I could see half-naked Chinese, with their big cone-shaped hats, working like animated mushrooms, thigh-deep in mud, planting rice in the flat watery fields against a background of green mountains.

We crept along until at last the mule stopped of himself, poked his head around his stern, whisked a fly away with his tail, and looked at me with distaste. The driver woke with a start, shouting automatically as if I were a full carload of passengers: "All out for Kapiolani Park!"

I thanked him politely as he lifted me down in front of the entrance to the Park and I asked him to read me a freshly painted sign at the side of the gates. He slowly read the words: "Fishing in the Park is strictly prohibited and will be punished with the full severity of the law.—Kalakaua, Rex."

I stood rooted to the ground as the driver, with a sleepy grin, drove the bobbing mule-car around a curve and out of sight, leaving me with my ball of twine, my pins, and my pockets empty of money. I stood for a time stunned. "Full severity of the law" meant only one thing when a king caught you. Your head was chopped off on a block of wood in the Tower of London and popped into a basket. Slowly I drew half circles in the dust with my big toe, waiting for my heart to quiet down.

By fine degrees courage returned to me. It came first in the shape of curiosity. I edged my way slowly through the gates, tip-toeing out of the blinding heat into the chill cathedral gloom of the park. I saw two Chinese gardeners sweeping the driveway. Again I stood still for a long time. Finding they paid no attention to me, I took a few cautious steps farther in and once more became rooted to the ground, for there, quite near me, squatting on his haunches, was a half-naked Chinese with the face of a joss-house mask. He was cutting the grass with an evil-looking scimitar. Standing still until he had worked himself out of sight round a tree, I dashed off the roadway across the lawn into a beautiful Chinese garden with gray stone lanterns, pagodas and frog-faced lions goggle-eyed with ferocity.

I came to a pond filled with water lilies, the edges of their enormous pads neatly turned up, like little fences. A moon-bridge arched over the still water and I climbed the slippery incline, which is very steep until the circle flattens out on top; here I lay on my stomach, quaking. Guilt had laid a cold hand on me. I was a robber in a royal domain.

Placing my straw hat beside me and slowly raising my head, I looked carefully about for sign of a human being, but apparently this garden was a place apart. It was empty of life save for a pink flamingo who stared at me suspiciously. I peered down into the pool below and saw a small white object which stared up at me with frightened eyes. It was my own face reflected among the lilies.

Then I saw them! I couldn't believe my good luck. I had found them at last, the noble goldfish of the Emperor of Japan. Prodigious fellows, obviously aristocrats of high degree, wearing feathery fins and tails like court trains, trailing clouds of glory.

Quickly I bent a pin, and fastening it to the end of my red, white and blue string I lowered it, hand over hand, into the liquid crystal below. The leisurely fish, as bright as porcelain, glided haughtily past my pin, not deigning to notice it. Why I thought a fish would swallow my baitless hook I do not know. It was a triumph of hope over experience, however, for after I had lain patiently on my stomach for a long time the miracle happened.

A large, dignified grand duke of a goldfish, attracted by the brightness of my pin, made the stupid mistake of thinking it was something good to eat. He slowly opened his bored face and swallowed it. A hard tug nearly toppled me off the bridge. I hauled up the sacred fish and soon had him indignantly flopping beside me, where he spat out the hook with disdain and would have flopped off the bridge had I not covered him with my straw hat. Again I peered around, now guilty in fact, for the deed was done.

The flamingo was still there, standing motionless on one leg, staring at me with an unblinking, accusing eye. In panic I hastily stuffed the fish into the crown of my hat, and jamming it on my head, with the victim struggling inside, I flew with the heels of terror out into the open road.

To my dismay I found the day almost spent as I ran before a following wind; the whole sky was afire with a red sunset which threw my gigantic shadow like a dancing hobgoblin far ahead of me on the wide road.

The awful voice spoke to me again. "There, what did I tell you? You have no money, so now you have an all-night walk in the dark."

But my only thought was how to keep my fish alive until I got him in our tub. I saw a wide irrigation ditch, which fed the paddy fields with water, running by the side of the road. Slipping down the bank, I removed my hat, and, holding the fish by his golden tail, I plunged him into the water, arguing that to a fish this was like a breath of air to a suffocated man.

I held him under until he grew lively again and then I went on my interminable journey, running fast along the road, slipping down to the side of the ditch to souse my imperial highness until he revived enough for the next lap. I don't know how many times I did this, or how many hundred feet I had advanced along the way, but my legs began to ache and my head swam with weariness and wet fish. Then suddenly I was in the midst of warning shouts, angry men's voices, stamping horses, jingling harness, military commands—a carriage had nearly run over me.

I was too young to know about palace revolutions and the necessity for armed escorts. I only knew I was terrified to find myself surrounded by grave men on horseback. An officer leaped from his saddle and stood before me.

I had the presence of mind to jam my prize under my hat as I was led to a shining C-spring victoria which smelled of elegance, varnish, polished leather, and well-groomed horses.

In it rode a fine figure of a man, calm and immaculate in white ducks and pipe-clayed shoes. He sat in noble repose, his strong face, his hands, and his clothes dyed crimson by the tropical sunset. My heart began to jump about, for I recognized the face which was stamped on all the silver coins of his island realm. He wore his famous hat made of woven peacock quills as fine as straw, with its broad band of tiny sea shells. He eyed me gravely as I stood in the road before him, wet to the skin, with muddy hands and feet, my fish violently protesting under my hat. Would he order his soldiers to execute me on the spot?

"Why, it's Mrs. Strong's little boy!" the deep voice was saying. "What are you doing so far away from home?"

I was speechless.

"Your mother must be very anxious. Come, get in and I'll take you home."

The officer deposited me, dirty and damp, on the spotless cushion beside the king. An order rang out and away we dashed, a fine cavalcade with outriders galloping ahead and men on horseback thundering behind.

His Majesty began to question me tactfully, trying, as is the way with kings, to put his guest at ease, but the fish was too much on my mind and head. I realized it would soon die if I held my tongue, but if I told, what would be my punishment? Try as I might, I couldn't hold back unmanly tears. The king removed his cigar in concern.

"Are you in pain, Austin?" he asked. I began to shake all over in an agony of indecision. "Won't you tell me what's the matter?"

I heard another and a craven voice blurting out of me.

"Oh, please don't cut off my head!" it cried.

The king replied gravely, "I have no intention of cutting off your head."

Removing my hat, I showed him his gift from the Emperor of Japan. The king raised a hand, the cavalcade came to a halt, again the officer was alongside. The king cried, "Stop at the nearest horse trough. Be quick!"

Away we flew, the king with his arm about me, trying vainly to comfort me as I saw my fish growing weaker and weaker. At last we drew up in front of a native hut. I jumped out and plunged my fish into an overflowing horse trough while the king and his men looked on with polite interest. A native was sent running for a large calabash, and the fish was put in it, his sacred life spared, his dignity restored.

I was rolled home in triumph, fast asleep against His Majesty's protecting shoulder, to be roused by shouts of laughter from my relieved parents, who were astounded by my royal return. They watched me with puzzled faces as, struggling with sleep, I staggered away from them to empty my golden prize into our tub.

No one ever knew why I stole that fish; wild horses couldn't drag an explanation from me. I woke very early the next day and crept out through the cool shadows of the morning across the wet lawn in my bare feet and peered anxiously into our tub. There, sure enough, was the grand duke swimming proudly in our shabby barrel, restoring face to my parents and raising their social standing in the society of my enemies.

There is no moral to this story—in fact it is a most unmoral one, for later that morning a smart equerry on horseback, dressed in a glistening uniform, dismounted before our gate. He came bearing a large gilt-bordered envelope on which was stamped the crown of Hawaii.

It was a royal grant to one Master Austin Strong, giving him permission to fish in Kapiolani Park for the rest of his days. It was signed "Kalakaua, Rex."

From "His Oceanic Majesty's Goldfish," Austin Strong, *Atlantic Monthly*, May 1944.

XLV

Henry Codman Potter

Shouting, gesticulating, hilarious throngs milled through the streets of Honolulu; ancient cannons boomed from the rim of Punchbowl; fusillades of firecrackers sputtered on the sidewalks; fire bells clanged in chorus with church bells; salutes rolled in from ships in the harbor; every factory whistle in or near the city tooted and screamed. The date was July 13, 1898. News had arrived that the Congress of the United States had voted just a week before to annex the Hawaiian Islands.

But the hilarity was by no means universal. It was a sad day for many a Hawaiian who saw annexation as an end to all hope for restoration of the monarchy; the splendid days of the kings were gone forever. And by no means was there unanimity among those who were supposed to be the beneficiaries of the territorial acquisition—the American people.

Few issues of the decade had been argued more bitterly. A southern bloc, supporting the interests of Louisiana sugar growers, fought annexation tooth and nail. Antiexpansionists cried, "Foul! American imperialism!" "We need Hawaii just as much, and a good deal more, than we did California," countered President McKinley. While opponents fought against taking in a cluster of remote Islands already inhabited by a forbidding number of Orientals, proponents maintained that unless the United States accepted the Islands at once, Japan would grab them. In the end, the day was won by persuasive militarists who saw the need for a mid-Pacific base, and by lobbyists for the Hawaiian sugar planters.

Yet even after the Islands were unconditionally annexed, the quarrel continued, with attempts to justify or condemn the *fait accompli*. Just after the turn of the century, New York's Episcopal Bishop Henry Codman Potter (1835–1908), "the People's Friend," widely respected author, one of the country's leading spokesmen for social reform and civic improvement, the visionary who initiated the construction of Manhattan's magnificent Cathedral of St. John the Divine, visited the Islands, assessed the political climate, and gave in measured words his verdict on the issue.

Foothold Between Coasts

I am not a disciple of a policy of imperialism, but I confess, in view of the situation as it existed in the Hawaiian Islands when they voted to seek annexation to the United States, I am unable to see what else we could have done than to grant that request. For their position in the Pacific indicated that if they are not strong enough to rule themselves, they belong rightfully under that protection which we, of all other peoples, can best give them.

Whatever earlier civilization, Spanish, English, or French, found them, seized them, or sought to enrich itself from them, we alone earliest recognized a duty to them, and sought, by bringing to bear upon them the highest and most transforming influences, to discharge it.

We alone strove to build up among them a civilization which had for its foundation some other motive than the passion of conquest or the love of gain. We alone gave them schools and teachers, and the good physician with the Christian home. We alone enriched them with those who, whatever may be said of their descendants, lived pure and noble lives, and did among them good and lasting work.

After these, it is true, have come the trader, the land-speculator, the sugar-planter, and the rest; and possibly it may be as well that the authority of the United States should stay in the Hawaiian Islands to regulate them, as well as to protect its own international rights.

International rights, I say, for as to the growing importance of these there can be no smallest doubt. One need not be dazzled or blinded by the glamor of imperial expansion in order to recognize that no republic such as ours can draw a line round its domestic territory and ignore its duties and its opportunities with reference to the rest of the world. We must trade with other countries than our own; and if we have anything good that they have not, we must needs wish, and even though there should be pecuniary profit in it, may rightly wish, to impart it to them.

But we cannot do this unless we can get at them, and we cannot get at them without the physical resources and conveniences which shall enable us to do so. Now, the Hawaiian Islands stand preeminently for one of these conveniences. No traffic with the great East can be maintained, except at almost ruinous cost, without some foothold between its coasts and ours for a Pacific coaling station, and no greater opportunity for the enlargement of certain departments of agriculture and trade than the Hawaiian Islands afford, could easily be discovered.

If we do our duty toward them, we shall find our interest in doing it, and to that duty and to those toward whom we are to discharge it, there is no great world power that is so near as we. Geographical, commercial and moral considerations here seem all to point one way.

But, alas! it would seem as if the people toward whom we are to discharge such duty would soon cease to be. There is one mysterious effect of civilization upon weaker races concerning which the historian and the psychologist have yet to give us more light. The United States, since its people first went to the Sandwich Islands, has carried on no exterminating war. With shame and confusion it must be owned that it has taught them many vices, or rather perhaps it would be more true to say it has corrupted them with the taint of forms of those vices which were distinctly its own.

But, on the other hand, it has given them the arts, and learning, and civic order, and the examples of industry and thrift. But it cannot be said that they have prized the learning highly or widely profited by it. For no reason which can be directly traceable to us, it must be owned that they are a decaying race, and their more recent statistics reveal this with dramatic significance. . . .

The eight islands composing the Hawaiian group have a total population of 107,000, of which, however, only 35,000 are Hawaiians. There are 10,000 people of mixed descent, in part Hawaiian; the rest are Chinese, Japanese, Portuguese and other Europeans, of which last, with Americans, there are 14,000. In other words, nearly two thirds of the people of these islands are other than Hawaiian. That this proportion is likely to be increased along the same line seems probable, and the time seems likely to come when the native Hawaiian, like the native North American Indian, will have disappeared.

Who they are who will ultimately be dominant in his place it is not easy to forecast. At any moment the United States may close its Hawaiian doors to those races which, of the Eastern world, are nearest to the islands, and which are now represented there by a large proportion of the population—some 24,000 Japanese and 15,000 Chinese, who today, in fact, taken together, make an element larger than that represented by the Hawaiians themselves or any other peoples.

As the eye ranges the distant hillsides which flank the rear of Honolulu, it is arrested by the shining patches of ordered verdure which, terrace upon terrace, climb up along their slopes, and the inquirer is told, in every instance, that these are the farms and market gardens of the Japanese, who have in so many like places taught the soil to yield its increase where it never did before.

Such qualities, in any people, are sources of power and wealth; and when it is remembered that behind the Japanese have come the Chinese, whose thrift in the Eastern world is a proverb like that of the French or Germans in the Western, it is plain that their influence upon the future of the Hawaiian Islands must be deep and lasting.

Already, in the case of the Chinese, has their capacity for agricultural work revealed itself in the vast sugar plantations which

American and other capital has acquired and is administering with characteristic skill and profit; and already there are tokens of the wealth which, aided by this foreign labor, these can extract from a rich soil and from singularly favorable climatic conditions.

So the problem is set: the mixture of races, energies, industries, and of the higher moral qualities which these various strains, ancestries, and activities stand for. There are other theaters in which the same drama is being played out under much broader and, it may be, more complex conditions, but none in which a more interesting or indeed dramatic experiment is being made.

It will be for the government and the people of the American republic to demonstrate that they are equal to a task in itself so delicate, and in its consequences so grave and important.

From "Impressions of the Sandwich Islands," Henry C. Potter, *Century Magazine,* September 1901.

XLVI

Ray Stannard Baker

In 1906 President Theodore Roosevelt delivered a famous address entitled "The Man with the Muck Rake," in which he deplored the sweeping and frequently unjust charges of corruption being made against public men and corporations by writers and political orators. Overnight a new word was coined—the "muckrakers"; and as it traveled across the country, it was applied to journalists of every color who attempted to expose in print any form of unsavory practice among the great trusts, in business generally, and in government or society, even though the critic was sincerely aiming at reform. Involuntarily the muckrakers became a new literary class.

One of the first prominent authors to acquire this rank was Ray Stannard Baker (1870–1946), an experienced analyst for *McClure's Magazine,* part owner and editor of the *American Magazine.* Baker considered himself a genuine social reformer, not an alarmist, rabble-rouser, or headline-seeker. Under the pen name "David Grayson," he was even better known and all but worshiped for his pleasant rural essays, *Adventures in Contentment* and *Great Possessions.* Later, during the last year of World War I, he earned worldwide notoriety when he was sent to Europe by his close friend President Woodrow Wilson to use his influence as a peacemaker. Still later, he won the Pulitzer Prize for two of his volumes of Wilson's official biography.

In 1911 Baker the muckraker arrived in the Islands to make a comprehensive study of the sugar industry and all its ramifications. What he found was at considerable variance with John Vandercook's summary of a quarter century later. Cynically entitled "Wonderful Hawaii: A World Experiment Station," the articles, published in the *American Magazine,* stand even today as conspicuous—and controversial—models in the mountainous library of muckraking literature. The sugar industry had come a long way since Henry Lyman inspected the bullock mill at Hilo or Mark Twain jested about the little experimental plantations.

The House of Lords

Hawaii has been called, and justly called, the Paradise of the Pacific. But it is a paradise not only of natural beauties and wonders; it is also a paradise of modern industrial combination. In no part of the United States is a single industry so predominant as the sugar industry is in Hawaii, and nowhere else, perhaps, has the centralized control of property reached a state of greater perfection. Hawaii furnishes a vivid illustration of the way in which private business organization in its final stages of development permeates, influences, and controls the life of a country.

Sugar is King in Hawaii to a far greater extent than cotton was in the old South. . . . Those rich, warm lands in all the islands are devoted almost exclusively now to the production of sugar cane. They are divided up and held mostly in large plantations, the number of which in the islands is about fifty. Some of them are veritable principalities, stretching for miles along the coast, the broad green fields reaching from the sea level to the height of 2,000 feet in the mountains. . . .

The largest of the ownerships is that of the Hawaiian Commercial and Sugar Company in the island of Maui with 35,000 acres, of which over 20,000 is cultivated in cane. It has an enormous equipment of the machinery of manufacture and transportation and an army of 3,200 workers, who, with their families live in twenty-four little villages or camps dotted about upon the great estate. . . . While this is the largest of the plantations, there are many others in the islands which produce from 15,000 to 40,000 tons of sugar annually. . . . With raw sugar selling at from $70 to $80 a ton, some idea of the magnitude of the operations may be formed.

Unlike the old South, where the cotton plantations were owned by individuals or by families who lived upon them in a sort of isolated grandeur, these great sugar estates of Hawaii are without exception owned by corporations. In a few cases the original or controlling owners of these corporations continue to live upon and manage the land, but in a majority of cases—and the tendency is constantly growing—the men who really control the plantations live in Honolulu and employ salaried managers to operate the land. Modern aristocracy is urban and absentee, not agricultural and local, as was that of the last century; the aristocrat is a financier rather than a farmer.

We thus have over fifty corporations controlling the sugar land of the Territory; but these corporations themselves are grouped together so that in all essential matters they act as a unit.

In the first place they are organized in the powerful Sugar Planters' Association, which, while it is nominally a voluntary organization, exercises the profoundest control over industry in the islands. . . . The Planters' Association is far more powerful than the territorial government; it has well been called the Hawaiian House of Lords.

Behind the Planters' Association, and really directing its operations, are the trustees, all of whom are representatives of the great sugar agencies or factors of the islands. There are nine such factors, but the great bulk of the sugar business is done by five of them—the so-called Big Five: Alexander & Baldwin, Brewer & Co., Castle & Cooke, Hackfeld & Co., and Theo. H. Davies & Co. These five powerful financial agencies represent as factors nearly all of the plantations on the islands. They finance the plantations, they buy the supplies, they attend to the shipping and the sale of the product.

Not only are these agencies the business representatives of the plantations, but more and more they are actually coming into the stock ownership or control of the plantations. I presume that from six to ten men connected with the agencies practically dictate the policies of the island sugar industry. . . . What is the result of this control? What are the advantages and disadvantages? An answer to these questions will not only explain Hawaiian conditions, but will illuminate the great problem of industral combination which confronts the nation on every hand.

I think no one can visit the islands without being impressed with the remarkable intelligence and high efficiency with which the sugar industry is directed. It has been in a high degree farming with brains. The planters have adapted themselves with wonderful flexibility and ingenuity to all manner of difficult conditions. Marvelous irrigation systems, ditches and flumes from mountain streams and great pumping plants have been developed. Conditions of soil and rainfall have been studied and the last perfection of modern farm machinery and modern methods of fertilizing have been introduced. . . .

Nor is this all. The Planters' Association maintains an extensive private experiment station in Honolulu, where a group of scientists is constantly at work experimenting in the production of better grades of cane and seeking better methods of planting and harvesting the crops. . . . In a hundred other ways the planters have shown remarkable constructive and organizing ability. They have begun a campaign to protect the forests and to plant more trees; they have developed private docks and private railroads; and they are seeking out or developing the very best methods for extracting the sugar in their great mills.

More than this, the combined planters have dealt minutely with the methods of shipping and selling. When they found that the sugar trust was robbing them, they got together and formed a corporation called the Sugar Factors' Company and bought a refinery in California in which they began to refine some of their own sugar and thus compete with the trust. It was only a small refinery, but it . . . has made the Hawaiian planters sharers in the profits which arise from that monopolistic combination. . . .

In other big ways—the handling of their credits, the purchasing of supplies in great quantities, their participation in the control of the company which makes most of their own sugar mill machinery

—in all these big, daring, constructive lines of activity, the combined planters of Hawaii have shown unusual ability in overcoming the disadvantages of distance and the rigors of world competition. . . .

It may be asked how it is possible for a comparatively few white men and their families, out of a population of nearly 200,000, thus to control so vast an industry. . . . Land, machinery, labor! Control these and you control the world!

Control is made easier in Hawaii, as it was in the old South, by the presence of a very large population of non-voting workmen. This not only includes that half of the population which is made up of Chinese and Japanese, but of thousands of ignorant Portuguese, Spanish, Russians, and others, who are not yet naturalized. Fully three-quarters of the population of Hawaii have no more to say about the government under which they are living than the old slaves. The total registered voters in the islands, indeed, is only 14,442 (in 1910). Of these, nearly 10,000 are native Hawaiians, and only 1,763 are American born. The remainder is made up of naturalized Portuguese, British, German and other whites, and 396 Chinese and 234 Japanese. Of the 234 registered Japanese, the highest number who ever voted in an election is thirteen. . . .

The Anglo-Saxon is not particular about having the *name* of power: what he looks for, always, are the *actualities* of power. . . . Thus the mayor of Honolulu, many of the territorial legislators, and many officers in all the islands are Hawaiians—and the road work and much other public work of the territorial government is done, at high wages, by native voters. But the offices of real power are practically all held by strong, quiet, able white men —who hold the government with a steady hand. . . . In short, while the government of Hawaii is in name an elective democracy, in actuality it is a government by a very limited aristocracy of wealth. A very few white men control the destinies of the islands and of its 200,000 diverse people. . . .

What does the dominant white group gain by its political control? Well, it gains practically every advantage it has. It is able by controlling politics to get the legislation necessary to protect its land holdings—especially the large tracts of government land it holds under lease; it keeps down taxes; it is able to provide money from the territorial funds to bring in laborers for its plantations, and above all to present a strong front in Congress every time the sugar tariff comes up for discussion. Hawaiian sugar comes into the United States free: that is, it is protected from foreign competition by a tariff of some $34 a ton. Without that tariff privilege, which is a tax paid by the consumers of the country, many of the sugar plantations of the islands would have to shut up shop.

The very great prosperity of the planters today, like that of some others of our law-made "trusts," is based not so much upon natural advantages, as upon legislative and political advantages. The enormous protective tariff on sugar has enabled them to open thousands of acres of land which they could not profitably cultivate without that tariff.

With a high protective tariff on sugar and, until recently, free trade in labor, the planters have brought in large numbers of Orientals who work at cheap wages, and live on a low scale. When commodities cannot come into a country, the people who make the commodities must come. The influx of such swarms of cheap laborers to develop an artificially stimulated industry has tended to drive out white labor . . . just as the poor whites before the [Civil] War fled from the Negro. . . .

We spend uncounted millions of dollars in fortifying the islands of Hawaii—far, far more in cash, perhaps, than the advantages of the sugar industry of the islands are worth to us. We must keep considerable bodies of troops there on the volcanic hills, and then, to protect our communications we must have the further protection of a big navy . . . and we must make heroic efforts to subsidize merchant ships that they may become fighting vessels in time of need. What a combination of costly protections in order that a few rich men should become still richer by producing sugar on lands where, without taxing the consumer of the sugar, it could not possibly be grown in competition with great sugar-producing countries like Cuba!

One wonders indeed what would have happened if Hawaii had never had a protective tariff on sugar. Certainly no such amount of land could have been opened for sugar production, but this might have given an opportunity for more white settlers to come in naturally and to practice a more diversified agriculture. No such domination of the politics of the islands would have been possible. The development would undoubtedly not have been so rapid, but it might have been steadier and in the long run more democratic. And immigrants would have come in slowly and could have been educated and assimilated without placing the institutions of the islands to the strain under which they are now laboring. . . .

To the outside visitor, indeed, the island life at the present time conveys a curious sense of unnatural strain and over stimulation. . . . The profits on sugar during the last few years have been enormous. On a product worth over $40,000,000 last year it is estimated that about one-third was clear profit. . . . The actual cost of producing sugar on one of the smaller plantations on the island of Hawaii this year was about $36 a ton. The value before shipment was nearly $70 a ton. . . . Is it any wonder that they talk of the success of the system in Hawaii?

But this is not all by any means. The same narrow group of men who own or control the plantations also own or control nearly everything else, . . . the fertilizer business, . . . the profitable Honolulu Iron Works, which has been successful in building high-grade sugar-mill machinery; they also control practically all the wholesale and most of the retail mercantile business of the territory. They are interested, back and forth and in and out, in the banks and trust companies, and they control, directly or indirectly, practically all the public utilities, telephones, electric light plants, railroads, and in some degree the steamship lines. If one venture proves unprofitable, they make it up on some other venture.

As in the old South, the system has been eminently successful for those in control of the land, the machinery, and the labor supply. Many of them have become very rich. They live in excellent style; they send their sons and daughters to Eastern colleges and universities; they themselves take frequent trips to Europe or to the United States, and they are as cultivated and as delightful a people generally as there are anywhere to be found in the world.

As to the remainder of the population—the vast majority who do the hard work of the islands—the system presents entirely different aspects. . . . Without capital, without rights of citizenship, without a Western education, the Orientals and most of the Portuguese, Filipinos, Puerto Ricans and others, of course, cannot acquire land. So they have two courses open to them; they may work on the plantations for wages, or they may lease small tracts of land, at the highest possible rentals, from small land owners.

Often you will find Hawaiians living in a sort of squalid idleness from the income of a bit of wet taro land, where a couple of old Chinamen are putting out rice with patient industry. Or you find Japanese families—men and women both—toiling with a passion of industry unequaled elsewhere upon this earth day after day and year after year on rented lands in order to make for themselves a little more money than they have to pay out to the man who owns the land and does nothing. And then the white man brings the charge against the Oriental that he sets a ruinously low standard of living!

It is, indeed, almost impossible for a white man—except a few Portuguese peasants, whose scale of living is not much above that of the Japanese—to remain on the land in Hawaii and do his own work. It is very much as it was in the South before the war: landless white men are either driven out entirely or else they become wage-earning overseers or clerks on the plantations. . . .

It is difficult for an outsider to form any adequate conception of the extent to which a feudal aristocracy, dominating the land, can direct or influence even in remote details the life, the income, the politics, the education and even the religion of the country. Not only does the plantation manager dominate the actual work on his own plantation but his domination extends to all the people who live around the plantation—to all the little settlements and to all the small groups of homesteaders and small farmers near about. . . .

Let me illustrate: Along nearly the whole northern and northeastern coast of the island of Hawaii extends a broad band of plantations. Among these plantations are quite a number of small villages with a few white men in each and many Japanese and

Portuguese. And back on the hills are a few small land owners and homesteaders who are nominally independent of the plantations. Many of the plantations have built wharves or landings in front of their mills and here vessels stop and discharge their freight. Some of this freight is ordered by the small merchants and independent homesteaders. The plantation fixes a scale of charges for landing goods from the vessel to the wharf. I have before me a list of the landing charges of the Honokaa Sugar Company: for lifting one barrel of cement, twenty cents; a bag of grain, ten cents; a barrel of whiskey, $2.50; a bicycle, fifty cents; a sewing machine, $1.00 and so on.

Let us now see how this works out in the case of a ton of barley shipped from San Francisco to Honokaa. The freight from San Francisco to Hilo, over 2,500 miles, is $2.75 a ton. There is still ocean competition from San Francisco. But at Hilo competition ends. All the inter-island shipping is practically monopolized by the Inter-Island Steamship Company, owned and controlled by the same interests as the plantations—an enormously profitable company.

When the ton of barley gets to Hilo, then, it is taken by the Inter-Island Steamship Company and pays $5 freight for a trip of sixty miles to Honokaa. It paid $2.75 for over 2,500 miles from San Francisco—and nearly twice as much for sixty miles to Honokaa. Here it is landed on the private wharf of the plantation corporation at ten cents a bag or $2 for a ton.

But the profit in such devices as these is not, after all, the main thing. The power, the control, which it gives the plantation corporation over all the people of the community: over the laborers, over the merchants, over the voters—that is the main thing. It enables them to dictate largely who shall thrive and who shall not; it enables them to discipline the unruly voter and crowd out any man who does not submit. But more than this, it increases very materially the cost of living to the people. . . . It is another way by which the controlling financial interests tax all the people. . . .

Some of the white settlers, or would-be settlers, have endeavored to escape from this universal control by opening new lines of activity. Certain lands unsuitable for cane were found to be excellent for pineapples and immediately quite a number of enterprising Americans came in and began to develop the land. Today the pineapple industry is the second most important in the islands—but the small, independent, thrifty citizen-owner is being now rapidly crowded out. Big corporations, with packing plants and transportation facilities, and backed largely by the same interests which are in control of sugar, are rapidly coming into the full control of the situation and Japanese laborers and Japanese renters are taking the places of white settlers. The same process is going forward with the pineapples as with the sugar cane. . . .

The trouble with feudalism is that the feudal lord must do everything himself. By withholding the industrial independence and social initiative of the people under him he also makes them supine in many other matters—as of sanitation, education, religion. They come to have no community life or activity. Thus many of the planters of Hawaii have gone to really astonishing lengths in developing all sorts of benevolent activities. This is especially true of the old missionary stock, which has a tender conscience, and responds readily to the sense of obligation which goes with great power.

I have rarely visited any place where there is as much charity and as little democracy as in Hawaii. Colleges, kindergartens, churches, missions, and social settlements flourish there with unexampled vigor. A year or so ago they wanted a new Y.M.C.A. building and went out with the intention of raising $100,000 in ten days, but so liberal was the giving that they got $143,000 in six days and had to close the subscriptions.

At the same time Honolulu has some of the worst slums in the world—and if poverty in the tropics is picturesque, its gnawings are none the less painful. For downright overcrowding and unsanitary conditions it would be hard to find anything worse than some of the rickety old tenements which I visited in the city of Honolulu. And one will find here, exactly as in the slums of Chicago or New York, earnest men and women trying to convert these miserable creatures to the religion of Him who laid down the Golden Rule. So heavily do the conditions rest upon some of the rich men of Honolulu, that in one or two instances they give from 40 to 60 percent of their income yearly to benevolences. . . .

In the case of one of the greatest of the plantations, where the corporation owns not only the agricultural land, but the railroad and all the land of the town (which is also a seaport), the manager has used his power of benevolent protection to the utmost degree. He has admitted no saloons, no gambling places, no houses of prostitution and he has been careful in renting stores only to especially approved tenants. He has allowed the building of no shacks or poor structures. He has permitted one church, one wholesale liquor store, one Japanese store, and one Portuguese store.

He dictates to the last degree the conduct of the place and its people—as also he dictates the politics. He and his family contribute liberally to all the Christian churches in that island; they maintain a fine settlement work, kindergartens and reading rooms, and for the white employees they have a big club house with bowling alleys, tennis courts and a swimming tank. The expenditures every year by this planter and his family for benevolent purposes must be very large. Every employee is directed at every turn and in nearly every detail of his life. I never knew a more complete nor more benevolent example of feudalism than this; and never more respectable and less democratic conditions. . . .

All the liberal changes in the laws which the progressives have been able to bring about, all their benevolences and philanthropies, all their missions and churches, have so far not appreciably changed the oligarchic system. Indeed, the aristocracy grows ever wealthier, the middle-class white settlers and workers become fewer, the peasant laborers more numerous, and the feudalistic system more firmly intrenched. . . .

The keynote, indeed, of our modern worldwide economic situation is the struggle for docile labor. . . . So urgent is the need of labor that two separate immigration bureaus are maintained in the islands. One is privately supported by the Planters' Association, the other by the territorial government. . . . The purpose of both organizations, of course, is to get cheap laborers. . . .

Those who favor white immigration are having to meet all sorts of difficulties. In the first place the Asiatic element in the islands is now overwhelmingly predominant, and any white worker who meets Asiatic competition must live on a very low scale. Moreover, most of the planters would much prefer the Oriental—who is docile and industrious and who cannot become a citizen and voter. . . . The great majority of the plantation interests—and their word is law—don't want men who are likely to become ambitious; they don't want citizens. They are even now agitating the idea of persuading the United States government to so modify its exclusion law as to let in a "few more" Chinese workers under a sort of contract system.

One of the chief troubles with the Japanese in the islands is that they rear large families, and the boys of these families, born on our soil, will soon be voters. And that introduces a perplexing if not alarming element in the situation. I asked one of the big planters on Maui whether he thought that the coming generation of Japanese would make intelligent citizens. "Oh, yes," he said, "they'll make intelligent citizens all right enough, but not plantation laborers—and that's what we want." . . .

One of the underlying ideas of the planters in supporting the really sincere work of the government immigration bureau in attempting to bring in white peasants from Europe is frankly to meet the now overwhelming Japanese element with many other diverse peoples, with diverse customs and prejudices. A strike of Japanese workmen on several plantations two years ago caused the Planters' Association to see a great light in this connection. A population having no common language, no common ambitions, and being fierce competitors in the labor market, is difficult to organize and it therefore becomes more unlikely that there can be any concerted movement that would tend to disturb conditions or shake the control of the small and closely associated and interrelated group of white men who dominate the islands. They approve the wisdom of Napoleon's motto, "Divide and you dominate." . . . The more the planters' interests can keep the workers struggling and fighting among themselves for places and work, the larger the profits of the business. . . .

The planters have been making conditions pleasanter for workmen; but in the main thing of all—wages, or a fair share in the product of the sugar industry—and in real independence, the mass of the people in Hawaii are probably not so well off as they were five years ago. More things are being done for them in a feudalistic way; but they are less able to do things for themselves and thus prepare for real citizenship. . . .

While wages of males have gone up slightly, though probably not enough to offset increased cost of living, the tendency in the islands has been to force more and more women and children into the fields and mills. This has been necessary owing to the low wages. Though the planters will show you lists of common laborers who receive as high as $22 to $25 a month . . . "the average actual earnings of these employees probably do not much exceed, if they exceed at all, $15 monthly." . . .

No one, indeed, can visit the islands without being impressed with the enormous amount of labor being done there by women. Often they come into the fields with small babies strapped to their backs. Sometimes they carry them while they work and sometimes they make a little tent of cloth and put the baby down on the ground, where I have seen them the center of swarming clouds of flies. Among the Japanese it is the women who work mostly in the fields, for the Japanese have a passion for education and send their young people to school until they are thoroughly prepared. Among the Portuguese, however, the women remain at home and the boys and girls are taken out of the schools very early and sent into the fields. . . .

The effort of the planters at all hazards to maintain the present feudalistic system not only leads to "dividing and dominating" the laborers, but it finds further and perfectly logical expression in the hostility to the proper education of the children of the foreigners. Education brings people together, gives them a common language and common motives and it makes them ambitious. As one planter expressed it to me: "It spoils good workmen; turns the young men away from the plantations, disturbs political conditions." . . . Notwithstanding the enormous profits of the sugar industry, the growing wealth and an almost passionate interest in charities and benevolences on the part of many rich people, the crucial element in our civilization—public education—is being neglected. . . .

Partly because of the inadequacy of the public schools, but more largely perhaps because they are a people intensely loyal to their own language and customs, the Japanese have established their own schools everywhere in the islands. They take all that the public school gives them, and also send their children to the Japanese schools. Although the wages of those who work average only about fifty cents a day, they tax themselves steadily and at high rates for the maintenance of schools.

Usually these schools in the country are situated near the public schools and the teachers are often educated men from Japan, sometimes Buddhist priests. In the same way, the Chinese maintain schools of their own and there are also a few Portuguese schools directed by Roman Catholic teachers, and even a Korean school or two. It is easier to get help from the rich interests in the islands for these private foreign schools than for the democratic public schools. . . .

Having thus provided the very conditions which tend to force most of the Japanese and Chinese to perpetuate their Oriental life and interests, the commonest charge brought against all these Oriental people is that they do not "Americanize," and that, therefore, they should neither have a part in the government which taxes them, nor an equality in payment with other races for their labor. . . .

Whether in the South, in connection with the Negro, or in Hawaii, in connection with the Oriental people . . . the note of pessimism is struck most strongly by the element which has a selfish interest in keeping the Negro or the Oriental "in his place," in making him work at low wages, and in preventing him from securing adequate education or opportunities to rise. The note of optimism on the other hand is struck by those who are in some way trying to serve or help; teachers and preachers, especially, who are meeting the other races on terms not of business, but of friendly contact. . . .

It is a curious thing how contact on a friendly basis with even the lowest and most miserable of people gives men hope for mankind and faith in democracy, while the relationships which involve exploitation of these same people make men suspicious and pessimistic.

From "Wonderful Hawaii" and "Human Nature in Hawaii," Ray Stannard Baker, *American Magazine,* November and December 1911.

XLVII

Rupert Brooke

Waikiki in 1913 was still a long way from acquiring renown as a Pacific tourist capital, but it was, in a quiet way, attracting an increasing number of occasional guests from the Mainland. Strangely enough, its most ardent publicists in the States were veterans of the Spanish-American War who had discovered Waikiki on their way to and from the Philippines, and who years later were coming back with their families. The place appealed to a great many Americans because it made no pretense of being a resort.

The fishing village character predominated; *haole* beachcombers could hobnob inconspicuously with the lackadaisical Hawaiians, join them in their canoeing, surf frolics, sunning, and singing. Despite the mosquitoes and the untidy shorefront, it was a beautiful spot, with the palm groves, the bold crown of Diamond Head rising to the east, and the distant Waianae mountains to the west. For a less fastidious breed of guests than those who insisted on staying at the Royal Hawaiian Hotel in the heart of Honolulu, there were now informal accommodations at Waikiki too—the weathered Seaside boarding house or the beginnings of a new hostelry called the Moana. A "Promotion Committee" of the Honolulu Chamber of Commerce and the Merchants' Association were even beginning to talk about the practicality of building a canal to drain the evil-smelling, mosquito-infested swamp just inland from the beach.

This was the Waikiki that the handsome, athletic, witty British poet,

Rupert Brooke (1887–1915), found on his long journey to the South Seas in 1913. Although the sonnet "Waikiki," inspired by the setting, is not of the quality of his poignant stanzas on World War I, in which he tragically died two years later, it stands as a fine souvenir of his Hawaiian visit.

Waikiki

Warm perfumes like a breath from vine and tree
    Drift down the darkness. Plangent, hidden from eyes,
    Somewhere an ukulele thrills and cries
And stabs with pain the night's brown savagery.
And dark scents whisper; and dim waves creep to me,
    Gleam like a woman's hair, stretch out and rise;
    And new stars burn into the ancient skies,
Over the murmurous soft Hawaiian sea.

And I recall, lose, grasp, forget again,
    And still remember, a tale I have heard, or known,
An empty tale, of idleness and pain,
    Of two that loved—or did not love—and one
Whose perplexed heart did evil, foolishly,
A long while since, and by some other sea.

From *The Collected Poems of Rupert Brooke* (New York: Dodd, Mead and Company, 1915).

XLVIII

Jack London

Jack London's tale of Ah Kim is, in essence, the biography of hundreds of Chinese who were persuaded to go to Hawaii as plantation laborers for five years and stayed for life. The common biographical elements are all present: the humble living standards in a remote Chinese village, the financial inducements of the recruiting agents, the crowded passage to the Islands, the disappointing existence on a plantation in Hawaii, the frugality, the homage to ancestors, the move to town as soon as the labor contract expired, the parental domination, eventual success in an independent business enterprise, and the long climb up the social ladder.

A majority of the Chinese immigrants returned with their savings to the homeland, but the few thousand who remained created Honolulu's Chinatown and the *Pake* settlements scattered throughout the Islands. Altogether they constituted the most industrious, the most ambitious, and the most resourceful of the early labor groups imported to work the plantations.

As demonstrated in "The Tears of Ah Kim," Jack London (1876–1916) had an uncommon talent for illuminating in a few paragraphs the sum and substance of a place, period, social group, event, or movement. He was the most virile of all the writers lured to tropical Hawaii. Twice he visited the Islands: for four months in 1907 on the projected round-the-world cruise of the *Snark*—which ended in Australia; and for almost a year in 1915–16, when he did more than anyone else of the era to revive the art of surf-riding and promote Waikiki as a lively resort.

Although his tales of the high seas and the Klondike gold rush country are more widely read, the stories set in Hawaii are no less engaging. "The Tears of Ah Kim" was completed at Waikiki on June 16, 1916.

The Tears of Ah Kim

There was a great noise and racket, but no scandal, in Honolulu's Chinatown. Those within hearing distance merely shrugged their shoulders and smiled tolerantly at the disturbance as an affair of accustomed usualness. "What is it?" asked Chin Mo, down with a sharp pleurisy, of his wife, who had paused for a second at the open window to listen. "Only Ah Kim," was the reply. "His mother is beating him again."

The fracas was taking place in the garden, in back of the living rooms that were in back of the store that fronted on the street with the proud sign above: Ah Kim Company, General Merchandise. The garden was a miniature domain, twenty feet square, that somehow cunningly seduced the eye into a sense and seeming of vastness.

There were forests of dwarf pines and oaks, centuries old, yet two or three feet in height, and imported at enormous care and expense. A tiny bridge, a pace across, arched over a miniature river that flowed with rapids and cataracts from a miniature lake stocked with myriad-finned, orange-miracled goldfish that in proportion to the lake and landscape were whales. On every side the many windows of the several-storied shack buildings looked down. In the center of the garden, on the narrow graveled walk close beside the lake, Ah Kim was noisily receiving his beating.

No Chinese lad of tender and beatable years was Ah Kim. His was the store of Ah Kim Company, and his was the achievement of building it up through the long years from the shoestring of savings of a contract coolie laborer to a bank account in four figures and a credit that was gilt edge. An even half century of summers and winters had passed over his head, and, in the passing, fattened him comfortably and smugly. Short of stature, his full front was as rotund as a watermelon seed. His face was moon-faced. His garb was dignified and silken, and his black silk skullcap with the red button atop, now, alas, fallen on the ground, was the skullcap worn by successful and dignified merchants of his race.

But his appearance, in this moment of the present, was anything but dignified. Dodging and ducking under a rain of blows from a bamboo cane, he was crouched over in a half-doubled posture. When he was rapped on the knuckles and elbows, with which he shielded his face and head, his winces were genuine and involuntary. From the many surrounding windows the neighborhood looked down with placid enjoyment.

And she who wielded the stick so shrewdly from long practice! Seventy-four years old, she looked every minute of her time. Her thin legs were encased in straight-lined pants of linen, stiff-textured and shiny black. Her scraggy gray hair was drawn unrelentingly and flatly back from a narrow, unrelenting forehead. Eyebrows she had none, having long since shed them. Her eyes, of pinhole tinyness, were blackest black. She was shockingly cadaverous. Her shriveled forearm, exposed by the loose sleeve, possessed no more of muscle than several taut bow-strings stretched across meager bone under yellow, parchment-like skin. Along this mummy arm, jade bracelets shot up and down and clashed with every blow.

"Ah!" she cried out, rhythmically accenting her blows in series of three to each shrill observation. "I forbade you to talk to Li Faa. Today you stopped in the street with her. Not an hour ago. Half an hour by the clock you talked. What is that?"

"It was the thrice accursed telephone," Ah Kim muttered, while she suspended the stick to catch what he said. "Mrs. Chang Lucy told you. I know she did. I saw her see you. I shall have the telephone taken out. It is of the devil."

"It is a device of all the devils," Mrs. Tai Fu agreed, taking a fresh grip on the stick. "Yet shall the telephone remain. I like to talk with Mrs. Chang Lucy over the telephone."

"She has the eyes of ten thousand cats," quoth Ah Kim, ducking and receiving the stick stingingly on his knuckles. "And the tongues of ten thousand toads," he supplemented ere his next duck.

"She is an impudent-faced and evil-mannered hussy," Mrs. Tai Fu accented.

"Mrs. Chang Lucy was ever that," Ah Kim murmured like the dutiful son he was.

"I speak of Li Faa," his mother corrected with stick emphasis. "She is only half Chinese, as you know. Her mother was a shameless Kanaka. She wore skirts like a degraded *haole* woman—also corsets, as I have seen for myself. Where are her children? Yet she has buried two husbands."

"The one was drowned, the other kicked by a horse," Ah Kim qualified.

"A year of her, unworthy son of a noble father, and you would gladly be going out to get drowned or be kicked by a horse."

Subdued chucklings and laughter from the window audience applauded her point.

"You buried two husbands yourself, revered mother," Ah Kim was stung to retort.

"I had the good taste not to marry a third. Besides, my husbands died honorably in their beds. They were not kicked by horses nor drowned at sea. What business is it of our neighbors that you should inform them I have had two husbands, or ten, or none? You have made a scandal of me before all our neighbors, and for that I shall now give you a real beating."

Ah Kim endured the staccato rain of blows, and said when his mother paused, breathless and weary: "Always have I insisted and pleaded, honorable mother, that you beat me in the house, with the windows and doors closed tight, and not in the open street or the garden open behind the house."

"You have called this unthinkable Li Faa the Silvery Moon Blossom," Mrs. Tai Fu rejoined, quite illogically and femininely, but with utmost success in so far as she deflected her son from continuance of the thrust he had so swiftly driven home.

"Mrs. Chang Lucy told you," he charged.

"I was told over the telephone," his mother evaded. "I do not know all voices that speak to me over that contrivance of all the devils."

Strangely, Ah Kim made no effort to run away from his mother, which he easily could have done. She, on the other hand, found fresh cause for more stick blows.

"Ah! Stubborn one! Why do you not cry? Mule that shameth its ancestors! Never have I made you cry. From the time you were a little boy I have never made you cry. Answer me! Why do you not cry?"

Weak and breathless from her exertions, she dropped the stick and panted and shook as if with a nervous palsy.

"I do not know, except that it is my way," Ah Kim replied, gazing solicitously at his mother. "I shall bring you a chair now, and you will sit down and rest and feel better."

But she flung away from him with a snort and tottered agedly across the garden into the house. Meanwhile recovering his skullcap and smoothing his disordered attire, Ah Kim rubbed his hurts and gazed after her with eyes of devotion. He even smiles, and almost might it appear that he had enjoyed the beating.

Ah Kim had been so beaten ever since he was a boy, when he lived on the high banks of the eleventh cataract of the Yangtze River. Here his father had been born and toiled all his days from young manhood to a towing coolie. When he died, Ah Kim, in his own young manhood, took up the same honorable profession. Farther back than all remembered annals of the family, had the males of it been towing coolies. At the time of Christ his direct ancestors had been doing the same thing, meeting the precisely similarly modeled junks below the white water at the foot of the cañon, bending the half mile of rope to each junk, and, according to size, tailing on from a hundred to two hundred coolies of them and by sheer, two-legged man power, bowed forward and down till their hands touched the ground and their faces were sometimes within a foot of it, dragging the junk up through the white water to the head of the cañon.

Apparently, down all the intervening centuries, the payment of the trade had not picked up. His father, his father's father, and himself, Ah Kim, had received the same invariable remuneration —per junk one-fourteenth of a cent, at the rate he had since learned money was valued in Hawaii. On long, lucky, summer days when the waters were easy, the junks many, the hours of daylight sixteen, sixteen hours of such heroic toil would earn over a cent. But in a whole year a towing coolie did not earn more than a dollar and a half.

People could and did live on such an income. There were women servants who received a yearly wage of a dollar. The net makers of Ti Wi earned between a dollar and two dollars a year. They lived on such wages, or, at least they did not die on them. But for the towing coolies there were pickings, which were what made the profession honorable and the guild a close hereditary corporation or labor union. One junk in five that was dragged up through the rapids or lowered down was wrecked. One junk in every ten was a total loss. The coolies of the towing guild knew the freaks and whims of the currents, and grappled and raked and netted a wet harvest from the river. They of the guild were looked up to by lesser coolies, for they could afford to drink brick tea and eat No. 4 rice every day.

And Ah Kim had been contented and proud until, one bitter spring day of driving sleet and hail, he dragged ashore a drowning Cantonese sailor. It was this wanderer, thawing out by his fire, who first named the magic name Hawaii to him. He himself had never been to that laborer's paradise, said the sailor; but many Chinese had gone there from Canton, and he had heard the talk of their letters written back. In Hawaii was never frost nor famine. The very pigs, never fed, were ever fat of the generous offal disdained by man. A Cantonese or Yangtze family could live on the waste of an Hawaiian coolie. And wages! In gold dollars, ten a month, or, in trade dollars, twenty a month, was what the contract Chinese coolie received from the white-devil sugar kings.

In a year the coolie received the prodigious sum of two hundred and forty trade dollars—more than a hundred times what a coolie, toiling ten times as hard, received on the eleventh cataract of the Yangtze. In short, all things considered, an Hawaiian coolie was one hundred times better off, and, when the amount of labor was estimated, a thousand times better off. In addition was the wonderful climate.

When Ah Kim was twenty-four, despite his mother's pleadings and beatings, he resigned from the ancient and honorable guild of the eleventh cataract towing coolies, left his mother to go into a boss coolie's household as a servant for a dollar a year and an annual dress to cost not less than thirty cents, and himself departed down the Yangtze to the great sea.

Many were his adventures and severe his toils and hardships ere, as a salt-sea junk sailor, he won to Canton. When he was twenty-six he signed five years of his life and labor away to the Hawaiian sugar kings and departed, one of eight hundred contract coolies, for that far island land, on a festering steamer run by a crazy captain and drunken officers and rejected of Lloyds.

Honorable, among laborers, had Ah Kim's rating been as a towing coolie. In Hawaii, receiving a hundred times more pay, he found himself looked down upon as the lowest of the low—a plantation coolie, than which could be nothing lower. But a coolie whose ancestors had towed junks up the eleventh cataract of the Yangtze since before the birth of Christ inevitably inherits one character in large degree; namely, the character of patience. This patience was Ah Kim's. At the end of five years, his compulsory servitude over, thin as ever in body, in bank account he lacked just ten trade dollars of possessing a thousand trade dollars.

On this sum he could have gone back to the Yangtze and retired for life a really wealthy man. He would have possessed a larger sum, had he not, on occasion, conservatively played che fa and fan-tan, and had he not, for a twelvemonth, toiled among the centipedes and scorpions of the stifling cane fields in the semi-dream of a continuous opium debauch. Why he had not toiled the whole five years under spell of opium was the expensiveness of the habit. He had had no moral scruples. The drug had cost too much.

But Ah Kim did not return to China. He had observed the business life of Hawaii and developed a vaulting ambition. For six months, in order to learn business and English at the bottom, he clerked in the plantation store. At the end of this time he knew more about that particular store than did ever a plantation manager know about any plantation store.

When he resigned his position he was receiving forty gold a month, or eighty trade, and he was beginning to put on flesh. Also, his attitude toward mere contract coolies had become distinctively aristocratic. The manager offered to raise him to sixty gold, which, by the year, would constitute a fabulous fourteen hundred and forty trade, or seven hundred times his annual earning on the Yangtze as a two-legged horse at one-fourteenth of a gold cent per junk.

Instead of accepting, Ah Kim departed to Honolulu and in the big general merchandise store of Fong & Chow Fong began at the bottom for fifteen gold per month. He worked a year and a half, and resigned when he was thirty-three, despite the seventy-five gold per month his Chinese employers were paying him. Then it was that he put up his own sign: Ah Kim Company, General Merchandise. Also, better fed, there was about his less meager figure a foreshadowing of the melon-seed rotundity that was to attach to him in future years.

With the years he prospered increasingly, so that, when he was thirty-six, the promise of his figure was fulfilling rapidly, and, himself a member of the exclusive and powerful Hai Gum Tong and of the Chinese Merchants' Association, he was accustomed to sitting as host at dinners that cost him as much as thirty years of towing on the eleventh cataract would have earned him. Two things he missed: a wife, and his mother to lay the stick on him as of yore.

When he was thirty-seven he consulted his bank balance. It stood him three thousand gold. For twenty-five hundred down and an easy mortgage he could buy the three-story shack building and the ground in fee simple on which it stood. But to do this left only five hundred for a wife. Fu Yee Po had a marriageable, properly small-footed daughter whom he was willing to import from China and sell to him for eight hundred gold plus the costs of importation. Further, Fu Yee Po was even willing to take five hundred down and the remainder on note at six percent.

Ah Kim, thirty-seven years of age, fat and bachelor, really did want a wife, especially a small-footed wife; for, Chinese born and reared, the immemorial small-footed female had been deeply impressed into his fantasy of woman. But more, even more and far more than a small-footed wife, did he want his mother and his mother's delectable beatings.

So he declined Fu Yee Po's easy terms, and at much less cost imported his own mother from servant in a boss coolie's house at a yearly wage of a dollar and a thirty-cent dress to be mistress of his Honolulu three-story shack building with two household servants, three clerks, and a porter of all work under her, to say nothing of ten thousand dollars' worth of dress goods on the shelves, that ranged from the cheapest cotton crêpes to the most expensive hand-embroidered silks. For be it known that even in that early day Ah Kim's emporium was beginning to cater to the tourist trade from the States.

For thirteen years Ah Kim had lived tolerably happily with his mother and by her been methodically beaten for causes just or unjust, real or fancied; and at the end of it all he knew as strongly as ever the ache of his heart and head for a wife, and of his loins for sons to live after him and carry on the dynasty of Ah Kim Company. Such the dream that has ever vexed men from those early ones who first usurped a hunting right, monopolized a sand bar for a fish trap, or stormed a village and put the males thereof to the sword. Kings, millionaires and Chinese merchants of Honolulu have this in common, despite that they may praise God for having made them differently and in self-likable images.

And the ideal of woman that Ah Kim at fifty ached for had changed from his ideal at thirty-seven. No small-footed wife did he want now, but a free, natural, out-stepping, normal-footed woman who somehow appeared to him in his daydreams and haunted his night visions in the form of Li Faa, the Silvery Moon Blossom. What if she were twice widowed, the daughter of a Kanaka mother, the wearer of white-devil skirts and corsets and high-heeled slippers? He wanted her. It seemed it was written

that she should be joint ancestor with him of the line that would
continue the ownership and management through the generations
of Ah Kim Company, General Merchandise.

"I will have no half *paké* daughter-in-law," his mother often
reiterated to Ah Kim, *paké* being the Hawaiian word for Chinese.
"All *paké* must my daughter-in-law be, even as you, my son, and
as I, your mother. And she must wear trousers, my son, as all the
women of our family before her. No woman in the she-devil skirts
and corsets can pay due reverence to our ancestors. Corsets and
reverence do not go together. Such a one is this shameless Li Faa.
She is impudent and independent, and will be neither obedient
to her husband nor her husband's mother. This brazen-faced Li
Faa would believe herself the source of life and the first ancestor,
recognizing no ancestors before her. She laughs at our joss sticks
and prayer papers and family gods, as I have been well told—"

"Mrs. Chang Lucy," Ah Kim groaned.

"Not alone Mrs. Chang Lucy, O son. I have inquired. At least a
dozen have heard her say of our joss house that it is all monkey
foolishness. The words are hers—she, who eats raw fish, raw squid
and baked dog. Ours is the foolishness of monkeys. Yet would she
marry you, a monkey, because of your store that is a palace and
of the wealth that makes you a great man. And she would put
shame on me, and on your father before you, long honorably
dead."

And there was no discussing the matter. As things were, Ah
Kim knew his mother was right. Not for nothing had Li Faa been
born forty years before of a Chinese father, renegade to all tradition, and of a Kanaka mother whose immediate forebears had
broken the taboos, cast down their own Polynesian gods, and
weak-heartedly listened to the preaching about the remote and
unimaginable god of the Christian missionaries.

Li Faa, educated, who could read and write English and
Hawaiian and a fair measure of Chinese, claimed to believe in
nothing, although in her secret heart she feared the *kahunas* (Hawaiian witch doctors), who she was certain could charm away
ill luck or pray one to death. Li Faa would never come into Ah

Kim's house, as he thoroughly knew, and kowtow to his mother and be slave to her in the immemorial Chinese way.

Li Faa, from the Chinese angle, was a new woman, a feminist, who rode horseback astride, disported immodestly garbed at Waikiki on the surf boards, and at more than one luau had been known to dance the hula with the worst and in excess of the worst, to the scandalous delight of all.

Ah Kim himself, a generation younger than his mother, had been bitten by the acid of modernity. The old order held, in so far as he still felt in his subtlest crypts of being the dusty hand of the past resting on him, residing in him; yet he subscribed to heavy policies of fire and life insurance, acted as treasurer for the local Chinese revolutionists that were for turning the Celestial empire into a republic, contributed to the funds of the Hawaii-born Chinese baseball nine that excelled the Yankee nines at their own game, talked philosophy with Katso Suguri, the Japanese Buddhist and silk importer, fell for police graft, played and paid his insidious share in the democratic politics of annexed Hawaii, and was thinking of buying an automobile.

Ah Kim never dared bare himself to himself and thresh out and winnow out how much of the old he had ceased to believe in. His mother was of the old, yet he revered her and was happy under her bamboo stick. Li Faa, the Silvery Moon Blossom, was of the new, yet he could never be quite completely happy without her.

For he loved Li Faa. Moon-faced, rotund as a watermelon seed, a canny business man, wise with half a century of living—nevertheless Ah Kim became an artist when he thought of her. He thought of her in poems of names, as woman transmuted into flowery terms of beauty and philosophic abstractions of achievement and easement. She was, to him, and alone to him of all men in the world, his Plum Blossom, his Tranquillity of Woman, his Flower of Serenity, his Moon Lily and his Perfect Rest. And as he murmured these love endearments of namings, it seemed to him that in them were the ripplings of running waters, the tinklings of silver wind bells, and the scents of the oleander and the jasmine.

She was his poem of woman, a lyric delight, a three dimensions of flesh and spirit delicious, a fate and a good fortune written, ere the first man and woman were, by the gods whose whim had been to make all men and women for sorrow and for joy.

But his mother put into his hand the ink brush and placed under it, on the table, the writing tablet.

"Paint," said she, "the ideograph of *to marry*."

He obeyed, scarcely wondering, with the deft artistry of his race and training, painting the symbolic hieroglyphic.

"Resolve it," commanded his mother.

Ah Kim looked at her, curious, willing to please, unaware of the drift of her intent.

"Of what is it composed?" she persisted. "What are the three originals, the sum of which is it: to marry, marriage, the coming together and wedding of a man and a woman? Paint them, paint them apart, the three originals, unrelated, so that we may know how the wise men of old wisely built up the ideograph of *to marry*."

And Ah Kim, obeying and painting, saw that what he had painted was three picture signs—the picture signs of a hand, an ear and a woman.

"Name them," said his mother; and he named them.

"It is true," said she. "It is a great tale. It is the stuff of the painted pictures of marriage. Such marriage was in the beginning; such shall it always be in my house. The hand of a man takes the woman's ear and by it leads her away to his house, where she is to be obedient to him and to his mother.

"I was taken by the ear, so, by your long honorably dead father. I have looked at your hand. It is not like his hand. Always have I looked at the ear of Li Faa. Never will you lead her by the ear. She has not that kind of ear. I shall live a long time yet, and I will be mistress in my son's house, after our ancient way, until I die."

"But she is my revered ancestress," Ah Kim explained to Li Faa.

He was timidly unhappy; for Li Faa, having ascertained that Mrs. Tai Fu was at the temple of the Chinese Aesculapius making

The last of the longhorns

a food offering of dried duck and prayers for her declining health, had taken advantage of the opportunity to call upon him in his store.

Li Faa pursed her insolent, unpainted lips into the form of a half-opened rosebud, and replied: "That will do for China. I do not know China. This is Hawaii, and in Hawaii the customs of all foreigners change."

"She is nevertheless my ancestress," Ah Kim protested, "the mother who gave me birth, whether I am in China or Hawaii, O Silvery Moon Blossom that I want for wife."

"I have had two husbands," Li Faa stated placidly. "One was a *paké*, one was a Portuguese. I learned much from both. Also am I educated. I have been to high school, and I have played the piano in public. And I learned from my two husbands much. The *paké* makes the best husband. Never again will I marry anything but a *paké*. But he must not take me by the ear—"

"How do you know of that?" he broke in suspiciously.

"Mrs. Chang Lucy," was the reply. "Mrs. Chang Lucy tells me everything that your mother tells her, and your mother tells her much. So let me tell you that mine is not that kind of ear."

"Which is what my honored mother has told me," Ah Kim groaned.

"Which is what your honored mother told Mrs. Chang Lucy, which is what Mrs. Chang Lucy told me," Li Faa completed equably. "And I now tell you, O Third Husband To Be, that the man is not born who will lead me by the ear. It is not the way in Hawaii. I will go only hand in hand, with my man, side by side, fifty-fifty, as is the *haole* slang just now. My Portuguese husband thought different. He tried to beat me. I landed him three times in the police court, and each time he worked out his sentence on the reef. After that he got drowned."

"My mother has been my mother for fifty years," Ah Kim declared stoutly.

"And for fifty years has she beaten you," Li Faa giggled. "How my father used to laugh at Yap Ten Shin! Like you, Yap Ten Shin had been born in China, and had brought the Chinese customs with him. His old father was forever beating him with a stick. He loved his father. But his father beat him harder than ever when he became a missionary paké. Every time he went to the missionary services, his father beat him. And every time the missionary heard of it he was harsh in his language to Yap Ten Shin for allowing his father to beat him. And my father laughed and laughed, for my father was a very liberal paké who had changed his customs quicker than most foreigners. And all the trouble was because Yap Ten Shin had a loving heart. He loved his honorable father. He loved the God of Love of the Christian missionary. But in the end, in me, he found the greatest love of all, which is the love of woman. In me he forgot his love for his father and his love for the loving Christ.

"And he offered my father six hundred gold for me—the price was small because my feet were not small. But I was half Kanaka. I said that I was not a slave woman, and that I would be sold to no man. My high-school teacher was a *haole* old maid who said love of woman was so beyond price that it must never be sold. Perhaps that was why she was an old maid. She was not beautiful. She could not give herself away.

"My Kanaka mother said it was not the Kanaka way to sell their daughters for a money price. They gave their daughters for love, and she would listen to reason if Yap Ten Shin provided luaus in quantity and quality. My paké father, as I have told you, was liberal. He asked me if I wanted Yap Ten Shin for my husband. And I said yes; and freely, of myself, I went to him. He it was who was kicked by a horse; but he was a very good husband before he was kicked by the horse.

"As for you, Ah Kim, you shall always be honorable and lovable for me, and some day, when it is necessary for you to take me by the ear, I shall marry you and come here and be with you always, and you will be the happiest paké in all Hawaii; for I have had two husbands, and gone to high school, and am most wise in making a husband happy. But that will be when your mother has ceased to beat you. Mrs. Chang Lucy tells me that she beats you very hard."

"She does," Ah Kim affirmed. "Behold!" He thrust back his loose sleeves, exposing to the elbow his smooth and cherubic forearms. They were mantled with black and blue marks that advertised the weight and number of blows so shielded from his head and face.

"But she has never made me cry," Ah Kim disclaimed hastily. "Never, from the time I was a little boy, has she made me cry."

"So Mrs. Chang Lucy says," Li Faa observed. "She says that your honorable mother often complains to her that she has never made you cry."

A sibilant warning from one of his clerks was too late. Having regained the house by way of the back alley, Mrs. Tai Fu emerged right upon them from out of the living apartments. Never had Ah Kim seen his mother's eyes so blazing furious. She ignored Li Faa, as she screamed at him: "Now will I make you cry. As never before shall I beat you until you do cry."

"Then let us go into the back rooms, honorable mother," Ah Kim suggested. "We will close the windows and the doors, and there you may beat me."

"No. Here shall you be beaten before all the world and this shameless woman who would with her own hand take you by the ear and call such sacrilege marriage! Stay, shameless woman."

"I am going to stay anyway," said Li Faa. She favored the clerks with a truculent stare. "And I'd like to see anything less than the police put me out of here."

"You will never be my daughter-in-law," Mrs. Tai Fu snapped.

Li Faa nodded her head in agreement. "But just the same," she added, "shall your son be my third husband."

"You mean when I am dead?" the old mother screamed.

"The sun rises each morning," Li Faa said enigmatically. "All my life have I seen it rise—"

"You are forty, and you wear corsets."

"But I do not dye my hair—that will come later," Li Faa calmly retorted. "As to my age, you are right. I shall be forty-one next Kamehameha Day. For forty years I have seen the sun rise. My father was an old man. Before he died he told me that he had observed no difference in the rising of the sun since when he was a little boy. The world is round. Confucius did not know that, but you will find it in all the geography books. The world is round.

Ever it turns over on itself, over and over and around and around. And the times and seasons of weather and life turn with it.

"What is, has been before. What has been will be again. The time of the breadfruit and the mango ever recurs, and man and woman repeat themselves. The robins nest, and in the springtime the plovers come from the north. Every spring is followed by another spring. The coconut palm rises into the air, ripens its fruit and departs. But always are there more coconut palms. This is not all my own smart talk. Much of it my father told me. Proceed, honorable Mrs. Tai Fu, and beat your son who is my Third Husband To Be. But I shall laugh. I warn you I shall laugh."

Ah Kim dropped down on his knees so as to give his mother every advantage. And while she rained blows upon him with the bamboo stick, Li Faa smiled and giggled, and finally burst into laughter.

"Harder! O honorable Mrs. Tai Fu!" Li Faa urged between paroxysms of mirth.

Mrs. Tai Fu did her best, which was notably weak, until she observed what made her drop the stick by her side in amazement. Ah Kim was crying. Down both cheeks great round tears were coursing. Li Faa was amazed. So were the gaping clerks. Most amazed of all was Ah Kim, yet he could not help himself; and, although no further blows fell, he cried steadily on.

"But why did you cry?" Li Faa demanded often of Ah Kim. "It was so perfectly foolish a thing to do. She was not even hurting you."

"Wait until we are married," was Ah Kim's invariable reply, "and then, O Moon Lily, will I tell you."

Two years later, one afternoon, more like a watermelon seed in configuration than ever, Ah Kim returned home from a meeting of the Chinese Protective Association to find his mother dead on her couch. Narrower and more unrelenting than ever were the forehead and the brushed-back hair. But on her face was a withered smile. The gods had been kind. She had passed without pain.

He telephoned first of all to Li Faa's number, but did not find her until he called up Mrs. Chang Lucy. The news given, the marriage was dated ahead with ten times the brevity of the old-line Chinese custom. And if there be anything analogous to a bridesmaid in a Chinese wedding, Mrs. Chang Lucy was just that.

"Why," Li Faa asked Ah Kim when alone with him on their wedding night, "why did you cry when your mother beat you that day in the store? You were so foolish. She was not even hurting you."

"That is why I cried," answered Ah Kim.

Li Faa looked at him without understanding.

"I cried," he explained, "because I suddenly knew that my mother was nearing her end. There was no weight, no hurt in the blows. I cried because I knew *she no longer had strength enough to hurt me*. That is why I cried, my Flower of Serenity, my Perfect Rest. That is the only reason why I cried."

From *On the Makaloa Mat,* Jack London (New York: Macmillan, 1920).

XLIX

William Somerset Maugham

For over a century people had thought of the Hawaiian Islands as a natural crossroads for East and West—a geographical crossroads for commerce, but not a residential point of convergence for the races of Occident and Orient. It was not planned that way; there was no plan; only out of the lack of planning did it become that, and everyone seemed a little surprised and chagrined when suddenly Honolulu was recognized as a common residence of Occidentals and Orientals.

At first white residents were not very proud of what had transpired; they avoided talking about it; but when visitors began acclaiming the mixture of races as one of the interesting features of the Islands, they too accepted the fact, and boasted a little of the not unhappy state of racial integration. It was at the dawn of this period that William Somerset Maugham (1874–1965) paused at Honolulu en route from England to Russia, to be thoroughly startled at what he found.

His novel *Of Human Bondage,* published in 1915, had made him famous; and eager to participate in events associated with the Great War, he had accepted appointment as a British secret agent—in the very natural role of well-known author traveling from country to country in search of new material for his writing. His mission was to accomplish what he could to keep the Bolsheviks from seizing power in Russia, but he masked his real objective by first visiting the United States, stopping briefly in Hawaii and touring the South Pacific before approaching Asia.

On this surreptitious journey he picked up incidents and local color for South Sea stories like *Rain* and *The Moon and Sixpence*. On Oahu he stumbled upon accounts of the ancient Hawaiian practice of praying enemies to death, and made that discovery the theme of his short story "Honolulu." In narrating the setting for the story he gave a vivid capsule description of the center of Honolulu as he himself saw it in 1916—a melting pot with an "incongruity which I felt from the beginning was its most striking characteristic."

Meeting Place of East and West

Nothing had prepared me for Honolulu. It is so far away from Europe, it is reached after so long a journey from San Francisco, so strange and so charming associations are attached to the name, that at first I could hardly believe my eyes. I do not know that I had formed in my mind any very exact picture of what I expected, but what I found caused me a great surprise.

It is a typical western city. Shacks are cheek by jowl with stone mansions; dilapidated frame houses stand next door to smart stores with plate glass windows; electric cars rumble noisily along the streets; and motors, Fords, Buicks, Packards, line the pavement. The shops are filled with all the necessities of American civilization. Every third house is a bank and every fifth the agency of a steamship company.

Along the streets crowd an unimaginable assortment of people. The Americans, ignoring the climate, wear black coats and high, starched collars, straw hats, soft hats, and bowlers. The Kanakas, pale brown, with crisp hair, have nothing on but a shirt and a pair of trousers; but the half-breeds are very smart with flaring ties and patent-leather boots. The Japanese, with their obsequious smile, are neat and trim in white duck, while their women walk a step or two behind them, in native dress, with a baby on their backs.

The Japanese children, in bright colored frocks, their little heads shaven, look like quaint dolls. Then there are the Chinese. The

men, fat and prosperous, wear their American clothes oddly, but
the women are enchanting with their tightly-dressed black hair,
so neat that you feel it can never be disarranged, and they are
very clean in their tunics and trousers, white, or powder blue, or
black. Lastly there are the Filipinos, the men in huge straw hats,
the women in bright yellow muslin with great puffed sleeves.

It is the meeting place of East and West. The very new rubs
shoulders with the immeasurably old. And if you have not found
the romance you expected, you have come upon something singularly intriguing. All these strange people live close to each other,
with different languages and different thoughts; they believe in
different gods and they have different values; two passions alone
they share, love and hunger. And somehow as you watch them,
you have an impression of extraordinary vitality.

Though the air is so soft and the sky so blue, you have, I know
not why, a feeling of something hotly passionate that beats like
a throbbing pulse through the crowd. Though the native policeman at the corner, standing on a platform, with a white club to
direct the traffic, gives the scene an air of respectability, you cannot but feel that it is a respectability only of the surface; a little
below there is darkness and mystery.

It gives you just that thrill, with a little catch at the heart, that
you have when at night in the forest the silence trembles on a
sudden with the low, insistent beating of a drum. You are all
expectant of I know not what.

There are certain places, surrounded by a halo of romance, to
which the inevitable disillusionment which you must experience
on seeing them gives a singular spice. You had expected something wholly beautiful and you get an impression which is infinitely more complicated than any that beauty can give you. It
is like the weakness in the character of a great man which may
make him less admirable but certainly makes him more interesting.

From *The Trembling of a Leaf*, W. Somerset Maugham (New York: Doubleday and Company, Inc., 1921).

L

Armine von Tempski

Next to Jack London, the most virile contributor to the literature of Hawaii was a woman, Armine von Tempski (1899–1940), who still stands as prima donna among Island-born creative writers. Dynamic daughter of the dynamic manager of Haleakala Ranch, she was born and brought up in the *paniolo* country of Maui, and expert horsemanship came as second nature to her. She rode intuitively, boldly, gracefully; and she wrote the way she rode: *Hula, Dust, Fire, Lava, Hawaiian Harvest, Ripe Breadfruit* and, best of all, her autobiography, *Born in Paradise.*

She was an author who did not have to lean on research; she drew from vivid memory and personal experience. Hers was an exciting life, and she knew how to make it exciting to others. The Hawaiians, the Portuguese, the Chinese, the Japanese, as well as *haoles* of all classes, were intimate acquaintances. Through living with them she gathered a feeling for their background, their family traditions, their pride, and their prejudices; she had firsthand knowledge of their problems, ambitions, weaknesses, their favorite pleasures, foods, sports, music; and her descriptions rang true. Her description of hunting wild cattle during her girlhood, from *Born in Paradise*, offers a fair representation of her racy style.

[409]

Tied to Death

Riding along, I stared at the vast shape of Haleakala looming blackly against the stars. The eager thud of hoofs, men's laughing voices about me, horses blowing out their nostrils, and the electrical *kiu* wind swooping down from the crater rim sent a queer surf running through my heart.

The beasts we were going after were longhorns gone wild, descendants of the stock landed in Hawaii in 1793 by Lord Vancouver. Weighing up to 1,600 pounds, savage, nimble as cats, they were ready to charge riders on sight. Roping them was as dangerous as lion- or tiger-hunting and required more precision from man and mount than pig-sticking in India. Yet whenever ranch work was slack Dad and the boys went up the mountain after wild bulls, for they raised havoc with the purity of registered bulls and wasted pasturage. After they were secured, they were tied to old oxen and dragged home to be castrated and trained for ox-wagons. Those that would not tame were slaughtered to supply extra beef for the ranch larder.

Watching the jaunty figures about me I knew I mustn't make mental pictures of what might occur on the rough slopes of Haleakala when dawn came. If I was going to lead a man's life with Dad, I must think man-thoughts and keep a grip on my emotions. But it was a difficult thing to do under the circumstances. I knew that Dad, and every self-respecting *paniolo,* rode —to translate an old Spanish term—"tied to death." To lose a lasso, or cast off from an animal once it had been roped was a *paniolo's* ultimate disgrace, even though failure to do so had cost many a man's and horse's life.

It didn't seem fantastic to me that necks and lives were risked unnecessarily by adherence to this code. It had produced the finest roper in the world. In 1908, Ikuwa Purdy, a part-Hawaiian *paniolo* from Parker ranch, had gone to Cheyenne and defeated Angus MacPhee, who had been champion roper of the world for five years in succession. Angus came to Hawaii the following year to get back his title, but Ikuwa beat him again and the big Wyoming man stayed on in the Islands. As well as being champion roper of the world for five years, Angus had been top bronc-buster in Buffalo Bill's Wild West show, but the first time he went out to rope wild cattle on Maui he declared that only the insane rode like *paniolos*.

I thought of the biggest wild-bull horns ever roped on Maui, which adorned the mantel at home. Over four inches in diameter at the base, the span from needle-tip to needle-tip was five feet three inches. Swipes from those horns had cost three valiant horses their lives and injured two men before Dad roped and killed the outlaw.

I knew from the contours of the cones and ridges we were passing that we were nearing the lava beds below the summit. There we would wait until the wild cattle returned from their night maraudings to seek the safety of wastelands which were too rough for men and horses to ride through. Getting to a commanding hilltop, Dad halted and studied the sky.

"About an hour to dawn," he announced. "Get a fire going, someone."

Eole touched a match to a *kawao* bush. Little tongues of flame licked greedily through the tiny leaves, sending up dense clouds of white smoke. The men secured the spare horses, brought along in case of accidents, to trees. I thawed out my stiff fingers before slacking Bedouin's girths. Men began squatting down and went carefully over their lassos, tossing them out coil by coil, hunting for possible kinks, which under terrific strain might snap the stout rawhides which were painstakingly braided in slack moments. Then with equal care they coiled up two fathom-lengths of thick manila rope, finished with heavy metal swivels, and tied them to their saddles. Each man carried three with which to tie up wild bulls after they had snubbed the animals to trees with lassos.

The wind coming from the summit had an eerie quality, as if it were blowing from black spaces between the stars. Gradually the Ghost Dawn welled into the sky and subsided. Stars enlarged

and faded. A pale daffodil light crept up behind the cold blue
shoulder of Haleakala. The world seemed big, empty, and awesome in the morning light. Above us, some five miles away, naked,
deluged by old lava flows, the summit of the dead volcano
towered.

Men began getting to their feet, watching the country below.
Shortly the wild cattle would begin working back from the pas-
tures and forests. To bolster up my spirits for what was ahead,
I whispered an old verse Dad had taught me.

> I trust my sword,
> I trust my steed,
> But most I trust
> Myself—in need!

Daddy grinned. "Right," he agreed. "And get this thoroughly
into your head. Once we start roping we won't have time to look
out for you. Keep a sharp watch out for lava pits. Some are easy
to see, others are hidden by brush. The horses are sure-footed
and know their business, but that doesn't excuse you from not
being on the job every instant. Remember old John Paris whom I
visited in Kona last summer?"

I nodded.

"One day he went up Hualalai to rope wild cattle and didn't
come back. For three days search parties scoured the mountain
for him. Finally a *paniolo* picked up his trail, which ended in a
patch of scrub. The *paniolo* went forward cautiously on foot.
There at the bottom of a forty-foot pit was old John, still alive
but weak from lack of food and water. His horse and, luckily for
old John, the bull he had been tied to, were killed by the fall. The
paniolo hauled him out with a lasso, but it was a close call."

I looked at Dad, swallowed, and managed a smile. I was not
at all sure, now, that I wanted to see him and the *paniolos* lasso-
ing wild bulls. I thought of the babies asleep at home, of my two
sisters. What would become of us if anything happened to Dad?

The *kawao* bush had burned to a heap of white ashes. Men
had ridden off and posted themselves on commanding ridges.

Only Dad, Holomalia the foreman, and I were left with the tied-up extra horses. With a sort of restrained eagerness, Dad and Holomalia began cinching up their saddles. Holomalia was riding Tradewind, a gray gelding eleven years old, in the height of his vigor and strength, as beautiful and courageous as Champagne. While Holomalia worked about him, the horse kept his eyes fixed on the country below, alert for the first sound or smell of wild cattle emerging from the woods. He looked like a charger scenting battle as he waited with lifted head and pricked ears, ready to spring away at the first signal.

Dad swung onto Champagne. "Remember, keep *above* the cattle, First Born," he cautioned. "When a bull charges uphill he hasn't enough momentum to knock a horse over or hurt him badly. If he charges and *you're* below, the weight of his body, added to the pitch of the land, will knock you galley west. You're an expert enough horsewoman to handle yourself properly in tight spots or I wouldn't have let you come out with us."

I scrambled into my saddle, my heart hammering, as I wondered how expert I *would* be in this new field. Clean wind rushed down from the mountain. Live, feel, dare, it taunted me. Tradewind froze to attention and I clamped into the saddle. A moment later Hauki, posted on the next ridge, called out, "Wild cattle below."

Bedouin began dancing about in circles, keyed up by the excitement which had suddenly charged the fragile blue morning. Holomalia watched critically, then satisfied that I could handle him, grinned. "Wait, swell-fun rope wild cattle. You see!" Then he became all business.

A herd of about forty wild cattle were standing at the edge of the forest. An enormous brindled bull, leading the herd, left the shelter of the trees and stood with lifted head, scenting the air. His huge up-sweeping horns looked like arms lifted for a wicked embrace. Harsh black curls grew in his forehead and crested his heavy shoulders. Evil and magnificent, reluctant to abandon cover, he stood, the Monarch of the Mountain; then as if he had made his decision, he began to cross the stretch of

open grassy ground lying between him and the safety of the
lava beds.

When he had advanced about fifty feet, he snuffed danger,
paused, and began lashing his sides with his tail, while he pawed
up dust and threw it over his shoulders. Behind him a dozen lesser
bulls, which he had awed into submission, watched him, waiting
for orders. He gave a low warning bellow and cows, heifers, and
a few small calves gathered in a close knot behind their males.
The truculent leader started forward again, stopping now and
then to stamp and shake his great horns.

After a few tense minutes the Monarch began streaking up the
long slope at a fast trot, which broke into a running canter, his
herd at his heels. When they were a couple of hundred yards
from the trees, Dad gave a shout and *paniolos* swooped in from
right and left. With wild cries they urged the herd toward a
more-or-less level space where ropes could be used to best advantage. For an instant the brindled outlaw and his mates were
startled and raced in the direction wanted; then they scattered
and began charging. The mountaintop echoed with the whine
of swinging lassos, dull bellows, shouts, and the fiery run of hoofs.

Jamming my heels into Bedouin's ribs, I headed him for a small
hill where I could watch without getting in the way. Brave and
beautiful Dad and the *paniolos* looked, leaning forward over their
pommels, swinging their great loops with rhythmic precision. The
brindled bull that everyone wanted to get streaked out sideways.
Eole, yelling like a maniac, raced to head him off. A tawny three-
year-old crossed Dad's bows and with a deft twist of his wrist his
noose whizzed out, closed about the bull's horns, snapped taut
and the animal went head over heels.

It struck the earth with a hollow thud, but was on its feet instantly, charging for Champagne. Dad dodged its rushes and,
after a little maneuvering, he got into position, feinting for the
bull to attack Champagne from the rear. Before its horns could
graze the glossy gray quarters, Dad was racing off, flipping his
lasso from side to side over his head, as he dashed for a *koa* tree.
Before I could see how he managed it, he had dodged around

and snubbed the bull's horns against the stout trunk. Champagne braced back, while the rest of the wild cattle went streaming on toward the mountain.

Eole, riding like a madman, was racing to head off the outlaw, while the rest of the *paniolos* tore among the charging cattle, swinging for the bulls. A mahogany-colored five-year-old charged Pili and one long wicked horn grazed his stirrup, but the impetus of the attack took the animal by and Pili roped it. Hauki was racing in pursuit of a steel-gray bull with long white horns that flashed off the early sunlight. The rest of the herd, realizing too late that they could never regain their wastelands, wheeled back for the comparative safety of the scattered forests below, *paniolos* who had not already secured animals tearing in pursuit.

I tried to hold Bedouin and wait for Dad but with a sideways wrench at the bit, he took off down the mountain after the herd and racing riders. Swooping through a hollow, I nearly ran over Holomalia tying up a rangy strawberry roan which must have weighed 1,500 pounds. Bedouin gave a convulsive sideways leap to avoid bowling over Tradewind, braced on his haunches while his master tied one of the heavy manila swivel-ropes about the great neck thrashing savagely against the tree trunk. "Wait one minute," Holomalia called, his white teeth flashing to a grin; "maybe I catch the big bull for you."

In less than a minute the strawberry roan was fastened solidly to the tree. Holomalia leaped into the saddle and Tradewind flattened out, trying to overtake the Mountain King which Eole had succeeded in turning back from the lava wastes. We could see the mammoth beast tearing down a ridge some distance away, intent on regaining the forests.

Leaping and plunging, our horses went up the steep side of the gulch and tore away. Below us fleeing cattle were crashing through the scrub bordering the forest. Neck and neck Tradewind and Bedouin sailed over logs, swerved to avoid lava holes too wide to leap, and splashed through boggy hollows. The rush of wind in our ears and the thud of flying hoofs and the bellowing of cattle filled the morning.

We slid down the steep side of a small gulch, leaped across the deep wash at the bottom, and scrambled up the farther side. Tradewind's small ears were pricked up, his dark eyes wild with excitement. While part of his superbly functioning horse-mind was busy with his footing, the rest was focused on the animal we were after. He knew his work and loved it—the dash, danger, and risk of it were ingrained in his soul. Faint shouts and thuds below told us other men were bringing cattle down, but Holomalia was bent on roping the old bull which had flouted capture for ten years. Reaching the crest of a hill we halted for a split second. The brindle bull was nowhere in sight.

"He's hiding," Holomalia announced in Hawaiian, sweeping the scrubby ridges ahead of us with expert eyes. Our lathered horses sniffed the wind, then Tradewind darted away like a silver javelin. Sure enough, the kawao bushes ahead of us whipped into motion and with an enraged bellow the Ancient One wheeled and charged. Just as his appalling horns were lowered for Tradewind, he sprang aside, evading the charge. Holomalia threw and his noose snapped fast about the massive up-sweeping horns.

For a few minutes there was a wicked tangle of horse, bull, and man as the Ancient One lunged and swung his heavy head with side-tosses which, had they landed right, would have disemboweled Tradewind. But expert from years of handling wild stock, the magnificent gray made inspired backward leaps, turns and stops. A dozen times I thought the bull's horns would reach their goal, but Tradewind managed to keep clear.

Finally he offered his haunches invitingly to the lowered horns. The bull roared and charged, but Tradewind sprang away and tore for some trees. With knotted tail, lowered head, bellowing and blowing great puffs of spray from his nostrils, the bull took after his retreating enemy. But Tradewind had maneuvered into position and deftly put a tree between himself and the wild bull. The lasso whined taut. Tradewind wheeled, propped and darted back around the tree, whanging the huge curly head with its death-dealing horns against the trunk.

When the bull's raging rushes and plunges to get free subsided

a little, Holomalia dismounted. Tradewind braced back on his
haunches, keeping the rope taut and the bull's head against the
tree, eyes and ears alert for possible mishaps which might imperil
Holomalia's life. Edging forward cautiously with the manila tie-
rope, Holomalia succeeded, after repeated tries, in getting it about
the bull's massive neck and tied him fast.

Signing to Tradewind that everything was finished, he stepped
back and the gray eased up on the lasso. Holomalia flashed in,
snatched up his rawhide and stepped back grinning as only a
paniolo can grin when he's succeeded in roping a famous outlaw.
Then with a quick grateful movement he pressed his hand on
Tradewind's reeking shoulder. "Fine," he said to his partner.

Swinging into the saddle, Holomalia started down the ridge
in the direction of the forests below, where faint shouts told us the
other men were still busy. We tore along the rough hogback and
a great bull leaped out of his hiding place in the scrub. His
lowered horns seemed to expand to twice their size as he came for
me. Our horses shied out in opposite directions, but the huge beast
passed so close I could feel the heat of his body. Bedouin swerved,
the bull vanished, and I felt my horse give a convulsive leap in
the air as he sailed over the corner of a lava pit which had en-
gulfed the bull.

"Never mind, us get him tomorrow," Holomalia yelled and we
tore on. This was life, this was living and glory, I thought. We
sped on down the rough shoulder of the mountain. Far ahead we
saw racing specks, then a wild cry from the left stopped us. In
the opening Eole was racing for a tree with a bull pursuing him.
His horse, which had come a cropper, was off in a distance.
Holomalia yelled and I shut my eyes. He was racing to Eole's
rescue—from *below*. Tradewind would be knocked off his feet if
the bull charged him.

I jerked Bedouin to a trembling standstill and against my will
my eyes opened. Eole, his face blanched with terror, sprang for
the limb of the tree, missed it, and dodged behind the trunk. The
bull roared, charged and swept past. When it wheeled to attack
a second time, it spied Tradewind. Tradewind flung up his head

protestingly when Holomalia jammed in the spurs, knowing it was a wrong maneuver, then submitted to his master's order. With flattened ears he rushed in. Holomalia threw, caught the bull as it was charging, wrenched Tradewind out sideways and tried to brace against the weight of the bull when it reached the end of the lasso. But Tradewind was on the sidehill. There was a sickening thud and horse and rider went down.

Holomalia was on his feet instantly, but Tradewind had the wind partially knocked out of him. The bull, which had pitched head over heels, scrambled up, mad to destroy. Tradewind gave a leap to his feet and wavered on wide-straggled legs. Snatching out his legging-knife, Holomalia slashed through his lasso, freeing his horse, then swung into the tree, shouting to distract the bull's attention to himself. But blind with fury, the bull struck Tradewind a terrific blow. One long horn disappeared into the gray flank. The bull tossed his head and ripped the horse open. Entrails dropped.

Dad and Hauki, attracted by the commotion, rushed in and, from above this time, they re-roped the bull. Tradewind stood braced, his magnificent muscles quivering, his noble head held high. Then his legs collapsed. Holomalia rushed to him. Muscles all over the horse's body were cramping and bunching as he kicked on the grass. Holomalia swooped for the knife he had dropped when he cut Tradewind free, then pressed his hand fiercely against the gray's shoulder. With a smothered oath he slipped the sharp blade in just behind the horse's ears, severing the spinal cord. A shiver passed through the silver-gray body and it was still.

Straightening up, Holomalia stared at the slow drops of blood falling from his knife point and frowned at his severed lasso as though he did not recognize it. Then, like a boy who is hurt, he scraped his arm across his wet eyes.

Paniolos crowded up. When Dad and Hauki finished tying the bull, they came forward. Dad laid his hand on Holomalia's rigid shoulder. "Don't grieve," he said in Hawaiian. "Tradewind has gone like a god—on the flood tide! To outlive your usefulness, to feel life passing you by, to sense your hold is slipping—that's tragedy. But to leap from Here to There, while life's still a rich song, is a blessing!"

Holomalia nodded, wiped his wet eyes on his wrist and began mechanically unstrapping the saddle from the gray body it still girdled, lying limply on the jewel-green grass.

From *Born in Paradise,* Armine von Tempski (New York: Duell, Sloan and Pearce, 1940).

LI

Thomas G. Thrum

In the heyday of the schooners and clippers anyone who crossed from San Francisco to Honolulu in nine or ten days marveled at the way modern transportation was shrinking the dimensions of the globe. Steamers and fast liners gradually trimmed that time to a week. In July 1883 the new *Mariposa* of the Oceanic Line, under forced draft, made the trip in five days and twenty hours—a record that stood for many years. Still, despite all this shortening of travel time, a cruise to Hawaii was only for the unhurried tourist. Even when the Matson steamer *Lurline* went into service in 1908, followed by the *Wilhelmina,* the *Matsonia,* and the *Maui*—sugar boats that also catered to first-class passengers—it was a major journey to Honolulu.

In 1910 Islanders saw their first airship when a daredevil, popularly known as "Bud" Mars, shipped a biplane, the *Skylark,* to Honolulu and performed hair-raising hops over the city. But not until 1912, when Glenn Curtiss was reported to have constructed a successful flying boat, did visionaries venture to predict that one day people might actually fly with the speed of the wind between the Islands, and in the distant future, perhaps even to the Mainland.

Skeptics scoffed at the idea. But the feats aviators performed during World War I made that dream less fantastic; and the starch was taken out of the slurs of scoffers in May 1919 when a flier named A. C. Read piloted a flying boat from Newfoundland to the Azores, then on to Portugal and England. If man could conquer the Atlantic in flight, he could conquer the Pacific. During the following years airhops grew longer and more daring. Richard Byrd was planning a skyride over the North Pole with Floyd Bennett, but eight months before that came off, two years before Charles Lindbergh astounded the world with his solo flight to Paris, Hawaii was propelled into aviation history.

Thomas George Thrum (1842–1932), Hawaii's busiest historian for more than half a century, had witnessed and described all the great changes in transportation to and from the Islands. Since 1875 he had been the foremost local annalist. He migrated to Honolulu in 1853 and became an authority on his new homeland the hard way, "jacking" at all trades, as store clerk, whaler, sugar planter, merchant, publisher, archaeologist, and author.

In 1875 he started publishing the *Hawaiian Annual,* an imaginative and literate almanac that came to be known as *"Thrum's,"* indispensable to any Island household. It catalogued major events of the previous year and in carefully documented articles related phases of newly explored Hawaiian history. Thrum helped to launch the magazine *Paradise of the Pacific;* he located and listed nearly five hundred *heiaus* scattered about the Islands; identified four hundred gods and goddesses; edited the Fornander Collection of Hawaiian Folklore, and compiled several volumes of myths and folktales. Then, with the casualness of a seasoned reporter, at the age of eighty-four, he chronicled the big event that ushered Hawaii into the era of transpacific flight—an era that was eventually to bring the Islands within a few hours of the Coast and transform its landscape, its economy, and its population.

Haven't Gas to Last Five Minutes

Of the three planes assigned and prepared for the flight to Hawaii from San Francisco, to start August 31st [1925], the PB-1 (designated the Boeing plane) was held back for further tests, and the two PN9 planes, numbers 3 and 1, set forth a little before 3 P.M. The start was made under favorable conditions and was witnessed by a vast throng at all observation points as the planes swung into San Francisco Bay and passed out through the Golden Gate at an altitude of about 150 feet, and at a speed of 80 miles an hour. An hour after their start they rose to 500 feet for their course.

The crew of the PN9 No. 1, the flag-plane, comprised Commander John Rodgers, Lieutenant B. J. McConnell, W. H. Bowlin, S. R. Pope, and O. G. Stantz. That of the PN9 No. 3 were: Lieutenant A. P. Snody, Lieutenant A. Girvin, N. H. Craven, C. J. Sutter, and C. W. Allen.

Along the course of their flight, U. S. naval craft were stationed 200 miles apart as a safeguard and to mark the way in smoke clouds by day and searchlights by night. These vessels, in the order of their alignment from the Coast, were: the *William Jones, McCawley, Mayer, Doyen, Langley, Reno, Farragut, Aroostook* and *Tanager,* the latter 130 miles from Honolulu.

Three hundred miles out of San Francisco, plane No. 3, piloted by Lt. A. P. Snody, was forced down and rode the waves several hours till found and picked up about 2 A.M. by the *William Jones,* which, with the *McCawley,* went to its aid. Messages at first indicated it would resume flight, as it was not in trouble, though experiencing difficulty in rising. But it was towed back to San Francisco, and came to grief in the Bay.

Plane No. 1, Commander Rodgers, made successful progress through the night, communicating frequently to flight headquarters, "Feeling fine. All OK," which was picked up by the several guard-ships. This continued till near Honolulu's noon hour, and expectation was rife that the crowning event of its arrival was almost in sight. Then came silence; then an ominous message of fuel getting low, and again that "We haven't gas to last five minutes." Its position at the time was between the *Aroostook* and the *Tanager,* some 300 miles from its goal, with the weather most unpropitious, the last message received being: "We will crack up if we have to land in the rough sea without motive power."

When it was learned that the plane had alighted at 1:34 P.M., search toward the adjudged locality was taken up by the *Farragut* and *Aroostook,* nearest guard-ships, followed by concerted naval maneuvers of ships and planes from Pearl Harbor and Lahaina. Thick weather interrupted the first night's plans, but at daybreak all efforts were resumed. Uncertainty of the exact position of the plane's alighting added materially to the difficulty of the search, and as day after day passed, the searching fleet, increased to 23 vessels, literally combed the sea between the islands and the adjudged locality of mishap, aided by six scouting planes.

Entering upon the fourth day, as also the fifth, and later, with still no word of discovery, the report of night flares having been seen by the *Whippoorwill* strengthened hope that was waning in many hearts. Meanwhile all available craft of sea and air were being added to the searchers, including some of the returning fleet from Australia.

Shortly after 5 P.M. of September 10th a radio message to the *Honolulu Advertiser* announced the arrival of Commander Rodgers and companions in their fuelless plane at Nawiliwili, Kauai, having been located by the submarine R-4, 15 miles northwest of that port, and towed thither with all hands aboard, well, but worn and hungry.

Thus Commander Rodgers and his crew in the PN9 No. 1 succeeded in the pioneer flight from the Pacific Coast to the Hawaiian Islands, though not exactly as planned.

On reaching shore the aviators were greeted by huge crowds, garlanded and conveyed to the Lihue Hotel where, under medical care, sustenance and rest were prescribed.

Great relief and much rejoicing throughout the city of Honolulu, and in naval and army circles followed the receipt of the glad tidings, and aid from Pearl Harbor was at once dispatched by the destroyer *MacDonough,* in case it should be required, with instructions to bring the intrepid fliers to the naval station as soon as they were able. Commander Rodgers planned to be towed to his goal in his plane to complete the voyage, but in this he was overruled. A good night's rest enabled them to board the *MacDonough* and, leaving Nawiliwili a little after 2 P.M. of the 11th, reached Pearl Harbor shortly after seven o'clock, a five hours' trip.

Sirens on warships blared, and crowds on ship and shore

cheered lustily as the vessel came up to its dock. Commander Rodgers and his crew, grouped on the bridge, acknowledged the welcome greetings of the throng, and waved to friends as search-lights lit up the shore. When the vessel was moored and the distinguished party disembarked, Commander Rodgers, leading the way, was greeted by Admiral John McDonald and by Governor and Mrs. Farrington, who decorated the fliers with floral *leis*. The exciting welcome by the many friends gathered was short-ened by the doctor's orders cautioning for quiet and rest.

The following day the heroes came to the city for a noon thanks-giving and welcome gathering on the grounds of the executive building, where some 5000 residents greeted them. Commander Rodgers and crew were met with congratulations on the steps of the capitol by Governor Farrington . . . and other representa-tives of army, navy and the territory. After an exchange of greet-ings the party moved to the grandstand where Bishop J. D. La Mothe offered the prayer of thanksgiving for their preservation and achievement. Then followed general presentations, wreath-decorating of the heroes and short addresses by Commander Rodgers and each of his fellow-fliers. And during it all the photog-raphers were not idle.

Commander Rodgers in his address expressed appreciation of the welcome and corrected the erroneous impression that they had been drifting. "We were sailing," he said; "we had taken some cloth from the plane which we made into a sail, whereby we were making two knots an hour, so we knew that sooner or later we would make port, and were about to succeed when somebody came along and found us."

From "Pacific Aviation Pioneers," Thomas G. Thrum, *1926 Hawaiian Annual,* Honolulu, December 1925.

LII

Sister Adele Marie

The cataclysm that broke over Pearl Harbor on the morning of December 7, 1941, affected citizens and soldiery alike. The date was a demarcation between an old and a new Hawaii. Until that morning the Islands had been a charming, lazy, unsophisticated retreat for a few Mainland holiday seekers. The bombs dropped on Pearl Harbor on December 7 were heard around the world. Millions, to whom the Harbor was only a name, and to whom Hawaii was a chain of Islands vaguely positioned somewhere between California and Asia, pinpointed the dots on their maps, though they still called them "Hawa-ya." Within hours, Hawaii forever lost its seclusion.

During the next five years Americans in uniform and in mufti, by the hundred thousand, swept into the Islands and transformed them. Hawaii would never again be the same. Many have chronicled that social, political, military, and political revolution, but no one more vividly and intimately than modest Sister Adele Marie (1901–) in *To You from Hawaii*. A member of the order of St. Joseph of Carondelet, she was among a company of Sisters sent to the Islands in 1938 to take over a large parochial school in a slum area of Honolulu.

In a letter-diary addressed to the Sisters of St. Joseph on the Mainland, she recorded fairly and wittily the details of life on the home front during the war years. The anxieties, the irritations, and the minor privations that she experienced were common to all civilians in Honolulu.

[425]

War Correspondent on the Home Front

I think I told you in one of my previous letters that three of us teach . . . catechism every Sunday morning at Schofield Barracks to the children of the army personnel. . . . On the morning of December seventh, Sister Frances Celine, Sister Martha Mary and I got into our taxi as usual, at seven-thirty, and set out for the Barracks.

As we neared the Pearl Harbor district, about 7:50 we noticed planes, scores of them, flying unusually low. Two planes swooped so close to our machine that we commented about the long red objects fastened beneath them. Our driver remarked that these were probably torpedo bombs on some of our new planes. Suddenly we heard the rat-a-tat-tat of guns. Planes soared on both sides of us, diving and soaring in an extraordinary way.

We drove on thinking all the time that sham maneuvers were taking place on a grand scale this cloudy Sunday morning. Little did we dream that those agile bombers were even then hurling destructive missiles. Once I glanced up from our Office book just in time to see a plane diving toward the earth with wings in vertical position. I didn't see it land, but we began to suspect something.

As we approached Schofield Barracks, a vast cloud of dense, black smoke arose from the horizon and crawled skyward. We thought at first that a cane field was on fire; yet, there was something ominous about that cloud. A few minutes later, we saw that some of the hangars at Wheeler Field were in flames. At the gate of the Barracks, our car was stopped by guards—something which had never happened before.

"Is this real, Officer, or only maneuvers?" I inquired. The expression of the guard's face was answer enough before he spoke.

"I'm afraid it's *real*, Sister," he replied. Then, with a nod to the driver, he said, "Get going, fast!"

We rode past the great hangars from which poured the thick column of smoke. Machines, army trucks, and tanks came pell-

melling down the road. Soldiers seemed to be running in all directions and the sharp rat-a-tat-tat of guns came in quick succession.
A soldier crouching under a tree yelled "Air raid!" at us, but
anxiety to reach the chapel made us heedless and we drove on.
We passed a demolished house upon which a bomb had fallen a
few moments before.

Much to our relief, we arrived whole and entire at the little
chapel which was always filled to capacity on Sunday morning;
but today it looked strangely empty. Four solders and a handful
of women and children formed the congregation. Mass began.
All during the Mass, men with strained looks on their faces drove
up to the little chapel and asked to take their children. One officer
had bullet holes through the rear end of his car. I was kept walking back and forth, escorting children to anxious parents.

A soldier ran up and shouted, "Have the women and children
ready to evacuate at a moment's notice. Tell the chaplain." I
glanced up at the altar. The Offertory had just begun. I sent the
word to Father O'Brien by the usher. He made the disquieting
announcement calmly and Mass went on. The firing of guns continued intermittently. After Mass the remaining members of the
congregation vanished quickly.

. . . Our taxi driver made the wise suggestion that we wait at
the taxi stand until the traffic was less congested. We agreed, and
our machine pulled in under cover. . . . The noise and action
were so distracting that somehow or other my brain didn't func-
tion quickly enough to register fear. I remember winding my
rosary around my wrist as the guns spat forth their deadly fire.
. . . When the shooting died down, we asked two or three of the
men if they thought it would be safer for us at the post chapel.

"You're as safe here as anywhere, Sisters," they answered
grimly.

One by one the taxi drivers were called off with their taxis. Our
driver informed us that he, too, had to leave as his post of duty
in this emergency was at an ammunition depot. We decided to
go with him. . . . Army vehicles screamed past us. Our car was
stopped many times by guards along the way. At one point some-

one yelled "Air raid! Take cover!" and we catapulted from our machine and rushed for a sugar cane field.

Far to our right were two airplanes engaged in a dog fight. Dark little smoke puffs from antiaircraft batteries hung high above us. When the planes retreated, we made for our machine and were about to resume the homeward journey when an officer informed our driver that all roads to Honolulu were closed. He ordered us back to Schofield, but on arriving at one of its gates, we were refused admittance, for all women were being evacuated.

We drove on to Wahiawa where we teach catechism. . . . Here we learned that a Japanese plane had crashed three hundred yards from the church. The pilot was burned to death in his wreckage. Our driver was informed that the big gray buses were permitted to get through into Honolulu. We decided to make another attempt . . . the sole occupants of a bus that could easily have carried thirty people.

The army monopolized the road. Motorcycles, ambulances, tanks, and trucks full of soldiers dashed past us with incredible speed. As we approached the Pearl Harbor district, we saw great clouds of smoke arising from two ships. One, the *Arizona,* I believe, was gradually sinking.

It was well that the distance and the dense screen of smoke hid from our view the tragedy of Pearl Harbor, charred bodies, mangled forms, trapped sailors, and men swimming through oily waters, a struggle between life and death. We could see our ships firing and being fired upon by dive bombers and torpedo planes. On shore, men were running and crouching and shooting up into a gray cloudy sky. . . . Our little Chinaman [the driver] was loquacious but he traveled quickly through a danger zone in which we could have been struck by shrapnel or machine gun fire. . . .

At noon we drove into Honolulu. Large groups of civilians, mostly men, stood at every street corner. They seemed bewildered, incredulous. The traffic was very heavy and everywhere policemen were forcing cars to park along the curbing so that the army might have the right of way. What a relief it was to come to the haven of our convent. . . .

Evening came, and, as a complete blackout had been announced over the radio, we retired early. . . . We have added an hour or more of extra prayers to our usual ones. This is our little contribution to the defense program. Most of us had just settled for the night's rest, after an exciting day, when suddenly, about nine o'clock cannons began to roar. We ran to the windows and looked westward toward Pearl Harbor. What a gigantic display of fireworks spread in a fan-like shape far into the sky. The booming of the guns shook not only our house but our hearts. Then all was ominously quiet and once more we took to our beds; but this time we didn't undress.

The night was interminable. Around five, the next morning, there was another raid of short duration; once again some of us stood at our windows looking out, horrified, yet fascinated by that awful exhibition of attack and defense fire. . . . Suddenly I was frozen to the spot by a loud, long-drawn-out swish . . . sh . . . sh . . . ! . . . I knew it was a bomb which had passed somewhere over our house. I knew it had fallen in the garden below; I knew that in a moment it was going to explode, . . . but my feet were paralyzed. Finally, they found wings and, in less time than it takes to write it, I was downstairs, in the chapel, and on my knees! . . . We heard later that it had crashed, with exhausted fury, no doubt, into a rock formation on the heights several blocks above us. . . .

December 8 . . . after Mass we came home, turned on the radio, and left it on practically all day, since vital announcements were being made from time to time. Men were called in for various jobs—electricians, engineers, mechanics, stevedores; in fact all workers in army and navy projects were told to report. . . . Blood donors were solicited by the medical corps; Red Cross units organized; schools were turned into emergency centers or temporary homes for evacuees from Schofield Barracks, Hickam Field, Fort Shafter, and other danger zones.

The police force began an active round-up of all persons engaged in subversive activities and the FBI became extremely vigilant. Countless short-wave sets, great quantities of ammunition, and scores of sampans were taken over by military authorities. Martial law prevailed. An order went forth that until further notice a complete blackout was imperative every night. Officers were given orders to shoot out any light and arrest those who failed to comply with this ruling. . . .

Headlights on cars operating at night have all been painted black with the exception of a two-and-a-half-inch circle below the headlight lens, which circle is painted blue. The tail lights are also blue. No person is allowed on the streets, highways or beaches, on foot or in vehicles, between 6 P.M. and 6 A.M. Exceptions are made, of course, for those required to be out because of employment. The carrying of lighted cigarettes, cigars, or pipes in the open during blackout is forbidden. Gasoline, vegetable seeds, drugs, and food stuffs are being rationed. The sale of liquor is prohibited.

We have marveled at the way these people have responded to the restrictions placed upon them by the pressure of martial law. Everyone has been aroused to a white heat of indignation by Japan's treacherous attack on that Sunday morning and all are determined to see that act fully avenged. The three words *Remember Pearl Harbor* have taken on a tremendous significance.

During the week that followed the attack, the great tragedy of Pearl Harbor was brought home to many Honoluluans by the sight of the trucks loaded with long rough wooden boxes which were taken to the scene of the disaster. We didn't see those trucks return. . . . Trenches were made for them at Nuuanu cemetery and also at Red Hill; and here, day after day, without pomp or ceremony, the defenders of Hawaii were laid to rest. . . .

Honolulu had no illuminated outdoor Christmas trees this year, and only a fortunate few had one indoors. The sixty thousand trees shipped from Washington and destined for Hawaii were lost on the *Mauna Ala*. . . . We spent a good hour on Christmas eve, setting up an artificial tree; but, somehow, it looked gaudy and misplaced . . . and even though our little tree made a brave show to display itself, we took it down and relegated it to a classroom cupboard.

Many Honoluluans must have missed the cup that cheers this year, too; and I fancy that egg-nogs weren't even mentioned, for the price of fresh eggs is exorbitant, and the "nog" is tucked away behind official padlocks. Someone remarked that in spite of the Japanese blitz the holiday spirit was in the air, but it's certainly not on the breath, for Hawaii has gone bone dry! Prohibition is with us again.

And so, Christmas has come and gone. True, there was a note of sadness in everyone's Christmas joy, but there was thankfulness too, for we have had peace during these holidays—peace amid a setting for war. Our gay, care-free city has been transformed into a veritable garrison. Great stacks of sand-bags are piled high in front of windows where *lei* sellers once sat with their baskets of lovely flowers; bomb shelters disfigure gardens and lawns; long strands of gummed paper are plastered in crisscross patterns on shop windows; sentries, armed to the teeth, walk our streets and in the dead of night one often hears them shout "Halt" to some rambling pedestrian or vehicle. Woe to the person who is not heedful of that command! We've had no school since the war started. Many of our schools have been taken over by the government for various purposes. But, in spite of barricades and barbed wire and gun emplacements and droning planes and martial law and blackouts, we have had peace—at the price of nerve-racking alertness. . . .

1942

What strange transformations war can bring about! In former years Honoluluans have greeted the New Year with a flamboyant burst of fireworks, with gaiety and laughter and noise. In former years we stood at our windows at midnight and looked out upon a scene that could have been taken for a bit of Fairyland. This year, on December 31 . . . how singularly still it was! Then a plane roared past; a rooster crowed. . . . The howling of a dog or the crowing of a rooster on these still unnatural nights is most disquieting. Invariably, one mistakes everything and anything for the air raid siren. And while we listened, the big clock in the Sisters' room struck twelve . . . and the New Year was born. . . .

January 15. A gala day in our house. Our Christmas mail has arrived! Cards, letters, packages, in spite of Nipponese subs. May God bless Uncle Sam's boats!

January 23. For the first time, no doubt, in the history of our Congregation, the Sisters of St. Joseph have had the experience of being finger-printed, of wearing gas masks, of donning helmets. From now on, every man, woman, or child on this island must, under penalty of fine, carry about on his person an identification card. . . . No matter where we go, that mask, like Mary's proverbial lamb, must accompany us. It is carried in an olive drab bag which is worn on the left side and held in place by a strap over the right shoulder. The helmets are to be issued to civilians in the near future. The mask, fortunately, is easy to don, but we wonder how we are going to manage the helmet. . . .

. . . Because of censorship regulations, I have had to omit much that would have made more interesting reading matter. However, with one eye (mentally) on the *censor* and the other on the typewriter, I proceed!

February 9. Daylight Saving Time has just gone into effect and our little world is turned *kapakahi,* as the Hawaiians say. There's a suppressed excitement in the air, too. Wednesday is an anniversary for the Emperor Hirohito and it is rumored that his loyal subjects wish to present the august Son of Heaven with a small gift; namely, a little group of islands in mid-Pacific. With a glint in our eyes, we wait. Singapore has almost fallen.

February 18. We attended a unique meeting today—the first of its kind, probably, on American territory. All teachers of both public and private schools met at McKinley auditorium to be instructed on what to do in the event of a gas attack. We learned many interesting but fearful facts about mustard, lewisite and phosgene gases. . . .

February 20. The *Aquitania* and the *Lurline* are in port. We hear that both ships are being loaded with Japanese and German aliens who are to be removed to the Mainland. The waterfront is now a restricted area, but we know ships still come and go. . . . Islands eggs are eighty-five cents a dozen. Our butter is a bit stale, but we have a good supply of it on hand. We haven't seen an orange since the blitz. Baking soda and onions are not to be

Waikiki—the new Hawaii

found on the market. Sister put in an order for starch, vinegar, matches, mayonnaise, vanilla, paper napkins and clothespins, but she was told that none of these articles were available until the next convoy came in. . . .

At two o'clock, on the morning of March 4, we were awakened out of a sound slumber by three or four terrific blasts. We leaped from our beds and out into the hall and there, with pounding hearts, awaited for the attack; but nothing happened. . . . We learned later . . . one lone, enemy plane had flown over the city at a high altitude, dropping the four "eggs" which shattered a few windows and shook thousands of stout hearts, and faint ones, too! No damage done . . . but near Roosevelt High School are the huge craters which prove what damage one bomb can do. . . .

March 7. I was about to sit down to do my report cards when the air raid signal sounded. Many people scuttled out to their bomb shelters but we stayed indoors. The day was rainy and gloomy and that constant shrill whistle lowered the mercury of one's disposition to below zero. The radio stations were off the air most of the morning. The all-clear signal came at 11:30. Army and Navy officials are very noncommittal. . . .

March 11. . . . Last night we heard over our local station the touching account of a spectacular adventure as told by the three men who just got into Pearl Harbor after being afloat in a tiny rubber boat somewhere in the South Pacific for thirty-nine days. They lived on raw fish and shark meat and drank the rain water which they managed to sop up in their clothing.

March 14. Another air raid alarm this morning. One can get used to everything—even sirens. Everyone is a bit jittery but prudently watchful.

March 25. . . . We've had a torrential downpour all week. The trenches are filled with water and toads. Just what would we do with the children in the event of an air raid alarm? . . .

April 9. Bataan has fallen. What next?

April 28. . . . A convoy came in. There's plenty of food in the market now. . . .

May 4. . . . It is rumored that a contingent of the Japanese

fleet is somewhere on high seas headed for Australia or for Hawaii.
. . .

May 7. Old Glory was lowered yesterday at Fort Mills on Corregidor. God help us. We thought Corregidor was impregnable. Our convoys still come and go; they bring vast loads of food and defense materials and take back sugar and evacuees. We have a splendid bomb shelter now. . . . It holds about sixteen people and is entirely underground. Public bomb shelters are being built around town on the average of fifteen a day. These new ones are long, igloo affairs which seem much more protective than the open-trench kind.

May 11. That mysterious Japanese fleet was met in the Coral Sea by the naval and air force of the United States. . . .

We are having some hot and sultry weather, due no doubt, to the eruption of the volcano, Mauna Loa, over in Hawaii. Blackout regulations can't control the goddess *Pele* when she goes on a rampage and she continues to spew smoke and flames hundreds of feet into the air. Islanders are fearful lest its fiery glow provide a beacon for Japanese raiders. The Military Government has banned, for the present, all publication concerning the volcano's activity; but rumors are abroad that Radio Tokyo has broadcast the fact. . . .

May 18. . . . The military governor, Lieutenant General Emmons, has repeatedly warned the territory to expect another and a heavier attack by the Japanese, and today everyone is apprehensive. The atmosphere is charged with tension. . . .

May 28. Reports filter in that Japanese marauders are on the loose somewhere in our area of the Pacific; but our fleet is out, and we can rest assured it isn't idle. . . .

June 6. The alert is over! The huge Japanese invasion fleet which was headed this way, complacently confident, no doubt, that Hirohito's colors would soon be raised over another choice bit of territory, was intercepted and routed at Midway by our Army, Navy and Marine forces. We breathe freely again, for a while at least. . . . This much we can be sure of now: that fortunate interception spared the people of this island from witnessing a dreadful conflict near or on our own shores. . . .

June 8. Vacation at last! We closed classroom doors with joy and unbounded relief. . . . Honolulu is jubilant, of course, over the Midway victory; but, by no means, is it less vigilant, for our military governor has issued the warning that the enemy will probably return in greater numbers and with every kind of weapon at his disposal. . . .

July 1. In another month our compound will be honeycombed with numerous bomb shelters, each large enough to accommodate fifty people. . . . Those for the use of the public are to be built on each side of the church; those for the use of our children or evacuees are to be on the playgrounds, in the rear of the school.

Hawaii has its own currency now. All regular United States currency has to be out of circulation by July 16, and is being replaced by the Hawaiian series of bills. . . . This change is merely a precautionary step to protect U.S. currency in the *very* remote event that Hawaii might be invaded and our money seized by the Japanese. . . .

July 25. For the past weeks onions have been as scarce as helium. Dehydrated foods are appearing on the market. The black, foul-smelling eggs imported from the Orient and which the Chinese considered such a delicacy are now a thing of the past. . . .

July 29. Equipped with gas masks and a goodly supply of rations, we took off for an outing to Kailua. . . . Before us was the vast expanse of the Pacific, and yet its waters were inaccessible because of barbed wire entanglements. . . . The army is asking for canine recruits which are to be trained for sentry and patrol duty. Judging from the nocturnal howling in our neighborhood, we must be surrounded by countless potential draftees. . . .

August 8. Senator Sanji Abe of Hilo, Hawaii, the first American of Japanese ancestry ever to sit in the territorial senate, has been arrested for violating the order prohibiting the possession of a Japanese flag. . . .

August 16. Two soldier lads dropped in last evening to chat, to do us a good deed by fixing our sagging clothesline, and to sample in an unstinted way our homemade cookies. Their barracks is just a block away. We hear that there's a fierce sea, land and air battle raging down around the Solomons. Strange that a seemingly insignificant spot in the vast Pacific should become a strategic battlefield in this global war. . . .

September 8. . . . The Japanese language schools, which in prewar days taught young Americans of Japanese ancestry the ways of Japan, have been closed since the blitz. May their doors remain closed forever. . . .

September 15. Today . . . we stepped into the cathedral for a quiet little visit before the Blessed Sacrament. . . . A sailor strode leisurely up the side aisle with his gas mask and cap in one hand and a bag of something that looked like doughnuts in the other. He deposited the bag on the step by the Communion railing while he lit a vigil light at our Lady's altar. Then he knelt, buried his face in his hands, and prayed. I think he must have been saying: "Gosh, dear Mother, this is tough! I'm kind of lonely; I miss the folks back home. I'm dying to get a crack at the Japs and yet I'm afraid of blood. Remember how hard it was for me to kill that chicken for Aunt Clara. This war business is a mess. See us through it, dear Mother of Christ. You loved your Son. Take care of us, His sailors." . . .

October 1. Those long-awaited dimout bulbs will be on sale Monday at 33¢ per bulb, one being allowed to each purchaser. . . .

November 10. . . . The shortage in labor has become acute. Today we registered the children who wish to work in the pineapple or sugar cane plantations. The public schools have now 1800 children, twelve years or over, working under faculty supervision on a four-day week schedule. Even the 650 prisoners of Oahu's jail have been put to work digging bomb shelters, planting gardens or aiding the OCD. There are no drones in Hawaii these days. The work accomplished on the islands since the attack on Pearl Harbor has been phenomenal. Great construction projects are forging steadily ahead under the auspices of the Army and Navy. Oahu is gradually becoming the greatest fortress in the Pacific. . . .

November 23. . . . Mass evacuation of the Japanese is out of the question. Such a move would certainly be disrupting to island economy as there are over 160,000 of them here.

November 26. Thanksgiving Day, and one of America's favorite holidays, but Hawaii has kept its shoulder to the wheel of war.

December 7. The first anniversary of the infamous attack on Pearl Harbor was observed in Hawaii by an outpouring of money for bonds—a veritable bond blitz. . . . The florists of Honolulu, and peculiarly enough most of them are Japanese, today closed their shops and placed this sign where all could read it: "We are closed because we are donating our day's flowers for the decoration of the graves of those who gave their lives on December 7th."

December 10. The spotlight of the nation is focused very steadily on our islands these days, for the territorial martial law is being challenged in various quarters. What *is* to be our political status? . . .

December 22. The Territory's December 7th war bond sales netted $5,000,000. A magnificent response. . . .

December 24. Christmas Eve, and our islands are swathed in darkness. Tonight, perhaps more than ever before, the thoughts of men are directed toward the one great Light which no blackout can ever dim; for, on this Christmas of 1942, across the blackest skies the world has ever known, the Star of Bethlehem sheds its radiance on war-weary hearts. . . .

1943

January 10. . . . Except for two candles on the altar, the church is in utter darkness these mornings when Father says Mass. I hold a flashlight for him while he gives us Holy Communion. A few days ago General Emmons said that Hawaii is one of the greatest fortresses on earth and safe against Japanese invasion. There is no doubting it. We *must* be safe, at night at least, for with this rigorous blackout, who on God's earth could ever find us. . . .

January 18. If ever you want to hear something that sounds for all the world like demoniacal howling, listen to an air raid alarm in the wee hours of the morning. When the sirens began to shriek, I think we all must have made a simultaneous leap from our beds. I turned on the radio hoping to hear that this was a practice alert;

but instead, ten dreaded words blared out the warning: "This is an air raid alarm! Take cover! Take cover!" Mother Virginia began the rosary aloud; I fear she got some distracted responses to her fervent Hail Marys. . . . We were on the point of leaving the house when, to our immense relief, the "All-Clear" sounded. . . . We laughed, and filed into the chapel to thank our Lord. . . .

February 4. This is the Chinese New Year, the traditional and most celebrated holiday of the Chinese people. Once again, because of the war, it will slip by without the usual fanfare of festivities and firecrackers. . . .

February 19. The Military Governor has granted the Royal Hawaiian Band the permission to give moonlight concerts. . . .

February 28. We witnessed some interesting maneuvers this morning. Honolulu's waterfront was blanketed in smoke produced by a chemical process. This is the second time we have had a smoke-screen test. . . .

April 3. Today a unique ceremony took place at Iolani Palace where Hawaii bade aloha to some 2800 young Americans of Japanese ancestry who volunteered for overseas combat service. Almost 20,000 people, mostly Japanese, jammed into the palace grounds to bid farewell to the boys and to bestow upon them a parting gift or a *lei*. . . .

May 1. Someone has said that Hawaii is wreathed in charm and beauty in spite of its heart of steel. Even a war-conscious Hawaii could not permit May Day to pass without some recognition. The familiar song *May Day Is Lei Day in Hawaii* was in the atmosphere regardless of barbed wire meshes and machine gun nests. . . .

May 23. All of the nineteen warships damaged in the Japanese attack on Pearl Harbor on that never-to-be-forgotten December seventh have been repaired and have left Hawaii under their own power with the exception of the *Arizona,* the *Oklahoma* and the *Utah.* The last two named are being salvaged; but the *Arizona,* damaged beyond repair, lies almost submerged in the waters of Pearl Harbor. One thousand seventy-one men gave their lives on this ill-fated ship. . . . Admiral Furlong has stated that had the enemy known at the time the true extent of the damage done, they would have returned the following week with an invasion force; and, in all possibility, we could not have repelled them. . . .

June 10. June is synonymous with graduations and flowers and farewells—even away out here in the Pacific. . . . Thirty-nine bright-eyed, dark-skinned boys and girls marched up the church aisle, under a long arch of flowers, to receive their diplomas. . . . They were indeed a true representation of Honolulu's polyglot population. Among them were Chinese, Japanese, Koreans, Portuguese, Puerto Ricans, Hawaiians, Filipinos, a Russian girl, and the ever-present *hapa haole* or part-white mixture. . . .

July 13. Honolulu is rejoicing. Tonight we shall revel in *light* and *air* at one and the same time. Modifications have been made in the blackout regulations which permit us to leave windows open and lights on until ten o'clock in any room not facing the sea. . . .

November 22. Another group of our boys has been sent out into the danger zone. The battle is raging in the Gilberts, two thousand miles southwest of us. Casualties are being brought back here for hospitalization. On our way home from Wahiawa this afternoon, we were delayed by a long line of Red Cross ambulances. . . .

November 30. Little by little, the appalling story of Tarawa is being revealed. Here is a battle that will go down in history as one of the most dramatic and macabre engagements of World War II. So heavily fortified was this little island garrison that the Japanese had boasted it would require a million men to capture it. On D-Day a few thousand of our troops assailed the Nipponese stronghold, and after three days of frightful onslaught, the atoll was in American hands. Our casualties were startlingly heavy, but those which the Japanese sustained were five times as great. A tiny atoll bathed in fire and blood. . . .

December 25. . . . For the first time since the blitz, we had a real Christmas tree, thanks to . . . lads of the 7th Air Corps. . . .

1944

February 17. Three thousand miles west of us lies Truk, the greatest Japanese naval base in the Pacific. Our bombers are now penetrating this enemy stronghold, but we hear that Japan considers Truk impregnable. . . .

April 11. Our Territory is flooded with money. Never before have I seen so much currency in the hands of school children. . . . During the past year our service men in the Territory have spent five million dollars in souvenirs. Prior to the war, we had about ninety-five stores in Honolulu which specialized in Hawaiian curios; now we have nearly three hundred. The amusing side of it all is that over eighty percent of our "Hawaiian curios" are manufactured in the States. . . .

April 28. . . . We hear that Charles A. Lindbergh is in town. . . . World personalities may pass this way, but Hawaii is too engrossed in martial tactics to take much more than a passing note of them. Its traditional greetings and hospitality of prewar days have given way to grim secrecy and stern realism. Countless ships silently enter Hawaiian harbors and as silently leave. The Royal Hawaiian Band is no longer at the pier; . . . there are no warm alohas, nor fragrant flower *leis,* nor lighthearted laughter. Hawaii is at war, and relentless reminders of this fact meet one at every turn. Yet these harsh reminders . . . cannot obscure, thank God, the bright threads of humor. . . . Two Maryknoll Sisters were getting on a bus, in the rear of which was a soldier who had been imbibing much too freely. When he saw the Sisters, he called out thickly, "Say, conductor, what branch of the Service is getting on now?" . . .

July 31. . . . We were greeted at the airport by the exciting rumor that President Roosevelt, Prime Minister Winston Churchill, Generalissimo Chiang Kai-shek and General Mac-Arthur were somewhere in the city, closeted in conference. Papers and radio have been discreetly silent on the matter . . . but two sergeants dropped in this evening and they punctured very definitely the bubble about Chiang Kai-shek and Churchill. . . . However, this much is incontestably true: tonight two of America's greatest men are resting their weary heads within the confines of this polyglot city on the Crossroads of the Pacific. . . .

December 24. A beautiful phonograph attachment for the radio, together with a cabinet and records, was delivered to us today with the compliments of "our soldier boys" who are now some-where near Saipan. . . . The blackout is a thing of the past; the curfew has been relaxed; and it will be our privilege to have mid-night Mass once again.

This afternoon two sergeants helped us decorate the Christmas trees, one in the community room and one in the front yard. Our twenty-eight-pound turkey (a gift from the butcher) was cooked at the barracks, for we had no pan large enough to hold such a Goliath of a bird. The ten GI's whom we have invited to a Christmas dinner will quickly and eagerly despoil Goliath of its beauty. . . .

1945

. . . Seven years have passed since we came to Hawaii. Our island world has undergone some radical changes since that day when we first touched Hawaiian soil. Honolulu, particularly, has been affected by the war. So great has been the influx of people that our streets are teeming with milling throngs of war workers and service personnel of both sexes.

The problems arising from housing conditions have become acute. On every available site a mushroom growth of buildings has sprung up—buildings for the use of the armed forces or for the newly arrived civilians. Island terrain is thickly dotted with count-less town-size encampments of Quonset huts, army tents, wooden shacks, or rambling barracks. Perhaps the saddest spots on our horizons are those numerous and hivelike hospitals into which pours a constant stream of war casualties. Honolulu has seen the real heroes of Tarawa, Kwajalein, Saipan, Tinian and Iwo Jima; the men whose mangled bodies have been reduced to human torsos and who are known in hospital parlance as "basket cases." . . .

January 12. I almost dislike going to town these days. Honolulu, with its boomtown aspect, is battening in a sea of feverish activity. The easy-going tenor of by-gone days is no more. Prosperity is leaving a spirit of sophisticated modernity in its wake. Even the old fish vendors, whose drawling, nasal cry used to delight my ear—even these, I say, have now adopted new methods as well as new wares. They sell hot dogs and hamburgers which are advertised not by that strange, wheedling cry that used to entice fish and *saimin* patrons, but by mute and prosaic freshly-painted signs: HOT DOGS 10¢, HAMBURGERS 15¢. . . .

February 12. The Italian prisoners of war were at our convent again today. In appreciation for our helping in lining his tabernacle, Father Dalsasso brought us an exquisite plaque which was made by the prisoners themselves. The bas-relief, in the *della Robbia* style, represents the Madonna and Child. . . .

April 13. America is bowed in grief. Our beloved President is dead. In these hours of crisis, the Nation mourns deeply for one who was her greatest leader and who gave his life in his efforts to bring about an enduring peace among the peoples of the world. . . .

May 7. This is V-E Day, but Hawaii has taken little more than scant note of the victory which thrills another part of the world. One of the Saipan veterans said to us this afternoon, "Peace in Europe! Sure that's swell news. But the war isn't over by a long shot. It's still close to home. It's still in our backyard, and things look pretty rugged out Tokyo-way." . . .

June 25. . . . A Territorial order came out yesterday requesting the return to the O.C.D. of all gas masks. It was with a heaven-be-praised feeling that we discarded these ugly reminders of what-might-have-been. According to O.C.D. reports, the Territory's bomb shelters, or "scare pukas," as the Hawaiians call them, are to be made away with in the very near future. Since Admiral Nimitz's headquarters are now in Guam, Hawaii is no longer considered as part of the war zone. . . .

August 9. Sitting before the radio last night I dialed from station to station, only to hear from each, snatches of alarming information concerning mankind's latest weapon, the atomic bomb. In almost awesome tones radio commentators pronounced it "the most terrible engine of destruction ever conceived"; "two hundred times more powerful than a six-ton block buster; a terrifying force, the full fury of which we cannot gauge"; "the most carefully guarded secret of World War II." The world may well stand aghast at the discovery which, undoubtedly, has initiated a new age in the history of mankind, the Atomic Age. Man now has in his grasp elements whose peacetime uses are infinite, but whose wartime potentialities are terrifying. . . .

August 14. At long last V-J Day has come! It is the eve of Mary's feast and the heart of a war-torn world sings with the Queen of Heaven:

> My soul magnifies the Lord, and
> my spirit rejoices in God our Saviour.

. . . Yet despite the cessation of hostilities, there is a feeling of apprehension in the air. In its wake the war has left ghastly scars and a foul leaven whose taint obscures the rays of peace. . . . It is regrettable that a pessimistic note should have crept into this last entry with its glorious announcement of PEACE. V-E Day and V-J Day are realities at last. There is a *Te Deum* resounding in my heart. The Censor, that specter who has shackled my garrulous pen for almost five years, is no more.

From *To You from Hawaii,* Sister Adele Marie (Albany, N.Y.: Fort Orange Press, 1950).

LIII

Bob Krauss

Ever since Hawaii came under the jurisdiction of the United States in 1898, the Islands had been tardy in reacting to great economic or social movements occurring on the Mainland. Whether it was a boom or a depression, the full effect did not reach Hawaii for months, even years. That pattern ended with World War II. December 7, 1941, propelled Hawaii into the fore; the blunt shock of wartime realities was felt there first. For four years Islanders were more intimately oriented to war than the residents of any other American region. And Hawaii did not need to wait for Mainland example in making adjustment to the aftermath of V-J Day.

In the boom years following the war, prodigious alterations took place on the periphery of practically every metropolis in the United States, and there were changes almost as dramatic in the landscape between the cities, as multilaned highways spread across the country, soon to be bordered by sprawling new residential developments and industrial complexes. The same was occurring in the Islands. If anything, this time Hawaii seemed to be setting the pace, rather than following a parade.

The Islands had experienced many earlier upheavals due to mass immigration, but never anything like what occurred between 1945 and 1965. Tens of thousands who thought they had discovered a potential paradise during the war returned as tourists or permanent residents. Their friends, and friends of friends, followed. The endless flow of newsprint on the territory's candidacy for statehood and its final admission as the fiftieth state lured thousands more. And the establishment of Oahu as headquarters for the largest unified military command in the world inevitably brought still more thousands.

To accommodate the influx, whole new towns sprang up in the Islands—in the same way that they were burgeoning on the Mainland. The cane fields, swamplands, *kiawe* thickets, and inaccessible valleys of one year were handsome residential areas the next; trunk highways, colossal apartment buildings, and commercial complexes transformed Honolulu; Waikiki Beach, which could boast of scarcely half a dozen better-class hostelries in 1945, was edged twenty years later with scores of multistoried hotels, as if deliberate attempt were being made to overreach the skyline of Miami; and in the neighboring islands remote beaches were converted within a season into plush tourist centers.

Twenty years created a different world of Hawaii—as different as comparable areas on the Pacific, Atlantic, and Gulf coasts were from their prewar images. It all happened too hurriedly to allow gestation time for a representative literature; rather the new era was heralded in racy journalese. Visitors, residents, and writers alike balked at the change; a few defended or disprized it. Bob Krauss (1924–   ), one of the most widely recognized Island spokesmen, columnist, journalist, and guidebook author, lined up with the defenders.

In Defense of the Boom

The most persistent lament of critics returning to paradise is, "Yeah, but it's not the old Hawaii." Then comes a blast at high-rise hotels, waterfront freeways, rush-hour traffic, bowling alleys, rocket-launching sites, clutter on Waikiki Beach, wax museums, tract housing, a grumpy bus driver, the price of Scotch and soda or whatever else the visiting beachcomber has decided doesn't fit his memory of the Islands.

At least once a year, "Yeah, but it's not the old Hawaii" gets into print. Sometimes the critic is an out-of-town architect, sometimes a visiting city planner, sometimes a university professor back on a sabbatical. . . . Each time letters came pouring in to the editors of Honolulu papers as the citizens of Hawaii either screamed "Foul!" or else covered themselves with sackcloth.

What most of them don't seem to realize is that this sort of thing has been going on almost since the first bird dropped the first seed on the first lava flow in Hawaii, and, human nature being what it is, there's no prospect that the next million years will be very different.

Take a few examples. When Captain James Cook discovered the Sandwich Islands, one of his junior officers was a bright, ambitious young fellow named George Vancouver. About fifteen years later Vancouver commanded his own expedition to Hawaii, where he found about thirty white beachcombers already teaching the natives bad habits, such as shooting at ships. As you read Vancouver's log, you can almost hear him saying to his first mate, "Yeah, they're still children of nature. But it's not the old Hawaii."

For the next thirty years, Hawaii was a sailor's paradise. The girls joyfully swam out to meet each ship. A man with a bright piece of calico became a sultan, and his wife back in New England need never hear about it. Then, in 1820, the missionaries came and outlawed prostitution. Worse still, they began writing home some of the more sensational details of sea captains' escapades. Imagine the disgust in the tone of a Nantucket sailor as he spread the word, "The weather's fine, but it's not the old Hawaii."

Next came the missionary's turn. In the business slump of the 1840's, collection plates in Eastern churches gathered smaller and smaller harvests. The Mission Board in Boston just couldn't meet the ministerial payroll out there in the Sandwich Islands. Orders finally arrived at Honolulu for all missionaries to become self-supporting. Hawaii's threadbare men of God did not complain as they tried to get other jobs, but it was obvious what they were thinking: "Sugar may be the coming crop, but it's not the old Hawaii."

If these examples haven't convinced you that "old Hawaii" is mostly a state of mind, let's try some history that is more easily recognizable. After all, everybody knows that it wasn't the sailors or the missionaries who *really* spoiled Hawaii. It was the boom— all those hotels and subdivisions and used-car lots. It's the boom that has ruined the natural splendor of Hawaii, scarred the land-scape, crowded the beaches, filled the air with smoke. The only problem with this most common of all criticisms is: Which boom are you talking about?

Consider the boom of 1876. . . . It was the year the Kingdom of Hawaii signed a Treaty of Reciprocity with the United States, permitting Hawaiian sugar to enter the United States duty free. Sugar profits soared. The boom scarred the landscape and filled the air with smoke. Everybody was building sugar mills and breaking land for cane. In their mad scramble for progress and profit, they very nearly plowed up Honolulu.

The number of sugar mills doubled within five years, increasing the demand for firewood to feed the steam engines that drove the rollers that ground the cane. To meet the demand, sugar planters nearly denuded the forests halfway up the mountain slopes. And so this boom resulted in a permanent blight on the face of Hawaii? Not exactly. Many of the sugar planters recognized the danger and started private reforestation projects, setting out hundreds of thousands of saplings on mountain slopes. Today, seventy-five years later, more than one tourist has pointed to those forests and exclaimed ecstatically, "Look at that natural beauty! That's old Hawaii." That same tourist would go home satisfied if he hadn't visited a field of glistening, leafy sugar cane.

The next explosion went off in 1898, touched off this time by annexation. Mainland money siphoned across the sea. Construc-tion volume hit new highs. Then a familiar thing happened. A lot of cheap tenements went up and critics howled in outrage. Today, when these same buildings, now over sixty years old, are being torn down for urban redevelopment, the same kind of critic is just as outraged because "They're tearing down old Hawaii."

. . . What is the old Hawaii? Apparently it is a state of nostalgia that has less to do with the facts than the emotions.

Start with the Hawaii the Polynesians discovered on a voyage up from Tahiti about 2,000 years ago. Imagine a "paradise" as grim and desolate as a raw lava flow. Imagine the mountains without trees, the beaches without shade, the valleys without those subtle modulations of cool green. Those pioneer Hawaiians began the process of beautification by bringing along breadfruit and coco palm, *hau* and *lauhala,* sugar cane and ti.

But you have only to look at the sketches made by the artist John Webber on Captain Cook's expedition to see how barren the Islands still were when white men first landed on these shores. The newcomers immediately set to work to add more beauty: hibiscus, plumeria, royal poinciana, African tulip, banyan, jacaranda, monkey-pod, bird of paradise, orchids.

The process took a long time, and even a century later Honolulu was far from being a beautiful city. Photographs at the Bishop Museum show narrow dusty streets, clapboard stores, mosquito-breeding swamps, mud flats, shabby beaches. Even Punchbowl, looking down upon this little huddle of houses, was not the inviting green slope it is today. It was bare shoulder of red dirt and rough lava.

Since that time, boom has followed boom in Hawaii. What have been the effects? Waialae-Kahala beyond Diamond Head used to be pig farms. About fifteen years ago the land was scarred by bulldozers for a housing development. Today tour drivers steer their buses through this section to show visitors flowering trees.

Lanikai and Kailua, across the mountains from Honolulu, only ten years ago were largely wilderness of *kiawe.* Now the area is one big subdivision. But it is also leafy shade trees and tall palms. Hawaii Kai, Henry Kaiser's new development near Koko Head, is still bare because it is so new. Yet in twenty-five years those houses, too, will be shaded by towering mangoes and by wide-spreading monkey-pods.

Anyone still burdened by the nagging of romantic nostalgia can always fly to Tahiti where many of the roofs are still thatched and the stores close for lunch; where the girls have golden-brown skins and quite a few families still live on breadfruit and fish. There, at last, you will know you have found the real Polynesia— until you run into somebody who has been there once before and he will say, "Yeah, but it's not the old Tahiti."

From "In Defense of the Boom," Bob Krauss, *Paradise of the Pacific,* December 1964.

LIV

Eileen McCann O'Brien

Polynesians, pioneer explorers, merchant adventurers, whalers, missionaries, the planters, proletarian throngs from the Orient and the Occident, multitudes in uniform, and millions of vacation-seeking transients all contributed to the legacy of the state of Hawaii. The character of a state, like the character of an individual, is the product of heredity and environment. For better or for worse, the two together shaped modern Hawaii.

The state was blessed with a natural environment about as desirable as mortal men could long for, and few commonwealths support a broader cross section of mankind. How well are these assorted peoples reacting to their collective heritage in the land of aloha? In 1946 Eileen McCann O'Brien, editor of *Paradise of the Pacific*, gave her answer to the question and at the same time posted a challenge as applicable in 1976 or 1996 as it was when she wrote it.

Challenge

Hawaii is known for a variety of things in other parts of the world. Some think of the islands in terms of tourist advertisements as a land of hula girls and ukulele music. Others have realistic associations connected with Pearl Harbor and the unpleasant war years.

. . . To many, Hawaii is simply a distant lotus land of balmy climate, flamboyant flowers and escape from realities.

The most fascinating and perhaps most significant aspect of Hawaii, however, is less widely known elsewhere. This is Hawaii's remarkable assimilation of vastly different races and cultures, a blend of the Occident, the Orient and Polynesia that gives Hawaii its individual flavor and, to many, its chief fascination. This blend of races and cultures has taken place both literally and figuratively, with the Hawaiians' spirit of aloha as the prompting urge.

The extent to which persons in Hawaii are judged by their conduct, rather than by the color of their skin or the faith they embrace, is perhaps unique in all the world.

This does not mean that all is "sweetness and light," that every man loves his neighbor as himself, that there is a complete absence of tensions based on racial and economic differences. But it does mean that there is equality of educational and economic opportunities for all, that there is no segregation of racial groups in living areas, that persons of mixed racial marriages and of all racial groups are in a large measure accepted on their individual merits. It means that the indefinable aloha of the Hawaiians—a gentle, kindly friendliness toward others—is a living reality in the islands of Hawaii.

A sociologist, the late Romanzo Adams, has written: "As the waters of the Pacific moderate temperature changes in Hawaii, the tradition of racial equality moderates the stresses incident to the assimilation of its peoples."

In a world tormented by fear, distrust and animosities, all manifestations of good will among men become doubly precious. The frantic search for peace in every land can never be successful unless this tradition and spirit are more universally accepted and practiced. It is to be hoped that Hawaii will preserve and cherish her achievements in inter-racial harmony, for in so doing it can set a pattern for the rest of the world.

From "Hawaii Sets a Pattern for the World," an editorial by Eileen McCann O'Brien, *Paradise of the Pacific*, December 1946.

GLOSSARY

This list includes common Hawaiian words used in the text; it does not include words with obsolete or erroneous spelling, most of which are defined as they appear.

As a rule, every syllable in Hawaiian ends with a vowel, and, except for a few vowel combinations, each letter has but one sound. *A* is pronounced as in f*a*r; *e* as in f*e*te; *i* as in mach*i*ne; *o* as in j*o*ke; *u* as in r*u*le; *ai* as in *ai*sle; *au* or *ao* as in s*au*erkr*au*t; *ei* as in v*ei*n; *oe* as *oy* in j*oy*. Most words are lightly accented on the next to last syllable.

'a'a—rough lava
aikane—friend
ali'i—chief, chieftess, royalty
aloha— love, greeting, hello, goodby
'a'ole—no, not; Certainly not!
'awa—narcotic drink

hala—pandanus or screw pine
hale—house, shelter
hana—work
haole—white person
hapa haole—part-white Hawaiian
hau—lowland tree related to hibiscus
haupia—pudding made of coconut cream and cornstarch or arrowroot
heiau—temple, paved or terraced platform of worship
holua—sled

hui—club, group, partnership
hula—dance

kahili—feather-decorated standard, symbolic of royalty
kahuna—priest, teacher, or other trained expert
kalo—taro
kama'aina—old timer, native
kamani—large hardwood tree
kanaka—man
kapakahi—out of order, one-sided, biased
kapu—tabu, taboo, forbidden, holy
kawao—variety of sweet potato
ke'a pua—to shoot arrows made of sugarcane tassels
ki—ti
kiawe—algarroba tree
kiu—cool, fresh northwest wind
koa—largest native tree, hard wood used for furniture, utensils, etc.
kua—house used for beating tapa
kukui—candlenut tree, which produces oily nuts used for illumination

lau hala—pandanus leaf used for weaving or thatching
lehua—*'ohi'a* tree or flower
lei—wreath or necklace of flowers, shells, feathers, etc.
lomilomi—massage
lu'au—feast
luna—overseer, boss

maika—stone-bowling game
maika'i—good, beautiful
maile—native trailing vine with fragrant leaves used for *leis*
maka'ainana—commoner, masses
makahiki—four-month winter festival period
malihini—stranger, newcomer
malo—loincloth
mauka—toward the mountains
mele—song, chant
Menehune—legendary little people
mo'olelo—story, history

mua—men's eating house
mu'a—bottle-necked drinking gourd

nei—this, here

'ohelo—low native shrub, the berries of which were sacred to Pele
'ohi'a—upland tree used for timber

pahoa—short dagger, sharp stone
Pake—China, Chinese
palalu—low-pitched, continuous sound
palapala—writing
pali—cliff, precipice, fortress
paniolo—cowboy
pau—finished, done
pa'u—shirt, sarong
pilikia—trouble, difficulty
poi—pasty food staple from taro root
pololu—long spear
puhenehene—game played with hidden stone
pu nui—large gun

wahine—woman, girl

KEY DATES IN HAWAIIAN ANNALS

c.200–c.1000   Colonization of Hawaiian Islands by Polynesians.

c.1200   Communication with South Pacific islands discontinued.

1778   Discovery of Hawaiian Islands by Captain Cook, who named them the Sandwich Islands.

1782   Accession of Kamehameha.

1792   First of three visits by Captain George Vancouver, foremost early benefactor in attempting to raise subsistence standards in the Islands.

1804   Hawaiian population decimated by mysterious epidemic disease.

1810   Islands united under one kingdom by Kamehameha.

1819   Accession of Kamehameha II (Iolani Liholiho) and Queen Kaahumanu, as joint rulers. Abolition of taboo system and idol worship.

1820   Arrival of first American missionaries and first whalers. Oral Hawaiian transformed into written language.

1825   Accession of Kamehameha III (Kauikeaouli), Queen Kaahumanu continuing as regent.

1835   First large-scale sugar plantation started at Koloa, Kauai.

1840   First constitution proclaimed, with provision for freedom of worship.

1846   Peak year of whaling industry, with 596 ships entering Hawaiian ports.

1848   The Great *Mahele*—division of the lands—by which Hawaiians of all classes won privilege of land ownership.

1851   Labor immigration started with importation of Chinese coolies.

1852   New constitution adopted, providing for franchise of all male citizens and for legislative and judicial systems.

1855   Accession of Kamehameha IV (Alexander Liholiho).

1861   American Civil War brought rapid decline in whaling trade.

1863   Accession of Kamehameha V (Lot).

1864   Constitution of 1852 abrogated by king and replaced by less liberal one.

1873   William C. Lunalilo elected king—last of the Kamehameha dynasty.

1874   David Kalakaua appointed king by legislature.

1876   Reciprocity Treaty with the United States ratified, giving unprecedented boost to Island sugar industry.

1886   Marketable pineapples introduced from Jamaica.

1887   Pearl Harbor ceded to United States as condition to renewal of Reciprocity Treaty. Demands of American residents for radical political reforms result in proclamation of new constitution, providing for "Cabinet Goverment."

1891   Accession of Queen Liliuokalani.

1893   Queen Liliuokalani deposed and monarchy abrogated. Provisional government instituted.

1894   Republic of Hawaii established.

1898   Hawaii annexed by the United States.

1899   Outbreak of bubonic plague in Honolulu. Chinatown burned.

1900   Territorial government inaugurated.

1911   Pearl Harbor opened as naval base.

1924   Immigration Act debarred further Japanese immigration.

1925   Flight of John Rodgers from West Coast to Hawaiian waters.

1929   Interisland flight service inaugurated.

1931   Massie Case brought flood of unfavorable publicity to Hawaii and series of Congressional investigations.

1936   Transpacific passenger service established by Pan American.

1941   Pearl Harbor attack, December 7. Islands placed under martial law.

1944   Martial law terminated by Presidential order on October 24.

1947   Unprecedented boom in tourist hotel construction begun.

1952   Citizenship eligibility extended to Japanese, Koreans, and Samoans.

1957   Pacific armed forces reorganized under centralized command of CINCPAC on Oahu, creating largest single unified military command in the world, covering over 40 percent of earth's surface.

1959   Hawaii admitted as 50th state.

1962   Tourist industry passed $150,000,000 mark annually.

■ MICHENER ■ MALO ■ ELLIS ■ FORNANDER ■ COLUM ■ LEDYARD ■ DIXON ■ JARVES ■

WESTMAR COLLEGE LIBRARY

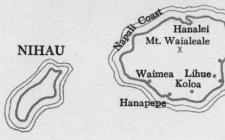

KAUAI

NIHAU

OAHU

■ MELVILLE ■ MACOUN ■ TWAIN ■ VANDERCOCK ■ BLISS ■ BIRD ■ NORDHOFF ■

LA FARGE ■ STRONG ■ POTTER ■ BAKER ■ BROOKE ■ LONDON ■ MAUGHAM ■ VON TEMPSKI ■ THRUM ■ ADELE MARIE ■ KRAUSS ■ O'BRIEN